PROTECTION FROM REFUGE

The places in which refugees seek sanctuary are often as dangerous and bleak as the conditions they fled. In response, many travel within and across borders in search of safety. As part of these journeys, refugees are increasingly turning to courts to ask for protection, not from persecution in their homeland, but from a place of 'refuge'. This book is the first global and comparative study of 'protection from refuge' litigation, examining, with a particular focus on gender, whether courts facilitate or hamper refugee journeys. Drawing on jurisprudence from Africa, Europe, North America and Oceania, Kate Ogg shows that courts have transitioned from adopting robust ideas of refuge to rudimentary ones. This trajectory indicates that courts can play a powerful role in creating more just and equitable refugee protection policies, but have, ultimately, compounded the difficulties inherent in finding sanctuary, perpetuating global inequities in refugee responsibility and rendering refuge elusive.

KATE OGG is Associate Professor at the Australian National University. Her research has been published in leading international journals, and she is co-editor of the acclaimed *Feminist Engagement with International Law*. Kate has presented her research at UNHCR Headquarters and given evidence on refugee law to the Parliament of Australia.

T0384872

Cambridge Asylum and Migration Studies

At no time in modern history have so many people been on the move as at present. Migration facilitates critical social, economic, and humanitarian linkages. But it may also challenge prevailing notions of bounded political communities, of security, and of international law.

The political and legal systems that regulate the transborder movement of persons were largely devised in the mid-twentieth century, and are showing their strains. New challenges have arisen for policymakers, advocates, and decision-makers that require the adaptation and evolution of traditional models to meet emerging imperatives.

Edited by a world leader in refugee law, this new series aims to be a forum for innovative writing on all aspects of the transnational movement of people. It publishes single or coauthored works that may be legal, political, or cross-disciplinary in nature, and will be essential reading for anyone looking to understand one of the most important issues of the twenty-first century.

Series Editor

James C. Hathaway, James E. and Sarah A. Degan Professor of Law, and Director of Michigan Law's Program in Refugee and Asylum Law, University of Michigan

Editorial Advisory Board

Alexander Betts, Leopold Muller Professor of Forced Migration and International Affairs, University of Oxford

Vincent Chetail, Professor of Public International Law, and Director of the Global Migration Centre, Graduate Institute of International and Development Studies, Switzerland

Thomas Gammeltoft-Hansen, Professor with Special Responsibilities in Migration and Refugee Law at the University of Copenhagen

Audrey Macklin, Professor and Chair in Human Rights Law, University of Toronto, Canada

Saskia Sassen, Robert S. Lynd Professor of Sociology, and Chair of the Committee on Global Thought, Columbia University

Books in the Series

The Child in International Refugee Law
Jason M. Pobjoy

Refuge Lost: Asylum Law in an Interdependent World
Daniel Ghezelbash

Demanding Rights: Europe's Supranational Courts and the Dilemma of Migrant Vulnerability
Moritz Baumgärtel

PROTECTION FROM REFUGE

From Refugee Rights to Migration Management

KATE OGG

Australian National University

CAMBRIDGE
UNIVERSITY PRESS

Shaftesbury Road, Cambridge CB2 8EA, United Kingdom

One Liberty Plaza, 20th Floor, New York, NY 10006, USA

477 Williamstown Road, Port Melbourne, VIC 3207, Australia

314–321, 3rd Floor, Plot 3, Splendor Forum, Jasola District Centre, New Delhi – 110025, India

103 Penang Road, #05–06/07, Visioncrest Commercial, Singapore 238467

Cambridge University Press is part of Cambridge University Press & Assessment, a department of the University of Cambridge.

We share the University's mission to contribute to society through the pursuit of education, learning and research at the highest international levels of excellence.

www.cambridge.org
Information on this title: www.cambridge.org/9781009011082
DOI: 10.1017/9781009024259

© Kate Ogg 2022

This publication is in copyright. Subject to statutory exception and to the provisions of relevant collective licensing agreements, no reproduction of any part may take place without the written permission of Cambridge University Press & Assessment.

First published 2022
First paperback edition 2023

A catalogue record for this publication is available from the British Library

Library of Congress Cataloging-in-Publication data
Names: Ogg, Kate, author.
Title: Protection from refuge : from refugee rights to migration management / Kate Ogg, Australian National University, Canberra.
Description: Cambridge, United Kingdom ; New York, NY : Cambridge University Press, 2022. | Series: Cambridge asylum and migration studies | Includes index.
Identifiers: LCCN 2021032148 (print) | LCCN 2021032149 (ebook) | ISBN 9781316519738 (hardback) | ISBN 9781009011082 (paperback) | ISBN 9781009024259 (ebook)
Subjects: LCSH: Refugees – Legal status, laws, etc.
Classification: LCC KZ6530 . O35 2021 (print) | LCC KZ6530 (ebook) | DDC 341.4/86–dc23
LC record available at https://lccn.loc.gov/2021032148
LC ebook record available at https://lccn.loc.gov/20210321493

ISBN   978-1-316-51973-8   Hardback
ISBN   978-1-009-01108-2   Paperback

Cambridge University Press & Assessment has no responsibility for the persistence or accuracy of URLs for external or third-party internet websites referred to in this publication and does not guarantee that any content on such websites is, or will remain, accurate or appropriate.

For Ron

CONTENTS

PREFACE

It is counterintuitive that some people may need protection *from* refuge. If a refuge is meaningful, then surely nobody needs to be protected from it. Conversely, a refuge from which people feel compelled to flee ought arguably not to be deemed a refuge at all.

Yet as Kate Ogg makes clear in this groundbreaking study, claims for protection from refuge are increasingly common and litigated. To understand this phenomenon, Ogg undertakes what Martha Minow refers to as a 'recasting project', drawing on lines of seemingly disparate cases from across jurisdictions to discover whether there is in fact a conceptual commonality that links them. Through examination of resistance to practices of mandatory encampment, the setting of regional asylum boundaries, containment policies, the relegation of Palestinian refugees to an institutionalised enclave and rules that compel refugee claimants to return home to face internal displacement, Ogg identifies a common thread: in none of these cases does the refugee believe that what is on offer is truly refuge worthy of the name.

This book argues that the legal response to the various manifestations of the failure of refuge has ebbed and flowed. While some courts have championed a full-throated understanding of asylum, others have, in Ogg's words, approached 'refuge as a scarce commodity and one stripped down to the barest minimum of protections'. Equally important, Ogg shows that, when refugees challenge that stripping-down exercise, courts are often disinclined to offer relief in other than circumstances deemed 'exceptional or extraordinary' – the definition of which rarely does justice to needs and aspirations defined by such concerns as gender, age or disability.

This is a marvellous book in so many ways. It takes law seriously – unearthing and engaging with the work of courts around the world on issues of critical importance to persons compelled to flee in search of protection, thus neatly complementing and completing stories of refugee journeys in the social science literature. It harnesses feminist legal analysis to posit an inclusive definition of what ought to count as truly adequate refuge and shows how adjudicative practice too often fails to meet that standard. Most fundamentally, it constructs a paradigm to understand and effectively to contest the fact that the places in which people seek protection are often as bleak and as dangerous as those which they fled.

James C. Hathaway
Editor, Cambridge Asylum and Migration Studies

ACKNOWLEDGEMENTS

This book was written on Ngunnawal and Ngambri country, which was stolen and sovereignty was never ceded. I pay my respects to the elders of the Ngunnawal and Ngambri people, past, present and emerging. I thank them for their continued generosity in welcoming all people who have come to live in and visit their ancestral lands.

I express my deepest gratitude to Professor Hilary Charlesworth for nurturing this project, which began as a PhD thesis. Thank you also to my associate supervisors, Professors Michelle Foster and Fiona Jenkins, for their guidance and encouragement. I also wish to thank Professors Catherine Dauvergne, Cathryn Costello and Dallal Stevens who examined the dissertation and provided invaluable feedback. This project emerged from the interdisciplinary research environment at the School of Regulation and Global Governance (RegNet). I thank Professors John Braithwaite, Veronica Taylor, Kate Henne and Anthea Roberts for their generous reflections that helped shape the research.

While working on this project I was fortunate to be hosted as an academic visitor by Professors James C. Hathaway, Jane McAdam and Cathryn Costello. I am indebted to each of them for the conversations that enriched the work. Thank you also to everyone at the University of Michigan Law School, Kaldor Centre for International Refugee Law and Refugee Studies Centre for their warm welcome and helpful comments on the research.

I am grateful to everyone at the Office of the United Nations High Commissioner for Refugees who provided feedback and an opportunity to present this research. Particular thanks go to Dr Madeline Garlick, Louise Aubin, Jean-François Durieux and Chanelle Taoi.

I express my gratitude to the ANU College of Law at the Australian National University (ANU). Thank you to those who have been mentors and supported my career, especially Professors Sally Wheeler, Kim Rubenstein, Don Rothwell, Penelope Mathew, Penelope Andrews, Susan Harris Rimmer, Fiona Wheeler, Jeremy Farrall, Ann Evans, Peta Spender, Pauline Ridge, Rebecca Monson, Vivien Holmes, Tony Connolly and Matthew Zagor.

I was blessed to have a wonderful publication team at Cambridge University Press. Thank you to Finola O'Sullivan, Becky Jackaman and Marianne Nield. I am also greatly indebted to the anonymous reviewers for their insightful feedback and suggestions.

Finally, to my family. This book would not have been possible without the unfailing love and support of my husband, Associate Professor Ron Levy. Thanks go to my parents, Patricia Eckford and Peter Ogg, for their love and for giving me every opportunity to pursue university study. My son, Josiah Levy, arrived into the world during the research for this book and propelled and disrupted it in ways both unexpected and delightful.

ABBREVIATIONS

CAT	Convention against Torture and Other Cruel, Inhuman or Degrading Treatment or Punishment, 10 December 1984, 1456 UNTS 85, in force 26 June 1987
CEDAW	Convention on the Elimination of All Forms of Discrimination against Women, 18 December 1979, 1249 UNTS 13, in force 3 September 1981
CRC	Convention on the Rights of the Child, 20 November 1989, 1577 UNTS 3, in force 2 September 1990
CRPD	Convention on the Rights of Persons with Disabilities, 30 March 2007, 2515 UNTS 3, in force 3 May 2008
ECHR	European Convention for the Protection of Human Rights and Fundamental Freedoms, 4 November 1950, ETS 5, in force 3 September 1953
EU	European Union
ICCPR	International Covenant on Civil and Political Rights, 16 December 1966, 999 UNTS 171, in force 23 March 1976
ICESCR	International Covenant on Economic, Social and Cultural Rights, 16 December 1966, 993 UNTS 3, in force 3 January 1976
IDP	internally displaced person
NGO	non-governmental organisation
Refugee Convention	Convention Relating to the Status of Refugees, 28 July 1951, 189 UNTS 137, in force 22 April 1954, as amended by the Protocol Relating to the Status of Refugees, 31 January 1967, 606 UNTS 267, in force 4 October 1967
UDHR	Universal Declaration of Human Rights, GA Res 217A (III), UN GAOR, UN Doc A/810 (10 December 1948)
UN	United Nations
UNGA	United Nations General Assembly
UNHCR	Office of the United Nations High Commissioner for Refugees
UNHCR Statute	Statute of the Office of the United Nations High Commissioner for Refugees, GA Res 428(V), UN Doc A/RES/428(V) (14 December 1950)
UNRWA	United Nations Relief and Works Agency for Palestine Refugees in the Near East

1

Journeys in Search of Refuge

1.1 Introduction

The word 'refugee' has its roots not in what people are escaping from, but in what they are seeking: refuge.[1] Today, the number of people searching for sanctuary in foreign lands is the highest ever recorded.[2] However, many of the places to which people flee are sites of refuge only in a nominal sense. They are often unsafe and insecure; provide little access to healthcare, education and employment; and have inadequate sanitation, shelter, food and water. Hathaway laments that 'people guilty of absolutely no crime except for doing what we have said they may do, which is to come seek asylum, find themselves in horrific conditions'.[3] These problems exist in places of so-called refuge in both higher- and lower-income countries. Carens explains that, despite being 'supposedly safe havens', in some refugee camps in the Global South, 'the deprivation and danger appear to be as bad as the conditions from which refugees fled'.[4] Recalling a refugee settlement known as the 'Jungle' in Calais, an Afghani refugee writes that it 'looked as though the world's toilet had been flushed and the mess washed up here'.[5] The conditions in some locales in which people seek refuge are so grim that many wish to return to the place from which they had initially fled.[6]

In response to these dangerous and bleak conditions of refuge, asylum seekers and refugees adopt various strategies. As Ramsay explains, '[e]ven in contexts of uncertainty, refugees ... imagine, and actively work toward, new futures'.[7] Some move from camp environments to urban areas due to the prospect of greater security, better living conditions and employment opportunities. Others are able to make much longer expeditions across one or a number of international borders in search of sanctuary. These voyages are often

---

[1] 'Refugee' derives from the Old French word réfugié, meaning 'gone in search of refuge': Glynnis Chantrill (ed), *The Oxford Dictionary of Word Histories* (Oxford University Press, 2002) 424.

[2] UNHCR, *Global Trends: Forced Displacement in 2019* (18 June 2020) 2 <www.unhcr.org/en-au/statistics/unhcrstats/5ee200e37/unhcr-global-trends-2019.html>.

[3] James Hathaway, 'The UN's "Comprehensive Refugee Response Framework": Actually a "Contingent Refugee Assistance Project"' (speech delivered at the Refugee Law Initiative Eighth International Refugee Law Seminar Series, 21 May 2018).

[4] Joseph Carens, 'Refugees and the Limits of Obligations' (1992) 6(1) *Public Affairs Quarterly* 31, 40.

[5] Gulwali Passarlay and Nadene Ghouri, *The Lightless Sky: An Afghan Refugee Boy's Journey of Escape to a New Life* (Atlantic Books, 2015) 292.

[6] Amnesty International, *EU: Asylum-Seekers Must Be Moved from Appalling Conditions* (14 December 2016) <www.amnesty.org.au/eu-asylum-seekers-must-be-moved-from-appalling-conditions/>; Georgina Ramsay, 'Benevolent Cruelty: Forced Child Removal, African Refugee Settlers, and the State Mandate of Child Protection' (2017) 40(2) *Political and Legal Anthropology Review* 245, 255.

[7] Georgina Ramsay, 'Incommensurable Futures and Displaced Lives: Sovereignty as Control over Time' (2017) 29(3) *Public Culture* 515, 516.

hindered by various mechanisms states use to constrain refugees' movements.[8] Factors such as age, gender, care responsibilities and disability increase the challenges refugees face in their quests for refuge. As a result, these journeys are rarely linear, but are instead 'fragmented'.[9] For example, those in need of protection sometimes become trapped in certain places, unable to travel onwards or return home. In other situations, refugees who feel they have found a place of refuge are forced to leave and must find ways to stay or return.

While there are studies of these fragmented journeys in fields such as anthropology, sociology and criminology,[10] there is little consideration of the role litigation plays. This is despite people in need of international protection increasingly turning to courts or other adjudicative bodies to continue their journeys in search of sanctuary. For example, a refugee may seek a court order granting them permission to leave the confines of a camp, or an asylum seeker living in the Jungle in Calais may initiate court proceedings in the UK seeking relocation there.

When refugees and asylum seekers bring these legal claims, they are seeking protection, not from persecution in their home country, but from a place of ostensible refuge. They want rescue from a place that raises serious protection concerns, but which is, notionally at least, serving as a place of refuge to hundreds or thousands of others. I refer to these actions as 'protection from refuge' claims and they are the focus of this book. While there are myriad studies of how courts interpret refugee definitions, in this first global and comparative study of protection from refuge jurisprudence, I examine how judges approach the remedy: refuge. I provide an account of how adjudicative decision-makers conceptualise refuge through a variety of legal prisms and arbitrate the clash between the search for sanctuary and the different ways states constrain refugees' mobility. I also consider whether these judicial approaches to protection from refuge claims assist or hinder refugees' (or particular refugees') journeys towards a safe haven with a particular focus on gender but also other factors such as youth, disability, sexuality and parenthood.

I outline, in Section 1.2, the 'protection from refuge' conundrum in more detail and discuss the frictions inherent in these legal claims. In Section 1.3, I identify where along a refugee journey these legal challenges can manifest, starting from what may be the first country of asylum to litigation that occurs farther afield. In Section 1.4, I highlight how bringing together what have traditionally been viewed as disparate areas of jurisprudence under the 'protection from refuge' rubric and adopting comparative and feminist methods of analysis provides unique insights on refugee law and the international protection regime more broadly. Finally, Section 1.5 outlines the scope of the work and how the protection from refuge framework developed in the book can inform future research.

---

[8] Thomas Spijkerboer, 'The Global Mobility Infrastructure: Reconceptualising the Externalisation of Migration Control' (2018) 20 *European Journal of Migration and Law* 452, 458.

[9] Michael Collyer, 'Stranded Migrants and the Fragmented Journey' (2010) 23(3) *Journal of Refugee Studies* 273, 275.

[10] See, e.g., Richard Black, 'Breaking the Convention: Researching the "Illegal" Migration of Refugees to Europe' (2003) 35(1) *Antipode: A Radical Journal of Geography* 34; Maria Cristina Garcia, *Seeking Refuge: Central American Migration to Mexico, the United States and Canada* (University of California Press, 2006); Mariana Nardone and Ignacio Correa-Velez, 'Unpredictability, Invisibility and Vulnerability: Unaccompanied Asylum-Seeking Minors' Journeys to Australia' (2016) 29(3) *Journal of Refugee Studies* 295; Susan Zimmermann, 'Irregular Secondary Movements to Europe: Seeking Asylum beyond Refuge' (2009) 22(1) *Journal of Refugee Studies* 74.

1.2   Protection from Refuge: Tensions and Queries

Protection from refuge claims are a burgeoning trend. They started to emerge in the early 2000s, but have increased in number over the first two decades of the twenty-first century and have arisen in Africa, Europe, North America, the Middle East and the Asia-Pacific region.[11] The majority of these claims are instigated in domestic courts and adjudicative tribunals, while others have been brought before supranational courts and UN treaty bodies. I include in the 'protection from refuge' rubric cases determined by an adjudicative decision-making body in which an asylum seeker or refugee is either resisting being sent to an alternative place of refuge or petitioning to be transferred from their current place of refuge to another. My definition of 'refugee' includes anyone recognised as a refugee under the Refugee Convention or a regional refugee instrument,[12] given complementary protection[13] or qualifying as a Palestinian refugee according to UNRWA.[14] While refugee status is declaratory as opposed to constitutive,[15] I use the term 'asylum seeker' to refer to a person who is seeking international protection, but whose status has not been confirmed. This book examines protection from refuge decisions handed down between 1 January 2000 and 31 December 2020.[16]

Protection from refuge claims are grounded in different aspects of international, regional and domestic law, which I outline in Section 1.3. What unites them is that all of the asylum seeker and refugee litigants are seeking the same outcome: to continue their journey in search of a place of genuine refuge. Despite differences in the ways protection from refuge cases are framed, they raise similar quandaries for decision-makers that have implications for the international protection regime more broadly. These tensions are reflected in the phrase 'protection from refuge', which may, at first, appear to be paradoxical. The term 'refuge' is associated with notions of safety and well-being. Why would a person seek protection from a place intended to provide security and shelter? The apparent contradiction arises because the word 'refuge' is used to refer to both the idea of providing a safe haven (refuge as a concept) and the site at which that sanctuary may be provided (refuge as a place).[17] In protection from refuge challenges, the ideal and the actuality of refuge both

---

[11] I discuss claims made in all of these regions, with the exception of the Middle East. The only relevant claim made in this region occurred in Israel but was withdrawn before final judgment – see note 85.

[12] For example, the Convention Governing the Specific Aspects of Refugee Problems in Africa, 10 September 1969, 1001 UNTS 45, in force 20 June 1974.

[13] Complementary protection is protection given to those who are 'fleeing serious harm but who do not fall within the technical legal definition of a "refugee"': Jane McAdam, *Complementary Protection in International Law* (Oxford University Press, 2007) 1.

[14] UNRWA's definition of a Palestinian refugee is outlined in Section 1.3.

[15] UNHCR, *Handbook on Procedures and Criteria for Determining Refugee Status under the 1951 Convention and the 1967 Protocol Relating to the Status of Refugees*, UN Doc HCR/IP/4/Eng/REV.1 (1979, re-edited 1992) [28]; James Hathaway, *The Rights of Refugees under International Law* (Cambridge University Press, 2005) 11 (see also James Hathaway, *The Rights of Refugees under International Law* (Cambridge University Press, 2nd ed, 2021)).

[16] The only exception to this is in Chapter 5, where I discuss *The Minister of Citizenship and Immigration and The Minister of Public Safety and Emergency Preparedness v The Canadian Council for Refugees et al* [2021] FCA 72. This judgment was handed down on 15 April 2021 shortly before this book went to press and was an appeal of a decision by the Federal Court of Canada handed down on 22 July 2020.

[17] The *Oxford English Dictionary* defines 'refuge' as meaning both 'shelter from pursuit or danger or trouble' and 'a person or place etc. offering this': RE Allen (ed), *The Concise Oxford Dictionary of Current English* (Clarendon Press, 8th ed, 1990) 1009. Grahl-Madsen makes the same point with the word 'asylum': Atle Grahl-Madsen, *The Status of Refugees in International Law: Volume 2* (AW Sijthoff-Leyden, 1966) 3.

enter the judicial arena. When refugees make these claims, they draw attention to the disparities between ideas of what refuge is supposed to be with the material reality of the place in which they are or will be located. In other words, they highlight the incongruities between refuge as a concept and as a place. In arbitrating these disputes, decision-makers have the opportunity to draw on frameworks available in international, regional and domestic law to elucidate the concept of refuge. For example, they may understand refuge as allowing refugees to thrive or merely survive. They could posit refuge as a legally binding obligation or as a discretionary act. Decision-makers must then determine the extent to which they can use these notions of refuge to cast judgment on spaces of refuge within or outside their borders.

Another conundrum inherent in these cases and reflected in this book's title is why a person must seek protection from a place of refuge. If a person does not feel secure in their current location, why can they not simply find alternative places of sanctuary? The reason why refugees often need to resort to legal processes to obtain protection from such places is due to the operation of containment mechanisms. Containment mechanisms are laws, policies or agreements that aim or are used to prevent refugees from moving within and across borders and restrict them to particular places of ostensible refuge.[18] They have been increasingly employed over the past three decades,[19] with wealthier states in particular having 'a near-obsession with migration control, spending billions of dollars each year in the hope of securing their borders'.[20] Some containment mechanisms, such as encampment policies, aim to reduce refugee mobility within a state's borders and prevent refugees living in local communities. There are also policies and practices that externalise migration control beyond a state's borders – they aim to prevent asylum seekers arriving or staying in a state's territory[21] and can exert 'control over the entire length of the journey'.[22] Examples of these transnational and cooperative forms of containment mechanisms are offshore processing, international agreements determining which state has responsibility for a refugee and joint surveillance, interception and policing practices.[23] Some scholars argue that the Refugee Convention is a containment mechanism because it only responds to a fraction of people in need of protection and it is sometimes applied in a restrictive manner.[24]

When refugees bring protection from refuge claims, they initiate a contest between their entitlement to refuge and states' interests in constraining refugees' ability to move within

---

[18] Andrew Shacknove, 'From Asylum to Containment' (1993) 5(4) *International Journal of Refugee Law* 516, 521–3.

[19] Thomas Gammeltoft-Hansen, 'International Refugee Law and Policy: The Case of Deterrence Policies' (2014) 27(4) *Journal of Refugee Studies* 574, 576.

[20] Thomas Gammeltoft-Hansen and James Hathaway, '*Non-Refoulement* in a World of Cooperative Deterrence' (2015) 53(2) *Columbia Journal of Transnational Law* 235, 236.

[21] Thomas Gammeltoft-Hansen, *Access to Asylum: International Refugee Law and the Globalisation of Migration Control* (Cambridge University Press, 2011) 2.

[22] Ibid 6.

[23] Azedeh Dastyari and Asher Hirsch, 'The Ring of Steel: Extraterritorial Migration Controls in Indonesia and Libya and the Complicity of Australia and Italy' (2019) 19 *Human Rights Law Review* 435, 436; Itamar Mann, 'Dialectic of Transnationalism: Unauthorized Migration and Human Rights' (2013) 54(2) *Harvard International Law Journal* 315, 334–5, 344.

[24] See, e.g., B. S. Chimni, 'The Geopolitics of Refugee Studies: A View from the South' (1998) 11(4) *Journal of Refugee Studies* 350, 356; Patricia Tuitt, *False Images: The Law's Construction of the Refugee* (Pluto Press, 1996) 69–71.

and across borders. The 'dissonance' between refugees' 'human needs and desires and generalised policies of migration control'[25] is what adjudicative decision-makers must arbitrate. Decision-makers' determinations of these conflicts will either disrupt or cement containment mechanisms. In this book I examine whether these judicial responses impede or facilitate refugees' journeys in search of refuge. I also consider if they assist or create additional hurdles for those who face the greatest difficulties in travelling in search of refuge, such as unaccompanied minors, refugees with disabilities and single female-headed families. I ask these questions against the background of how scholars, UN actors and refugees understand refuge, and I turn to this in the next section.

1.3   What Is Refuge and What Are the Different Types of Protection from Refuge Claims?

The word 'refuge' is widely used in refugee and forced migration scholarship,[26] but it is 'rarely distinctly defined'.[27] This book provides the first detailed study of how adjudicative decision-makers conceptualise refuge. In particular, I identify how they understand the objectives, nature, threshold and scope of refuge. In Chapter 2, I outline how scholars from a variety of disciplines, UN institutions and refugees envision these aspects of refuge (in order to highlight refugees' perspectives I draw on memoirs written by people with lived experience of displacement). This provides the background against which I examine how adjudicative decision-makers approach refuge and address the discrepancies between ideas of refuge and the reality.

The analysis in Chapter 2 indicates that there are commonalities across scholarship from different disciplines with respect to the starting points for elucidating what refuge is or should be. The literature on refuge also indicates that the concept is a robust one. Scholarship, UN materials and refugee memoirs provide sophisticated accounts of what refuge is intended to achieve beyond the 'absolute priority on "saving lives"'.[28] There are also well-developed understandings of the nature of refuge as a remedy, legal status, duty, right and process. Scholars, UN institutions and refugees understand refuge to have a broad scope, encompassing a wide range of needs, desires and hopes. The standard of what is deemed to be adequate refuge is usually a high one, surpassing the basic duties of guaranteeing safety and providing essentials for the sustenance of life. Furthermore, the conceptualisation of refuge presented in the literature is dynamic in the sense that there are

---

[25] Gammeltoft-Hansen and Hathaway (n 20) 237.

[26] See, e.g., Catherine Besteman, *Making Refuge: Somali Bantu Refugees and Lewiston, Maine* (Duke University Press, 2016); Alexander Betts and Paul Collier, *Refuge: Transforming a Broken Refugee System* (Allen Lane, 2017); Elena Fiddian-Qasmiyeh (ed), *Refuge in a Moving World: Tracing Refugee and Migrant Journeys Across Disciplines* (UCL Press, 2020) 1; Daniel Ghezelback, *Refuge Lost: Asylum Law in an Interdependent World* (Cambridge University Press, 2018); Klaus Neumann, *Refuge Australia: Australia's Humanitarian Record* (UNSW Press, 2005); Silvia Pasquetti and Romola Sanyal (eds), *Displacement: Global Conversations on Refuge* (Manchester University Press, 2020); David Scott Fitzgerald, *Refuge Beyond Reach: How Rich Democracies Repel Asylum Seekers* (Oxford University Press, 2019).

[27] Georgina Ramsay, *Impossible Refuge: The Control and Constraint of Refugee Futures* (Routledge, 2018) 156.

[28] Jean-François Durieux, 'Three Asylum Paradigms' (2013) 20(2) *International Journal on Minority and Group Rights* 147, 162.

considerations of the ways it may differ for people of different genders, sexualities and ages, as well as those with disabilities and care responsibilities. To highlight the discrepancies between refuge as a concept and as a place, in Chapter 2 I also discuss literature that examines the conditions in which many refugees live. I focus in particular on the places of ostensible refuge that are the subject of the protection from refuge claims examined in this book.

I explore how decision-makers respond to the disjunctures between ideas and actualities of refuge in Chapters 3–7, in which I survey protection from refuge claims made at different points in a refugee journey. I start in Chapter 3 with legal challenges that arise in what may be a first country of asylum or a place of refuge relatively close to home. This chapter examines forced encampment litigation. I focus on Kenya, which is where most forced encampment litigation has occurred. These cases have been initiated by refugees living in urban areas resisting being forcibly sent to a refugee camp, as well as refugees living in camps seeking permission to leave. They are grounded in domestic, regional and international human rights and refugee law. I examine how Kenyan judges use these legal frameworks as prisms to articulate the functions and nature of refuge. I show that Kenyan courts have understood refuge as a process as well as a human rights remedy that must allow refugees to live a liveable life in the present, have hope for the future and heal from past trauma. This extends understandings of refuge when compared to the academic literature. Judges arrive at these sophisticated understandings of refuge when they identify and reflect on irreducible aspects of refugeehood.

However, in more recent cases, Kenyan judges have moved away from this approach and instead focus on the uniqueness of the protection from refuge litigants. This results in conceptualising refuge as a limited commodity that, akin to welfare, must be given to those most in need or most deserving. Nevertheless, in line with adopting feminist methods of analysis (which I describe in Section 1.4), I highlight that, in identifying the anomalous refugee, Kenyan courts have addressed protection concerns relating to gender, age and disability in a sensitive and nuanced manner.

I continue my examination of the use of human rights arguments to secure protection from a place of refuge in Chapter 4, where I look to Europe. Most of these protection from refuge claims are brought by those who have made longer, often transcontinental journeys. They are using human rights law to request or challenge a transfer made pursuant to the EU's Dublin System[29] or other containment practice. These cases are brought before the European Court of Human Rights or domestic adjudicative decision-making bodies pursuant to the ECHR. They have also been brought before UN treaty bodies. While these cases do not directly call into question the validity of European containment practices, they have potential to set precedents that jeopardise their continued operation.

Unlike Kenya's forced encampment litigation, which has received scant scholarly attention, there are numerous studies of this jurisprudence. Most analyses are written from the perspective of how it develops (or, with respect to UN treaty body jurisprudence, compares to) European human rights law, especially regarding migrants' rights.[30] In Chapter 4,

---

[29] The Dublin System determines the EU member-state responsible for hearing an asylum claim. It was adopted in 2003 and recast in 2013. There was a proposal for its reform in 2016. However, in 2020 the European Commission announced that the Dublin System would be abolished and the proposal for its reform was withdrawn. At the time of writing, the Dublin System was still in force.

[30] Moritz Baumgärtel, *Demanding Rights: Europe's Supranational Courts and the Dilemma of Migrant Vulnerability* (Cambridge University Press, 2019); Başak Çalı, Cathryn Costello and Stewart Cunningham, 'Hard Protection through Soft Courts? Non-Refoulement before the United Nations Treaty Bodies' (2020) 21

I depart from the existing scholarship by opening a different line of enquiry. I examine how the case law develops judicial understandings of refuge and what it says, through the prism of different areas of human rights law, about international refugee law and the remedy it offers. My analysis is also unique in that I critically examine the jurisprudence from a gender perspective. The leading legal and sociolegal examinations of this case law do not take a feminist or intersectional approach. Briddick notes that women are 'conspicuously absent or underrepresented' in Dublin System cases[31] and that 'consideration of gender has been noticeably absent from debates on Europe's re-bordering'.[32]

The human rights arguments available to refugee and asylum seeker litigants to plead in the European context are more limited than in Kenya. Most protection from refuge claims are based on the right to be free from torture and inhuman and degrading treatment, the right to family life, the right to an effective remedy and the right against collective expulsion: rights not in the Refugee Convention and rights that would be considered far below the standard of adequate protection when compared to the legal literature on refugee protection (outlined in Chapter 2). I deepen the analysis made in Chapter 3 by highlighting that, in initial and early European protection from refuge claims, decision-makers identified common aspects of refugeehood and used the above-noted rights to engage with the functions and nature of refuge. Similar to Kenyan case law, there was an understanding that refuge is a remedy that must address present, future and past vicissitudes of displacement, but decision-makers now search for the 'good' or 'peculiarly vulnerable' refugee. This has resulted in decision-makers approaching refuge as a scarce commodity and one stripped down to the barest minimum of protections. Unlike their Kenyan counterparts, in searching for the exceptional refugee, most decision-makers approach questions of gender, age and disability in a nominal manner.

In Chapter 5, I continue with the journeys of refugees who have travelled beyond what may be their first country of asylum in search of sanctuary farther afield, but I examine cases they have initiated that directly challenge regional containment instruments. This has occurred in four parts of the world: North America (an agreement between the US and Canada), Asia-Pacific (agreements between Australia and Malaysia, Australia and Papua New Guinea and Australia and Nauru), Europe (the Dublin System and an agreement between Europe and Turkey) and Libya (an agreement between Libya and Italy).[33] Human rights arguments are present in these cases, but they are less central. The arguments pleaded traverse many areas of domestic, regional and international law. In

---

(3) *German Law Review* 355; Marie-Bénédicte Dembour, *When Humans Become Migrants: Study of the European Court of Human Rights with an Inter-American Counterpoint* (Oxford University Press, 2015).

[31] Catherine Briddick, 'Some Other(ed) "Refugees"?: Women Seeking Asylum under Refugee and Human Rights Law' in Satvinder Juss (ed), *Research Handbook on International Refugee Law* (Edward Elgar, 2019) 281, 287.

[32] Ibid 284.

[33] With respect to the EU, I examine cases before the Court of Justice of the European Union that directly challenge the validity and operation of the Dublin System such as *N S v Secretary of State for the Home Department and M E v Refugee Applications Commissioner, Minister for Justice, Equality and Law Reform* [2011] ECR I-13905. These cases are different from the cases discussed in Chapter 4, most of which are challenges made before the European Court of Human Rights under the ECHR. Unlike the cases discussed in Chapter 5, the cases in Chapter 4 do not directly call into question the Dublin System's validity, and the European Court of Human Rights does not have jurisdiction to make such a determination: Cathryn Costello, 'Courting Access to Asylum in Europe: Recent Supranational Jurisprudence Explored' (2012) 12(2) *Human Rights Law Review* 287, 307.

deciding these cases, judges must determine the extent to which they will take regional law, international law or foreign jurisprudence into account in setting the threshold for adequate refuge. Another contentious issue is whether these legal frameworks permit them to pass judgment on other states' laws and policies. Therefore, the main theme in Chapter 5 is the role that cartographic and juridical borders play in protection from refuge challenges. I examine the ways decision-makers position and manoeuvre juridical borders in constructing ideas of refuge and determining the legality of states' attempts to prevent refugees crossing international borders in search of refuge. I observe that, when courts consider the significance of refugeehood and expand their juridical borders to permit assessment of sites of refuge in other states, they set high thresholds for refuge and characterise it as a duty owed by states. These powerful conceptualisations of refuge disrupt the continuation of containment agreements.

However, in most cases examined in Chapter 5, courts ignore the salience of refugee status and retract their juridical borders. This means that there is no minimum standard of refuge set in these protection from refuge cases and refuge morphs from an obligation to a discretion. Refugees become trapped in the resisted place of refuge, unable to continue their journey except in exceptional or extraordinary circumstances. What is considered exceptional is highly gendered with the narrow frameworks developed sidelining experiences of male and also many female refugees. The extraordinary circumstances needed to trigger these legal frameworks also have significant gendered consequences, placing both men and women at significant and different forms of risk.

In Chapters 6 and 7, I examine protection from refuge claims that arise under the Refugee Convention. These claims are also brought by those who have made long journeys to countries in the Global North. However, instead of being sent to or trapped in a nearby country within the region, these litigants face the prospect of being returned to a place of ostensible refuge in the Global South. Human rights arguments are present in these claims, and the role of borders is significant, but another factor at play is Global North states' concerns that potentially significant numbers of people may use the Refugee Convention to transfer their place of refuge from a lower- to a higher-income country.[34] To assist a dissection of decision-makers' approaches to these claims, I draw on literature written from third-world approaches to international law, critical race and postcolonial perspectives that position the Refugee Convention as a containment mechanism.

I embark on this line of investigation in Chapter 6, in which I examine cases that are instigated by Palestinian refugees. Palestinians are the only group of refugees who do not come within the UNHCR's mandate and instead have their own UN body that provides protection and assistance – UNRWA. The history behind the different treatment of Palestinian refugees is discussed in Chapter 6. UNRWA defines Palestinian refugees as those whose normal place of residence was Palestine during the period 1 June 1946 to 15 May 1948, and who lost both home and means of livelihood as a result of the 1948 conflict, as well as descendants of men who meet this criteria.[35] UNRWA is also mandated to provide protection and assistance to other displaced persons, including those displaced as

---

[34] Chimni (n 24) 351; Penelope Mathew, 'The Shifting Boundaries and Content of Protection: The Internal Protection Alternative Revisited' in Satvinder Juss (ed), *The Ashgate Research Companion to Migration Law, Theory and Policy* (Ashgate, 2013) 189, 206.

[35] UNRWA, *Consolidated Eligibility and Registration Instructions (CERI)* (May 2006) 2 <www.unrwa.org /sites/default/files/ceri_24_may_2006_final.pdf>.

a result of the 1967 Israel–Arab conflict and subsequent hostilities.[36] UNRWA uses the term 'Palestinian refugee' to encompass the groups it is mandated to protect and assist as well as those who come within UNRWA's definition of a Palestinian refugee.[37]

Some Palestinian refugees leave an UNRWA area of operation (Jordan, Lebanon, Syria, the Gaza strip, East Jerusalem or the West Bank) and seek refugee protection elsewhere. In making these journeys, they confront article 1D of the Refugee Convention, which applies only to Palestinian refugees and is described as an exclusion[38] or 'contingent inclusion' clause.[39] Article 1D provides that Palestinian refugees are excluded from protection under the Refugee Convention unless their UN protection or assistance has ceased for any reason. I explain in detail article 1D and the debates on its interpretations in Chapter 6. Decision-makers' approach to these claims determines whether Palestinian refugees should return to an UNRWA region to receive international protection or be entitled to remain in the country where they made the article 1D claim and receive protection as Convention refugees.

When decision-makers reflect on the nature of Palestinian refugeehood and expand their juridical borders, they come close to setting a broad scope of refuge for Palestinian refugees and characterising refuge as a right, duty and act of international solidarity. In particular, a 2019 Aotearoa/New Zealand decision may open the door to a protection-sensitive approach to article 1D, at least for those Palestinian refugees who travel to the Antipodes. However, most decision-makers determine these claims in a way that truncates the scope of refuge for Palestinian refugees, positions refuge not as a right but as an act of benevolence and entrenches article 1D as a containment mechanism. This inhibits Palestinian refugees' ability to find a place of refuge outside the UNRWA region unless their circumstances are deemed exceptional in some way. A feminist analysis of the case law indicates that the approach to exceptionality in article 1D jurisprudence creates additional barriers for female Palestinian refugees. This is because it prioritises those who have been specifically targeted with a form of harm manifesting in the public sphere but disregards harms most likely to occur behind closed doors.

In Chapter 7, I analyse cases in which decision-makers have to determine whether a person can seek refuge in an IDP camp. These cases arise under article 1A(2) of the Refugee Convention and are made by putative refugees. A putative refugee is a person outside their country of origin or habitual residence, whose circumstances indicate they satisfy one aspect of the refugee definition in the Refugee Convention (a well-founded fear of being persecuted for reasons of race, religion, nationality, membership of a particular social group or political opinion), but who have not yet established another part of the definition (that they are unable to avail themselves of the protection of their country of origin or habitual residence). In most jurisdictions, decision-makers will ask whether the putative refugee can relocate to another part of their country of origin or habitual residence in which they will have protection. This is an internal protection alternative ('IPA') enquiry.[40] In some of these cases, the putative refugee has pleaded that, if they internally

---

[36] Damian Lilly, 'UNRWA's Protection Mandate: Closing the "Protection Gap"' (2018) 30(3) *International Journal of Refugee Law* 444, 446.

[37] Ibid 446.

[38] James Hathaway and Michelle Foster, *The Law of Refugee Status* (Cambridge University Press, 2nd ed, 2014) 513, 515.

[39] Guy Goodwin-Gill and Susan Akram, 'Brief *Amicus Curiae* on the Status of Palestinian Refugees under International Law' (2000) 11 *Palestine Yearbook of International Law* 187, 191.

[40] See Jessica Schultz, *The Internal Protection Alternative in Refugee Law* (Brill, 2019) 15–7 for a discussion of other terminologies, including 'internal flight alternative' and 'internal relocation'. I use 'internal

relocate, they would have no option but to live in an IDP camp. Decision-makers must then determine if an IDP camp is an acceptable internal protection alternative. These cases have arisen in the UK and Aotearoa/New Zealand.[41] It is possible to consider all putative refugees facing an IPA assessment as prospective IDPs[42] (IDPs are people who have fled their homes but remain within their state).[43] However, in these particular cases, refuge as a place and concept collide because the putative refugee is resisting the prospect of seeking refuge in an IDP camp, a place intended to provide refuge to significant numbers of people displaced from their homes.[44]

When these claims initially came before courts and tribunals in the early 2000s, decision-makers reflected on the situations of those living in IDP camps. They set a broad scope for adequate refuge and approached decisions with an ethic of international cooperation. But subsequently, there has been a transition in which decision-makers produce rudimentary notions of refuge. They give it a narrow scope – limiting it to bare survival rights – and there is a shift from understanding that refuge involves a nation-state bestowing protection to positioning refuge as something individuals can forge themselves. The understanding that refuge is an act of international solidarity has dissipated from the jurisprudence. Protection from life in an IDP camp will only be granted if the putative refugee can establish that they are exceptionally vulnerable. Feminist methods of analysis highlight that decision-makers' notional approaches to the interactions between gender and vulnerability have resulted in problematic outcomes for refugees of all genders.

In the concluding chapter, I reflect on the patterns in the ways decision-makers across all of these jurisdictions, grappling with different legal instruments and doctrines, approach and determine protection from refuge claims. Across the globe, decision-makers have transitioned from sophisticated to impoverished understandings of refuge, from approaches that disrupt containment mechanisms to those that cement them and from decisions that facilitate to ones that impede refugee journeys. However, some recent jurisprudence indicates that there may be a shift back towards more protection-sensitive decisions.

---

protection alternative' because it highlights what should be decision-makers' main concern: whether the putative refugee will have *protection* if they relocate.

[41] I conducted a search of IPA jurisprudence on LexisNexis, Westlaw and Refworld. The issue of internal relocation to an IDP camp has arisen in some decisions in which the individuals are not entitled to refugee protection. See note 92 for an example. As outlined on page 18, protection from refuge claims made by those whose claims for international protection have been unsuccessful are outside the scope of this book.

[42] Schultz (n 40) 7.

[43] IDPs are those 'who have been forced or obliged to flee or to leave their homes or places of habitual residence, in particular as a result of or in order to avoid the effects of armed conflict, situations of generalized violence, violations of human rights or natural or human-made disasters, and who have not crossed an internationally recognized state border': Guiding Principles on Internal Displacement, UN ESCOR, UN Doc E/CN.4/1998/53/Add.2 (22 July 1998) [2].

[44] Principle 12(2) of the Guiding Principles on Internal Displacement (n 43) provides that IDPs 'shall not be interned in or confined to a camp' unless 'absolutely necessary'. However, this 'addresses the use of closed camps which [IPDs] cannot leave, and has to be distinguished from the practice of using camps to host large numbers of such persons': Walter Kälin, 'Guiding Principles on Internal Displacement: Annotations' (Paper No 32, American Society of International Law Studies in Transnational Legal Policy, 2008) 32. In most contexts, IDP camps are intended to be sites of protection for IDPs and many are staffed by representatives from various international organisations: Brookings Institution, *Protecting Internally Displaced Persons: A Manual for Law and Policy Makers* (October 2008) 63 <www.unhcr.org/50f955599.pdf>.

The ways courts are arbitrating protection from refuge challenges has significant implications for refugee law and the international protection regime more broadly. In particular, two of the most pressing problems in refugee protection are protracted encampment situations and that the majority of the world's refugees are hosted by states least able to do so.[45] Courts cannot comprehensively address these dilemmas, and there is scepticism about the long-term utility of using litigation as a tool to reshape refugee protection policy.[46] Nevertheless, the significance of courts as arbitrators of conflicts between refugee journeys and states' containment mechanisms is unlikely to abate. As states shift from earlier forms of *non-entrée* practices, such as interception, to more externalised and cooperative forms of border control, new legal challenges will emerge.[47] Courts can, depending on the way they determine these claims, alter or reinforce the current inequities in location of and responsibility for refugees. In Chapter 8, I highlight the approaches to protection from refuge claims likely to help to create a more just and equitable system of refugee protection and those that compound existing injustices and inequities. I make these observations while acknowledging that protection from refuge claims across the globe are grounded in different legal frameworks. Bringing these divergent areas of case law together in the one study is an integral aspect of my methodology, which I outline in the next section.

1.4   Methodology: Tracing Litigation across the Refugee Journey

By tracing the different points at which protection from refuge claims can arise in refugee journeys, I am conducting what Minow calls a 'recasting project': a study that gathers 'more than one "line" of cases across doctrinal fields' to 'show why they belong together' and offer 'a new framework or paradigm' in which they can be examined.[48] While analyses of case law are commonly categorised according to the legal framework in which actions are grounded,[49] I bring together cases on the basis of similarities in what the litigants are seeking. Thus, this project has methodological parallels with studies of remedies. Remedies scholars collate jurisprudence with reference to what a court orders or grants, as opposed to specific causes of action, and draw together cases framed in different areas of law such as contract, tort, equity and property.[50] Zakrzewski highlights the significance of such approaches by underlining that all civil litigants come to lawyers or courts wanting a remedy, and it is the lawyer's job to work backwards and assist them to obtain that remedy by pleading their case using the appropriate cause of action.[51] Translated to refugee law, the

[45] Developing regions host 85 per cent of the refugees under the UNHCR's mandate: UNHCR (n 2) 2. Also, in Europe, southern border states host disproportionate numbers of refugees due to the operation of the Dublin System: Madeline Garlick, 'The Dublin System, Solidarity and Individual Rights' in Vincent Chetail, Philippe De Bruycker and Francesco Maiani (eds), *Reforming the Common European Asylum System: The New European Refugee Law* (Brill, 2016) 156, 165–6.
[46] Baumgärtel (n 30) 79; Cathryn Costello, *The Human Rights of Migrants and Refugees in European Law* (Oxford University Press, 2015) 232.
[47] Gammeltoft-Hansen and Hathaway (n 20) 236, 244.
[48] Martha Minow, 'Archetypal Legal Scholarship: A Field Guide' (2013) 63(1) *Journal of Legal Education* 65, 66.
[49] Rafal Zakrzewski, *Remedies Reclassified* (Oxford University Press, 2005) 5.
[50] See, e.g., Peter Birks, 'Personal Property: Proprietary Rights and Remedies' (2000) 11(1) *Kings College Law Journal* 1; Michael Tilbury, *Principles of Civil Remedies* (Butterworths, 1990).
[51] Zakrzewski (n 49) 1.

litigants in protection from refuge cases all seek what they believe to be a genuine place of refuge. Their representatives use the legal frameworks available to them to achieve this objective. The legal frameworks will differ depending on the refugee's status and circumstances and whether they are in, for example, Kenya, Greece, Canada, Australia or Papua New Guinea. There are significant distinctions between the ways protection from refuge cases are framed and the jurisdictions and institutional cultures of the decision-making bodies that determine them. These are acknowledged and discussed throughout the book. Nevertheless, at the core of these claims, refugees and asylum seekers are using the legal frameworks available to them to resist transfer to or seek rescue from a place of refuge.

While there are a plethora of studies on the ways decision-makers have interpreted refugee definitions,[52] bringing protection from refuge cases into conversation with each other enables an examination of how they draw the contours and content of the remedy: refuge. The best-known study of the rights refugees are entitled to is Hathaway's seminal 2005 publication (the second edition was published in 2021),[53] in which he elucidates a refugee rights regime through synthesising entitlements in the Refugee Convention with rights in the ICCPR and ICESCR. However, when refugees seek courts' assistance in securing transfer to or rescue from a place of refuge, it is rare that they can directly plead these rights. As noted earlier, they often have to resort to other, and often local, legal instruments to frame their case. Hathaway says that, '[d]espite its length', his study 'is no more than a first step in the development of a clear appreciation of how best to ensure the human rights of refugees under international law'.[54] In this book, I take another step. Rather than starting my enquiry, as Hathaway does, with reference to international legal instruments, I begin with the legal claims refugees have brought in their attempts to secure a place of genuine refuge. While many of these claims do not directly invoke the Refugee Convention, I show that courts bring local and regional legal frameworks into conversation with international refugee law and sometimes in a way that deepens our understanding of refugee protection. As Knop explains, there is a process of translation that occurs when domestic and regional courts refer to international law alongside domestic and regional law.[55] This process of translation can produce new meanings and enrich our understanding of international law obligations.

While cutting across different areas of jurisprudence can offer new frameworks or paradigms, it is not without its challenges. Adopting a recasting methodology requires analysis of areas of law that are often considered distinct. As discussed earlier, this book brings together jurisprudence and literature on people with refugee status pursuant to the Refugee Convention, those granted complementary protection, Palestinian refugees, putative refugees and IDPs. The legal frameworks that apply to these categories of protection

---

[52] See, e.g., Michelle Foster, 'Non-Refoulement on the Basis of Socio-Economic Deprivation: The Scope of Complementary Protection in International Human Rights Law' (2009)(2) *New Zealand Law Review* 257; Constance MacIntosh, 'When Feminist Beliefs Became Credible as Political Opinions: Returning to a Key Moment in Canadian Refugee Law' (2005) 17 *Canadian Journal of Women and the Law* 135; Jenni Millbank, 'From Discretion to Disbelief: Recent Trends in Refugee Determinations on the Basis of Sexual Orientation in Australia and the United Kingdom' (2009) 13(2/3) *International Journal of Human Rights* 391; Hugo Storey and Rebecca Wallace, 'War and Peace in Refugee Law Jurisprudence' (2001) 95 *American Journal of International Law* 349.
[53] Hathaway (n 15).   [54] Ibid 991.
[55] Karen Knop, 'Here and There: International Law in Domestic Courts' (2000) 32(2) *New York University Journal of International Law and Politics* 501, 504.

seekers are different. From an international law perspective, protection for Convention refugees and those with complementary protection is governed by the rights in the Refugee Convention, supplemented by international human rights law.[56] Palestinians were excluded from the Refugee Convention when it came into force and some scholars and courts take the view that they remain excluded. As noted earlier, they are the only group of refugees not to come under the UNHCR's mandate and, instead, receive protection and assistance from UNRWA. In examining the protection available to Palestinian refugees, Albanese and Takkenberg look across statelessness law, international humanitarian law, human rights law and UNRWA's mandate.[57] Protection of IDPs is outlined in the Guiding Principles on Internal Displacement[58] and, in Africa, the Convention for the Protection and Assistance of Internally Displaced Persons in Africa.[59] There is no legal framework as such that applies to putative refugees but there are various legal tests, grounded in refugee and human rights law, that are applied to determine whether a putative refugee will have adequate protection if they internally relocate within their country of origin. Each of the aforementioned legal frameworks and principles are discussed in Chapter 2.

Limiting the case studies in this book to Convention refugees or those with complementary protection (jurisprudence in Chapters 3–5) would have been more intellectually pure. Chapters 6 and 7 necessitate consideration of the different legal frameworks and principles applicable to Palestinian refugees, putative refugees and IDPs. Nevertheless, in Chapter 2 and throughout the book, I show that, while there are different categories of people entitled to protection and distinct legal frameworks that apply to them, there are similarities with respect to understandings of what that protection should be. In particular, ideas about what refuge should achieve and what it should contain are paralleled across legal frameworks, scholarship and jurisprudence, addressing Convention refugees, those with complementary protection, Palestinian refugees, putative refugees and IDPs.

Further, if this book did not include protection from refuge claims made by Palestinian refugees and putative refugees fearing life in an IDP camp, some things would have been lost. Kagan bemoans 'Palestinian exceptionalism', by which he means that Palestinian refugees are treated as an anomalous group of refugees and rarely discussed alongside other refugees.[60] By including a chapter on Palestinian refugees, this book pushes against this pattern. Consideration of putative refugees fearing life in an IDP camp in Chapter 7 aligns with scholarship that problematises the distinction between refugees and IDPs on the grounds that both groups are often fleeing for similar reasons but only some have managed to cross an international border.[61] The reason for the distinction between IDPs and refugees, from an international law perspective, is that, due to the limits of state sovereignty, the Refugee Convention cannot apply to a person

---

[56] Hathaway (n 15); McAdam (n 13).

[57] Francesca Albanese and Lex Takkenberg, *Palestinian Refugees in International Law* (Oxford University Press, 2nd ed, 2020).

[58] The Guiding Principles (n 43) 'consolidate into one document the legal standards relevant to the internally displaced drawn from international human rights law, humanitarian law and refugee law by analogy': Francis Deng, 'Preface' in Kälin (n 44).

[59] 23 October 2009, in force 16 December 2012.

[60] Michael Kagan, 'The (Relative) Decline of Palestinian Exceptionalism and Its Consequences for Refugee Studies in the Middle East' (2009) 22(4) *Journal of Refugee Studies* 417.

[61] See, e.g., Andrew Shacknove, 'Who Is a Refugee?' (1985) 95(2) *Ethics* 274; Patricia Tuitt, 'Refugees, Nations, Laws and the Territorialization of Violence' in Peter Fitzpatrick and Patricia Tuitt (eds), *Critical Beings: Law, Nation and the Global Subject* (Ashgate, 2004) 37, 48.

within the borders of their homeland. The jurisprudence discussed in Chapter 7, in traversing ideas of protection under the Refugee Convention and protection of IDPs, provides an opportunity to unsettle these (some would say arbitrary) categories of protection seekers.

In examining protection from refuge claims made in different jurisdictions and by different categories of people with or seeking international protection, I draw on comparative legal analysis as a methodology. Comparative legal analysis involves searching for similarities and differences across legal systems and, in particular, looking for 'differences in an area of perceived similarities, and for similarities in an area of perceived difference'.[62] This book is an invitation to readers to both appreciate the specific legal frameworks pleaded in each type of protection from refuge claim and look beyond these differences to consider how these cases arbitrate the objectives, nature, threshold and scope of refuge. In this sense, this book is a response to the concern that much refugee law scholarship is 'relentlessly local' in that it 'tend[s] to frame questions and answers within national or regional frameworks'.[63] Developing tools and terminology to identify and analyse shifting judicial standards of refugee protection is important. Durieux suggests that 'to define refugees is to say as much about "who we are" as about "who they are" – it goes to the identity of the definer'.[64] Similarly, where we set the ambit of refuge – whether we are generous or uncharitable – is a reflection of the principles we hold. Studying courts' views is important because their role is to give 'clear messages to states as to what is and what is not permitted under human rights law' and 'nip in the bud arbitrariness and a descent into totalitarianism and exclusivism'.[65]

This book also adds a new dimension to refugee law scholarship because I analyse this jurisprudence by drawing on feminist approaches to international law. Feminist legal methodology involves 'looking beneath the surface of law to identify the gender implications of rules and the assumptions underlying them'.[66] This requires interrogating the positive rules of law and the issues deemed 'irrelevant or of little significance'.[67] These silences or legal boundaries often ignore or 'distort the concerns that are more typical of women than men'.[68] Nevertheless, asking the woman question, or 'asking the gender question',[69] does not mean focussing only on women. It includes an analysis of the different ways in which law impacts upon people of all genders as well as members of marginalised groups such as people with disabilities, children, the elderly and people who are lesbian, gay, bisexual, transgender, gender diverse, intersex, queer, asexual and questioning.[70] There is a large literature on refugee decision-makers' approaches to questions of gender, but the overwhelming majority of these studies focus on how they interpret refugee definitions and

---

[62] Gerhard Danneman, 'Comparative Law: Studies of Similarities or Differences?' in Mathias Reimann and Reinhard Zimmermann (eds), *The Oxford Handbook of Comparative Law* (Oxford University Press, 2006) 384, 406.

[63] Efrat Arbel, Catherine Dauvergne and Jenni Millbank, 'Introduction, Gender in Refugee Law – From the Margins to the Centre' in Efrat Arbel, Catherine Dauvergne and Jenni Millbank (eds), *Gender in Refugee Law: From the Margins to the Centre* (Routledge, 2014) 1.

[64] Durieux (n 28) 151.   [65] Dembour (n 30) 508.

[66] Katharine Bartlett, 'Feminist Legal Methods' (1990) 103(4) *Harvard Law Review* 829, 843.

[67] Hilary Charlesworth, 'Feminist Methods in International Law' (1999) 93 *American Journal of International Law* 379, 381.

[68] Alice Edwards, *Violence against Women under International Human Rights Law* (Cambridge University Press, 2010) 30.

[69] Ibid 30.   [70] Bartlett (n 66) 831.

grounds for complementary protection.[71] What is missing is an assessment of the role of gender in decision-makers' conceptualisations of refuge and approaches to refugees' searches for sanctuary.

In their assessment of gender in refugee law scholarship and advocacy, Arbel, Dauvergne and Millbank state that renewed focus on gender in refugee law is vital, because 'while much has been accomplished, in the most recent years ground has also been lost'.[72] In this book, I answer this call by examining whether the ways decision-makers approach protection from refuge claims, and in particular, what they deem crucial and irrelevant, disadvantages certain refugees in their journeys in search of refuge. In their analysis of refugee status assessment, Arbel, Dauvergne and Millbank argue that, after decades of sustained feminist engagement with refugee law, jurisprudence has moved from being gender blind and being 'a much better fit for men than for women'[73] to a situation where 'decision-makers in Western refugee receiving countries routinely put gender on the tick-box of topics for consideration'.[74] In this book, I examine whether there has been a similar trajectory with respect to judicial approaches to the concept of refuge and contests between refugees' entitlement to refuge and states' interests in constraining refugees' mobility.

By switching the focus from refugee definitions to the remedy (refuge), this book illustrates that, in some contexts, refugee law decision-makers have not made the basic progression from gender-blind decisions that create legal tests more fitting for men than women to including gender as an important unit of analysis. Nevertheless, while some protection from refuge challenges are arbitrated in this manner, in others, decision-makers acknowledge that gender as well as factors such as sexuality, youth and disability are important factors that must be considered. This puts these protection from refuge decisions in line with refugee status assessments where decision-makers 'routinely' consider questions of gender.[75] However, most decision-makers are not engaging with questions of gender in any substantive way, but are approaching them in a perfunctory manner. These desultory approaches to gender in protection from refuge claims raise the same query Arbel, Dauvergne and Millbank ask in the refugee status assessment context: when 'the argument can no longer be for jurisprudential inclusion', how do we facilitate 'more meaningful, more complicated, more substantive analysis'?[76] The jurisprudence analysed in this book

---

[71] Arbel, Dauvergne and Millbank provide the most recent collection of scholarship on decision-makers' approaches to gender concerns and describe their project as 'an international comparative project on gender-related persecution and [refugee status determination]': (n 63) 9. There is only one chapter in their edited collection concerning what I call protection from refuge challenges, Arbel's study of litigation on a containment agreement between Canada and the US, on which I draw in Chapter 5. Edwards 'traces the history of feminist engagement with refugee law and policy' from 1950 to 2010: Alice Edwards, 'Transitioning Gender: Feminist Engagement with International Refugee Law and Policy 1950-2010' (2010) 29(2) *Refugee Survey Quarterly* 21. Her analysis focusses on the refugee definition. Anderson and Foster explain that '[w]hile [refugee status determination] has been (perhaps inevitably) dominated by feminist *legal* scholarship, such analysis is much less prevalent, even largely absent, in some respects of the wider refugee experience': Adrienne Anderson and Michelle Foster, 'A Feminist Appraisal of Refugee Law' in Cathryn Costello, Michelle Foster and Jane McAdam (eds), *The Oxford Handbook of International Refugee Law* (Oxford University Press, 2021) 60, 69.

[72] Arbel, Dauvergne and Millbank (n 63) 14. See also Catherine Dauvergne, 'Women in Refugee Jurisprudence' in Cathryn Costello, Michelle Foster and Jane McAdam (eds), *The Oxford Handbook of International Refugee Law* (Oxford University Press, 2021) 728.

[73] Arbel, Dauvergne and Millbank (n 63) 3.   [74] Ibid 1.   [75] Ibid 1.   [76] Ibid 6.

provides some counterintuitive insights on moving towards a more meaningful, compli-cated and substantive gender and intersectional analysis in refugee law jurisprudence.

1.5   Scope

While this is a global and comparative study, it is not an exhaustive one. Within the confines of a single book, I cannot address all aspects and manifestations of protection from refuge scenarios. In this section, I highlight the issues and jurisprudence that lie outside the scope of this work and also how the protection from refuge framework developed in this book can be deployed to inform future research.

The question this book poses is: *how* do decision-makers approach and determine protection from refuge claims? To answer this question, in each case study I identify the methods of reasoning judges and other adjudicative decision-makers use in arbitrating protection from refuge claims. In this sense, this book sits alongside other studies in the field that trace changes in judicial reasoning.[77]

It is beyond this book's scope to investigate *why* decision-makers adopt particular approaches. As noted earlier, one of the findings is that there has been a shift in how decision-makers approach protection from refuge claims. Courts are constrained by codi-fied law, rules of interpretation, the way the litigants frame their case and, where *stare decisis* applies, earlier precedent. Yet, in almost all of the jurisprudence examined in this book, courts had a choice in how to determine the arguments pleaded.[78] Indeed, in most court challenges, there are numerous outcomes open to the judges and the result is a consequence of both legal reasoning and choice.[79] Explaining why a particular decision was made presents methodological challenges for legal researchers, in particular because judicial deliberations are conducted in confidence. In most cases, the best a researcher can do is to provide 'informed guesses'.[80]

There are a number of methodological models in refugee law scholarship for how to confront this dilemma. Mann tracks the trajectory of judicial responses to unauthorised migration but does not interrogate or comment on judges' motivations.[81] Spijkerboer, in his analysis of refugee jurisprudence in the Court of Justice of the European Union, speculates on the political motivations behind the Court's decisions.[82] Similarly, Dembour, in her analysis of the European Court of Human Rights' approaches to migrant rights, notes that the reasons why the Court takes specific approaches is outside the scope of her study but provides 'potential explanations'.[83] Going further, Baumgärtel and Ticktin interview judges to gain direct insights into the reasons for their decisions.[84]

Given the global focus of this book, the approach I take lies between that of Mann and Spijkerboer and Dembour. I focus predominately on the reasoning adopted and, where appropriate, offer suggestions about the underlying judicial motivations. The reasons for

---

[77] Dembour (n 30) 22; Mann (n 23).

[78] The only exception is some of the Australian cases in Chapter 5, in which High Court of Australia was confined by changes to the Migration Act 1958 (Cth).

[79] Dembour (n 30) 20; Thomas Spijkerboer, 'Bifurcation of People, Bifurcation of Law: Externalisation of Migration Policy before the EU Court of Justice' (2017) 31(2) *Journal of Refugee Studies* 216, 232.

[80] Dembour (n 30) 419.   [81] Mann (n 23).   [82] Spijkerboer (n 79).   [83] Dembour (n 30) 9.

[84] Baumgärtel (n 30); Miriam Ticktin, 'Policing and Humanitarianism in France: Immigration and the Turn to Law as State of Exception' (2005) 7(3) *International Journal of Postcolonial Studies* 346.

the changes observed in each case study demand further scholarly attention and require a different methodological repertoire than the one employed here. This book, by tracking these disconcerting shifts across multiple jurisdictions, provides the groundwork for these future studies.

This book addresses most, but not all, protection from refuge claims. As described earlier, I have selected case studies that allow for an examination of legal challenges made at various stages of a refugee journey, initiated in different parts of the world and governed by divergent legal frameworks. Nevertheless, the rubric developed in this book can be applied to other legal challenges that raise the protection from refuge conundrum. In this book, I do not consider cases that have been initiated but withdrawn before final judgment due to changes in government policy.[85] An examination of the strategic value of such litigation would enrich understandings of the roles of courts in addressing protection from refuge scenarios. With respect to cases concerning safe third country rules in domestic legislation unconnected with a bilateral agreement, these are not included in this book. This is because in many jurisdictions judicial review of safe third-country decisions is heavily curtailed[86] and, in others, legislation significantly restricts the considerations courts and other decision-making bodies can take into account when determining whether the third country is indeed safe.[87] While there have been comparisons of safe third-country legislation and practices,[88] these restrictions make comparative assessments of judicial approaches difficult and ill-suited to the questions this book addresses. However, an emerging issue in the European context is the extent to which the European Court of Human Rights is willing to interfere with domestic safe third-country provisions.[89] An analysis of this

---

[85] The Israeli government made arrangements to relocate asylum seekers to undisclosed countries in Sub-Saharan Africa. A legal challenge was commenced and the Israeli Supreme Court issued a temporary injunction against the transfers. The proceeding was withdrawn when the Israeli government called off the removals. See Ruvi Ziegler, 'Benjamin Netanyahu's U-turn: No Redemption for Asylum Seekers in Israel', *The Conversation* (online 9 April 2018) <https://theconversation.com/benjamin-netanyahus-u-turn-no-redemption-for-asylum-seekers-in-israel-94441>. As this book was being written, the Biden Administration announced that it had initiated the process of terminating safe third-country agreements between the US, Guatemala, Honduras and El Salvador (entered into by the Trump Administration). I do not consider legal challenges to these agreements commenced prior to this announcement because only preliminary matters were determined and no final judgments had been handed down.

[86] Legislation in the UK allows for the removal of asylum seekers to a safe third country without substantive consideration of their claim: Asylum and Immigration (Treatment of Claimants, etc.) Act 2004 s 33, sch 3. If the Secretary of State certifies that a person is proposed to be removed to the safe third country, the asylum seeker cannot bring an appeal alleging that the transfer would breach the Refugee Convention: Asylum and Immigration (Treatment of Claimants, etc.) Act 2004 sch 3, pts 2.5(3)(a), 3.10(3), 4.15(3).

[87] For example, sections 36(4)–36(5A) of Australia's Migration Act 1958 (Cth) limit decision-makers' considerations to: whether the asylum seeker would have a well-founded fear of being persecuted for a Refugee Convention ground in the third country, would be at real risk of suffering significant harm in the third country, has a well-founded fear that the third country would return them to another country where they will be persecuted for a Refugee Convention ground or has a well-founded fear of being returned to a country where there is a real risk they would suffer significant harm.

[88] Violeta Moreno-Lax, 'The Legality of the "Safe Third Country" Notion Contested: Insights from the Law of Treaties' in Guy Goodwin-Gill and Philippe Weckel (eds), *Migration & Refugee Protection in the 21st Century: International Legal Aspects* (Martinus Nijhoff, 2015) 665; Jane McAdam, 'Migrating Laws? The "Plagiaristic Dialogue" Between Europe and Australia' in Hélène Lambert, Jane McAdam and Maryellen Fullerton (eds), *The Global Reach of European Refugee Law* (Cambridge University Press, 2013) 25, 28–35.

[89] *Ilias and Ahmed v Hungary* (Fourth Section, Application No 47287/15, 14 March 2017) and *Ilias and Ahmed v Hungary* (Grand Chamber, Application No 47287/15, 21 November 2019) indicate that the

new area of jurisprudence using the methods and terminology developed in this book would add to understandings of courts' use of human rights law to engage with notions of refugee protection. Finally, I do not examine cases in which refugees are challenging detention and they are not detained pursuant to a bilateral or regional containment agreement.[90] In most of these cases, courts and other decision-making bodies are concerned with issues such as whether detention is lawful or arbitrary and not wider issues of refugee protection. Nevertheless, cases concerning escape from immigration detention may warrant examination of how decision-makers use legal frameworks to facilitate or hinder refugee journeys.[91]

There are also cases that do not quite fit into the protection from refuge framework adopted in this book but an analysis of which would add to our understanding of judicial notions of refuge. There are some protection from refuge cases brought by litigants who have not claimed or have been denied international protection.[92] I do not to examine these cases because I wish to explore the functions, nature, scope and threshold of refuge for those who are or may be entitled to some form of international protection. The ways decision-makers conceptualise refuge for those otherwise not entitled to international protection is a topic that is starting to receive attention.[93] Another set of cases that could illuminate judicial understandings of refuge are cases in which refugees challenge their host states' policies on, for example, access to healthcare or welfare.[94] I do not include these cases because they do not involve a refugee litigant demanding to be rescued from or transferred to a specific place of refuge and I seek to explore the ways judicial ideas of refuge facilitate or impede refugees' journeys. Nevertheless, the concepts and methods of analysis developed in this book could be used to critically assess the ideas of refuge reflected in these decisions and whether they respond to the particular needs of refugees from more marginalised backgrounds.

Finally, I only examine cases that have come before adjudicative decision-making bodies and reached the stage where a decision has been delivered. Many factors determine whether an asylum seeker or refugee is able to access courts or other decision-making bodies to secure protection from a place of refuge. In particular, refugees in many jurisdictions do not

European Court of Human Rights is willing to consider transfers via safe third-country provisions to be in violation of article 3 of the ECHR.

[90] See, e.g., *Amuur v France* (1996) III Eur Court HR 850; *Plaintiff M76 2013 v Minister for Immigration, Multicultural Affairs and Citizenship* (2013) 251 CLR 322; *Refugee and Migratory Research Unit v Government of Bangladesh* Writ Petition No. 10504 of 2016, Bangladesh Supreme Court, 31 May 2017.

[91] See, e.g., *R (B & Others) v SSFCA* [2005] QB 643; ΑΡΙΘΜΟΣ:682/2012 ΠΡΑΚΤΙΚΑ ΚΑΙ ΑΠΟΦΑΣΗ ΤΟΥ ΜΟΝΟΜΕΛΟΥΣ ΠΛΗΜΜΕΛΕΙΟΔΙΚΕΙΟΥ ΗΓΟΥΜΕΝΙΤΣΑΣ Συνεδρίαση της 2ης Οκτωβρίου 2012.

[92] An example of such a case is *Sufi and Elmi v UK* [2012] 54 EHRR 9. The European Court of Human Rights considered whether a Somali man whose application for refugee status had been refused and a Somali refugee who had lost the protection of the Refugee Convention due to art 33(2) could be deported. The Court held that levels of violence in Mogadishu presented a real risk of treatment contrary to art 3 of the ECHR: [250]. The Court then considered the prospect of internal relocation to IDP camps in Somalia as well as to the Dadaab refugee camp in Kenya. It concluded that conditions in both camps raised a real risk of treatment contrary to art 3 of the ECHR: [291]–[292].

[93] Bríd Ní Ghráinne, 'Complementary Protection and Encampment' (2021) 21(1) *Human Rights Law Review* 54.

[94] See, e.g., *Canadian Doctors for Refugee Care, The Canadian Association of Refugee Lawyers, Daniel Garcia Rodrigues, Hanif Ayubi and Justice for Children and Youth v Attorney General of Canada and Minister of Citizenship and Immigration* [2014] FC 651; *Kreis Warendorf v Ibrahim Alo and Amira Osso v Region Hannover* (Cases 443/14 and 444/14) ECLI:EU:C:2016:127.

receive free legal representation.[95] Even when legal representation is available, factors such as language difficulties, youth, gender, disabilities, restrictions on freedom of movement, illiteracy and mistrust of legal authorities can inhibit an asylum seeker or refugee's access to legal services.[96] The use of courts to seek protection from a place of ostensible refuge can exacerbate inequities between refugees who have access to legal representation and those who do not.[97] An important question for future research is to consider who has access to adjudicative decision-making bodies in protection from refuge contexts.

1.6 Conclusion

While scholars have investigated refugees' journeys within and across borders and outlined various understandings of what refuge should be, there has been little work on judicial conceptualisations of refuge and how these may facilitate or impede refugees' searches for sanctuary. This is despite refugees and asylum seekers in a number of jurisdictions turning to courts and other decision-making bodies to either resist or seek transfer to an alternative place of refuge. This book is the first study to draw together these protection from refuge claims and examine how decision-makers approach and determine them. In doing so, it sheds light on judicial ideas of refuge and the role adjudicative bodies play in refugees' journeys.

This study identifies a pattern across the various jurisdictions in which protection from refuge claims are made. When decision-makers reflect on the nature of refugeehood and use the legal frameworks pleaded to address the predicaments faced by refugees and asylum seekers, judicial ideas of what refuge should be go beyond basic notions of safety and survival and advance ideas of refuge outlined by scholars and UN institutions. These judicial conceptualisations of refuge are also responsive to the particular needs of refugees of different genders, sexualities and ages, as well as to the difficulties faced by refugees with care responsibilities and disabilities. In these jurisprudential moments, refuge becomes a potent concept and one that refugees can wield to disrupt the continuation of containment mechanisms and continue their searches for refuge within and across borders.

However, most of these victories have been ephemeral. Decision-makers reverse or dilute initial protection from refuge successes by reframing the legal issues in ways that excise consideration of refuge as a concept, of refuge as a place or of both. While the reasons for this change must be assessed with respect to what is occurring in each particular jurisdiction, the common outcome of this reframing is that decision-makers shift from purposive and broad understandings of refuge to rudimentary ones. Once this occurs, the protection from refuge litigant must prove that they are exceptional in some way. Decision-makers' approaches to identifying the 'atypical' refugee often create additional hurdles for women, men, parents, children and those with disabilities to use courts to seek a safe place of refuge.

[95] Stephen Anagost, 'The Challenge of Providing High Quality, Low Cost Legal Aid for Asylum Seekers and Refugees' (2000) 12(4) *International Journal of Refugee Law* 577.
[96] Andika Ab. Wahab and Aizat Khairi, 'Right to Justice and Legal Aid Barriers to the Vulnerable Non-Citizens in Malaysia' (2020) 16(1) *Malaysian Journal of Society and Space* 13; Jacqueline Bhabha, 'Seeking Asylum Alone: Treatment of Separated and Trafficked Children in Need of Refugee Protection' (2004) 42(1) *International Migration* 141, 143; Mary Anne Kenny, Nicholas Proctor and Carol Grech, 'Mental Health and Legal Representation for Asylum Seekers in the "Legacy Caseload"' (2016) 8(2) *Cosmopolitan Civil Societies Journal* 84.
[97] Baumgärtel (n 30) 78.

This disengagement from the concept of refuge and search for the extraordinary refugee transforms these judgments from refugee protection to migration management decisions. These judicial approaches impede refugees' journeys in search of refuge, perpetuate the current injustices and global inequities in refugee responsibility and render refuge, as both a concept and a place, elusive.

   Nevertheless, some very recent jurisprudence indicates that the tide may be turning and courts will once again provide a forum where refugee rights can triumph over containment mechanisms, enabling refugees to continue their journeys in search of sanctuary. It is hoped that this book, by identifying the methods of judicial reasoning that produce robust ideas of refuge and gender-sensitive decisions, provides some guidance for the future conduct and analysis of protection from refuge litigation.

Refuge as a Concept and a Place

2.1   Introduction

'No, I am not ruined yet. Looking out over the natural landscape, looking out over the grandeur before me, I can erase all the sinking feelings of weakness, of desolation, of inferiority. I am able to replace them with hope and joy'.[1] These are the words of Behrouz Boochani, a Kurdish refugee, describing his flight from Australia's Christmas Island to Papua New Guinea's Manus Island. This passage reflects the fragmented journeys many refugees endure – in this case being forcibly transferred from one host country to another. It also encapsulates the tensions between refuge as an idea and as a physical location: the protection concerns on both Christmas Island and Manus Island are well documented but Boochani expresses the need to mentally escape from this material reality and exhibit a sense of hopefulness.

In this chapter, I outline how scholars from a variety of disciplines, UN institutions and refugees approach and understand the notion of refuge. I also highlight the discrepancies between these ideas and the reality. This provides the backdrop against which I discuss how adjudicative decision-makers envision refuge and navigate the disjunctures between refuge as a concept and place in the following chapters. In Section 2.2, I explain why I use the word 'refuge' as opposed to similar terms commonly employed in the literature. In Section 2.3, I identify the five dominant intellectual inroads scholars use when articulating what refuge is or should be for those with or seeking international protection. In Sections 1.4–1.7 I draw on scholarship, UN materials and refugee memoirs to build a picture of the objectives, nature, scope and threshold of refuge. Across all of these sections, I ask the gender question by exploring literature that looks at what women are seeking when they search for refuge. Much of this scholarship provides a different perspective to understandings of refuge that do not specifically consider gender. I also cover material that gives insights on the nature of refuge sought by children and refugees with disabilities. Finally, in Section 1.8, I highlight what life is like in a number of sites of refuge, focussing on the places subject to the protection from refuge litigation examined in this book.

While the material discussed in this chapter is multi-disciplinary and wide-ranging, some limits must be acknowledged. First, because I am examining the concept of refuge with specific reference to those entitled to or seeking international protection, I do not consider more general theories of hospitality.[2] Second, this specific focus sidelines practices and concepts of refuge with respect to other forms of cross-border movement. For example, in many parts of the world there are people who cross borders as a form of 'subsistence

---

[1]   Behrouz Boochani, *No Friend But the Mountains: Writing from Manus Prison* (Pan Macmillan, 2018) 100.
[2]   See, e.g., Jacques Derrida and Anne Dufourmantelle, *Of Hospitality: Anne Dufourmantelle Invites Jacques Derrida to Respond*, tr Rachel Bowlby (Stanford University Press, 2000).

migration'.[3] They are usually not seeking international protection but rather move back and forth between their homeland and neighbouring countries.[4] Another example is the migration of people from lower- to higher-income countries seeking better economic opportunities. Achiume argues that former colonial states should permit their entry, not as refugees, but as a form of distributive and corrective justice.[5] People moving across international boundaries for different reasons often use the same channels – a phenomenon known as 'mixed migration'.[6] Nevertheless, these journeys are treated separately in international law[7] and scholarship. This chapter highlights that scholars from a variety of disciplines agree that, despite patterns of mixed migration, a special form of refuge should be granted to those who have or are seeking international protection.

As discussed in Chapter 1, this book addresses different categories of people in need of protection – people with or seeking protection under the Refugee Convention, those granted complementary protection, Palestinian refugees, putative refugees and IDPs. This necessitates consideration of the different legal frameworks that apply across these categories. The analysis in this chapter indicates that there are overlapping ideas about the objectives and content of refuge across the principles applicable to these different categories of people in need of protection. Overall, this chapter indicates that refuge as a concept is robust and highly developed. However, there is often a stark disparity between ideas of what refuge should be and the conditions those seeking refuge endure.

2.2   Refuge, Sanctuary, Asylum and International Protection: Synonymous Terms?

The words 'asylum', 'sanctuary' and 'refuge' have similar etymologies. Asylum derives from the Latin form of the Greek word *asylos*,[8] which means inviolability.[9] It was first used to describe 'some place or territory, large or small, where a person may not be seized by his [or her or their] pursuers'.[10] The term sanctuary is closely linked to asylum and 'comes from the Latin word for a sacred place'.[11] Certain places of worship in ancient Egypt, Greece and Rome provided sanctuary to runaway slaves and those accused of crimes.[12] Refuge originates from the Latin word *refugium*, which means a place to flee to.[13] One of its earliest uses is

---

[3]   Lindsey Carte, Claudia Radel and Birgit Schmook, 'Subsistence Migration: Smallholder Food Security and the Maintenance of Agriculture through Mobility in Nicaragua' (2019) 185 *The Geographic Journal* 180, 187.

[4]   Ibid.   [5]   E Tendayi Achiume, 'Migration as Decolonization' (2019) 71(6) *Stanford Law Review* 1509.

[6]   UNHCR, *Refugee Protection and Mixed Migration: A 10 Point Plan of Action* (1 January 2007) <www.unhcr.org/en-au/the-10-point-plan-in-action.html>.

[7]   For example, the type of migration Achiume (n 5) discusses would not be covered by the Refugee Convention or treaties providing complementary protection but may be covered by aspects of the International Convention on the Protection of the Rights of all Migrant Workers and Members of their Families, 18 December 1990, 220 UNTS 3, in force 1 July 2003.

[8]   Atle Grahl-Madsen, *The Status of Refugees in International Law: Volume 2* (AW Sijthoff-Leyden, 1966) 3; Matthew Price, *Rethinking Asylum: History, Purpose, and Limits* (Cambridge University Press, 2009) 26; Linda Rabben, *Give Refuge to the Stranger: The Past, Present, and Future of Sanctuary* (Left Coast Press, 2011) 18.

[9]   Price (n 8) 26; Rabben (n 8) 18.   [10]   Grahl-Madsen (n 8) 3.   [11]   Rabben (n 8) 18.   [12]   Ibid 18.

[13]   Collette Daiute, 'Narrating Refuge' (2017) 13(1) *Europe's Journal of Psychology* 1, 5.

in the Hebrew Bible, in which there were six cities of refuge where those accused of manslaughter were protected from avengers.[14]

In more recent contexts, these terms are often used synonymously. The Refugee Convention drafters considered these words to have congruity. The Peruvian delegate suggested that the word 'asylum' in the preamble should be changed to 'refuge' because, in the Latin American context, 'asylum' was used for what he described as political refugees, whereas refuge was granted to ordinary refugees.[15] However, the French representative countered that in France there was no distinction between the concepts of asylum, refuge and sanctuary.[16] The Chilean representative agreed that the word 'asylum' had the same meaning as 'refuge' even in a Latin American context.[17] Today, the UNHCR speaks of people seeking or being granted refuge,[18] asylum,[19] sanctuary[20] or international protection.[21] The authors surveyed in this chapter use one or all of these terms, and often interchangeably.

Nevertheless, I predominantly employ the word 'refuge' for two reasons. First, the term 'sanctuary' is more often associated with religious traditions of providing protection, whereas 'asylum' and 'international protection' are more likely to be used to refer to legal responses to people fleeing serious harm.[22] 'Refuge' is more generic and can encompass both. While one of the aims of this book is to examine judicial understandings of refuge, in doing so I do not want to overlook the similarities between legal approaches to refuge and those from outside the field of law. Due to the interdisciplinary nature of this chapter, refuge is a more fitting and flexible term. Second, there is a close linguistic connection between the words 'refuge' and 'refugee'. As noted in Chapter 1, 'refugee' derives from the Old French *réfugié*, which means 'gone in search of refuge'. In the following section, I discuss the ways scholars conceptualise refuge, and it will become apparent that the content of refuge is sometimes informed by the circumstances of those seeking it.

2.3   Conceptualising Refuge: Where to Begin?

There are a number of starting points for imagining what refuge is or should be. A survey of scholarship on refuge, sanctuary and asylum indicates five dominant approaches, which I describe as historical and cultural, experiential, rights-based, philosophical and categorical. I outline each next in Sections 2.3.1–2.3.5, but they are not mutually exclusive. Scholars often draw on more than one to outline their ideas of refuge. I identify these different inroads to theorising refuge so I can compare them to the ways decision-makers approach

---

[14] Moshe Greenberg, 'The Biblical Conception of Asylum' (1959) 78(2) *Journal of Biblical Literature* 125.
[15] UN Economic and Social Council, *Ad Hoc Committee on Refugees and Stateless Persons, Summary Record of the One Hundred and Sixty-Seventh Meeting*, UN Doc E/AC.7/SR.167 (22 August 1950) 5.
[16] Ibid 6.   [17] Ibid 6.
[18] The UNHCR's mission statement speaks of the need for refugees to 'find safe refuge in another state': UNHCR, *Global Report 2017* (June 2018) 4 <http://reporting.unhcr.org/sites/default/files/gr2017/pdf/GR2017_English_Full_lowres.pdf>.
[19] The UNHCR speaks of the importance of 'preserving the character of asylum': ibid 16.
[20] The UNHCR refers to an asylum seeker as 'someone whose request for sanctuary has yet to be processed': UNHCR, *Asylum-Seekers* <www.unhcr.org/en-au/asylum-seekers.html>.
[21] The UNHCR (n 20) refers to a refugee as someone who 'seeks international protection'.
[22] Rabben (n 8) 196.

the concept of refuge. While an obvious hypothesis may be that courts adopt rights-based thinking, there is potential for decision-makers to be influenced by other viewpoints.

2.3.1 Historical and Cultural

One method for understanding the concept of refuge adopted by scholars across a number of disciplines is to refer to ancient, religious and cultural practices of providing safety. This is sometimes used to inform principles behind contemporary ideas of refuge. For example, Mathew and Harley commence their discussion of the 'moral and philosophical underpinnings of refugee protection' by referring back to ancient Greek traditions of granting refuge in temples[23] and exploring the practices of refuge in Islam, Judaism, Christianity and Buddhism.[24] They suggest that, while sovereignty, as opposed to religion, is now the basis for asylum,[25] these '[p]rinciples of humanity and hospitality' continue to be 'important rationales for asylum'.[26] Gil-Bazo surveys historical and religious practices of granting asylum to build an argument that the right to asylum is a general principle of international law.[27] Arboleda[28] refers to the history of displacement and refugee protection in Africa to inform the Convention Governing the Specific Aspects of the Refugee Problems in Africa (OAU Refugee Convention).[29]

Historical practices of refuge are also used to uncover the role refuge plays in international relations or law reform. For example, Price traces the practice of asylum in ancient Greece and early modern Europe to show that it was originally 'a legal defense to extradition' and, thus, 'depended upon a judgment that another state targeted the asylum-seeker for harm in a manner inconsistent with its rightful authority'.[30] He draws on this history to argue that the current practice of asylum has a political dimension – it acts to condemn and reform persecutory regimes.[31] Nyaoro discusses how Pan-Africanism, which he describes as an 'emancipation ideology' that emphasises the 'historical injustices against African people',[32] influenced the development of the OAU Refugee Convention.

Studies of religious and cultural practices of refuge are also used to challenge dominant understandings of refugee protection. Chatty argues that, in some Middle Eastern countries, the Islamic notion of *karam* (generosity and hospitality) 'effectively operates to provide the asylum-seeker with sanctuary and refuge in an environment where international protection does not exist'.[33] She suggests that this duty-based approach to refuge should be melded

---

[23] Penelope Mathew and Tristan Harley, *Refugees, Regionalism and Responsibility* (Edward Elgar, 2016) 70.
[24] Ibid 70–3.
[25] S Prakash Sinha, *Asylum and International Law* (Martinus Nijohff, 1971) 15, 16 cited in ibid 73.
[26] Mathew and Harley (n 23) 73.
[27] Maria-Teresa Gil-Bazo, 'Asylum as a General Principle of International Law' (2015) 27(1) *International Journal of Refugee Law* 3, 17–23.
[28] Eduardo Arboleda, 'Refugee Definition in Africa and Latin America: The Lessons of Pragmatism' (1991) 3(2) *International Journal of Refugee Law* 185. See also Marina Sharpe, 'Organization of African Unity and African Union Engagement with Refugee Protection: 1963-2011' (2013) 21(1) *African Journal of International and Comparative Law* 50, 55.
[29] 10 September 1969, 1001 UNTS 45, in force 20 June 1974.   [30] Price (n 8) 14.   [31] Ibid 14, 70.
[32] Dulo Nyaoro, 'The Development of Refugee Protection in Africa: From Cooperation to Nationalistic Prisms' in Elisabeth Wacker, Ulrich Becker and Katherina Crepaz (eds), *Refugees and Forced Migrants in Africa and the EU* (Springer, 2019) 13, 19.
[33] Dawn Chatty, 'The Duty to be Generous (Karam): Alternatives to Rights-Based Asylum in the Middle East' (2017) 5 *Journal of the British Academy* 177, 196.

with the 'international rights-based protection approaches to refuge'.[34] Odhiambo-Abuya insists that refugee protection in Africa must 'amalgamate the international system with the African custom of hospitality'.[35] Ignatieff suggests that Canada's refugee resettlement programme is successful, not because of Canadian's allegiance to international law and refugee rights, but because the programme 'appeals specifically to the hospitality and generosity of ordinary Canadian families'.[36] Stephens reflects on Māori approaches to refugee protection to ground an argument for expanding refugee community sponsorship programmes in Aotearoa/New Zealand.[37]

2.3.2 Experiential

A different approach to understanding refuge is to explore what refugees themselves are searching and hoping for. This is most often seen in ethnographic work. Zimmermann's study of Somali refugees' journeys across Africa and Europe evidences that these refugees are seeking safety 'as well as quality of life and certainty in exile'.[38] Ramsay investigates how female refugees from Central Africa experience and imagine displacement[39] and argues that a crucial aspect of refuge for women is 'connection to others and relationship building'.[40] Besteman's work with Somali refugees resettled in the US indicates that they want to create 'meaning in their new context'.[41]

There are examples of what I call an experiential approach to envisioning refuge outside anthropological studies. Some scholars take refugee testimony to assess the ways refugees conceptualise refuge. For example, Paik examines legal testimony given by refugees in a well-known US case[42] and argues that they wanted more than provision of enough food, water and shelter to survive.[43] They resisted being the mere objects of humanitarian assistance[44] and sought 'recognition as full human subjects'.[45] The use of refugee narratives is also present in psychological literature. For example, Daiute draws on stories from refugee children to argue that a crucial part of refuge is the ability to 'imagine a beautiful future'.[46]

Another experiential approach to defining refuge is to unpack the motivations behind those offering it. Oomen's study of cities of refuge examines how local authorities and residents push back against national governments in providing shelter to asylum seekers.[47]

---

[34] Ibid 178.

[35] Edwin Odhiambo-Abuya, 'A Critical Analysis of Liberalism and Postcolonial Theory in the Context of Refugee Protection' (2005) 16 *King's Law Journal* 263, 290.

[36] Michael Ignatieff, *The Ordinary Virtues: Moral Order in a Divided World* (Harvard University Press, 2017) 217.

[37] Murdoch Stephens, *Expanding Community Sponsorship in Aotearoa New Zealand* (February 2020) 40–4 <www.swbc.org.nz/wp-content/uploads/2020/02/PDF-B.pdf>.

[38] Susan Zimmermann, 'Irregular Secondary Movements to Europe: Seeking Asylum beyond Refuge' (2009) 22(1) *Journal of Refugee Studies* 74.

[39] Georgina Ramsay, *Impossible Refuge: The Control and Constraint of Refugee Futures* (Routledge, 2018) 1.

[40] Ibid 207.

[41] Catherine Besteman, 'Refuge Fragments, Fragmentary Refuge' (2014) 15(4) *Ethnography* 426.

[42] *Sale v Haitian Centers Council Inc* 509 US 155, 133 (1993).

[43] A Naomi Paik, 'Testifying to Rightlessness: Haitian Refugees Speaking from Guantánamo' (2010) 28(3) *Social Text* 39, 53.

[44] Ibid 53–4.   [45] Ibid 41.   [46] Daiute (n 13) 2.

[47] Barbara Oomen, 'Rights, Culture and the Creation of Cosmopolitan Cityzenship' in Rosemarie Buikema, Antoine Buyse and Antonius Robben (eds), *Cultures, Citizenship and Human Rights* (Routledge, 2020) 121, 131.

In doing so, they draw on human rights law to defend their position.[48] Rehaag examines the provision of sanctuary to refugees in Canadian churches and suggests that religious actors generate norms of refuge that align with how the Canadian government understands refugee protection.[49]

2.3.3 Rights-Based

Dominant in legal scholarship is the use of international human rights and refugee law to build a positivist picture of refuge. Hathaway draws on the rights in the Refugee Convention, as well as the ICCPR and ICESCR to provide a comprehensive outline of the 'common corpus of refugee rights which can be asserted by refugees in any state party to the Refugee Convention or Protocol'.[50] McAdam looks to the Refugee Convention as 'a form of *lex specialis*' and argues that it should be applied to those who are granted complementary protection.[51] Adding to these studies on rights available to all refugees, there is scholarship on the ways human rights law may respond to the protection needs of women refugees,[52] child refugees[53] and refugees with disabilities.[54] There are also regional rights-based approaches to refugee protection. Sharpe looks across the Refugee Convention, OAU Convention and African human rights law to outline refugee protection in Africa.[55] Costello[56] and Giuffré[57] provide examinations of the rights of refugees and migrants in European law.

There are also rights-based studies of other categories of people in need of protection. As noted in Chapter 1, Palestinians are the only group of refugees to not come within the UNHCR's mandate and instead receive protection and assistance from UNRWA. A positivist approach to refuge for Palestinian refugees can be seen in Albanese and Takkenberg's study of the rights they are entitled to under UNRWA's mandate, statelessness law, and international humanitarian and human rights law.[58]

---

[48] Ibid.

[49] Sean Rehaag, 'Bordering on Legality: Canadian Church Sanctuary and the Rule of Law' (2009) 26 *Refuge* 43.

[50] James Hathaway, *The Rights of Refugees under International Law* (Cambridge University Press, 2005) 8. See also James Hathaway, *The Rights of Refugees under International Law* (Cambridge University Press, 2nd ed, 2021).

[51] Jane McAdam, *Complementary Protection in International Refugee Law* (Oxford University Press, 2007) 1.

[52] See, e.g., Chaloka Beyani, 'The Needs of Refugee Women: A Human-Rights Perspective' (1995) 3(2) *Gender and Development* 29; Malinda Schmiechen, 'Parallel Lives, Uneven Justice: An Analysis of Rights, Protection and Redress for Refugees and Internally Displaced Women in Camps' (2003) 22(2) *Saint Louis University Public Law Review* 473.

[53] See, e.g., Mary Crock, 'Justice for the Migrant Child: The Protective Force of the Convention on the Rights of the Child' in Said Mahmoudi et al (eds), *Child-friendly Justice: A Quarter of a Century of the UN Convention on the Rights of the Child* (Brill, 2015) 221; Thoko Kaime, 'From Lofty Jargon to Durable Solutions: Unaccompanied Refugee Children and African Charter on the Rights and Welfare of the Child' (2004) 13(3) *International Journal of Refugee Law* 336; Ciara Smyth, *European Asylum Law and the Rights of the Child* (Routledge, 2014).

[54] Mary Crock et al, *The Legal Protection of Refugees with Disabilities* (Edward Elgar, 2017) chs 9–12.

[55] Marina Sharpe, *The Regional Law of Refugee Protection in Africa* (Oxford University Press, 2018).

[56] Cathryn Costello, *Human Rights of Migrants and Refugees in European Law* (Oxford University Press, 2015).

[57] Mariagiulia Giuffré, *The Readmission of Asylum Seekers under International Law* (Hart, 2020).

[58] Francesca Albanese and Lex Takkenberg, *Palestinian Refugees in International Law* (Oxford University Press, 2nd ed, 2020) ch III.

Bartholomeusz[59] and Lilly[60] build a rights-based picture of the protection available to Palestinian refugees through analyses of UNRWA's evolving mandate with Lilly arguing that it is very similar to the type of protections available to Convention refugees.[61]

With respect to the rights available to IDPs, one of the earliest publications is Kälin's annotations[62] of the Guiding Principles on Internal Displacement.[63] This instrument defines IDPs as people within their own homeland 'who have been forced or obliged to flee or to leave their homes or places of habitual residence, in particular as a result of or in order to avoid the effects of armed conflict, situations of generalized violence, violations of human rights or natural or human-made disasters, and who have not crossed an internationally recognized state border'.[64] Abebe looks to international law, the Convention for the Protection and Assistance of Internally Displaced Persons in Africa ('Kampala Convention'),[65] and African human rights treaties to build a picture of IDP rights in Africa.[66] Adeola considers regional approaches to IDP protection.[67] Fawole analyses the Kampala Convention from a children's rights perspective.[68]

A rights-based approach to refuge also exists for putative refugees. As noted in Chapter 1, putative refugees are persons outside their country of origin or habitual residence, whose circumstances indicate they satisfy one part of the refugee definition (a well-founded fear of being persecuted for reasons of race, religion, nationality, membership of a particular social group or political opinion), but who have not yet established another aspect of the refugee definition (that they are unable or unwilling to avail themselves of the protection of their country of origin or habitual residence). Decision-makers will ask if they can relocate to another part of their homeland where they will have protection. Hathaway and Foster suggest that the rights in the Refugee Convention should serve as a guide to the type of protections that should be available in the prospective place of internal relocation.[69] Mathew[70] and Shultz[71] propose a slightly broader enquiry: decision-makers should investigate whether the putative refugee would have their international human rights protected.

---

[59] Lance Bartholomeusz, 'The Mandate of UNRWA at Sixty' (2009) 28(2–3) *Refugee Survey Quarterly* 452.

[60] Damian Lilly, 'UNRWA's Protection Mandate: Closing the "Protection Gap"' (2018) 30(3) *International Journal of Refugee Law* 444.

[61] Ibid 463–9.

[62] Walter Kälin, 'Guiding Principles on Internal Displacement: Annotations' (Paper No 32, American Society of International Law Studies in Transnational Legal Policy, 2008).

[63] *Guiding Principles on Internal Displacement*, UN ESCOR, UN Doc E/CN.4/1998/53/Add.2 (22 July 1998) ('Guiding Principles'). The Guiding Principles 'consolidate into one document the legal standards relevant to the internally displaced drawn from international human rights law, humanitarian law and refugee law by analogy': Francis Deng, 'Preface' in Kälin (n 62) v.

[64] Guiding Principles (n 63) [2].   [65] 23 October 2009, in force 16 December 2012.

[66] Allehone Abebe, *The Emerging Law of Forced Displacement in Africa: Development and Implementation of the Kampala Convention on Internal Displacement* (Routledge, 2016).

[67] Romola Adeola, *The Internally Displaced Person in International Law* (Edward Elgar, 2020) ch 4.

[68] Charissa Fawole, 'A Critical Analysis of the Kampala Convention from a Children's Rights Perspective' (2020) *Refugee Survey Quarterly* (advance).

[69] James Hathaway and Michelle Foster, *The Law of Refugee Status* (Cambridge University Press, 2nd ed, 2014) 358; First Colloquium on Challenges in International Refugee Law, 'Michigan Guidelines on the Internal Protection Alternative' (1999) 21 *Michigan Journal of International Law* 134 ('Michigan Guidelines on the IPA').

[70] Penelope Mathew, 'The Shifting Boundaries and Content of Protection: The Internal Protection Alternative Revisited' in Satvinder Juss (ed), *The Ashgate Research Companion to Migration Law, Theory and Policy* (Ashgate, 2013) 189, 193–5.

[71] Jessica Schultz, *The Internal Protection Alternative in Refugee Law* (Brill, 2019) 212–13.

2.3.4   Philosophical

A further way of conceptualising refuge is to draw on ethics or philosophy. A number of scholars do this to justify providing refuge. For example, Goodwin-Gill's study of temporary refuge cites Rawls's idea of a natural duty of 'helping another when he [or she] is in need or jeopardy, provided that one can do so without excessive risk or loss to oneself'.[72] Noll draws on the Kantian right to hospitality to explain why states have an obligation to offer refugee protection.[73] Odhiambo-Abuya resists the application of liberal, Western philosophy in the context of refugee protection in Africa and invites African scholars to 'think local' and employ Indigenous African norms when addressing displacement.[74] Hosein suggests that an autonomy approach provides the strongest philosophical grounding for a right to remain in the host country.[75] López-Farjeat and Coronado-Angulo draw on ethics of recognition to propose that, in certain contexts, ethical obligations towards refugees supersede sovereignty.[76]

Some scholars go further and use ideas in the fields of ethics and philosophy to articulate the *content* of what states should offer those in need of international protection. Betts and Collier's study of refuge refers to a 'famous moral thought experiment' regarding what a bystander should do when they discover a child in a pond asking for help.[77] Building on this scenario, they argue that states not only have an 'unambiguous duty of rescue'[78] but also an obligation to restore refugees' 'circumstances as near to normality as it is practically possible'.[79] Gibney draws on Locke and Walzer to develop a principle of 'humanitarianism' that should guide liberal democratic nations in their asylum policies.[80] Humanitarianism provides that 'states have an obligation to assist refugees when the costs of doing so are low'[81] and can also be used to determine 'how refugees and asylum-seekers can be rightfully treated'.[82] Kritzman-Amir takes a different approach and refers to feminist ideas about ethics of care and theories of utilitarianism to frame refuge as a shared responsibility.[83] She suggests that states' varying capacities to provide refuge is a prime consideration in determining which state should be responsible for refugees.[84]

---

[72] John Rawls, *A Theory of Justice* (Harvard University Press, 1971) 114 cited in Guy Goodwin-Gill, 'Nonrefoulement and the New Asylum Seekers' in David Martin (ed), *The New Asylum Seekers: Refugee Law in the 1980s* (Kluwer, 1988) 105, 110.

[73] Gregor Noll, 'Why Refugees Still Matter: A Response to James Hathaway' (2007) 8(2) *Melbourne Journal of International Law* 536, 544–7.

[74] Odhiambo-Abuya (n 35) 273.

[75] Adam Omar Hosein, 'Refugees and the Right to Remain' in David Miller and Christine Straehle (eds), *The Political Philosophy of Refuge* (Cambridge University Press, 2020) 114, 130–1.

[76] Luis Xavier López-Farjeat and Cecilia Coronado-Angulo, 'Group Asylum, Sovereignty, and the Ethics of Care' (2020) 9(8) *Social Sciences* 142.

[77] Alexander Betts and Paul Collier, *Refuge: Transforming a Broken Refugee System* (Allen Lane, 2017) 99.

[78] Ibid 99.   [79] Ibid 102.

[80] Matthew Gibney, *The Ethics and Politics of Asylum: Liberal Democracy and the Response to Refugees* (Cambridge University Press, 2004) 231–3.

[81] Ibid 231.   [82] Ibid 249.

[83] Tally Kritzman-Amir, 'Not in My Backyard: On the Morality of Responsibility Sharing in Refugee Law' (2009) 34(2) *Brooklyn Journal of International Law* 355, 363–372.

[84] Ibid 362, 372.

2.3.5 *Categorical*

Another method is to unpack what refuge is or should be by reference to the categories of people seeking international protection or to the defining features of refugeehood. Durieux states that fixing the label of refugee on a person or group (whether or not they come within a legal definition of a refugee) requires a response from the international community.[85] Therefore, it is necessary to clarify 'the normative meaning of refugeehood' to understand what response is appropriate.[86] Demonstrating what can be called a categorical approach to elucidating refuge, Durieux posits that those who have a well-founded fear of persecution (as opposed to, e.g., those who flee natural disasters) are entitled to not only 'protection against deportation' but also a 'guarantee of admission and inclusion'.[87]

A number of scholars also adopt a categorical approach by referring to the persecution aspect of refugee definitions to delineate the contours of refuge. Hathaway points to the persecution requirement to justify why those who come within the definition of a refugee in article 1A(2) of the Refugee Convention ('Convention refugees') are entitled to a special form of international protection.[88] Price argues that the requirement to establish a well-founded fear of persecution means that Convention refugees suffer 'a distinctive kind of harm that calls for confrontation and condemnation'.[89] Thus, refuge has an 'expressive dimension [that] differentiates it from other modes of refugee assistance, which are focused exclusively on meeting refugees' need for protection'.[90] Conversely, McAdam highlights the similarities between Convention refugees and those who may not have a well-founded fear of persecution, but cannot otherwise avail themselves of the protection of their country, to argue that both should be entitled to 'privileged treatment'.[91]

Some scholars look beyond legal definitions of refugees to understand the essence of refugeehood and the appropriate response. Shacknove argues that the idea of refugeehood should be extended to those whose governments cannot meet their basic needs.[92] Accordingly, refuge encompasses 'international restitution of these needs'.[93] Taking an even broader viewpoint, Gibney describes refugees as people who have not only lost state protection but have also been deprived of their 'social world'.[94] Therefore, refuge is not only about restoring their basic needs but should also offer a place in which refugees can rebuild 'communities, associations, relationships'.[95]

The different ways in which scholars conceptualise refuge will serve as a guide to understanding how decision-makers approach the notion of refuge. Next, I turn to discussing ideas about what refuge is designed to achieve for individual refugees, host states and the

[85] Jean-François Durieux, 'Three Asylum Paradigms' (2013) 20(2) *International Journal on Minority and Group Rights* 147, 148.

[86] Ibid 148.

[87] Ibid 156. See also Jane McAdam and Tamara Wood, 'The Concept of "International Protection" in the Global Compacts on Refugees and Migration' (2021) 23(1) *Interventions: International Journal of Postcolonial Studies* 2, 10.

[88] James Hathaway, 'Is Refugee Status Really Elitist? An Answer to the Ethical Challenge' in Jean-Yves Carlier and Dirk Vanheule (eds), *Europe and Refugees: A Challenge?* (Kluwer Law, 1997) 79.

[89] Price (n 8) 14.   [90] Ibid 14.   [91] McAdam (n 51) 198. See also Wood and McAdam (n 87).

[92] Andrew Shacknove, 'Who Is a Refugee?' (1985) 95(2) *Ethics* 274.   [93] Ibid 284.

[94] Matthew Gibney, 'Refugees and Justice between States' (2015) 14(4) *European Journal of Political Theory* 448, 460.

[95] Ibid 460.

international community. In the next section, I include, in addition to academic scholarship, UN materials and refugee memoirs.

2.4   What Are Refuge's Functions?

While the notion of refuge may have originated from ancient practices of providing safety, contemporary understandings have developed to encompass objectives beyond protection from serious harm. Descriptions of refuge's additional purposes range from restoration of 'social and economic independence',[96] ensuring refugees can live a dignified life,[97] providing 'a taste of the substance of the citizenship'[98] and finding a 'solution to refugeehood'.[99] However, there is no overarching theory of the objectives refuge should fulfil. As already discussed, scholars have assembled examinations of refuge according to other concerns such as the rights in the Refugee Convention or the categories of people entitled to international protection.

In this book, and in particular Chapters 3 and 4, I discuss the ways in which decision-makers adopt a purposive approach to refuge and how their perceptions of refuge's objectives align with and depart from the understandings of scholars, the UN and refugees. Examining purposes and functions is one way of categorising remedies.[100] While there is no dedicated study of what refuge is designed to achieve, the pattern that emerges across the literature is that refuge has three functions, which can be described as restorative, regenerative and palliative. Further, there is a temporal dimension to refuge's functions. Scholars, UN institutions and refugees speak of the need to live a rewarding life while displaced, have hope for the future and cope with traumatic experiences and memories. In Sections 2.4.1–2.4.3, I explore refuge's restorative, regenerative and palliative objectives by outlining ideas about how they align with refugees' present, future and past.

2.4.1   Being Reborn in Exile: Restoration of a Meaningful Life

The creation of a new life is a common motif for refuge in refugee memoirs. Passarlay, an Afghan refugee, speaks about being 'born again'.[101] Ahmedi, also an Afghan refugee, writes about wanting 'to have a life'.[102] Keitetsi, a former Ugandan child soldier, describes resettlement in Denmark as being given 'a new life'.[103] Hakakian, a Jewish Iranian refugee, says that to be a refugee is to 'begin anew'[104] and be 'recast as a brand-new human

---

[96] UNHCR Executive Committee, *Local Integration and Self-Reliance*, UN Doc EC/55/SC/CRP.15 (2 June 2005) [11].

[97] Colin Harvey, 'Is Humanity Enough? Refugees, Asylum Seekers and the Rights Regime' in Satvinder Juss and Colin Harvey (eds), *Contemporary Issues in Refugee Law* (Edward Elgar, 2013) 68, 74; UNHCR Executive Committee, *Conclusion No 93 (LIII)*, UN Doc A/AC.96/973 (8 October 2002) preamble.

[98] Harvey (n 97) 72.   [99] Hathaway and Foster, *The Law of Refugee Status* (n 69) 1.

[100] See Burrows' functional taxonomy of remedies: Andrew Burrows, *Remedies for Torts and Breach of Contract* (Oxford University Press, 3rd ed, 2005).

[101] Gulwali Passarlay and Nadene Ghouri, *The Lightless Sky: An Afghan Refugee Boy's Journey of Escape to a New Life* (Atlantic Books, 2015) 322.

[102] Farah Ahmedi and Tamim Ansary, *The Other Side of the Sky* (Simon and Schuster, 2005) 148.

[103] China Keitetsi, *Child Soldier* (Souvenir Press, 2004) 238.

[104] Roya Hakakian, *Journey from the Land of No: A Girlhood Caught in Revolutionary Iran* (Three Rivers Press, 2004) 14.

engine'.[105] This rebirth involves much more than being free from one's persecutors. Ahmedi explains, '[y]ou might suppose that a person who has escaped from suffering and oppression and the threat of death will be grateful and content simply to exist after that and want nothing more. But the human heart easily grows restless. ... I had come to long for something more than the mere absence of pain'.[106]

Scholars across a number of disciplines share the idea that refuge is intended to provide refugees with a life worth living, as opposed to the mere preservation of life. Hathaway and Foster contend that the rights in the Refugee Convention 'have a restorative function, facilitating the re-establishment of *a life*'.[107] Gibney argues that refuge involves rebuilding a 'meaningful social world'.[108] Betts and Collier state that refuge is about restoring 'basic features of a normal life'.[109] Zimmerman writes of refuge as being able to 'have a "life" rather than just to be alive'.[110] There is also an understanding that building a rewarding and meaningful life while displaced involves giving back what may have been lost through persecution and displacement but also providing conditions in which a refugee can grow and develop. Thus, we can see articulations of the restorative and regenerative functions of refuge during exile; I elaborate on both next.

2.4.1.1   Restoring Refugees to a Position Where They Can Be Alive and Have a Life

One restorative aspect of refuge is the re-establishment of a safe, secure and free existence. The importance of immediately feeling safe in the country of refuge is reflected in refugee memoirs. Bashir, a Sudanese refugee, in writing about her escape to the UK recalls the moment of being 'inside this machine that would fly me away to safety'[111] and that '[m]y first priority had to be to get into England – for that meant I was safely out of Sudan. . . . [H]ow I would live, my future – all of that could wait'.[112] When Keitetsi was told that she could stay in South Africa but would not receive housing or help in finding employment, her response was, 'I didn't care, as long as I had escaped my pursuers'.[113] Ahmedi was overjoyed about the prospect of being resettled because in the US: '[n]o one will attack me – the law won't allow it'.[114]

Restoration of a sense of security, safety and freedom as an important aspect of refuge is also evident in other sources. The UNHCR states that one of the aims of the Refugee Convention is achievement of a 'peaceful life'[115] and that '[r]efugees' rights to security and personal safety underpin the entirety of the provisions of the [Refugee] Convention'.[116] Goodwin-Gill argues that refugee protection is concerned with 'life, liberty and security of person'.[117] The importance of restoring safety, security and freedom in the context of displacement can be seen in the Refugee Convention's *travaux préparatoires* with respect to the host state's obligation to issue identity papers to refugees.[118] The representative from

---

[105] Ibid 15.   [106] Ahmedi and Ansary (n 102) 197.
[107] Hathaway and Foster, *The Law of Refugee Status* (n 69) 356 (emphasis added).
[108] Gibney (n 94) 460.   [109] Betts and Collier (n 77) 102.   [110] Zimmerman (n 38) 88.
[111] Halima Bashir and Damien Lewis, *Tears of the Desert: A Memoir of Survival in Darfur* (Harper Collins, 2008) 313.
[112] Ibid 316–17.   [113] Keitetsi (n 103) 251.   [114] Ahmedi and Ansary (n 102) 137.
[115] UNHCR, 'Statement by Prince Sadruddin Aga Khan, United Nations High Commissioner for Refugees, to the United Nations Economic and Social Council' (Speech delivered to ECOSOC, 26 July 1976).
[116] UNHCR Executive Committee, *Note on International Protection*, UN Doc A/AC.96/951 (13 September 2001) [15].
[117] Guy Goodwin-Gill, *The Refugee in International Law* (Oxford University Press, 2nd ed, 1996) 16.
[118] art 27.

the International Refugee Organization stated that '[a] person without papers was a pariah subject to arrest for that reason alone'.[119] The US representative emphasised the importance of identity papers to ensure that refugees 'would be free from the extra hardships of a person in possession of no papers at all'.[120]

Another restorative aspect of refuge is ensuring that refugees have the means to sustain life. The UNHCR states that refugees must have 'an adequate and dignified means of subsistence'.[121] The UNHCR's Executive Committee stresses the need for host states to ensure that refugees' 'basic support needs, including food, clothing, accommodation, and medical care ... are met'.[122] Goodwin-Gill and McAdam highlight the importance of 'provisions with respect to subsistence',[123] and Hathaway emphasises that refugees are entitled to 'basic survival' rights.[124] Crock et al. start their discussion of rights for refugees with disabilities by discussing 'the rights to sustenance and other basic needs'.[125]

Further, the restorative function of refuge is understood to encompass refugees having choices about their lives' directions. The Refugee Convention's drafters stressed the importance of refugees being able to 'perform the acts of civil life' (such as marriage, adoption, acquiring property and opening bank accounts).[126] The UNHCR Executive Committee understands that the Refugee Convention is designed to 'progressively restore the social and economic independence needed' for refugees to 'get on with their lives'.[127] Betts and Collier speak about refuge restoring the conditions in which refugees can exercise autonomy.[128] Hathaway states that the rights in the Refugee Convention 'afford refugees a real measure of autonomy and security to devise the solutions which *they* judge most suited to *their own* circumstances and ambitions'.[129] Reflecting on the relationship between refuge and choice, Keitetsi explains that, once she was resettled as a refugee, 'I no longer had to live my life for others, and no force makes me act against my will'.[130]

Beyond the re-establishment of safety, sustenance and choice, Passarlay's and Ahmedi's memoirs provide insights on the restorative aspects of refuge for child refugees, in particular, the need to restore a sense of childhood. Both left Afghanistan as minors; Passarlay was unaccompanied and Ahmedi travelled with her mother, but often found herself effectively in the parental role due to her mother's ill health. When Passarlay was finally able to start school in the UK, he felt 'like a child again'.[131] Ahmedi explains that, in the process of leaving Afghanistan, seeking refuge in Pakistan and being resettled in the US, 'I was forced

---

[119] UN Economic and Social Council, *Ad Hoc Committee on Refugees and Stateless Persons, Summary Record of the Thirty-Eighth Meeting*, UN Doc E/AC.32/SR.38 (26 September 1950).

[120] Ibid.

[121] UNHCR, *Statement by Ms Erika Feller, Director, Department of International Protection, UNHCR, at the Fifty-Fifth Session of the Executive Committee of the High Commissioner's Programme* (7 October 2004) <www.unhcr.org/en-au/admin/dipstatements/429d6f8e4/statement-ms-erika-feller-director-department-international-protection.html>.

[122] UNHCR Executive Committee, *Executive Committee Conclusion No 93* (n 97) (b)(ii).

[123] Guy Goodwin-Gill and Jane McAdam, *The Refugee in International Law* (Oxford University Press, 3rd ed, 2007) 396.

[124] Hathaway (2005), *The Rights of Refugees* (n 50) 84.   [125] Crock et al (n 54) 189.

[126] UN Economic and Social Council, *Ad Hoc Committee on Statelessness and Related Problems, Memorandum by the Secretary-General*, UN Doc E/AC.32/2 (3 January 1950). They introduced the right to administrative assistance in art 25 of the Refugee Convention.

[127] UNHCR Executive Committee (n 96) [11].   [128] Betts and Collier (n 77) 7.

[129] James Hathaway, 'Forced Migration Studies: Could We Agree Just to "Date"?' (2007) 20 *Journal of Refugee Studies* 347, 364 (emphasis in original).

[130] Keitetsi (n 103) 272.   [131] Passarlay and Ghouri (n 101) 342.

to grow up very suddenly'.[132] After being resettled, she befriends an older couple and explains that they 'are letting me live a little of my childhood now, even though I am past the time for it. They let me behave in very childish ways sometimes – I make demands and act silly'.[133]

While there is a recognition that the prime concern of refuge is to meet refugees' needs,[134] there is also consideration of how it may be restorative in a more global sense. Some political theorists and legal scholars argue that refuge functions as a form of reparation or corrective justice for the harm and injustice done to refugees by individual states or the global community.[135] This conceptualisation of refuge as reparation is particularly relevant in contexts where the host country may have, directly or indirectly, contributed to refugees being unable to return to their homeland.[136] While restoration of a meaningful life for refugees and repairing global injustices are important objectives, ideas of refuges go beyond this and stress its regenerative functions, which I discuss next.

2.4.1.2   Not Just Surviving, but Thriving in Exile

Beyond restoring refugees to a position where they can lead a liveable life, scholars, UN institutions and refugees understand refuge to be a rejuvenating process allowing refugees to develop and grow. For example, Ramsay's work with refugees in Uganda and Australia shows that they want to 'live lives of regenerative possibility'.[137] Zimmermann's study of Somali refugees indicates that they travel across Africa and Europe searching for a place where they can 'achieve something in exile'.[138] UNRWA states that part of its mission is 'to help Palestinian refugees achieve their full potential in human development terms under the difficult circumstances in which they live'.[139] Betts and Collier argue that the international community should adopt a human development approach for all refugees.[140] This means that '[f]or the period refugees are in limbo, we should be creating an enabling environment that nurtures rather than debilitates'.[141] Accordingly, refuge should encompass 'all of the things that allow people to thrive and contribute rather than merely survive'.[142]

Legal scholars highlight the ways the Refugee Convention gives refugees the opportunity to develop, as opposed to merely survive, in the host country. Edwards reminds us that refugees have the right not just to seek, but to enjoy, asylum.[143] This means that refugees should benefit in some way from their experience of refuge.[144] Edwards gives as an example the right to work in the Refugee Convention, which provides refugees with an opportunity to improve 'language and other skills'.[145] Another indication of the idea that refuge is intended to be a time of growth and creativity is the Refugee Convention drafters' insistence

---

[132] Ahmedi and Ansary (n 102) 210.   [133] Ibid 210.

[134] Goodwin-Gill and McAdam (n 123) 10; Mathew and Harley (n 23) 80.

[135] Kate Ogg, 'Backlashes Against International Commitments and Organisations: Asylum as Restorative Justice' (2021) 38(1) *Australian Yearbook of International Law* 230; James Souter, 'Towards a Theory of Asylum as Reparation for Past Injustice' (2014) 62(2) *Political Studies* 326; Michael Walzer, *Spheres of Justice* (Basic Books, 1983).

[136] Gibney (n 94) 460; Souter (n 135) 339.   [137] Ramsay (n 39) 81.   [138] Zimmermann (n 38) 83.

[139] UNRWA, *Report of the Commissioner-General of (UNRWA), Programme Budget, 2008–2009*, UN GAOR, Supp No 13A, UN Doc A/62/13/Add.1 (6 August 2007) [2].

[140] Betts and Collier (n 77) 144.   [141] Ibid 144.   [142] Ibid 144.

[143] Alice Edwards, 'Human Rights, Refugees, and the Right "To Enjoy" Asylum' (2005) 17(2) *International Journal of Refugee Law* 293. The UDHR provides that everyone 'has the right to seek *and to enjoy* in other countries asylum from persecution' (emphasis added).

[144] Edwards (n 143) 302.   [145] Ibid 320.

on protection of refugees' artistic rights and industrial property.[146] They recognised that such outputs are 'the creation of the human mind and recognition is not a favour'.[147]

When discussing refuge's regenerative function, there is a tendency to describe it in economic terms. The UNHCR stresses that the rights in the Refugee Convention 'are essential to establishing refugees' self-sufficiency and allowing them to contribute to, rather than depend upon, the country of asylum'.[148] The UNHCR also encourages states to implement assistance programmes that 'integrate strategies for self-reliance and empowerment'.[149] Hathaway and Cusick state that the socio-economic rights in the Refugee Convention are designed to 'ensure that refugees are able quickly to become self-sufficient in their country of refuge'.[150]

There is no doubt that gaining employment and being able to contribute to the host country is an important facet of refuge for many refugees. This comes through strongly in Bashir's memoir. She writes that, once she was safely in the UK, she 'wanted to contribute to this society. I was a trained medical doctor, and I knew this country needed doctors'.[151] However, it is important not to overemphasise the economic aspect of refuge's regenerative objectives. Skran and Easton-Calabria encourage scholars and policymakers to think of self-reliance more broadly than economic independence and include political, legal and social factors.[152] Providing an insight into what female refugees resettled in Australia want to achieve, Ramsay observes that their prime objective is to become pregnant and build a family.[153] By doing this, they are 'actualising . . . the regenerative potentiality of finally being secure and safe enough to bear and rear children'.[154] Inhorn's work with refugees in Detroit indicates that creating a family is a priority for both men and women.[155] These broader ideas about the ways refuge can be rejuvenating are also reflected in refugee memoirs. While Bashir wanted to contribute to her host country through employing her medical skills, she was not allowed to work. Rather, it was the birth of her son that gave her 'the spirit and the will to live'.[156] Providing an adolescent's perspective of the regenerative aspect of refuge, Ahmedi writes: 'I had come to crave some activity that would interest my mind. I wanted some fun'.[157]

Refuge is also understood to be regenerative not just for individual refugees but, in some cases, also for their communities in exile. Mishra investigates the role of secondary and higher education for Tibetan refugees in India in building a sense of 'being Tibetan'.[158] Dudley's study of Karenni refugees in Thailand looks at how the community builds a sense of 'home' during displacement.[159]

---

[146] art 14.   [147] UN Economic and Social Council (n 126).
[148] UNHCR Executive Committee (n 116) [57].
[149] UNHCR, *Agenda for Protection* (3rd ed, October 2003) <www.unhcr.org/protection/globalconsult/3e637b194/agenda-protection-third-edition.html>.
[150] James Hathaway and Anne Cusick, 'Refugee Rights Are Not Negotiable' (1999–2000) 14(2) *Georgetown Immigration Law Journal* 481, 485.
[151] Bashir and Lewis (n 111) 341.
[152] Claudia Skran and Evan Easton-Calabria, 'Old Concepts Making New History: Refugee Self-Reliance, Livelihoods and the "Refugee Entrepreneur"' (2020) 33(1) *Journal of Refugee Studies* 1, 5.
[153] Ramsay (n 39) 157.   [154] Ibid 157.
[155] Marcia Inhorn, *America's Arab Refugees: Vulnerability and Health on the Margins* (Stanford University Press, 2018) ch 3.
[156] Bashir and Lewis (n 111) 4.   [157] Ahmedi and Ansary (n 102) 197.
[158] Mallica Mishra, *Tibetan Refugees in India: Education, Culture and Growing Up in Exile* (Orient Blackswan, 2014).
[159] Sandra Dudley, *Materialising Exile: Material Culture and Embodied Experience among Karenni Refugees in Thailand* (Berghahn Books, 2010).

Not only is refuge supposed to be rejuvenating for refugee communities, it is also understood to be regenerative for host countries. Mathew and Harley argue that one reason for providing refuge is that 'refugees are not just a short-term "burden" but are likely to make valuable contributions to their host countries'.[160] Supporting this are studies that highlight the ways in which refugees enhance the social, civic and economic life of the countries in which they are granted refuge.[161]

While one of refuge's functions is to create a rewarding and meaningful life during refugeehood, a person is not expected to be a refugee forever. Another aspect of refuge's temporality is that it looks to the future. In the following section, I discuss refuge's next objective: creating hope.

2.4.2   Dreaming of and Creating a Future

Refuge's rejuvenating function is not limited to refugees' experience of displacement; it also flows over into generating aspirations for the future. Haines' history of refugees in the US argues that if refuge 'fails to provide a basis for hope for the future, then it is a poor refuge indeed'.[162] This is also a central theme in refugee memoirs. Reflecting on her refugee journey, Ahmedi explains that when she was living as a refugee in Pakistan:

> I had no source of hope out of which to nourish my struggle. When you see some possibility of getting out getting out of a pit, you can draw strength from the idea of where you will be once you get out: You see a goal worth fighting for. If the best you can hope for is to sink more slowly, struggle comes to feel pointless.[163]

For Ahmedi, hope came when she had the chance of resettlement in the US, where she could 'build a future'.[164] Wek, a Sudanese refugee, recalls that, when she left for the UK, she 'carried almost nothing, other than our family's hopes for the future'.[165] Later, when she was working in New York, the US Committee for Refugees and Immigrants contacted Wek asking for her assistance in a campaign for Sudanese refugees. She explains that this was 'heaven sent' because '[t]hey were offering hope. They too believed in the possibilities for the future'.[166]

Scholars who take an experiential approach to understanding refuge speak of the importance of imagining and working towards a future. Ramsay says that refugees want to 'actively create a future' as opposed to 'simply surviving in asylum'.[167] Their everyday existence is organised to achieve 'a future in which their lives [will] be "better"'.[168] Reflecting on her experience in counselling refugee children, Daiute writes about the ways they narrate their aspirations and imagine different futures.[169] She argues that through this process child refugees create a sense of refuge.[170]

---

[160]   Mathew and Harley (n 23) 83.

[161]   See, e.g., Graeme Hugo, Department of Immigration and Citizenship, *A Significant Contribution: The Economic, Social and Civic Contributions of First- and Second-Generation Humanitarian Entrants* (2011) <www.dss.gov.au/sites/default/files/documents/01_2014/economic-social-civic-contributions-booklet2011.pdf>; International Monetary Fund, *The Refugee Surge in Europe: Economic Challenges* (January 2016) <www.imf.org/external/pubs/ft/sdn/2016/sdn1602.pdf>.

[162]   David Haines, *Safe Haven? A History of Refugees in America* (Stylus Publishing, 2010) 48.

[163]   Ahmedi and Ansary (n 102) 123.   [164]   Ibid 137.

[165]   Alek Wek, *Alek: The Extraordinary Life of a Sudanese Refugee* (Virago Press, 2007) 152.

[166]   Ibid 232.   [167]   Ramsay (n 39) 81.   [168]   Ibid 38.   [169]   Daiute (n 13) 7.   [170]   Ibid 8.

Discussions of solutions to refugeehood are another way of expressing this aspect of refuge's functions. Betts and Collier posit that refugees are 'entitled to expect' not only rescue and restoration of autonomy but also 'an eventual route out of limbo'.[171] Stevens argues that the 'ultimate goal of refugee protection must be to achieve a satisfactory solution for the refugee'.[172] Hathaway explains that an important role of the refugee protection regime is to 'find a way to bring refugee status to an end – whether by means of return to the country of origin, resettlement elsewhere, or naturalization in the host country'.[173] He also emphasises that refugee law allows refugees to take the lead in creating their futures: 'the Refugee Convention gives priority to allowing refugees to make their own decisions . . . to take the time they need to decide when and if they wish to pursue a durable solution'.[174] One of the UNHCR's functions is to find durable solutions for refugees.[175] Scholars argue that, similar to Convention refugees, Palestinian refugees are entitled to durable solutions.[176] Schultz emphasises that a putative refugee will only have an internal protection alternative if it provides 'a durable solution rather than a currently safe refuge'.[177]

Refuge may also operate to engender hope, not just for refugees but for the future of the international community. While granting refugee protection is most commonly understood to be an apolitical act,[178] Price argues that, by providing refuge, nation-states are not just caring for refugees, but condemning the country of origin's laws, policies and actions.[179] Thus, refuge is part of a 'broader political program designed to reform the abusive state'.[180] It is one way the international community can address the 'root causes of refugee flows' and promote 'the rule of law and human rights'.[181]

While inspiring hope for the future is an essential function of refuge, refugees do not let go of the past and, sometimes, their past cannot be separated from their experience of exile and aspirations for the future. Next, I continue my exploration of refuge's functions and temporality by discussing the ways in which it addresses history, memories and trauma.

2.4.3   Living with the Past

In this section, I suggest that refuge has a palliative function. Hathaway also contends that refugee protection is palliative; by this he is referring to the provision of surrogate state protection[182] and the fact that refugee protection is apolitical.[183] I am using the term 'palliative' in a different and more literal sense – one of the aims of refuge is to allow refugees to heal from or deal with past trauma even though the act of providing refuge cannot necessarily address the factors that caused this pain.

A common theme in refugee memoirs is the links between the past, present and future. Many refugee memoirs address the tension between looking to the future in their place of

---

[171] Betts and Collier (n 77) 7.
[172] Dallal Stevens, 'What Do We Mean by "Protection"?' (2013) 20(2) *International Journal of Minority and Group Rights* 233, 241.
[173] Hathaway (2005) (n 50) 913.   [174] Ibid 914.   [175] UNHCR Statute ch I, para 1, ch II, paras 8(c), 9.
[176] Albanese and Takkenberg (n 58) ch VIII; Bartholomeusz (n 59) 469–73.   [177] Schultz (n 71) 212.
[178] *Declaration of Territorial Asylum*, GA Res 2312, UN Doc A/RES/2312(XXII) (14 December 1976) preamble; Grahl-Madsen (n 8) 27.
[179] Price (n 8) 167.   [180] Ibid 75.   [181] Ibid 70.
[182] Hathaway (2005) (n 50) 5; James Hathaway, 'Reconceiving Refugee Law as Human Rights Protection' (1991) 4(2) *Journal of Refugee Studies* 113, 117 ('Reconceiving Refugee Law').
[183] Hathaway, 'Reconceiving Refugee Law' (n 182) 117.

refuge and not being able to leave their past behind them. When Ahmedi was resettled in the US, she writes that it was like 'flying into my future – and yet – the past won't let me go. Not completely. Not yet'.[184]

Some refugees write about the importance of taking the past with them into exile. Bashir says that, when boarding the plane that would take her to the UK, '[a]ll I had were my memories'.[185] Hakakian explains that '[w]hen you become a refugee, abandon all your loves and belongings, your memories become your belongings. Images of the past, snippets of old conversations, furnish the world within your mind. When you have nothing left to guard, you guard your memories. . . . Remembering becomes not simply a preoccupation but a full-time occupation'.[186]

Others speak of being unable to escape memories of the past. Keitetsi, a former child soldier and now a refugee in Denmark, writes:

> [b]ut even with all of this freedom, I still have the fear that I had to carry every day of the desperation that I saw in almost any soldier . . . I was there, and I don't need to imagine their pain. I know it, and still feel the abuse, and humiliation, scars which my body and soul will carry forever.[187]

Refugees' previous experiences and their connections to understandings of the present and future are also themes in historical, psychological and anthropological scholarship. Stråth posits that refugees' reflections on their experiences are 'always made from a changing present, constantly provoking new views of the past and new outlines of future horizons'.[188] Daiute argues that making sense of their past is 'a dimension of refuge' for refugee children.[189] She explains that, when doing this, her clients often engage in 'future narrating', which is 'a means of describing what may be past but re-cast toward the future'.[190] Gemignani's research with refugees from the Former Yugoslavia indicates that many avoid talking about the past 'not as an attempt to erase the past' but to 'build a stronger future by still using the past'.[191] However, some refugees also actively engage with their memories because it gives them hope for the future.[192]

While the aforementioned examples focus on how individual refugees navigate the past and its relationship to healing, Malkki investigates the ways groups of refugees who continue their communities in exile address the past. In her anthropological work with Hutu refugees in a refugee camp and urban setting, Malkki observes different approaches to history and memory.[193] For the Hutu community living in a camp setting, a 'shared body of knowledge about their past in Burundi' informed 'virtually all aspects of contemporary social life'.[194] The past 'was seen as a source of power, knowledge, and purity'.[195] It enabled them to make sense of past violent events[196] and imagine their future.[197] However, the

---

[184] Ahmedi and Ansary (n 102) 123.   [185] Bashir and Lewis (n 111) 312.   [186] Hakakian (n 104) 14.

[187] Keitetsi (n 103) 272.

[188] Bo Stråth, 'Constructionist Themes in the Historiography of the Nation' in James Holstein and Jaber Gubrium (eds), *Handbook of Constructionist Research* (Guilford Press, 2008) 627, 629.

[189] Daiute (n 13) 8.   [190] Ibid 9.

[191] Marco Gemignani, 'The Past if Past: The Use of Memories and Self-Healing Narratives in Refugees from the Former Yugoslavia' (2011) 24(1) *Journal of Refugee Studies* 132, 142.

[192] Ibid 145.

[193] Liisa Malkki, *Purity and Exile: Violence, Memory, and National Cosmology Among Hutu Refugees in Tanzania* (University of Chicago Press, 1995) 153, 233–4.

[194] Ibid 53.   [195] Ibid 233.   [196] Ibid 97.   [197] Ibid 59.

urban Hutu community saw their past as 'a problem that had to be erased or subdued' and they did not want it to 'define the present'.[198]

There is also scholarship that recognises that the experience of displacement can be in and of itself distressing and destabilising, especially when parts of the host community are unwelcoming. This literature also examines how different actors can assist refugees to address current and past trauma. Based on interviews with Bosnian refugees in the US, Keyes and Kayne highlight that, along with memories of the past, other major stressors include coping with culture shock and feelings of not belonging in or being inferior within their new communities.[199] They suggest techniques professionals can employ to promote a sense of belonging that are respectful of the unique ways in which each refugee will go through a process of adaptation. There are also studies on how the challenges facing refugee children relate to both past experiences and their precarious status in the host community and how professionals can help to build resilience.[200]

In legal scholarship, there is much less focus on how refuge may address the past and achieve a sense of healing than on the ways it protects refugees while in exile and creates hopes for a secure future. Nevertheless, there is some indication in legal literature that healing from past trauma may be one aspect of refuge. There is recognition of the need to consider past suffering in material addressing putative refugees. The UNHCR suggests that in judging the appropriateness of an internal protection alternative, 'past persecution and its psychological effects' must be taken into account.[201] Mathew argues that 'it should be accepted that a putative refugee has the right to special consideration with respect to human rights violations … because of the fact that she has already been displaced by persecution'.[202] Schultz also insists that past persecution should 'constitute a valid exception to the expectation of return in relocation cases'.[203]

Further, there is consideration of the healing dimensions of refuge in situations where refugee status may have ceased,[204] but where there are 'compelling reasons'[205] against returning a refugee to their homeland due to previous persecution. Some of the Refugee Convention's drafters were of the view that states need to 'take particular account of the psychological hardship that might be faced by the victims of persecution were they returned to the country responsible for their maltreatment'.[206] While there is debate about whether the compelling reasons exception to cessation of refugee status still

---

[198] Ibid 233.

[199] Emily Keyes and Catherine Kayne, 'Belonging and Adapting: Mental Health of Bosnian Refugees Living in the United States' (2004) 25(8) *Issues in Mental Health Nursing* 809.

[200] For a summary of scholarship, see Karolin Krause and Evelyn Sharples, 'Thriving in the Face of Severe Adversity: Understanding and Fostering Resilience in Children Affected by War and Displacement' in Elena Fiddian-Qasmiyeh (ed), *Refuge in a Moving World: Tracing Refugee and Migrant Journeys Across Disciplines* (UCL Press, 2020) 306.

[201] UNHCR, *Guidelines on International Protection No 4: 'Internal Flight or Relocation Alternative' Within the Context of Article 1A(2) of the 1951 Convention and/or 1967 Protocol relating to the Status of Refugees*, UN Doc HCR/GIP/03/04 (23 July 2003) [25].

[202] Mathew (n 70) 204.   [203] Schultz (n 71) 250.

[204] Article 1C(5) of the Refugee Convention provides that the 'Convention shall cease to apply to any person under the terms of Section A if he [or she or they] can no longer, because the circumstances in connection with which he [or she or they] has been recognised as a refugee have ceased to exist, continue to refuse to avail himself [or herself or themself] of the protection of the country of his [or her or their] nationality'.

[205] Refugee Convention art 1C(5).   [206] Hathaway and Foster (n 69) 493–4.

applies,[207] some jurisdictions have chosen to adopt it.[208] The UNHCR's view is that the compelling reasons exception should apply to those who 'have suffered grave persecution, including at the hands of elements of the local population' and, in particular, children's experiences of persecution should be given special consideration.[209] Having outlined refuge's restorative, regenerative and palliative purposes and how they address the past, present and future, in the next section I consider the different ways in which the practice of refuge is characterised.

2.5   What Is the Nature of Refuge?

Hathaway posits that the refugee regime 'establishes a situation-specific human rights remedy'.[210] However, the term 'remedy' is used in a variety of different contexts and does not have a single, settled meaning.[211] Remedies scholars highlight that it can refer to a procedure, the assertion of a right, insistence on performance of a duty, relief sought or outcome given.[212] With respect to refugee and forced migration scholarship, we can similarly see that refuge as a remedy is characterised in a variety of ways and I outline these in this section. The purpose of this discussion is to provide a starting point for investigating how adjudicative decision-makers understand the nature of refuge.

One meaning of the term 'remedy' is the way in which the law addresses a problem or injustice.[213] Hathaway uses the term in this sense when he describes the rights in the Refugee Convention as a human rights remedy. He explains that the Refugee Convention provides a 'deliberate and coherent system of rights' specifically designed to address the predicament of refugeehood.[214] Similarly, McAdam stresses that the rights in the Refugee Convention are specially 'tailored to the precarious legal position of non-citizens whose own country of origin is unable or unwilling to protect them'.[215] The idea of surrogate or substitute state protection, endemic in legal understandings of refugee protection,[216] is also a characterisation of refuge as a response to a wrong. Surrogate protection requires host countries to provide 'the protection which the refugee's own state, by definition, cannot or will not provide'.[217] In essence, it gives refugees the status and political membership they have lost.[218] Oomen in her study of 'cities of refuge' highlights that it is sometimes local authorities and communities that foster this sense of political membership.[219]

---

[207] Hathaway and Foster (n 69) explain that the compelling reasons consideration only applies to those who were given refugee status pursuant to prior agreements: 490. However, Goodwin-Gill and McAdam (n 123) argue that the compelling reasons exception can apply to contemporary refugees: 148–9.

[208] See Hathaway and Foster (n 69) 492.

[209] UNHCR, Guidelines on International Protection No 3: Cessation of Refugee Status under Article 1C(5) and (6) of the 1951 Convention Relating to the Status of Refugees (the 'Ceased Circumstances' Clauses), UN Doc HCR/GIP/03/03 (10 February 2003) [20].

[210] Hathaway (2005) (n 50) 1000. See also Hathaway (n 129) 353.

[211] Peter Birks, 'Personal Property: Proprietary Rights and Remedies' (2000) 11(1) Kings College Law Journal 1; Rafal Zakrzewski, Remedies Reclassified (Oxford University Press, 2005) 7.

[212] Birks (n 211) 3; Zakrzewski (n 211) 7.   [213] Attorney General v Blake [2001] AC 268, 284.

[214] Hathaway (2005) (n 50) 4.   [215] McAdam (n 51) 5–6.

[216] Goodwin-Gill and McAdam (n 123) 10; Hathaway (2005) (n 50) 5; Schultz (n 71) 120-1. Courts have also adopted this language. See, e.g., Attorney General v Ward [1993] 2 SCR 689, 692; Horvath v SSHD [2000] 3 All ER 577, 583.

[217] Goodwin-Gill and McAdam (n 123) 10.   [218] Harvey (n 97) 88.   [219] Oomen (n 47) 123.

Another way in which scholars characterise the remedial nature of refuge is as the provision of a legal status.[220] Harvey explains that refugee law is distinct from other areas of human rights law, because of the 'centrality it attaches to a legally endorsed status'.[221] Whereas human rights are founded on the belief in the 'inherent dignity and of the equal and inalienable rights of all members of the human family',[222] the provision of a legal status for refugees is a reminder that rights are often only realised through citizenship.[223] McAdam also stresses that it is through the provision of legal status that refuge is realisable.[224] Scholarship on refugees' perspectives on refuge also indicates the importance of legal status. For example, in Odhiambo-Abuya's study of refugees in Kenya, one of his interviewees states, '[i]t is better if you have status; status is everything. Without status you have nothing. .... With status, it is good. You can move freely with confidence and even go to school'.[225]

The remedial nature of refuge can also be characterised as a right, duty or responsibility. Asylum has traditionally been conceived as a right of states to grant, but whether it is a right of individuals 'remains one of the most controversial matters in refugee studies'.[226] While the UDHR only provides a right to *seek* asylum,[227] Moreno-Lax argues that, at least in the European context, refugees have a right to access international protection.[228] Gil-Bazo's analysis of asylum as a general principle of international law indicates that 'the right to asylum is enshrined in most constitutions of countries across different legal traditions'.[229] She suggests that 'the long historical tradition of asylum as an expression of sovereignty has now been coupled with a right of individuals to be granted asylum of constitutional rank'.[230]

Describing the other side of the coin, Betts and Collier describe refuge as a duty to rescue.[231] Durieux insists that admission of refugees is 'a positive duty'.[232] Mathew and Harley speak of 'taking responsibility for refugees'.[233] Providing a historical and cultural perspective, Rabben highlights that, in some contexts, offering refuge is understood to be a religious duty.[234] She refers to Stowe's *Uncle Tom's Cabin*, in which the character Mary justifies harbouring a runaway slave to her husband on religious grounds: 'Now, John, I don't know anything about politics, but I can read my Bible; and there I see that I must feed the hungry, clothe the naked, and comfort the desolate; and that Bible I mean to follow'.[235]

There is also a sense that refuge should be a shared duty or responsibility. There is a large literature on ideas of international cooperation in delivering refugee protection.[236]

[220] Goodwin-Gill and McAdam (n 123) 456; Grahl-Madsen (n 8); Harvey (n 97) 74; Hathaway and Foster (n 69) 17; McAdam (n 51) 1, 198.
[221] Harvey (n 97) 72.   [222] UDHR preamble.   [223] Harvey (n 97) 72.   [224] McAdam (n 51) 456.
[225] Edwin Odhiambo-Abuya, 'United Nations High Commissioner for Refugees and Status Determination Imtaxaan in Kenya: An Empirical Survey' (2004) 48(2) *Journal of African Law* 187, 196.
[226] Gil-Bazo (n 27) 10.   [227] art 14(1).
[228] Violeta Moreno-Lax, *Accessing Asylum in Europe: Extraterritorial Border Controls and Refugee Rights under EU Law* (Oxford University Press, 2017) ch 9.
[229] Gil-Bazo (n 27) 23.   [230] Ibid 28.   [231] Betts and Collier (n 77) 97.   [232] Durieux (n 85) 155.
[233] Mathew and Harley (n 23) 70.   [234] Rabben (n 8) ch 5.
[235] Harriet Stowe, *Uncle Tom's Cabin* (John P Jewett, 1852) quoted in Rabben (n 8) 94.
[236] See, e.g., Rebecca Dowd and Jane McAdam, 'International Cooperation and Responsibility Sharing to Protect Refugees: What, Why and How?' (2017) 66(4) *International and Comparative Law Quarterly* 863; Agnès Hurwitz, *The Collective Responsibility of States to Protect Refugees* (Oxford University Press, 2009); Gil Loescher, *Beyond Charity: International Cooperation and the Global Refugee Crisis* (Oxford University Press, 1996); Gregor Noll, 'Risky Games? A Theoretical Approach to Burden Sharing in the Asylum Field' (2003) 16(3) *Journal of Refugee Studies* 236; Kate Ogg, 'International Solidarity and Palestinian Refugees: Lessons for the Future Directions of Refugee Law' (2020) *Human Rights Law*

Hathaway and Neve describe refugee protection as a 'human rights remedy' that states have 'a shared commitment ... to provide'.[237] They advocate for common but differentiated duties (e.g. wealthier countries providing aid to states hosting large numbers of refugees).[238] Mathew and Harley investigate the potential for regional responses to give rise to responsibility-sharing among states.[239] Nyanduga stresses the importance of international cooperation in the OAU Refugee Convention and suggests that it reflects principles of comity between African countries.[240]

Offering a different perspective, Ignatieff insists that, while asylum may be, from the perspective of international law, a right or duty, it should be conceptualised as 'a gift that a citizen makes as a matter of sovereign discretion'.[241] He explains that positioning asylum as a right 'removes the power of the citizen to determine who is worthy of the gift'[242] and will inhibit the development of a culture of welcome.[243]

In anthropological scholarship, refuge is often characterised as a process. As part of her study of Somali refugees resettled in the US, Besteman argues that refuge is not bestowed, but gradually made through efforts of refugees and the host society.[244] Ramsay's observation of refugees resettled in Australia also leads her to characterise refuge as a journey that involves actions on behalf of refugees and the wider community.[245] Both scholars caution against understanding refuge as a goal or end point. Besteman seeks to 'challenge the conception of refuge as relief or resolution, the end of the journey'.[246] Ramsay explains that 'when refuge is taken to be a process rather than a distinct "solution", it becomes a possibility'.[247]

Descriptions of refuge as a duty, responsibility or process give rise to the question of who is responsible for providing protection. Foster, writing in the context of transferring refugees to third countries, stresses that the Refugee Convention outlines 'protection obligations' that are 'specifically addressed to states'.[248] This means that protection can only be provided by a state and not an NGO or international organisation.[249] Taking a slightly different position, Schultz posits that, in an internal protection alternative inquiry, a non-state actor can be deemed to provide protection but only if they have 'an ability to enforce the rule of law and ensure basic rights protection'.[250] In many regions, international organisations and NGOs play a lead role in refugee protection. Stevens notes that in the Middle East refugee protection is provided by the UNHCR, UNRWA and NGOs.[251] Nah highlights the important role NGOs play in refugee protection in the Asia-Pacific region

---

Review (advance); Phil Orchard, *A Right to Flee: Refugees, States, and the Construction of International Cooperation* (Cambridge University Press, 2014).

[237] James Hathaway and Alexander Neve, 'Making International Refugee Law Relevant Again: A Proposal for Collectivized and Solution-Oriented Protection' (1997) 10 *Harvard Human Rights Journal* 115, 117.

[238] Ibid 118.   [239] Mathew and Harley (n 23) ch 3.

[240] Bahame Tom Mukiyra Nyanduga, 'Refugee Protection under the 1969 OAU Convention Governing the Specific Aspects of Refugee Problems in Africa' (2004) 47 *German Yearbook of International Law* 85, 93.

[241] Ignatieff (n 36) 210.   [242] Ibid 211.   [243] Ibid 216.

[244] Catherine Besteman, *Making Refuge: Somali Bantu Refugees and Lewiston, Maine* (Duke University Press, 2016).

[245] Ramsay (n 39) 157.   [246] Besteman (n 41) 426.   [247] Ramsay (n 39) 207.

[248] Michelle Foster, 'Protection Elsewhere: The Legal Implications of Requiring Refugees to Seek Protection in Another State' (2007) 28 *Michigan Journal of International Law* 223, 237.

[249] Ibid.   [250] Schultz (n 71) 210.

[251] Dallal Stevens, 'Rights, Needs or Assistance? The Role of the UNHCR in Refugee Protection in the Middle East' (2016) 20(2) *The International Journal of Human Rights* 264, 265.

where many states are not signatories to the Refugee Convention.[252] There is a new focus in scholarship on how refugees themselves create organisations and networks that deliver protection.[253]

Throughout the case studies in the following chapters, I examine whether decision-makers understand the nature of refuge as a response to a wrong, a legal status, a duty, a responsibility, a right or a process, or perhaps characterise it in different ways. In the next section, I turn to the ambit of refuge: what it must contain to realise its objectives and remedial nature.

2.6   What Is the Scope of Refuge?

The scope of refuge is understood to be broad, but indeterminate, and context specific. Its content varies depending on factors such as age, gender, sexuality and disability as well as the host state's circumstances and the length of time the refugee is in the host state. In Section 2.6.1, I outline ideas about the contours of refuge for Convention refugees. In Section 2.6.2, I show that there are similar understandings of the scope of refuge for Palestinian refugees. In Section 2.6.3, I address ideas about the scope of refuge for putative refugees and IDPs. In the following chapters, I use these to guide my assessment of decision-makers' approaches to what refuge encompasses.

2.6.1   Scope of Refuge for Convention Refugees

Anthropological studies of what refugees are searching for in exile indicate that personal safety is only one motivating factor.[254] They also want socio-economic security,[255] education and work prospects,[256] freedoms and tolerance,[257] homes and stability,[258] the ability to build a family[259] and a sense of community.[260] They are not only escaping serious harm but are also trying to recreate a feeling of 'wholeness'.[261] Betts and Collier explain that '[e]xternal provision of food, clothing, and shelter is absolutely essential in the aftermath of having to run for your life. But over time, if it is provided as a substitute for access to jobs, education, and other opportunities, humanitarian aid soon undermines human dignity and autonomy'.[262]

Legal scholarship on the content of refugee protection maps onto these studies of refugees' wants and needs. The Refugee Convention provides rights to, for example,

---

[252] Alice Nah, 'Networks and Norm Entrepreneurship amongst Local Civil Society Actors: Advancing Refugee Protection in the Asia Pacific Region' (2016) 20(2) *The International Journal of Human Rights* 223.

[253] Kate Pincock, Alexander Betts and Evan Easton-Calabria, *The Global Governed? Refugees as Providers of Protection and Assistance* (Cambridge University Press, 2020).

[254] See, e.g., Zimmermann (n 38) 74.

[255] Joëlle Moret, Simone Baglioni and Denise Efionayi-Mäder, 'The Path of Somali Refugees into Exile: A Comparative Analysis of Secondary Movements and Policy Responses' (Paper No 46, Swiss Forum for Migration and Population Studies, 2006) 10.

[256] Zimmermann (n 38) 88.   [257] Besteman (n 244) 30.

[258] Nadya Hajj, *Protection amid Chaos: The Creation of Property Rights in Palestinian Refugee Camps* (Columbia University Press, 2016); Zimmermann (n 38) 88.

[259] Inhorn (n 155) ch 3; Ramsay (n 39) 157–9.   [260] Ramsay (n 39) 207.   [261] Besteman (n 41) 426.

[262] Betts and Collier (n 77) 136.

education,[263] work,[264] welfare[265] and housing,[266] and scholars highlight that these rights are framed in a way specifically moulded to respond to refugees' predicaments.[267] Nevertheless, the Refugee Convention is not the only source of refugee rights and is inadequate on its own. McAdam highlights that 'the conceptualization of protection [the Refugee Convention] embodies has necessarily been extended by developments in human rights law'.[268] Scholars invoke rights in subsequent human rights treaties to articulate a comprehensive protection regime for refugees. Hathaway argues that rights to physical security in the ICCPR can be imported to address gaps in the Refugee Convention.[269] Additionally, there is no positive right to family unity in the Refugee Convention, but Hathaway and Edwards highlight that refugees can claim rights to family unity under the ICCPR, ICESCR and CRC.[270]

There is also a well-developed understanding that certain refugees have particular protection needs and the scope of refuge must accommodate this. There are many publications on the protection risks for women.[271] There are also discussions of refugee children's special protection needs and studies on the protections provided to child refugees through the CRC and other human rights instruments.[272] The UNHCR's Executive Committee calls on states to improve existing protection programmes by taking women, children and elderly refugees' distinctive needs into account.[273] The UN, UNHCR, UNHCR's Executive Committee and scholars also consider the risks faced by refugees with disabilities and the interrelationship between the Refugee Convention and the CRPD in addressing their protection needs.[274] Crock et al. highlight the importance of healthcare and rehabilitation services for refugees with

---

[263] art 22.   [264] arts 17, 18, 19, 24.   [265] art 23.   [266] art 21.

[267] Hathaway (2005) (n 50) highlights that many of the special protections in the Refugee Convention are not reflected in subsequent human rights instruments, such as 'recognition of personal status, access to naturalization, immunity from penalization for illegal entry, the need for travel and other identity documents, and especially protection from *refoulement*': 121. Also, the socio-economic rights in the Refugee Convention, unlike most of the rights in the ICESCR, are not to be progressively realised but are immediately enforceable: James Hathaway, 'Refugees and Asylum' in Brian Opeskin, Richard Perruchoud and Jillyanne Redpath-Cross (eds), *Foundations of International Migration Law* (Cambridge University Press, 2012) 177, 188–90. McAdam (n 51) highlights that the Refugee Convention's 'provision of identity and travel documents does not have a parallel in general human rights law': 203.

[268] McAdam (n 51) 5.   [269] Hathaway (2005) (n 50) 448–50.

[270] Hathaway (2005) (n 50) makes reference to family rights in articles 17, 23(1)–(2) and 24 of the ICCPR and article 10 of the ICESCR: 540–60. Edwards (n 143) adds articles 10 and 22 of the CRC: 311.

[271] See, e.g., Beyani (n 52); Jane Freedman, 'Mainstreaming Gender in Refugee Protection' (2010) 23(4) *Cambridge Review of International Affairs* 589; UNHCR, *UNHCR Handbook for the Protection of Women and Girls* (1st ed, January 2008) <www.unhcr.org/47cfa9fe2.pdf>; UNHCR, *Sexual and Gender-Based Violence Against Refugees, Returnees and Internally Displaced Persons: Guidelines for Prevention and Response* (May 2003) <www.unhcr.org/en-au/protection/women/3f696bcc4/sexual-gender-based-violence-against-refugees-returnees-internally-displaced.html>.

[272] See, e.g., Crock (n 53) 221; Guy Goodwin-Gill, 'Protecting the Human Rights of Refugee Children: Some Legal and Institutional Possibilities' in Jaap Doek, Hans van Loon and Paul Vlaardingerbroek (eds), *Children on the Move: How to Implement Their Right to Family Life* (Martinus Nijhoff, 1996) 97; Ben Saul, 'Indefinite Security Detention and Refugee Children and Families in Australia International Human Rights Law Dimensions' (2013) 20 *Australian International Law Journal* 55.

[273] UNHCR Executive Committee (n 97) (b)(iii).

[274] Crock et al. (n 54); UNHCR Executive Committee, Standing Committee, *The Protection of Older Persons and Persons with Disabilities*, UN Doc EC/58/SC/CRP.14 (6 June 2007); UNHCR Executive Committee, *Conclusion No 110 (LXI)*, UN Doc A/AC.96/1095 (12 October 2010); *Operations of the United Nations Relief and Works Agency for Palestine Refugees in the Near East*, GA Res 69/88, UN Doc A/Res/69/88 (16 December 2014) [14].

disabilities.[275] There have also been examinations of the particular risks for lesbian, gay, bisexual, transgender, queer, asexual and intersex refugees and the protections that may be provided to them by refugee and international law.[276]

The scope of refuge for Convention refugees reflects ideas of the temporality of refuge. With respect to refugees being able to build a future, there is agreement that refuge must include rights of solution.[277] However, there is debate about what these rights are. The UNHCR's three durable solutions are voluntary repatriation (where a refugee chooses to return to their country of origin and can do so safely and with dignity), local integration (the refugee remains in the host country and goes through process of legal, economic and social integration) and resettlement (a refugee is transferred from their current place of refuge to a third country and usually granted permanent residency).[278] Based on the provisions of the Refugee Convention, Hathaway argues that the rights to solution are voluntary re-establishment in the country of origin,[279] voluntary repatriation after a fundamental change of circumstances in the country of origin,[280] resettlement[281] and naturalisation.[282]

Perhaps less well developed in legal scholarship is how the content of refuge may enable refugees to address their past. Nevertheless, there is some acknowledgement that refuge must encompass healing from trauma. For example, article 25 of the EU's Directive on the Standards for the Reception of Applicants for International Protection[283] specifies, '[m]ember States shall ensure that persons who have been subjected to torture, rape or other serious acts of violence receive the necessary treatment for the damage caused by such acts, in particular access to appropriate medical and psychological treatment or care'. A similar sentiment is reflected in the OAU Refugee Convention's preamble, which notes that the signatory states are 'desirous of finding ways and means of alleviating [refugees'] misery and suffering'.

While refuge is understood to address a wide range of refugees' needs and includes a broad sweep of rights, there is also recognition that the content of refuge must correspond with the host country's circumstances and length of time the refugee remains there. Comparing the content of refuge to the duty to rescue a drowning child, Betts and Collier argue that the extent of any additional obligations 'depends on what it is feasible for us to do'.[284] They posit that host states should 'restore ... basic features of normal life' such as

---

[275] Crock et al (n 54) 201–7.

[276] Volker Türk, 'Ensuring Protection to LGBTI Persons of Concern' (2013) 25(1) *International Journal of Refugee Law* 120; UNHCR, *The Protection of Lesbian, Gay, Bisexual, and Intersex Asylum-Seekers and Refugees* (22 September 2010) <https://data2.unhcr.org/en/documents/details/45897>; UNHCR, *Protecting Persons with Diverse Sexual Orientations and Gender Identities: A Global Report on UNHCR's Efforts to Protect Lesbian, Gay, Bisexual, and Intersex Asylum-Seekers and Refugees* (December 2015) <https://cms.emergency.unhcr.org/documents/11982/43697/UNHCR+Division+of +Global+Protection%2C+Protecting+Persons+Of+Diverse+Sexual+Orientations+And+Gender +Identities%2C2015/86b46bac-d8f4-4654-b4e0-8658a76194b7>.

[277] James Hathaway, 'Refugee Solutions, or Solutions to Refugeehood?' (2007) 24(2) *Refuge* 3, 4.

[278] UNHCR, *Framework for Durable Solutions for Refugees and Persons of Concern* (May 2003) [12] <www.unhcr.org/en-au/partners/partners/3f1408764/framework-durable-solutions-refugees-persons-concern.html>. In implementing these durable solutions, the UNHCR and states have been criticised for prioritising their own interests over refugees' rights and wishes: see, e.g., Marjoleine Zieck, *UNHCR and Voluntary Reparation of Refugees: A Legal Analysis* (Nijhoff, 1997).

[279] Hathaway (2005) (n 50) 918.   [280] Ibid 953–4.   [281] Ibid 963.   [282] Ibid 977.

[283] Directive 2013/33/EU of the European Parliament and Council of 26 June 2013 Laying Down Standards for the Reception of Applicants for International Protection (Recast) [2013] OJ L 180/96-105/32.

[284] Betts and Collier (n 77) 101.

a home, employment and community to the extent they are able to.[285] Gibney acknowledges that there are 'limits [on] what one can reasonably demand of states in their response to refugees and asylum-seekers'.[286] He suggests that states may, in some situations and on a case-by-case basis, curtail certain refugee rights if in doing so they will 'preserve the integrity of asylum or ... increase the number of refugees who receive protection'.[287] The Refugee Convention has a complex method of determining the content of refuge with respect to host states' resources and the strength of the refugee's bond with the host state. There are only a few absolute rights in the Refugee Convention; most are granted on the same terms as nationals, favoured non-citizens or other non-citizens generally in the same circumstances. Also, the Refugee Convention grants 'enhanced rights as the bond strengthens between the particular refugee and state party in which he or she is present'.[288] Basic rights, such as *non-refoulement*, are granted once the refugee is subject to a state's jurisdiction. Another tranche of rights applies once refugees are in the host state's territory. A further set of rights accrue once the refugee is lawfully staying in the host state. The final rights apply to refugees with durable residency.[289]

2.6.2 Scope of Refuge for Palestinian Refugees

There is less written on the content of refuge for Palestinian refugees, but there is an understanding that it is similarly broad. While Akram argues that there is a protection gap for Palestinian refugees because UNRWA's does not have a protection mandate,[290] Bartholomeusz,[291] Lilly[292] and Albanese and Takkenberg[293] argue that UNRWA's mandate has evolved to include protection activities. With respect to UNRWA's protection mandate, Bartholomeusz[294] draws on UNGA resolutions to suggest that it covers the provision of 'basic subsistence support',[295] food aid,[296] healthcare,[297] education[298] and housing for Palestinians whose homes were demolished or razed by Israeli forces;[299] improving 'the

---

[285] Ibid 102.   [286] Gibney (n 80) 249.   [287] Ibid 252.   [288] Hathaway (2005) (n 50) 154.

[289] Ibid 154–5.

[290] Susan Akram, 'Palestinian Refugees and their Legal Status: Rights, Politics and Implications for a Just Solution' (2002) 31 *Journal of Palestine Studies* 36. The UN body initially charged with protection of Palestinian refugees was the UN Conciliation Commission for Palestine (UNCCP). The UNCCP still exists but has been inactive since the mid-1960s. I discuss the history of the UNCCP's and UNRWA's creation and their respective mandates in Chapter 6. See also Itamar Mann, 'The New Palestinian Refugees', *EJIL: Talk! Blog of the European Journal of International Law* (19 May 2021) <www.ejiltalk.org/the-new-palestinian-refugees/> in which he highlights that Palestinian refugees are not entitled to citizenship or local integration.

[291] Bartholomeusz (note 59).   [292] Lilly (note 60).   [293] Albanese and Takkenberg (note 58) 399.

[294] Bartholomeusz (note 59).

[295] Reference to basic subsistence support is made in UNRWA's 2008–2009 Programme Budget subsequently approved by a UNGA resolution: UNRWA (n 139) [72]. UNGA's approval of the budget specifically mandates all activities contained in the budget: Bartholomeusz (n 59) 462.

[296] Reference to food aid is made in UNRWA's 2008–2009 Programme Budget subsequently approved by a UNGA resolution: UNRWA (n 139) [79]. As already noted (n 295), UNGA's approval of the budget specifically mandates all activities contained in the budget.

[297] UN Secretariat, *Secretary-General's Bulletin, Organization of the United Nations Relief and Works Agency for Palestine Refugees in the Near East*, UN Doc ST/SGB/2000/6 (17 February 2000) note 1.

[298] Ibid.

[299] *Protection of Palestine Refugees*, GA Res 38/83A, UN Doc A/Res/38/83 A (15 December 1983) (I)[6]; *Protection of Palestine Refugees*, GA Res 44/47A, UN Doc A/Res/44/47A (8 December 1989) (I)[6].

quality of life' for Palestinians living in camp environments[300] and health conditions in camps;[301] and addressing the needs of poor Palestinian refugees who do not have access to the banking sector.[302] While UNRWA's protection mandate is usually seen in terms of protection of economic and social rights, scholars highlight that it also extends to protection of civil and political rights such as physical security.[303] In particular, while UNRWA is not responsible for security and law and order in camp settings,[304] the UNGA has resolved that UNRWA 'undertake effective measures to guarantee the safety and security and the legal and human rights of the Palestinian refugees in the occupied territories'.[305]

Scholars also discuss UNRWA's human development mandate.[306] UNGA resolutions confirm UNRWA's role in the 'provision of services for the well-being and human development of the Palestine refugees'.[307] The UN defines human development as 'a process of enlarging people's choices' which requires 'political, economic and social freedom [and] opportunities for being creative and productive, and enjoying personal self-respect and guaranteed human rights'.[308] As part of its human development mandate, UNRWA engages in provision of credit for enterprise and income-generating opportunities.[309]

Far from asserting a protection gap, Albanese and Takkenberg's position is that Palestinian refugees are entitled, under international law, to the same or even greater protections than Convention refugees.[310] In outlining the scope of protection for Palestinian refugees, they look across international humanitarian law, statelessness law, international refugee law and international human rights law.[311] Albanese and Takkenberg argue that UNRWA's protection mandate started to expand significantly in the late 1990s partly due to international recognition that the prospect of a Palestinian state would not be soon achieved.[312]

Another important aspect of the scope of refuge for Palestinian refugees is the recognition that it differs according to factors such as gender, age and disability. Bartholomeusz[313]

---

[300] Reference to improving the quality of life is made in UNRWA's 2008–2009 Programme Budget subsequently approved by a UNGA resolution: UNRWA, (n 139) [90]. As noted (n 295), UNGA's approval of the budget specifically mandates all activities contained in the budget.

[301] Reference to improving health conditions in camps is made in UNRWA's 2008–2009 Programme Budget subsequently approved by a UNGA resolution: UNRWA (n 139) [67]. As noted (n 295), UNGA's approval of the budget specifically mandates all activities contained in the budget.

[302] Reference to addressing the needs of poor refugees is made in UNRWA's 2008–2009 Programme Budget subsequently approved by a UNGA resolution: UNRWA (n 139) [79]. As noted (n 295), UNGA's approval of the budget specifically mandates all activities contained in the budget.

[303] Bartholomeusz (n 59) 469; Lex Takkenberg, *The Status of Palestinian Refugees in International Law* (Oxford University Press, 1998) 301.

[304] The host country remains responsible for these issues. See UNRWA, *Frequently Asked Questions* <www.unrwa.org/who-we-are/frequently-asked-questions>.

[305] *Special Identification Cards to All Palestine Refugees*, GA Res 37/120J, UN Doc A/Res/37/120J (16 December 1982) [1].

[306] Bartholomeusz (n 59) 452, 464; Takkenberg (n 303) 301.

[307] See, e.g., *Assistance to Palestine Refugees*, GA Res 63/91, UN Doc A/Res/63/91 (5 December 2008) [3]; *Assistance to Palestine Refugees*, GA Res 62/102, UN Doc A/Res/62/102 (17 December 2007) [3]. UNRWA (n 139) describes its mission as, 'to help Palestinian refugees achieve their full potential in human development terms under the difficult circumstances in which they live': [2].

[308] UN Development Programme, *Human Development Report 1990* (Oxford University Press, 1990) 10.

[309] Reference to credit provision is made in UNRWA's 2008–2009 Programme Budget subsequently approved by a UNGA resolution: UNRWA (n 139) [82]. As noted (n 295), UNGA's approval of the budget specifically mandates all activities contained in the budget.

[310] Albanese and Takkenberg (n 58) 170. [311] Ibid ch III. [312] Ibid 424–5.

[313] Bartholomeusz (n 59) 466.

highlights that UNRWA's protection mandate extends to addressing the needs and rights of women and children in accordance with the CEDAW and CRC.[314] The UNGA has also extended UNRWA's mandate to encompass the rights of Palestinian refugees with disabilities in line with the CRPD.[315]

These studies of the scope of refuge for Palestinian refugees reflect the temporal nature of refuge and, in particular, the idea that it must allow refugees to look towards the future. This is evident in UNRWA's human development mandate, its mandate to provide education and business development opportunities and the recognition that Palestinian refugees are entitled to durable solutions.[316] While acknowledging that many Palestinian refugees do not receive these protections in practice, Albanese and Takkenberg insist that 'the interconnectedness of the various areas of law can result in greater protection of Palestinian refugees'.[317]

2.6.3 Scope of Refuge for Putative Refugees and IDPs

As already noted, putative refugees are those who have a well-founded fear of being persecuted for a Convention reason but who have not yet established that they are unable to avail themselves of the protection of their country of origin or habitual residence. Decision-makers will ask whether they can relocate to another part of their homeland where they will be protected. There is debate about the appropriate way to discern the scope of protection in this context, but agreement that it must be much broader than negating the risk of persecution.[318] Mathew[319] and Schultz[320] argue that international human rights law should inform whether the putative refugee would have protection in the internal protection alternative. Hathaway and Foster contend that this approach may be 'unwieldy'[321] and suggest that the scope of protection can be determined with reference to the rights outlined in the Refugee Convention.[322] Despite this disagreement, pursuant to both approaches, refuge includes the rights and protections necessary to rebuild normal lives,[323] including access to 'employment, public welfare, and education'.[324] Schultz highlights that decision-makers must take account of specific protection needs arising from gender, youth, disability and statelessness.[325]

The UNHCR sets a narrower scope for what constitutes refuge in internal protection alternative cases: 'basic human rights standards, including in particular, non-derogable rights'.[326] The UNHCR elaborates that 'a person should not be expected to face economic

---

[314] *Operations of the United Nations Relief and Works Agency for Palestine Refugees in the Near East*, GA Res 59/119, UN Doc A/Res/59/119 (10 December 2004) [7]; *Operations of the United Nations Relief and Works Agency for Palestine Refugees in the Near East*, GA Res 62/104, UN Doc A/Res/62/104 (17 December 2007) [8]; *Operations of the United Nations Relief and Works Agency for Palestine Refugees in the Near East*, GA Res 63/93, UN Doc A/Res/63/93 (5 December 2008) [9].

[315] *Operations of the United Nations Relief and Works Agency for Palestine Refugees in the Near East*, GA Res 69/88, UN Doc A/Res/69/88 (16 December 2014).

[316] As already noted, scholars highlight that Palestinian refugees are entitled to durable solutions: Bartholomeusz (n 59) 469–73; Albanese and Takkenberg (n 58) ch VIII.

[317] Albanese and Takkenberg (n 58) 128.

[318] Hathaway and Foster (n 69) 344–50; Michigan Guidelines on the IPA (n 69); Schultz (n 71) ch 6.

[319] Mathew (n 70) 193–5.

[320] Schultz (n 71) 212–13. Schultz also posits that international humanitarian law is relevant.

[321] Hathaway and Foster (n 69) 354.   [322] Ibid 356.   [323] Ibid 356; Schultz (n 71) 217.

[324] Michigan Guidelines on the IPA (n 69) [22].   [325] Schultz (n 71) 228.   [326] UNHCR (n 201) [28].

destitution or existence below at least an adequate level of subsistence'[327] or 'live in conditions of severe hardship'.[328]

As highlighted in Chapter 1, the sharp lines that lawyers draw between different categories of people in need of protection blur in practice and also collide in protection from refuge scenarios. The putative refugees considered in this book (Chapter 7) are also prospective IDPs because they assert that, if they do return home and internally relocate, they will have no choice but to live in an IDP camp. The international community has recognised that IDPs have specific protection needs through the development of the Guiding Principles on Internal Displacement.[329] There is some support for reference to the Guiding Principles in international protection alternative cases.[330] Additionally, in Africa there is the Kampala Convention. Many African states have enacted domestic legislation implementing provisions in the Guiding Principles and Kampala Convention.[331]

The Guiding Principles on Internal Displacement and the Kampala Convention indicate that the scope of refuge for IDPs is wide-ranging and differs depending on factors such as gender, age and disability. For example, the Guiding Principles confirm rights to life,[332] liberty and security of person,[333] freedom of movement,[334] an adequate standard of living,[335] medical care[336] and education[337] for IDPs during displacement. It also outlines rights specifically tailored to the situation of IDPs such as the right to move freely in and out of camps[338] and right to be free from forced return or resettlement.[339] The Kampala Convention stresses that states have a number of obligations with respect to IDPs, including preventing sexual and gender-based violence against IDPs[340] and providing special protection to unaccompanied children, female heads of households, the elderly and persons with disabilities.[341]

The scope of refuge for IDPs also includes solutions to displacement.[342] Section V of the Guiding Principles outlines solutions of return, resettlement and reintegration. There is no strong legal basis for IDPs being entitled to such rights,[343] but, nevertheless, their inclusion indicates that internal displacement should not be a permanent state of affairs. The Kampala Convention obliges states to 'seek lasting solutions to the problem of displacement by promoting and creating satisfactory conditions for voluntary return, local integration or relocation on a sustainable basis and in circumstances of safety and dignity'.[344] The inclusion of durable solutions in the Guiding Principles and the Kampala Convention reflects ideas of refuge's temporality; in particular, that it must encompass hope for a different and better future.

---

[327] Ibid [29].   [328] Ibid [30].

[329] Phil Orchard, *Protecting the Internally Displaced: Rhetoric and Reality* (Routledge, 2019) 6.

[330] Elizabeth Ferris, 'Internal Displacement and the Right to Seek Asylum' (2008) 27(3) *Refugee Survey Quarterly* 76, 88; Bríd Ní Ghráinne, 'The Internal Protection Alternative Inquiry and Human Rights Considerations – Irrelevant or Indispensable?' (2015) 27(1) *International Journal of Refugee Law* 29, 37.

[331] For example, Kenya has The Prevention, Protection and Assistance to Internally Displaced Persons and Affected Communities Act (2012). For an examination of other domestic laws implementing the Kampala Convention, see International Committee of the Red Cross, *The Kampala Convention: Key Recommendations Ten Years On* (December 2019) <www.icrc.org/en/document/kampala-convention-key-recommendations-ten-years>.

[332] Guiding Principles (n 63) principle 10.   [333] Ibid principle 12.   [334] Ibid principle 14.

[335] Ibid principle 18.   [336] Ibid principle 19.   [337] Ibid principle 23.   [338] Ibid principle 14(2).

[339] Ibid principle 15(d).   [340] Kampala Convention art 9(1)(d).   [341] Ibid art 9(2)(c).

[342] For a discussion of the right to return for IDPs, see Megan Bradley, 'Durable Solutions and the Right of Return for IDPs: Evolving Interpretations' (2018) 30(2) *International Journal of Refugee Law* 218.

[343] Kälin (n 62) 69.   [344] art 11(1).

Overall, scholarship and UN materials indicate that the scope of refuge for Convention refugees, Palestinian refugees, putative refugees and IDPs is broad, but cannot be definitively drawn. Writing in 1966, United Nations High Commissioner for Refugees Felix Schnyder explained that 'the sum total of the rights, benefits and obligations due to refugees by virtue of rules of international law – cannot be reduced to a single, let alone simple, formula'.[345] Schnyder was writing in relation to the different statuses granted to refugees from the Russian revolution and post-World War II refugees. However, his statement is perhaps even more accurate today with the entry into force of the ICCPR, the ICESCR, regional refugee and human rights treaties and specialised international human rights instruments such as the CEDAW, the CRC and the CRPD, which all contain rights relevant to refugee protection and, for Palestinian refugees, UNRWA's evolving mandate. Providing a contemporary perspective, Albanese and Takkenberg state that 'current concepts of protection [for refugees] refer to a broad range of activities aimed at obtaining full respect for the rights of the individual in accordance with relevant bodies of international law, taking into account the specific needs of the individual'.[346] Nevertheless, another query is whether there is a minimum standard for adequate refuge. I turn to this question next.

2.7 What Is the Threshold for Adequate Refuge?

While refuge is understood to have a broad scope, one issue is whether there is a minimum standard of refuge that can be considered sufficient. In this book, and in particular Chapter 5, I examine where decision-makers set the bar for adequate refuge. The idea that there is a minimal standard for adequate refuge is addressed in legal scholarship with respect to Convention refugees. Scholars argue that the rights in the Refugee Convention are not aspirational, but represent the minimum standard of rights protection.[347] McAdam explains that the Refugee Convention's drafters settled on a 'middle course' in the sense that the rights in the Refugee Convention are 'beyond the lowest common denominator', but standards more favourable to refugees were avoided due to concerns that 'fewer states would ratify it'.[348] By taking this approach, the drafters believed that the Refugee Convention would 'give refugees a minimum number of advantages which would permit them to lead a tolerable life in the country of reception'.[349]

---

[345] Felix Schnyder, Foreword in Atle Grahl-Madsen, *The Status of Refugees in International Law: Volume 1* (AW Sijthoff-Leyden, 1966).

[346] Albanese and Takkenberg (58) 405.

[347] The Declaration of States Parties to the 1951 Convention and/or its 1967 Protocol Relating to the Status of Refugees confirms that the Refugee Convention and its amending Protocol provide the 'minimum standards of treatment that apply to persons falling within its scope': UNHCR, *Declaration of States Parties to the 1951 Convention and/or its 1967 Protocol Relating to the Status of Refugees*, UN Doc HCR/ MMSP/2001/09 (16 January 2002) preamble [2]. This position is also supported by Goodwin-Gill and McAdam (n 123), who describe the Refugee Convention as offering 'the most basic guarantees': 506. Hathaway (2005) (n 50) also emphasises that the rights in the Refugee Convention are 'the core minimum judged necessary' because they 'restore to refugees the basic ability to function within a new national community': 107.

[348] McAdam (n 51) 30.

[349] UN Economic and Social Council, *Ad Hoc Committee on Statelessness and Related Problems, Summary Record of the Twenty-Second Meeting*, UN Doc E/AC.32/SR.22 (14 February 1950) comment of the Chairman [14].

In support of this position, the Michigan Guidelines on Protection Elsewhere[350] stipulate that a host state can only transfer a refugee to a third country[351] if, 'in practice', they will be treated in accordance with articles 2–34 of the Refugee Convention.[352] This position is premised on the principle that a state cannot 'contract out' of its international legal obligations.[353] This approach to the minimum standard of adequate protection preserves refuge's future focus, because many of the provisions in the Refugee Convention, such as the rights to work,[354] education[355] and durable solutions,[356] enable refugees to imagine and plan the future directions of their lives.

The UNHCR's understanding of effective protection has been inconsistent. Its 2003 conclusion states that effective protection requires 'accession to and compliance with the 1951 Convention and/or 1967 Protocol … unless the destination country can demonstrate that the third State has developed a practice akin to the 1951 Convention and/or its 1967 Protocol'.[357] However, in a 2004 statement on effective protection and 2013 guidance on refugee transfers, the UNHCR does not specify that the third country must comply with the rights in the Refugee Convention.[358] Stevens criticises the UNHCR's approach to effective protection because it does not contain all the rights in the Refugee Convention and 'suggests that a lesser form of protection exists, which, though imperfect, is, nonetheless, in some way permissible'.[359] In its more recent guidance on safe third countries and irregular movement, the UNHCR has stressed the need for host countries to comply with the protection standards in the Refugee Convention.[360] These are high standards for adequate refuge but, in practice, they are rarely met. Next, I turn to these discrepancies between ideas of refuge and the reality.

2.8   The Reality of Refuge

While the aforementioned scholarship projects ideas about what refuge should look like, studies of and testimonies about places of refuge provide a different picture. As Sharpe

---

[350] Fourth Colloquium on Challenges in Refugee Law, 'The Michigan Guidelines on Protection Elsewhere' (2007) 28(2) *Michigan Journal of International Law* 207.

[351] The predominant view is that such transfers are lawful under the Refugee Convention as long as the asylum seeker or refugee is protected: Foster (n 248) 237; Michigan Guidelines on Protection Elsewhere (n 350) [1]; UNHCR, *Summary Conclusions on the Concept of 'Effective Protection' in the Context of Secondary Movements of Refugees and Asylum Seekers (Lisbon Expert Roundtable, 9–10 December 2002)* (February 2003) [12]; UNHCR Executive Committee, *Conclusion No 85 (XLIX)*, UN Doc A/53/12/Add.1 (9 October 1998) [aa]; cf Violeta Moreno-Lax, 'The Legality of the "Safe Third Country" Notion Contested: Insights from the Law of Treaties' in Guy Goodwin-Gill and Philippe Weckel (eds), *Migration & Refugee Protection in the 21st Century: International Legal Aspects* (Martinus Nijhoff, 2015) 665.

[352] Michigan Guidelines on Protection Elsewhere (n 350) [2], [8].   [353] Foster (n 248) 268.

[354] arts 17, 18, 19, 24.   [355] art 22.   [356] See Hathaway (2005) (n 50) 918, 953–4, 963, 977.

[357] UNHCR Executive Committee (n 351) [15(e)].

[358] UNHCR, *Guidance Note on Bilateral and/or Multilateral Transfer Arrangements of Asylum-Seekers* (May 2013) <www.refworld.org/docid/51af82794.html>; UNHCR, Statement by Ms Erika Feller (n 121).

[359] Stevens (n 172) 248.

[360] UNHCR, *Legal Considerations Regarding Access to Protection and a Connection between the Refugee and the Third Country in the Context of Return or Transfer to Safe Third Countries* (April 2018) [3], [4] <www.refworld.org/docid/5acb33ad4.html>; UNHCR, *Guidance on Responding to Irregular Movement of Refugees and Asylum Seekers* (September 2019) [11], [18] < www.refworld.org/docid/5d8a255d4.html>.

observes, it is often the case of 'rhetoric over reality'.[361] There are, of course, publications that highlight the ways in which refugees have worked to re-establish their lives and communities after displacement.[362] Nevertheless, sitting alongside these important testaments to refugee resiliency, there are myriad publications, reports and memoirs on the dangers and deprivations in places of so-called refuge. I cannot do justice to this extensive literature here. Instead, to highlight the disjunctures between refuge as a concept and as a place, I outline the main concerns in the substantial literature documenting conditions in sites of ostensible refuge. I focus on the locales subject to protection from refuge litigation examined in Chapters 3–7. This provides the background against which I explore, in the remainder of the book, the ways courts respond to the incongruities between ideas and realities of refuge.

While refuge is, first and foremost, intended to provide a place of safety, for many people seeking sanctuary the cycle of violence continues. Studies of life in IDP and refugee camps evidence that there are threats to physical security,[363] especially for women and girls.[364] IDP camps are often targeted for attacks,[365] and there is a risk of abduction by militant groups.[366] The disruption of displacement and encampment can exacerbate domestic violence for IDPs and refugees.[367] The ways in which many refugee and IDP camps have been designed have not prioritised safe access to sanitation facilities, in particular for women and girls.[368]

Sites of so-called refuge in Global North countries can also be violent places. For example, asylum seekers in Calais' Jungle have been subject to violence and police abuse[369] and there have been allegations of sexual abuse by NGO volunteers.[370] There is mounting

[361] Sharpe (n 28) 94.   [362] See, e.g., Haines (n 162) 174; Hajj (n 258).

[363] See, e.g., Barbara Harrell-Bond and Guglielmo Verdirame, *Rights in Exile: Janus-Faced Humanitarianism* (Berghahn Books, 2005); Arafat Jamal, 'Minimum Standards and Essential Needs in a Protracted Refugee Situation: A Review of the UNHCR Programme in Kakuma, Kenya' (Report 2000/05, Evaluation and Policy Analysis Unit, UNHCR, 2000) 18; Maja Janmyr, *Protecting Civilians in Refugee Camps: Unable and Unwilling States, UNHCR and International Responsibility* (Martinus Nijhoff, 2014); Edwin Odhiambo-Abuya and Charles Ikobe, 'Wasted Lives: Internally Displaced Persons Living in Camps in Kenya' (2010) 1 *International Humanitarian Legal Studies* 233, 244–5; UNRWA, *Jenin Camp* <www.unrwa.org/where-we-work/west-bank/jenin-camp>.

[364] Sharon Carlson, 'Contesting and Reinforcing Patriarchy: An Analysis of Domestic Violence in the Dzaleka Refugee Camp' (Working Paper No 23, Refugee Studies Centre, University of Oxford, 2005) 27–33; Roseanne Njiru, 'Political Battles on Women's Bodies: Post-Election Conflicts and Violence Against Women in Internally Displaced Persons Camps in Kenya' (2014) 9(1) *Societies Without Borders* 48, 55–6; UN International Children's Emergency Fund ('UNICEF'), *The Situation of Palestinian Children in the Occupied Palestinian Territory, Jordan, Syria and Lebanon* (2010) <www.unicef.org/oPt/PALESTINIAN_SITAN-final.pdf>.

[365] UNHCR, *UNHCR's Grandi: Failures Behind Nigeria IDP Camp Tragedy Must Be Identified* (18 January 2017) <www.unhcr.org/en-au/news/press/2017/1/587f6a734/unhcrs-grandi-failures-behind-nigeria-idp-camp-tragedy-must-identified.html>.

[366] *End of Mission Statement by the United Nations Special Rapporteur on the Human Rights of Internally Displaced Persons, Mr. Chaloka Beyani, on His Visit to Nigeria, 23 to 26 August 2016* (22 January 2016) <https://ohchr.org/EN/NewsEvents/Pages/DisplayNews.aspx?NewsID=20427>.

[367] Carlson (n 364).

[368] Dale Buscher, 'Refugee Women: Twenty Years On' (2010) 29(2) *Refugee Survey Quarterly* 4.

[369] Surindar Dhesi, Arshad Isakjee and Thom Davies, *An Environmental Health Assessment of the New Migrant Camp in Calais* (2015) 2 <www.birmingham.ac.uk/Documents/college-les/gees/research/calais-report-oct-2015.pdf>.

[370] May Bulman, 'Calais Jungle Volunteers Accused of "Sexually Exploiting" Camp's Refugees', *Independent* (online 22 September 2016) <www.independent.co.uk/news/world/europe/calais-jungle-volunteers-sex-refugees-allegations-facebook-care4calais-a7312066.html>.

documentation of the violence[371] and police abuse[372] experienced by refugees in the Greek Islands. Physical insecurity is also a serious concern with respect to Australia's offshore processing centres in Nauru and Papua New Guinea. Many refugees have been the victims of grave acts of violence both within these centres and after release into the community.[373] There is evidence that refugees have endured sexual violence in Nauru and Manus Island.[374] Most infamously, in a series of violent incidents at the Manus Island detention centre in February 2014, staff assaulted numerous detainees, and one asylum seeker was killed.[375]

In addition to high levels of violence, many people seeking international protection live in poverty and have no or minimal access to essential services, education and employment. Many refugees and IDPs who live in a camp struggle to continue their education and careers,[376] seek basic healthcare[377] and do not have adequate shelter, sanitation, food and water.[378] The extent to which host states allow Palestinian refugees to access work and education differs,[379] but many Palestinian refugees feel that they have no future because of a dearth of study and employment opportunities.[380]

There are similar concerns for refugees and asylum seekers in higher-income countries. For example, many refugees in Italy are socially marginalised[381] and live in 'inhumane

---

[371] Human Rights Watch, *Greece: Inhumane Conditions at Land Border* (27 July 2018) <www.hrw.org /news/2018/07/27/greece-inhumane-conditions-land-border?mc_cid=0e50786a23&m c_eid=677b225ed4>; UNHCR, 'Refugee Women and Children Face Heightened Risk of Sexual Violence amid Tensions and Overcrowding at Reception Facilities on Greek Islands' (Press Briefing, 9 February 2018) <www.unhcr.org/en-au/news/briefing/2018/2/5a7d67c4b/refugee-women-children-face-heightened-risk-sexual-violence-amid-tensions.html>.

[372] Human Rights Watch (n 371).

[373] A refugee was raped after being released from immigration detention in Nauru and placed into shared housing arranged and paid for by the Australian government: *Plaintiff S99/2016 v Minister for Immigration and Border Protection* [2016] FCA 483, [82]. There have been a number of reports of refugees on Manus Island being attacked after release from immigration detention: Human Rights Watch, *Australia/PNG: Refugees Face Unchecked Violence* (25 October 2017) <www.hrw.org/news/2017/10/25/australia/png-refugees-face-unchecked-violence>.

[374] Committee on the Elimination of Discrimination Against Women, *Concluding Observations on the Eighth Periodic Report of Australia*, UN Doc CEDAW/C/AUS/CO/8 (20 July 2018) [53]; Philip Moss, *Review into Recent Allegations Relating to Conditions and Circumstances at the Regional Processing Centre in Nauru* (Department of Immigration and Border Protection, 6 February 2015) 23–51; Senate Select Committee on the Recent Allegations Relating to Conditions and Circumstances at the Regional Processing Centre in Nauru, Parliament of Australia, *Taking Responsibility: Conditions and Circumstances at Australia's Regional Processing Centre in Nauru* (2015).

[375] Senate Legal and Constitutional Affairs References Committee, Parliament of Australia, *Incident at the Manus Island Detention Centre from 16 February to 18 February 2014* (December 2014) ch 5; Robert Cornall, Review into the Events of 16–18 February 2014 at the Manus Regional Processing Centre (Department of Immigration and Border Protection, 23 May 2014) 62–3.

[376] Harrell-Bond and Verdirame (n 364) 215, 253–9; Simon Turner, 'Angry Young Men in Camps: Gender, Age and Class Relations Among Burundian Refugees in Tanzania' (Working Paper No 9, UNHCR, New Issues in Refugee Research, June 1999); UNHCR, *The Situation of Palestinian Refugees in Lebanon* (February 2016) <www.refworld.org/pdfid/56cc95484.pdf>.

[377] Harrell-Bond and Verdirame (n 364) 241–52; UNHCR (n 377).

[378] Odhiambo-Abuya and Ikobe (n 363) 246–7; Harrell-Bond and Verdirame (n 363) 225–40; Henri Rueff and Alain Viaro, 'Palestinian Refugee Camps: From Shelter to Habitat' (2010) 28(2–3) *Refugee Survey Quarterly* 339, 356.

[379] Akram (n 290) 44–5.   [380] UNHCR (n 376).

[381] Médecins Sans Frontières, *Informal Settlements: Social Marginality, Obstacles to Access to Healthcare and Basic Needs for Migrants, Asylum Seekers and Refugees* (2018) 6–7 <www.msf.org/sites/msf.org/files/out_of_sight_def.pdf>.

conditions' without access to food, water, shelter or healthcare.[382] Reports of conditions for refugees in Greece indicate that there is a lack of adequate sanitation,[383] little or no access to healthcare,[384] inadequate provision of food and water,[385] overcrowded conditions,[386] no services for pregnant women and new mothers[387] or refugees with disabilities.[388] In the US, refugees are not provided with adequate and appropriate assistance to gain employment.[389] Detainees in Australia's offshore processing centres have limited access to healthcare and education,[390] live in overcrowded conditions with inadequate sanitation[391] and often do not have sufficient food and water.[392]

Another significant concern across many places of ostensible refuge is deprivation of liberty. One of the manifest problems with encampment is that it significantly restricts freedom of movement, which can inhibit family reunification and access to vital services.[393] Many Global North countries implement immigration detention. Greece imposes blanket detention policies and significant restrictions on freedom of movement.[394] The US practises immigration detention[395] and some asylum seekers 'languish in detention for long periods of time'.[396] Australia also has a regime of immigration detention and many refugees and asylum seekers are detained for significant periods.[397]

While refuge is intended to be temporary and provide a space to rebuild lives, many live in protracted situations of displacement – a 'long-lasting and intractable state of limbo' where people's 'lives may not be at risk, but their basic rights and essential economic, social and psychological needs remain unfulfilled after years in exile'.[398] With respect to protracted periods of encampment, Betts and Collier explain that 'if camp life endures for too long it may lead to long-term reliance upon aid, exacerbate vulnerability, and erode people's capacities for independence'.[399] A representative from the International Organization for Migration says of an IDP camp in Sudan that 'the effects of continued displacement can be seen in the eyes of the women – a sense of stagnancy and lack of hope and dreams is felt as they become accustomed to camp life'.[400] Boochani, writing as a refugee in Australia's offshore processing centre on Manus Island, documents the boredom and frustration experienced by those incarcerated there.[401] The longest-standing protracted refugee

---

[382] Ibid 14.   [383] Human Rights Watch (n 371).   [384] Ibid.

[385] Human Rights Watch, *Greece: Asylum Seekers Locked Up* (14 April 2016) <www.hrw.org/news/2016/04/14/greece-asylum-seekers-locked>.

[386] Human Rights Watch (n 371).   [387] Ibid.   [388] Ibid.

[389] Besteman (n 244); Haines (n 162); Inhorn (n 155) 82.

[390] Australian Human Rights Commission, *Asylum Seekers, Refugees and Human Rights: Snapshot Report (Second Edition)* (2017) 37 <https://humanrights.gov.au/our-work/asylum-seekers-and-refugees/publications/asylum-seekers-refugees-and-human-rights-0>.

[391] Ibid 35.   [392] Ibid 35.

[393] UNHCR (n 376); Marjoleine Zieck, 'Refugees and the Right to Freedom of Movement: From Flight to Return' (2018) 39(1) *Michigan Journal of International Law* 21, 116.

[394] Human Rights Watch (n 371).

[395] Daniel Hartoum, 'America's Modern Day Internment Camps: The Law of War and Refugees of Central America's Drug Conflict' (2015) 21(1) *Texas Journal on Civil Liberties & Civil Rights* 61, 65.

[396] Ibid 66.   [397] Australian Human Rights Commission (n 391).

[398] UNHCR Executive Committee, *Protracted Refugee Situations*, UN Doc EC/54/SC/CRP.14 (10 June 2004) [3].

[399] Betts and Collier (n 77) 137.

[400] Amani Osman, *From a Home to a Camp: Life as an IDP in Sudan* (IOM, 14 October 2015) <http://weblog.iom.int/home-camp-life-idp-sudan>.

[401] Boochani (n 1) 121.

situation is for Palestinian refugees.[402] As Lilly explains, 'the stumbling block is the absence of the political conditions that are necessary to achieve durable solutions' for Palestinian refugees.[403]

The reasons why many people in need of protection do not enjoy genuine sanctuary are varied and complex. It is outside the scope of this book to provide an account of the wealth of literature examining why IDPs and refugees often do not find adequate protection. Scholars have drawn attention to a global shift towards framing refugees as a threat to security;[404] the reduction of and inequitable levels of funding for refugee protection;[405] lack of accountability for actions by international organisations and NGOs[406] and that the global refugee regime lacks an effective international enforcement mechanism.[407] I do not delve into this scholarship in detail because when refugees come to courts seeking protection from a place of inadequate refuge, they provide evidence of the dangers and deprivations in these locales but not the multifaceted economic, political, social and structural causes of these conditions as described in scholarship. These decision-making bodies are then tasked with determining whether a refugee or asylum seeker is entitled, pursuant to the legal frameworks pleaded, to be saved from the place of resisted refuge.

2.9   Conclusion

In this chapter, I have shown that the concept of refuge is a robust one. There are different approaches to theorising refuge, but there is a shared understanding that it has restorative, regenerative and palliative functions that address refugees' past, present and future. Refuge operates as a response to the particular dilemmas of those in need of protection and is variously expressed as a remedy, right, duty, process and status. It has a broad and flexible scope that responds to the specific needs of women, children and refugees with disabilities. The standard for adequate refuge is a high one, encompassing much more than mere

---

[402] Lilly (n 60) 444.   [403] Ibid 462.

[404] See, e.g., B.S. Chimni, 'Globalization, Humanitarianism and the Erosion of Refugee Protection' (2000) 13(3) *Journal of Refugee Studies* 243; Selina March, 'Manufacturing Fear: Examining the Social Component of Anti-Immigration Policies within Counter-Terrorism Discourse' in James Simeon (ed), *Terrorism and Asylum* (Brill, 2020); Lilly (n 60) 451.

[405] See, e.g., Steven Roper and Lilian Barria, 'Burden Sharing in the Funding of the UNHCR: Refugee Protection as an Impure Public Good' (2010) 54(4) *Journal of Conflict Resolution* 616; Ogg (n 236); Raimo Vayrynen, 'Funding Dilemmas in Refugee Assistance: Political Interests and Institutional Reforms in the UNHCR' (2001) 35(1) *International Migration Review* 143.

[406] See, e.g., Miriam Bradley, 'UNHCR and Accountability for IDP Protection in Columbia' in Kristin Bergtora Sandvik, Katja Lindskov Jacobsen (eds), *UNHCR and the Struggle for Accountability: Technology, Law and Results-Based Management* (Routledge, 2016); Anita Ho and Carol Pavlish, 'Invisibility of Accountability and Empowerment in Tackling Gender-Based Violence: Lessons from a Refugee Camp in Rwanda' (2011) 24(1) *Journal of Refugee Studies* 88; Maja Janmyr, *Protecting Civilians in Refugee Camps: Unwilling and Unable States, UNHCR and International Responsibility* (Martinus Nijhoff, 2014); Volker Turk and Elizabeth Eyster, 'Strengthening Accountability in the UNHCR' (2010) 22(2) *International Journal of Refugee Law* 159.

[407] Katie O'Byrne, 'Is There a *Need* for Better Supervision of the Refugee Convention?' (2013) 26(3) *Journal of Refugee Studies* 330. Under the Refugee Convention there is no body that can hear and determine complaints from individuals. Pursuant to art 38, states can refer disputes to the International Court of Justice but no such disputes have been heard and determined by the Court.

survival. However, many people who seek protection find themselves in places where the conditions may be comparable to or worse than the places they fled.

In protection from refuge claims, the ideal and reality of refuge both enter the judicial domain. In the rest of the book, I draw on the ideas of refuge outlined in this chapter to examine how decision-makers conceptualise refuge and navigate the discrepancies between refuge as a concept and as a place. I assess the implications these judicial approaches to protection from refuge claims have for refugees' (or particular refugees') ability to move within and across borders to find sanctuary.

3

Using Human and Refugee Rights to Resist Encampment

3.1 Introduction

One of the most powerful voices against encampment is Harrell-Bond, who contends that 'refugee camps are not good for anyone. No-one freely chooses to move into a refugee camp to stay. Everyone who can gets out of them as quickly as possible'.[1] The refugee litigants described in this chapter are trying to do exactly this: they are starting court proceedings and pleading human and refugee rights to avoid forced relocation to a refugee camp, or to leave the confines of a camp. In doing so, they are using courts in their quest to stay in or reach a place in which they believe they can enjoy a sense of refuge. However, their rights arguments collide with states' justifications for confining refugees in their territory to a camp, in particular on national security grounds.

Forced encampment litigation is most prominent in Kenya.[2] The purpose of this chapter is to discuss how Kenyan judges approach and determine these legal challenges. In particular, I highlight the ways in which they use human rights law to conceptualise the functions and nature of refuge. I argue that, when courts draw on an abstract idea of refugeehood and then use the refugee litigant's circumstances to inform rights arguments, human rights law can be used to engage with ideas of refuge in a sophisticated manner. This proves powerful in challenging encampment policies. However, when refugees' individual circumstances are used to draw comparisons between refugees, the concept of refuge is diluted and human rights arguments lose their force in the face of states' justifications for encampment.

In Section 3.2, I situate Kenyan forced encampment jurisprudence within the broader literature on refugees making human rights claims against their host states. In Section 3.3, I start my analysis of the jurisprudence by examining the first Kenyan forced encampment case: the 2013 decision of *Kituo Cha Sheria v Attorney General* ('*Kituo Cha Sheria*') in the High Court of Kenya.[3] I suggest that the Court constructed ideas of refuge, not in a rights-based manner, but in a similar way to what I described in Chapter 2 as categorical and experiential approaches to understanding refuge. Through this reasoning, the Court engaged with the restorative, regenerative and palliative functions of refuge and characterised refuge as a remedy, legal status and process. While none of the refugee litigants in *Kituo Cha Sheria* were women, I suggest that the judgment projected ideas of refuge that were cognisant of and sensitive to refugees of all genders and backgrounds. This was

---

[1] Barbara Harrell-Bond, 'Are Refugee Camps Good for Children?' (Working Paper 29, UNHCR, 2000) 1.
[2] There is some forced encampment litigation in other countries. See, e.g., *Ex Parte Nsabimana v Department of Poverty and Disaster Management Affairs* (High Court of Malawi, Application 19/2006, 17 April 2008).
[3] [2013] eKLR (High Court of Kenya, Constitutional and Human Rights Division).

a significant victory because it quashed a Kenyan forced encampment directive and came close to ruling that encampment is in violation of the Refugee Convention. In Section 3.4, I show that there has been a change in the way Kenyan courts approach forced encampment litigation post *Kituo Cha Sheria*. There is now a focus on finding the exceptional refugee, which has diminished judicial conceptions of refuge in Kenya to far below the standards discussed in Chapter 2. This shift has also diluted the potential for rights arguments to challenge the legality of forced encampment policies and now Kenyan courts determine whether individual refugees can be saved from camp life on a case-by-case basis. Nevertheless, I highlight that Kenyan judges have taken sensitive and sophisticated approaches to questions of gender, parenthood and childhood when identifying the exceptional case that warrants rescue from a refugee camp.

3.2 Refugees' Human Rights Claims

Kenyan forced encampment jurisprudence has received scant attention in scholarship. There are some references to this case law with respect to Kenyan courts' interpretation of freedom of movement in the Refugee Convention.[4] There are also analyses from the perspective of Kenyan constitutional law[5] and urban refugees.[6] However, there is no broader examination of the significance of the jurisprudence from the perspective of refugee protection.[7]

In forced encampment litigation, refugees, as non-citizens, use human and refugee rights in the legal challenges they bring against the host state. This reflects scholars' observations on the ways refugee law differs from human rights law. As Gammeltoft-Hansen explains:

> refugee law is specific in dealing solely with the relationship between the state and the subjects of another state. This relation may still be played out vertically within the host state, yet the fact that it is concerned solely with foreigners and not a state's own subjects means that the refugee regime, in certain ways, differs from the ordinary modus operandi of the broader human rights regime.[8]

While it is difficult to disagree with Baumgärtel that 'entitlements of non-citizens in the absence of a social contract is arguably what the idea of human rights is all about',[9] when an alien makes a rights claim against a host state, it can give rise to tensions among the outsider's human rights, the human rights of the local population and the state's duty to

---

[4] Cathryn Costello, Yulia Ioffe and Teresa Büchsel, 'Article 31 of the 1951 Convention Relating to the Status of Refugees' (PPLA/2017/01, UNHCR Legal and Protection Policy and Research Series, July 2017) 6.

[5] Robert Nanima, 'An Evaluation of Kenya's Parallel Legal Regime on Refugees, and the Courts' Guarantee of their Rights' (2017) 21 *Law Democracy and Development* 42.

[6] Laurence Juma, 'Encampment, Refoulement, Refugee Protection and Urban Refugee Rights' (2018) 33(2) *Southern African Public Law* 1.

[7] Global South decision-making has been ignored in refugee law scholarship: Cathryn Costello, Michelle Foster and Jane McAdam, 'Introducing International Refugee Law as a Scholarly Field' in Cathryn Costello, Michelle Foster and Jane McAdam (eds), *The Oxford Handbook of International Refugee Law* (Oxford University Press, 2021) 1, 2.

[8] Thomas Gammeltoft-Hansen, *Access to Asylum: International Refugee Law and the Globalisation of Migration Control* (Cambridge University Press, 2011) 25–6.

[9] Moritz Baumgärtel, *Demanding Rights: Europe's Supranational Courts and the Dilemma of Migrant Vulnerability* (Cambridge University Press, 2019) 7.

protect both.[10] These tensions take on a greater salience in countries where many citizens live below the poverty line and have difficulty accessing basic resources and services. Such conflicts between refugees and locals have been examined in the Kenyan context.[11]

Complicating these quandaries is that forced encampment jurisprudence in Kenya, while it addresses Refugee Convention rights, is more centred on human rights in the Constitution of Kenya 2010 ('Kenyan Constitution'). The Bill of Rights in Kenya's Constitution includes what has been described as 'a near exhaustive catalogue of entitlements' that traverses civil and political and economic, social and cultural rights.[12] Part 2 of the Bill of Rights outlines these rights and then Part 3 addresses how they apply to what are described as vulnerable groups, including children, persons with disabilities and minorities (refugees are not specifically mentioned). In outlining general human rights and then how they apply to people in specific circumstances, Kenya's Bill of Rights has links to what Mégret describes as 'one of the most interesting and least studied puzzles of the contemporary development of international human rights'.[13] That is, human rights law is founded on 'the *sameness and unity* of human beings', but the existence of group-specific human rights is 'at least partly making a point about *difference and pluralism*'.[14] In the context of writing about the CRPD, Mégret suggests that this and other group-based human rights instruments recognise 'that there are, within humanity, a number of groups of human beings whose distinct claims to human rights are based on irreducible experiences that require a tailoring of the general rights regime'.[15] He refers to this as the 'pluralization of human rights'.[16]

Both of the aforementioned tensions are embedded in Kenyan-forced encampment jurisprudence. First, refugees are initiating litigation against a host state that has, in comparison to other states, especially in the Global North, a more limited capacity to provide for both refugees and its own citizens. Second, the petitioners are also not just making human rights claims; they are claiming special protection as refugees under the Refugee Convention and the Kenyan Constitution. Next, I analyse how the High Court of Kenya, in Kenya's first forced encampment case, grappled with these tensions and, in doing so, built a robust picture of refuge.

3.3   Categorical and Experiential Approaches to Conceptualising Refuge

The first Kenyan forced encampment case, *Kituo Cha Sheria*, challenged the legality of a 2012 Kenyan government directive requiring all refugees in Kenya to move to one of Kenya's two refugee camps ('Directive'). The Directive was a response to a series of terror

---

[10]   Yasemin Soysal, *The Limits of Citizenship: Migrants and Postnational Membership in Europe* (University of Chicago Press, 1995) 7–8.

[11]   Jecinta Anomat Ali and Witchayanee Ocha, 'East Africa Refugee Crises: Causes of Tensions and Conflicts between the Local Community and Refugees in Kakuma Refugee Camp, Kenya' (2018) 5(1) *Journal of Social Science Studies* 298.

[12]   John Osogo Ambani and Morris Kiwanda Mbondenyi, 'A New Era of Human Rights Promotion and Protection in Kenya? An analysis of the Salient Features of the 2010 Constitution's Bill of Rights' in Morris Kiwanda Mbondenyi et al (eds), *Human Rights and Democratic Governance in Kenya: A Post-2007 Appraisal* (Pretoria University Law Press, 2015) 17, 22.

[13]   Frédéric Mégret, 'The Disabilities Convention: Human Rights of Persons with Disabilities or Disability Rights?' (2008) 30(2) *Human Rights Quarterly* 494, 515.

[14]   Ibid 496 (emphasis in original).   [15]   Ibid 514.   [16]   Ibid 495.

attacks in urban areas.[17] While the Directive applied to all refugees in Kenya, its target was Somali refugees whom the government believed to be behind the attacks.[18] The case was brought by Kituo Cha Sheria, an NGO, and seven refugees living in Nairobi who were, pursuant to the Directive, subject to forced relocation to a camp. They argued that they had rebuilt their lives in Nairobi and forced relocation to a refugee camp would be a violation of their refugee and human rights. Their challenge was successful, and the High Court of Kenya's decision was upheld on appeal.

In Section 3.3.1, I show that the Court adopted a categorical approach to conceptualising refuge. In doing so, I draw parallels between the Court's reasoning and Mégret's identification, discussed earlier, of the pluralization of human rights. In Section 3.3.2, I discuss how other aspects of the judgment, which also address rights in the Kenyan Constitution, exhibit an experiential construction of refuge, and this deepened the Court's engagement with ideas of refuge's objectives and nature. In Section 3.3.3, I analyse how the Court interpreted Refugee Convention rights and suggest that it imbued them with deeper and richer understanding of states' protection obligations.

3.3.1 Understanding Refugeehood

In *Kituo Cha Sheria*, the High Court of Kenya adopted what I describe in Chapter 2 as a categorical approach to conceptualising refuge. The judge started his analysis by identifying what it means to be a refugee and, in particular, common experiences of refugeehood. Before considering the petitioners' substantive arguments, Justice Majanja recognised that '[r]efugees are a special category of persons who are, by virtue of their situation, considered vulnerable'.[19] Article 21(3) of the Kenyan Constitution provides that Kenya has a 'duty to address the needs of vulnerable groups'. While refugees are not mentioned in article 21(3), the Court was satisfied that they are a vulnerable group.[20]

In explaining why refugees are a vulnerable group, the Court identified three core aspects of refugeehood. First, refugees 'have been forced to flee their homes as a result of persecution, human rights violations and conflict'.[21] Second, '[t]hey or those close to them, have been victims of violence on the basis of very personal attributes such as ethnicity or religion'.[22] Third, they are 'vulnerable due to lack of means, support systems of family and friends and by the very fact of being in a foreign land where hostility is never very far away'.[23] Thus, the Court did not consider legal definitions of a refugee, but identified aspects of refugeehood most likely experienced by the majority of refugees.

Justice Majanja then drew on these common aspects of refugeehood in interpreting the rights pleaded. An example is the Court's approach to the right to dignity in the Kenyan Constitution. The Court stated that the right to dignity:

> has to be understood against the backdrop of appreciating the vulnerability of refugees and the suffering they have endured, the trauma and insecurity associated with persecution and flight, the need and struggle to be independent and the need to provide for themselves and their families and the struggle to establish normalcy in a foreign country.[24]

Through the prism of the right to dignity, the Court recognised that refugees, having left their communities and everyday lives, need to establish a sense of normalcy. The Court

---

[17] *Kituo Cha Sheria* [2013] (n 3) [5].   [18] Nanima (n 5) 46.   [19] *Kituo Cha Sheria* [2013] (n 3) [34].
[20] Ibid [34].   [21] Ibid [40].   [22] Ibid [40].   [23] Ibid [40].   [24] Ibid [68].

ruled that the Directive was in breach of refugees' right to dignity, because refugees would 'be uprooted from their homes and neighbourhoods' and this would disrupt the 'normalcy' they have established.[25] The Court explained that '[f]amily, work, neighbours and school all contribute to the dignity of the individual'.[26]

Through this reasoning, the Court used the right to dignity in a similar way to which a remedy is often understood: a response to a wrong or harm. It moulded the right to dignity in the Kenyan Constitution, a right applicable to everyone in Kenya, to respond to refugees' specific circumstances – in this case, the need to rebuild their lives and live an ordinary existence. Thus, with respect to the nature of refuge, the judgment has parallels to the scholarship discussed in Chapter 2 that describes refuge as a human rights remedy.

Applying Mégret's ideas, discussed earlier, in *Kituo Cha Sheria* the High Court of Kenya identified experiences common to most refugees such as trauma, living in an unfamiliar country and family separation. It then used these irreducible experiences of refugeehood to take a right applicable to everyone in Kenya (dignity) and interpret it in a way that addresses these specific circumstances and needs.

Further, the Court's categorical interpretation of the right to dignity in the Kenyan Constitution invokes refuge's restorative, regenerative and palliative functions. The recognition that education and employment are necessary for refugees to live with dignity reflects an appreciation that one of refuge's objectives is to rebuild what may have been lost as a result of displacement. By highlighting that neighbourhood and community relationships are part of the right to dignity, the Court conveyed an understanding that refugees must also create new connections and become part of the fabric of the host country's social and cultural life. Moreover, by analysing these factors 'against the backdrop' of refugees' suffering and past trauma, the Court recognised that re-establishment of a normal life and forming communal relationships are integral to healing from past trauma. Thus, embedded in this interpretation of the right to dignity is an appreciation that refuge's restorative and regenerative functions cannot be separated from its palliative objective. The judgment reflects an awareness of refuge's temporality and the ways it should simultaneously address refugees' past, present and future.

The Court's recognition of the importance of 'normalcy' for refugees also channels the concept of durable solutions through the constitutional right to dignity. As discussed in Chapter 2, there is widespread recognition that refugees should not live in limbo, but there is disagreement as to the nature and form of durable solutions. It is outside the scope of this work to resolve these different approaches but the divided opinion partly stems from neither the Refugee Convention nor the UNHCR statute explicitly outlining the available durable solutions for refugees. The High Court of Kenya's judgment does not discuss the various types of solutions but instead offers a purposive approach through the prism of the right to dignity. The judgment underlines the need for refugees to live a normal, everyday existence in a community in which they are well integrated and have a sense of security that their rebuilt lives will not be disrupted. It also highlights the crucial role of the Nairobi community in providing surrogate protection, which has resonance with studies of how local authorities can foster inclusion.[27] The Court's purposive approach to durable solutions through the right to dignity in the Kenyan Constitution is an example of what Knop refers to

---

[25] Ibid [68].   [26] Ibid [68].

[27] Barbara Oomen, 'Rights, Culture and the Creation of Cosmopolitan Citizenship' in Rosemarie Buikema, Antoine Buyse and Antonius Robben (eds), *Cultures, Citizenship and Human Rights* (Routledge, 2020) 121.

as 'translation': using domestic law to engage with and give deeper meaning to international obligations.[28]

While this categorical approach to rights produced rich understandings of refuge, there is danger in conceptualising refuge with reference to refugees' irreducible experiences. Writing from a feminist perspective, Ramsay warns that the refugee label 'renders the personal lives of peoples who have fled their homes dissolvable into easily recognised tropes' and 'serves to homogenise and generalise what are the diverse experiences of peoples who have been forced to flee their homes'.[29] Nevertheless, in *Kituo Cha Sheria*, the High Court of Kenya walked a fine line between recognising that there are circumstances common to all refugees, but that the ways they are experienced differ with respect to factors such as age, gender, disability and family responsibilities. This is evident in the Court's assessment of whether the Directive infringed the right to fair administrative action in article 47 of the Kenyan Constitution.[30] The Court interpreted this right in a way that responded not only to refugees' specific needs but also to their particular needs. The Court reasoned that, by virtue of the right to fair administrative action, '[e]very person who acquires refugee status under [Kenyan] law is entitled to be treated as such'.[31] The Court ruled that a blanket directive that did not take into account individual circumstances such as refugees with serious health conditions or those with children was a violation of the right to fair administrative action.[32] This reasoning shows an awareness that, while there are irreducible aspects of refugeehood (such as flight, past trauma and the need to rebuild a life in exile), these challenges manifest differently depending on refugees' particular circumstances.

With respect to considerations of disability, the Court did not refer to the CRPD. Nevertheless, its approach to the constitutional right to fair administrative action is in line with what Motz calls a 'disability-sensitive' approach to judicial reasoning in the refugee context – one that aligns with the way the CRPD positions disability.[33] The CRPD's 'paradigm shift' is that it replaces a medical model of disability (understanding disability as different from what is thought to be normal and needing to be fixed) with a social and human rights-based model (the recognition that society must change to accommodate persons with a disability, who are not objects of charity but people endowed with rights).[34] In its determination of the right to fair administrative action, the Court referred to the second petitioner who had diabetes, hypertension and asthma. He would be

---

[28] Karen Knop, 'Here and There: International Law in Domestic Courts' (2000) 32(2) *New York University Journal of International Law and Politics* 501, 504, 534.

[29] Georgina Ramsay, *Impossible Refuge: The Control and Constraint of Refugee Futures* (Routledge, 2018) 62.

[30] Section 10 of the Refugee Act (2006) provides that any person aggrieved by a Commissioner for Refugee Affairs' decision can appeal to the Appeal Board. The High Court of Kenya accepted that the Directive was an administrative decision made under the Refugee Act but held that 'such decisions must meet constitutional standards': *Kituo Cha Sheria* [2013] (n 3) [61]. The judgment focussed on whether the Directive was consistent with the right to fair administrative action in article 47 of the Kenyan Constitution rather than administrative law principles of fairness embedded in the Refugee Act's administrative appeal provisions.

[31] *Kituo Cha Sheria* [2013] (n 3) [62].   [32] Ibid [62], [65].

[33] Stephanie Motz, 'The Persecution of Disabled Persons and the Duty of Reasonable Accommodation' in Céline Bauloz, Meltem Ineli-Ciger, Sarah Singer and Vladislava Stoyanova (eds), *Seeking Asylum in the European Union: Selected Protection Issues Raised by the Second Phase of the Common European Asylum System* (Brill, 2015) 141. See also Stephanie Motz, *The Refugee Status of Persons with Disabilities* (Brill, 2021).

[34] Motz 'The Persecution of Disabled Persons' (n 33) 145–6.

considered as having a disability within the meaning of article 1 of the CRPD, which provides that persons with a disability include 'those who have long-term physical, mental, intellectual or sensory impairments which in interaction with various barriers may hinder their full and effective participation in society on an equal basis with others'. The Court positioned the second petitioner's access to medical treatment as a right that could not be taken away 'without due process of the law'.[35] In recognising that forced encampment would disrupt his access to healthcare, the Court highlighted both the rights-based nature of the petitioner's medical needs and that Kenya's laws and policies needed to accommodate his access to medical care.

The High Court of Kenya's categorical approach also proved potent in the contest between human rights and state interests. Most of the rights pleaded in *Kituo Cha Sheria* are qualified rights, meaning they are subject to permissible limitations. In the Court's proportionality assessment, it placed weight on the fact that the petitioners were refugees and ideas about refuge's functions were channelled through fundamental principles of human rights law such as fairness, equality and freedom. The High Court of Kenya found that protection of national security was the Directive's main rationale.[36] It acknowledged that, when the government acts in the interest of national security, it must 'be given some margin of appreciation'.[37] However, the Court stated that, by creating a blanket policy, Kenya was 'tarring a group of persons known as refugees with a broad brush of criminality', which is 'inconsistent with the values that underlie an open and democratic society based on human dignity, equality and freedom'.[38] The Court further explained that the government needed to show that 'a specific person's presence or activity in the urban areas is causing danger to the country and that his or her encampment would alleviate the menace'.[39] The connection the Court drew between labelling all refugees as criminals and infringing the values of dignity, equality and freedom reflects the notion that host states are the surrogate protectors of refugees' human rights. This idea proved powerful against justifications for forced encampment policies. The High Court of Kenya acknowledged that creating a refugee policy that responds to 'the special circumstances of urban refugees' may be costly, but stressed that 'there will always be costs involved in ensuring that the Constitution is complied with'.[40]

On appeal, the Kenyan Court of Appeal took a similar approach. It ruled that the High Court of Kenya 'struck the proper balance' in weighing the petitioners' rights against the interest of national security[41] and upheld the initial ruling.[42] It further held that the High Court of Kenya did not err in quashing the Directive.[43] In its reasoning, it stressed that the Directive targeted 'innocent' people whose 'only crime appears to be that they fled for their lives and freedom and sought refuge in Kenya'[44] and that forced encampment would '[strike] at the very heart of their dignity and worth, their self-respect and their essential humanity'.[45] The Court used excoriating language in describing the Directive as a 'knee-jerk reaction' and 'a high-handed decision quite oblivious to and uncaring about the ensuing hardships that the target group of persons would thereby be exposed to'.[46] The Court of Appeal's association between refugees' coming to Kenya to seek refuge and the Kenyan

---

[35] *Kituo Cha Sheria* [2013] (n 3) [62].   [36] Ibid [85].
[37] *Randu Nzai Ruwa v Minister, Internal Security* [2012] eKLR [53], cited in *Kituo Cha Sheria* [2013] (n 3) [85].
[38] *Kituo Cha Sheria* [2013] (n 3) [87].   [39] Ibid [87].   [40] Ibid [92].
[41] *Attorney General v Kituo Cha Sheria* [2017] eKLR 33 ('*Kituo Cha Sheria* [2017]').   [42] Ibid 34.
[43] Ibid 39.   [44] Ibid 36.   [45] Ibid 36.   [46] Ibid 35.

government acting with no concern for their welfare also reflects the idea that host states are the substitute protectors of refugees' human rights. Next, I show how amalgamating categorical with experiential reasoning deepens understandings of refuge's objectives and nature.

3.3.2   Understanding Refugees

In addition to categorical reasoning, the High Court of Kenya in *Kituo Cha Sheria* engages heavily with the refugee litigants' testimonies. The Court outlined each petitioner's particular circumstances early in its judgment[47] and stated that understanding their backgrounds was essential for making the determination.[48] This method of reasoning is similar to experiential approaches to understanding refuge described in Chapter 2. The High Court of Kenya narrated each petitioner's connections to the Nairobi community through religion, charity work, employment and business ownership. For example, the sixth petitioner was a Congolese refugee and a bishop at a church, which had over 300 parishioners from Congolese and Kenyan communities.[49] The second petitioner provided translation services[50] and the fourth petitioner was a French teacher.[51] There was also recognition of the petitioners having rebuilt their lives in Nairobi.[52] The Court noted the third petitioner was 'fully integrated in Nairobi'.[53] With respect to the sixth petitioner, the Court stressed that he and his family had 'established [themselves] in Nairobi and built a social network'.[54] There was also consideration of the petitioners' race and nationality. For example, the fourth petitioner was a Rwandese Hutu and was concerned that he would be targeted if forced to relocate to a camp due to an assumption that he took part in the Rwandan genocide.[55] The fifth petitioner was an Ethiopian refugee who feared forced relocation to one of Kenya's refugee camps due to their proximity to Ethiopia.[56] The Court also took account of the petitioners' past experiences. For example, it noted that the sixth petitioner's family members were killed in Katumba refugee camp.[57]

Additionally, when discussing the refugee petitioners' particular circumstances, the High Court of Kenya placed emphasis on family life. The Court stressed that many of the petitioners were married and had children and grandchildren in Nairobi. The Court noted that the second petitioner's children attended school in Nairobi and had 'established friends and playmates',[58] while the sixth petitioner had children and grandchildren who had 'all studied and continue to study in Nairobi and relocating them to the camp will greatly interrupt their smooth learning'.[59]

The Court drew on the petitioners' particular circumstances in its assessment of their rights arguments. This combined categorical and experiential reasoning allowed for a deeper engagement with the concept of refuge. For example, in its reasoning with respect to the right to fair administrative action in the Kenyan Constitution, the Court stressed that, for the petitioner whose family members were killed in a refugee camp, 'the threat of going back to a refugee camp brings back haunting memories'.[60] Thus, through the prism of the generally applicable human rights in the Kenyan Constitution, the Court engaged with refuge's palliative function. It recognised that refuge should provide a space for healing from

---

[47] *Kituo Cha Sheria* [2013] (n 3) [14]–[21].   [48] Ibid [13].   [49] Ibid [18].   [50] Ibid [14].
[51] Ibid [16].   [52] Ibid [20].   [53] Ibid [15].   [54] Ibid [18].   [55] Ibid [16].   [56] Ibid [17].
[57] Ibid [18].   [58] Ibid [14].   [59] Ibid [18].   [60] Ibid [64].

not only past persecution but also other types of painful experiences, and that the host state should avoid putting refugees in situations where they would be re-traumatised.

The Court's experiential approach also illuminates refuge's regenerative functions for refugees and the host community. This is evident in the Court's rejection of the Kenyan government's argument that the Directive would protect and promote refugees' welfare. The Court dismissed this argument on the grounds that the petitioners and other urban refugees were contributing to the Nairobi community and confining them to camps would inhibit their ability to do this.[61] This indicates that, for refugees, a place of genuine sanctuary should enable them to not just rebuild but grow their lives, and that the host country benefits from this process of rejuvenation.

Further, this combined categorical and experiential reasoning frames the nature of refuge not only as a remedy but also as a legal status. Through the right to fair administrative action, the Court highlighted the significance of refugees having a recognised legal status. One reason for the Court's ruling that the Directive interfered with this right was that it provided for the closure of refugee registration centres in urban areas.[62] This would mean that many refugees would not be able to renew their identity papers, which undermined the rights and protections to which they are entitled.[63]

The judgment also reflects an understanding that refuge is a process and one that predominately unfolds at the local community level. The Court ruled that the Directive was in violation of the right to fair administration action because it took away 'accrued or acquired' rights without taking into account individual circumstances.[64] While the idea of accruing rights may be antithetical to the notion that human rights are inalienable,[65] the Court was referring to the petitioners having found employment, schools and healthcare providers in Nairobi. The Court reasoned that it would be unfair to disrupt refugees' efforts in creating a sense of sanctuary in Nairobi by a blanket policy that did not take into account individual circumstances. This reflects the idea that refuge is a process that involves the state but also the local community and refugees themselves. As outlined in Chapter 2, while there is a recognition that it is states that formally owe protection obligations, it is often local authorities that take a lead role in fostering a sense of sanctuary. Further, a person can find refuge in a particular city even when the nation-state may be unwelcoming. The Court, by focussing on the petitioners' everyday activities such as work and school, positioned Nairobi as the place of refuge.

The High Court of Kenya's use of experiential reasoning responds to Malkki's concerns that, when people are generically referred to as refugees, they 'stop being specific persons and become pure victims in general'.[66] Malkki argues that, once this occurs, they no longer have 'the authority to give credible narrative evidence or testimony about their own condition' and are rendered 'universal man, universal woman, universal child'.[67] The High Court of Kenya, by starting its analysis with identifying aspects of refugeehood likely to be experienced by most refugees but then devoting a number of pages in the judgment to describing each petitioners' unique circumstances, allowed the petitioners' personal narratives to be heard.

---

[61] Ibid [82].   [62] Ibid [65].   [63] Ibid [65].   [64] Ibid [62].

[65] The UDHR's preamble describes human rights as 'inalienable'. See Louis Henkin, *The Age of Rights* (Columbia University Press, 1990) 2–3.

[66] Liisa Malkki, 'Speechless Emissaries: Refugees, Humanitarianism, and Dehistoricization' (1996) 11(3) *Cultural Anthropology* 377, 378.

[67] Ibid 378.

Nevertheless, there are risks in adopting experiential reasoning. In *Kituo Cha Sheria*, the High Court of Kenya came close to adopting an approach whereby those who had proved that they had contributed to the economic life of Nairobi were exemplary and deserving refugees who should not be forced to endure life in a refugee camp. The Court described the petitioners as 'productive residents'[68] who were 'independent and . . . contributing to the economy',[69] and stated that 'confining . . . persons of independent means . . . who are employed or carry on their business to refugee camps does not serve to solve the insecurity problem'.[70] Perhaps one of the reasons the Court characterised the petitioners in this manner was due to an awareness of anti-refugee sentiment in some parts of Kenyan society, especially with respect to competition for resources. While employment and contributing to the host community are core aspects of refuge's restorative and regenerative functions, prizing autonomy and self-sufficiency could prioritise particular refugee narratives. The seven petitioners in *Kituo Cha Sheria* were gainfully employed or successful entrepreneurs, but not all refugees have 'the language skills, educational background, and professional experience to be attractive to potential employees outside of self-created businesses'.[71] Lauding economic independence and entrepreneurship can also distract from structural barriers and lack of legal protections that make it difficult for refugees to access employment or start businesses.[72]

More generally, focussing on independence and self-sufficiency risks adopting a gendered understanding of refuge because not all refugees can achieve these ideals and the challenges are often greater for women and girls. Fineman critiques the assumption that the goal for individuals and families should be to become economically independent.[73] The consequence of prizing self-sufficiency is that those who rely on state support are heavily stigmatised.[74] Fineman argues that dependency as opposed to autonomy is by far the more natural state: each person is dependent on others at many stages of life (e.g. childhood, old age and periods of disability or illness).[75] Those who exit the workforce to provide care for others also become dependent on the state.[76] In the refugee resettlement context, Ramsay argues that host countries impose 'neoliberal logics of individualisation and self-sufficiency' on refugees by stressing the need to work and become self-sufficient.[77] She explains that for many female refugees this can provide 'exciting possibilities' to 'fulfil aspirations for further education' and 'employment', but it also means that 'the value of their lives is measured in terms of economic productivity and self-reliance rather than sociality and acts of regeneration'.[78] As highlighted in the refugee memoirs discussed in Chapter 2, some female refugees see displacement as a time to build their career and gain new skills but others are more focussed on growing their family and creating a nurturing home environment. Idealising autonomy and self-sufficiency can be problematic because refugees are not given the freedom to enjoy asylum in the way that suits their needs but are instead pressured to conform to neoliberal values of economic productivity.[79] Prioritising independence and self-sufficiency is also antithetical to the nature of refuge embedded in the Refugee Convention.[80] The model of surrogate state protection inscribed in the

---

[68] *Kituo Cha Sheria* [2013] (n 3) [68].   [69] Ibid [82].   [70] Ibid [88].   [71] Ramsay (n 29) 86.

[72] Gray Meral, 'Assessing the Jordan Compact One Year On: An Opportunity or a Barrier to Better Achieving Refugees' Right to Work' (2020) 33(1) *Journal of Refugee Studies* 42.

[73] Martha Fineman, *The Autonomy Myth: A Theory of Dependency* (New Press, 2004).   [74] Ibid 31.

[75] Ibid 35.   [76] Ibid 35–6.   [77] Ramsay (n 29) 202.   [78] Ibid 154.   [79] Ibid 193.

[80] Kate Ogg, 'The Future of Feminist Engagement with Refugee Law: From the Margins to the Centre and Out of the "Pink Ghetto"?' in Susan Harris Rimmer and Kate Ogg (eds), *Research Handbook of Feminist Engagement with International Law* (Edward Elgar, 2019) 175, 192–3.

Convention is not one that assumes or prizes self-reliance. Instead, the presumption is that all refugees are going to be in need of state assistance and this assistance should increase, not decrease, the longer the refugee remains in the host state.[81]

Did the High Court of Kenya in *Kituo Cha Sheria* elevate independence and autonomy above other values and create a neoliberal conceptualisation of refuge? The Court came close to such an approach in its analysis of the predicament faced by the seventh petitioner – a legal academic.[82] The Court noted that, due to his 'professional background, the petitioner's services can only be offered in an environment where there are law faculties hence confinement to the camp would suffocate his means of survival'.[83] The Court explained that forced relocation to a refugee camp would be a breach of the rights to fair administrative action, work and dignity.[84] The connection between work and dignity has been recognised in the refugee law context.[85] However, the judgment indicates that the reason this refugee could not be forced to relocate to a refugee camp was not because of his inherent right to dignity or work, but because he had professional qualifications that would be of no utility in a camp setting. The Court's approach to this issue prompts the question of whether the outcome would have been different if this particular refugee was not a legal academic, but instead unemployed or carried out manual labour that could have continued in a camp environment. Nevertheless, tainting the entire judgment in this manner would be unfair because at a number of points the Court stressed that the rights to fair administrative action and dignity also respond to refugees with health conditions that require specialised medical treatment and the needs of families caring for children.[86]

Did the Court, by using experiential reasoning, create a gendered precedent through stressing the petitioners' economic contributions? No female refugees were represented in *Kituo Cha Sheria*. Despite this, the Court included women's experiences by referring to some of the petitioners' female family members. For example, the Court described the sixth petitioner's wife (also a refugee) as 'a business woman' who sold textiles and educated the 'children from the proceeds of her business'.[87] The Court noted that the couple had a daughter who was transitioning from primary to secondary school and another in university.[88] This is significant, because the Court acknowledged both women's caring roles as well as their endeavours as entrepreneurs and students. While female refugees have different priorities (some wishing to stay at home and others wanting to continue their education and careers), they are often depicted primarily in the caregiving role.[89] Nevertheless, judicial prioritisation of economic contributions could serve to disadvantage any future female litigants wanting to challenge forced encampment policies. Some do not wish to participate in the marketplace, and those who do (or have no choice), often face similar gender-related barriers to working or starting businesses experienced by many women such as discrimination, pregnancy and breastfeeding and cultural expectations that they be the primary caregivers. Betts and Collier highlight that '[s]elf-reliance does not have uniform effects for everyone ... [s]ome thrive while others merely survive'[90] and that female refugees often earn significantly less than male refugees.[91] However, the Court buttressed its focus on the economic contributions made by urban refugees with other

---

[81] Ibid 193.   [82] *Kituo Cha Sheria* [2013] (n 3) [63].   [83] Ibid [19].   [84] Ibid [63].
[85] Alice Edwards, 'Human Rights, Refugees, and the Right "To Enjoy" Asylum' (2005) 17(2) *International Journal of Refugee Law* 293, 320.
[86] *Kituo Cha Sheria* [2013] (n 3) [62], [68].   [87] Ibid [18].   [88] Ibid [18].   [89] Ogg (n 80) 188–9.
[90] Alexander Betts and Paul Collier, *Refuge: Transforming a Broken Refugee System* (Allen Lane, 2017) 166.
[91] Ibid 167.

considerations such as contributions to Nairobi's social and religious life[92] as well as family responsibilities and health conditions.[93] Thus, the Court established an efficacious precedent for refugees with different experiences of asylum, but its particular focus on economic contributions indicates the risks associated with experiential reasoning.

Overall, when judges blend the abstract or metaphysical notion of refugeehood with individual refugees' unique circumstances, this allows for a deeper connection with the concept of refuge. However, in doing this there is a danger that courts may value certain refugee narratives over others, such as the exemplary refugee who contributes to the host country's economy. This risks making protection from refuge claims useful only for certain refugees who can fit these moulds and thwarting the concept of refuge by, for example, prioritising neoliberal values of economic independence and ignoring its broader palliative, restorative and regenerative objectives. This indicates that refugee litigants' individual circumstances can inform this abstract notion of refugeehood, but only to demonstrate the particular ways their rights would be infringed – not to make distinctions between refugees based on concepts such as self-sufficiency. So far, I have only considered how the Court interpreted rights in the Kenyan Constitution. Next, I consider its approach to Refugee Convention rights.

3.3.3 Understanding Refugee Rights

The analysis in the previous sections indicates that, by adopting categorical reasoning or a blended categorical and experiential approach, general human rights can be interpreted in a manner that responds to refugees' protection needs. What does this mean for refugee rights? Are they redundant or do they bolster protection from refuge claims?

With respect to the connections between refugee rights and the notion of refuge, categorical and experiential reasoning still serve as a bridge to ideas about refuge's objectives and sharpen the force of rights arguments against state interests. This is evident in the first instance and appeal decisions in *Kituo Cha Sheria* with respect to *non-refoulement*. The Directive did not state that refugees would be expelled from Kenya. Nevertheless, the High Court of Kenya found the Directive to be in violation of Kenya's *non-refoulement* obligations.[94] In coming to this determination, the Court used both categorical and experiential reasoning. It noted that refugees who have been living in the host country for long periods had 'established roots and significant connections with local communities'.[95] Being forced to relocate to a camp environment and, thus, 'being exposed to conditions that affect their welfare negatively' may 'lead to a situation that forces some of the petitioners to leave the country'.[96] The Court then explicitly referred to the fifth petitioner, who feared relocation to a refugee camp because 'he would be subjected to the same persecution that he was subjected to in the Congo'.[97] The Court found that the fifth petitioner 'and others in like situations' would be forced to leave Kenya.[98] The Court ruled that both situations would amount to constructive *refoulement*.[99]

Through this amalgamation of categorical and experiential reasoning, the judgment provides that refugees should not be forced to choose between life in a refugee camp where they will lose the life they have built or returning to their homeland where their life or freedom would be threatened. While Durieux argues that *non-refoulement* should not be

---

[92] *Kituo Cha Sheria* [2013] (n 3) [18].   [93] Ibid [62], [68].   [94] Ibid [75].   [95] Ibid [73].
[96] Ibid [73].   [97] Ibid [73].   [98] Ibid [73].   [99] Ibid [74]–[75].

considered refugee law's foundational principle because it is a negative obligation[100] and refuge necessitates welcome into the host community,[101] the High Court of Kenya utilised *non-refoulement* to encompass the positive obligations associated with refuge. Through the principle of *non-refoulement*, the Court invoked refuge's restorative and regenerative functions, in particular, that it should allow refugees to rebuild their lives and create new relationships. In doing so, it also drew connections between *non-refoulement* and durable solutions through the recognition that a refugee who has integrated into the local community should not be forced to choose between life in a camp and returning to their country of origin. This demonstrates an appreciation that a refugee's return to their homeland must be a genuinely voluntary one and not forced upon them through their host country's change in policy. On appeal, the Kenyan Court of Appeal gave even greater force to the principle of *non-refoulement*. It declared that *non-refoulement* is a peremptory norm of international law[102] and stated that 'it is not open for the State to go against a peremptory norm of international law and its having done so is alone sufficient to justify the quashing of the Directive'.[103]

Another right pleaded in *Kituo Cha Sheria* was freedom of movement. The Court acknowledged that the petitioners had freedom of movement rights under the Kenyan Constitution, African Charter on Human and People's Rights,[104] ICCPR and Refugee Convention.[105] However, these freedom of movement rights are not identical. The Court highlighted the differences between freedom of movement rights in article 39 of the Kenyan Constitution and article 26 of the Refugee Convention. Article 39(1) of the Kenyan Constitution provides that 'every person has the right to freedom of movement', but article 39(3) states that only Kenyan citizens have the 'right to enter, remain in and reside anywhere in Kenya'. The Attorney-General argued that refugees do not have the right to choose their own places of residence, because the Kenyan Constitution only bestows that right on citizens. However, Kenya is a monist country. The Court stated that article 39 of the Kenyan Constitution must be read in conjunction with article 26 of the Refugee Convention,[106] which provides that refugees lawfully in the host state's territory[107] have the right to choose their places of residence.

The High Court of Kenya held that the Directive violated refugees' right to choice of residence in article 26 of the Refugee Convention.[108] Its categorical and experiential

---

[100] Jean-François Durieux, 'Three Asylum Paradigms' (2013) 20(2) *International Journal on Minority and Group Rights* 147, 155.

[101] Ibid 156.

[102] *Kituo Cha Sheria* [2017] (n 41) 26. There is debate on whether *non-refoulement* is a peremptory norm: Jean Allain, 'The *Jus Cogens* Nature of *Non-Refoulement*' (2002) 13(4) *International Journal of Refugee Law* 533; Cathryn Costello and Michelle Foster, '*Non-Refoulement* as Custom and *Jus Cogens*? Putting the Prohibition to the Test' (2015) 46 *Netherlands Yearbook of International Law* 273.

[103] *Kituo Cha Sheria* [2017] (n 41) 35.

[104] 27 June 1981, CAB/LEG/67/3 rev 5, 21 ILM 58 (1982), in force 21 October 1986.

[105] *Kituo Cha Sheria* [2013] (n 3) [51].   [106] Ibid [51].

[107] The Court does not discuss whether the seven refugee petitioners are lawfully in Kenya within the meaning of the Refugee Convention. However, it cites (at [54]) the Human Rights Committee's conclusion that, for the purposes of freedom of movement, 'an alien who entered the State illegally, but whose status has been regularized, must be considered lawfully within a State': *General Comment No 27: Freedom of Movement (Article 12)*, UN Doc CCPR/C/21/Rev.1/Add.9 [4]. Given that the petitioners had been living in Kenya for many years and had refugee status leaves no doubt that they were lawfully in the country for the purposes of article 26 of the Refugee Convention. For an analysis of when a refugee is lawfully in the host state's territory, see Costello, Ioffe and Büchsel (n 4) 6.

[108] *Kituo Cha Sheria* [2013] (n 3) [59].

approach to this right reinforces ideas about refuge's objectives by drawing connections between constraints on freedom of movement and other protection concerns. The Court examined the consequences for refugees of having their freedom of movement curtailed.[109] The Court explained that forcing all refugees to reside in camps and the consequent closure of urban refugee registration centres would have 'deleterious effects' on refugees' other rights and freedoms.[110] The Court highlighted that:

> New arrivals have nowhere to report their intention to apply for asylum or seek refugee status. . . . Those whose identification documents have expired or are about to expire are put to great costs and expense to have the same renewed at peril to their livelihoods. Undocumented refugees and asylum seekers are left exposed to police harassment, extortion, arbitrary arrest and eventual prosecution for being in the country illegally. Undocumented refugees and asylum seekers within urban set ups cannot access humanitarian services from organisations that provide humanitarian services which require identification as a pre-requisite for qualification of services. Some undocumented refugee children are denied access to public services such as schools and hospitals.[111]

In this part of its judgment, the Court used the right to freedom of movement in the Refugee Convention to invoke other rights such as refugee identity documents, physical security, freedom from arbitrary arrest, education and healthcare. This is the inverse of what the Court did with the rights to dignity and fair administrative action, and it reinforces ideas about refuge's objectives. The Court's emphasis on the connections between refugee identity documents and avoiding police harassment reflects one aspect of refuge's restorative function: ensuring refugees' safety and legitimate presence in the host state. While there is no explicit right to healthcare in the Refugee Convention, the association the Court drew between identity documents and access to hospitals also reflects the restorative objective of refuge, in particular, that the host state must act as a surrogate provider of essential services. In recognising that identity documents are essential for children to access education, the Court engaged both with refuge's restorative function (that it should enable refugees to re-establish a normal, everyday life) and regenerative objective (that refugees should be able to grow, develop and build a future).

At no point in the judgment did the Court directly consider whether Kenya's policy of encampment or the conditions in the camps infringe refugee or human rights law. The Kenyan government argued that sections 16, 17 and 25 of the Refugee Act (2006)[112] 'presupposes that all refugees and asylum seekers should ordinarily reside in gazetted refugee camps'.[113] The petitioners did not challenge the constitutional validity of the Act but rather the constitutionality of the Directive requiring them to relocate to a refugee camp. Thus, there was no direct challenge to Kenya's policy of encampment.

Nevertheless, in its analysis of freedom of movement, the High Court of Kenya came close to setting a precedent that would render not only forced relocation of urban refugees to camps inconsistent with Kenya's international refugee law obligations, but also put into question the legality of encampment more generally. While the rights to freedom of movement in the Refugee Convention are qualified rights, the grounds on which states

---

[109] Ibid [60].   [110] Ibid [60].   [111] Ibid [60].

[112] Section 16(2) provides the Minister responsible for refugee affairs with the power to designate places for refugees to reside. Section 17 outlines refugee camp officers' functions and authorities. Section 25(f) states that it is an offence for a refugee to reside outside a designated area.

[113] *Kituo Cha Sheria* [2013] (n 3) [25].

can limit these rights are less flexible than the grounds in general human rights instruments such as the ICCPR. The rights to freedom of movement in article 26 of the Refugee Convention are 'subject to any regulations applicable to aliens generally in the same circumstances'. This means that, for a forced encampment policy to be valid under the Refugee Convention, it must apply not only to refugees but also to 'aliens generally in the same circumstances' which has been interpreted to mean other admitted non-citizens.[114] The likelihood that Kenya would include within a forced encampment policy other admitted non-citizens such as tourists or those with work or study visas is highly improbable. Thus, under the framework of the Refugee Convention, the Kenyan government would have no realistic grounds on which to justify a forced encampment policy.

This is different from the grounds on which a state can justify restrictions on freedom of movement under the ICCPR. Pursuant to article 12(3), these rights can be curtailed if those restrictions are provided by law; are necessary to protect national security, public order, public health or morals or the rights and freedoms of others; and are consistent with the other rights in the ICCPR. Under the ICCPR's framework, it is possible that the Kenyan government could justify a policy of forced encampment for refugees. It would have to justify the policy on the grounds of, for example, public order. It would also have to ensure that such a policy does not offend the principle of non-discrimination in articles 2(1) and 26 of the ICCPR.[115] Distinctions on one of the grounds enumerated in articles 2(1) and 26 are permissible as long as they are reasonable and objective, and achieve a purpose legitimate under the ICCPR.[116] Thus, under the ICCPR framework, the Kenyan government has more flexible grounds on which to justify a forced encampment policy for refugees than it does under the Refugee Convention. This indicates that the rights in the Refugee Convention, designed to address refugees' specific needs, can be particularly potent in challenging state interests.

The Kenyan Court of Appeal upheld the High Court of Kenya's decision that the Directive violated refugees' rights to freedom of movement.[117] It confirmed that the first instance judge was correct in reading article 39 of the Kenyan Constitution in conjunction with article 26 of the Refugee Convention on the grounds that article 2(6) of the Kenyan Constitution provides that international treaties ratified by Kenya form part of Kenyan law.[118] In dismissing the Attorney-General's appeal, the Court stressed that it is the duty of all courts to apply the provisions of Kenya's constitutional Bill of Rights (which, by virtue of article 2(6), encompasses international human rights) 'in a bold and robust manner', even if the consequences are 'disruptive' to ensure that 'no aspect of social, economic or political life should be an enclave insulated from the bold sweep of the Bill of Rights'.[119]

---

[114] James Hathaway, *The Rights of Refugees under International Law* (Cambridge University Press, 2005) 197. See also James Hathaway, *The Rights of Refugees under International Law* (Cambridge University Press, 2nd ed, 2021).

[115] Article 2(1) of the ICCPR provides that rights shall be granted 'without distinction of any kind, such as race, colour, sex, language, religion, political or other opinion, national or social origin, property, birth or other status'. There is authority for the proposition that 'alienage' can be considered an 'other status': Human Rights Committee, *General Comment No 15: The Position of Aliens under the Covenant*, UN Doc HRI/GEN/1/Rev.1 (11 April 1986) [2].

[116] Human Rights Committee, *General Comment No 18: Non-Discrimination*, UN Doc HRI/GEN/1/Rev.6 (10 November 1989) [13].

[117] *Kituo Cha Sheria* [2017] (n 41) 23.   [118] Ibid 14.   [119] Ibid 11.

By quashing the Directive,[120] the first instance and appeal decisions were a triumph of human and refugee rights over a state's desire to constrain refugees' movements and inhibit their quests for refuge. They were victories not just for the seven refugee petitioners but for all refugees living in Kenya's urban centres. The first instance decision was also potentially a victory for all refugees in Kenya when taking into account its reasoning on the right to freedom of movement, which came close to providing a precedent indicating that Kenya's practice of encampment was inconsistent with its human rights obligations. Next, I consider the disparities between the approach taken in *Kituo Cha Sheria* and later Kenyan forced encampment jurisprudence.

3.4   From Categorical and Experiential to Exceptionality Reasoning

Since the judgment by the High Court of Kenya in *Kituo Cha Sheria*, there has been a change in the way Kenyan courts approach forced encampment litigation. In Section 3.4.1, I show that there is no longer a strong focus on refugeehood. In Section 3.4.2, I suggest that this results in a judicial search for the exceptional refugee, which has diluted judicial conceptu- alisations of refuge. In Section 3.4.3, I highlight how this shift has weakened the potential for rights arguments to challenge encampment policies.

3.4.1   The Individualisation of Rights Claims

In forced encampment challenges initiated after *Kituo Cha Sheria*, Kenyan courts aban- doned a categorical approach to rights arguments. They did not start their reasoning by considering the irreducible experiences of refugeehood and how this may inform the interpretation and application of human and refugee rights. Instead, they moved directly to enquiring as to how forced encampment would affect each individual refugee and whether, on a case-by-case basis, this would amount to a violation of their human rights.

This shift first occurred in the High Court of Kenya's 2014 judgment in *Samow Mumin Mohamed v Cabinet Secretary et al* ('*Samow Mumin Mohamed*').[121] In this case, ten urban refugees unsuccessfully challenged a second Kenyan government directive requiring all refugees to relocate to one of Kenya's refugee camps ('Second Directive'). The petitioners attempted to frame their case in line with the precedent set by *Kituo Cha Sheria*. They argued that the Second Directive violated their fundamental rights and freedoms, including constitutional rights to dignity and fair administrative action.[122] However, in determining their claims, the Court did not place any significance on the petitioners' refugee experience and, unlike in *Kituo Cha Sheria*, did not undertake its rights assessment against the backdrop of refugees being vulnerable persons within the meaning of the Kenyan Constitution article 21(3). Instead, the Court found against the refugee petitioners because they did not demonstrate 'how the Directive affects their individual circumstances to the extent that their fundamental rights and freedoms are violated'.[123]

The High Court of Kenya adopted the same test in the 2015 case of *Refugee Consortium of Kenya v Attorney General* ('*Refugee Consortium of Kenya*'),[124] in which the Second Directive

---

[120] Ibid 4; *Kituo Cha Sheria* [2013] (n 3) [100].
[121] [2014] eKLR (High Court of Kenya, Constitutional and Human Rights Division).   [122] Ibid [16].
[123] Ibid [27].
[124] [2015] eKLR (High Court of Kenya, Constitutional and Human Rights Division) [44].

was challenged by an NGO and a refugee petitioner acting in a representative capacity. In this subsequent challenge to the Second Directive, the High Court of Kenya clarified that, in *Samow Mumin Mohamed*, 'the Court did not ... make a declaration that the [Second] Directive and press statement are unconstitutional, but held that the Petitioners in that case had failed to demonstrate how the Directive affects their individual circumstances'.[125] The Court then explained that it would consider 'whether or not the Petitioners in this matter have made a convincing case that it infringes upon their rights and fundamental freedoms'.[126]

What is evident in this trajectory is a shift in judicial approaches to forced encampment challenges. At no point in *Kituo Cha Sheria* did the High Court of Kenya require the seven refugee petitioners to prove individually that due to their specific circumstances their human and refugee rights would be violated. The Court referred to the petitioners' individual circumstances but only to demonstrate how the Directive would violate their human and refugee rights. While in *Samow Mumin Mohamed* the Court emphasised that the petitioners did not bring the claim in any representative capacity,[127] neither did the petitioners in *Kituo Cha Sheria*. Nevertheless, at a number of points in the *Kituo Cha Sheria* judgment, the Court referred to the petitioners and other refugees in their situation.[128] This and the fact that the Court quashed the Directive indicate that it did not require the petitioners in *Kituo Cha Sheria* to establish how the Directive would affect their individual circumstances to the extent that their fundamental rights and freedoms would be violated.

Nanima suggests that the petitioners in *Samow Mumin Mohamed* were unsuccessful because they did not plead their claim with requisite clarity,[129] but this is unconvincing. It is possible that the petitioners in *Samow Mumin Mohamed* did not argue their cases with the same degree of detail and precision as the petitioners in *Kituo Cha Sheria*, who had the pro bono assistance of a specialist legal advice centre. However, the same judge, Justice Majanja, decided both cases and, as outlined earlier, took distinctly different approaches to both challenges. One distinguishing factor that may explain the change in judicial approach is that, in *Kituo Cha Sheria*, the UNHCR appeared as amicus curiae, whereas it did not submit an amicus curiae brief in *Samow Mumin Mohamed*. The judgment in *Kituo Cha Sheria*, while it did not heavily refer to the UNHCR's amicus submission, was in line with the arguments the UNHCR made with respect to *non-refoulement* and freedom of movement. The UNHCR's amicus arguments in *Kituo Cha Sheria* would have been directly applicable to *Samow Mumin Mohamed*. Justice Majanja presided over both cases. This indicates that the international attention on the legal challenge in *Kituo Cha Sheria*, created through the UNHCR's participation as amicus, may have been a factor in swaying the Court's decision.

3.4.2   The Exceptional Refugee

The loss of a categorical approach and the shift in judicial reasoning, whereby challenges to forced encampment are considered on a case-by-case basis, means that decision-makers look for exceptionalities beyond refugeehood. This is evident in the High Court of Kenya's 2015 judgment in *Refugee Consortium of Kenya*. The second petitioner was a refugee who was forcibly relocated to Dadaab Refugee Camp pursuant to the Second Directive. She and other refugees were taken to the camp after attending a church service. She had left her six

---

[125] Ibid [44].   [126] Ibid [44].   [127] *Samow Mumin Mohamed* (n 121) [20].
[128] *Kituo Cha Sheria* [2013] (n 3) [68], [100].   [129] Nanima (n 5) 62, 66.

children at home during the church service and was not allowed to see them before she was forcibly transferred to the camp. She remained separated from them while living in the camp. She brought the petition on behalf of her six children and forty-eight other children separated from their parents as a result of the same incident. The Court started its analysis by referring back to *Kituo Cha Sheria* and acknowledging that refugees are vulnerable persons within the meaning of the Kenyan Constitution.[130] It then noted that '[i]n addition to vulnerabilities which a person may face by virtue of being a refugee, the difficulties of a person's situation is extrapolated if that person is also a child and belongs to another group of "vulnerable persons"'.[131]

While the Court recognised the compounding effects of youth and refugeehood, the Court's reasoning indicates that, if not for this additional vulnerability, the petitioners would not have been successful. The Court held that there had been a breach of the constitutional right to fair administrative action.[132] However, unlike in *Kituo Cha Sheria*, where the Court broadly considered encampment's effects on families, employment, access to healthcare, renewal of identity papers and previous trauma associated with camp environments, the Court in *Refugee Consortium of Kenya* limited its consideration to the second petitioner's and other parents' arrest and forced relocation after the church service while their children were at home. The Court reasoned that their right to fair administrative action was breached because the 'affected parents were arrested while in Church, denied the opportunity to make arrangements for the care of their minor children, detained and removed to the Refugee Camps'.[133] This is different from the Court's reasoning in *Kituo Cha Sheria* on the right to fair administrative action, in which it found that '[e]very person who acquires refugee status under our law is entitled to be treated as such. The Government Directive ... being a blanket directive, is inconsistent with the provisions of ... international law'.[134] Under the reasoning in *Kituo Cha Sheria*, it is the government's obligation to take into account individual circumstances. However, in *Refugee Consortium of Kenya*, the Court changed its reasoning in a way akin to shifting the burden of proof by requiring the petitioners to show why forced encampment affected their individual circumstances to such an extent that their fundamental freedoms were infringed.

Nevertheless, the High Court of Kenya, when considering refugees' individual circumstances, demonstrated sensitivity towards the ways containment policies affect women, parents and children. This is most apparent in its assessment of the petitioners' argument that the forced relocation of refugee parents to camps and subsequent separation from their children amounted to a breach of children's rights to parental care, education and protection from neglect.[135] The Court referred to children's rights in the CRC, the Kenyan Constitution and domestic legislation (Children Act 2010).[136] The Court placed emphasis on article 9 of the CRC, which provides that children must not be separated from their parents unless it is in their best interests and highlighted how the forced relocation of the petitioners' to a refugee camp was in violation of this right. It noted that some of the children were being breastfed at the time the Kenyan government forcibly relocated their mothers to Dadaab Refugee Camp and these infants 'consequently suffered malnutrition'.[137] The Court stressed that many of the children had to leave school because their parents were unable to pay school fees.[138] Also, some were placed in dangerous positions because they had no

---

[130] *Refugee Consortium* (n 124) [45].   [131] Ibid [46] (emphasis in original removed).   [132] Ibid [58].
[133] Ibid [58].   [134] *Kituo Cha Sheria* [2013] (n 3) [62].   [135] *Refugee Consortium* (n 124) [66].
[136] Ibid [59].   [137] Ibid [60].   [138] Ibid [60].

income and their new guardians were not able to provide for them financially.[139] The Court concluded that the 'effect of the separation has been to deprive the children of the right to family life and parental care which they had previously enjoyed'.[140]

Further, the Court held that it was not appropriate for the children to be sent to a refugee camp with their parents. The Court drew on South African jurisprudence[141] in holding that the principle of acting in the child's best interests, embedded in all the previously noted instruments, is 'a right not just a guiding principle' that 'requires the law to make the best effort to avoid, where possible, any breakdown of family life or parental care that may threaten to put the children at increased risk'.[142] The Court referred to evidence that only 40 per cent of refugee children in Kenya's camps were enrolled in school. The Court reasoned that while 'it may be in the best interest of an infant to be reunited with her mother in a refugee camp, the same will not necessarily be true for a 16 year old who might not be able to either work or to go to school'.[143] Thus, the Court concluded that Kenya is required to conduct individualised assessments of children's best interests before forcibly removing parents to a refugee camp.[144] This individualised assessment must include 'a clear and comprehensive assessment of the child's identity, including his or her nationality, upbringing, ethnic cultural and linguistic background, particular vulnerabilities and protection needs'.[145]

While the Court in *Refugee Consortium of Kenya* took great care to understand the implications of forced encampment on children of different ages, a transition from categorical reasoning informed by core or unifying aspects of refugeehood to one where decision-makers look for some form of exceptionality beyond refugeehood renders rights arguments less efficacious in challenging forced relocation to a refugee camp. This shift means that only certain refugees can successfully use court processes in their quest to avoid forced relocation to a refugee camp. At no point did the Court indicate that the Second Directive would imperil all refugee children's lives and safety. This is in line with its insistence at the beginning of the judgment that the petitioners had to prove that the Second Directive infringes their fundamental rights and freedoms 'in the specific circumstances and pleadings in [the] case'.[146] While this case was a victory for the second petitioner and the other families she represented, it was not a victory for all refugees subject to forced relocation to a refugee camp. Unlike in *Kituo Cha Sheria*, the High Court of Kenya did not quash the Second Directive, but only made an order for reunification in relation to the second petitioner and the other families she represented.[147]

This exceptionality approach can also lead to impoverished understandings of refuge. For example, in *Samow Mumin Mohamed*, the Court did not address the ten refugee petitioners' arguments regarding the ways forced encampment would be a violation of their human rights such as the right to dignity. Instead, the Court assessed whether the petitioners would face persecution if forcibly transferred to refugee camps or whether their businesses would be disrupted. The Court found that 'unlike in the *Kituo Cha Sheria Case*, the petitioners have not established a basis for persecution if they return to the camps'.[148] However, in *Kituo Cha Sheria*, only 'some of the petitioners' established that they would be persecuted if forcibly relocated to refugee camps.[149] *Samow Mumin Mohamed* confines the concept of refuge to

---

[139] Ibid [60].   [140] Ibid [60].   [141] *Sonderup v Tondelli and Another* (CCT53/00) [2000] ZACC 26.
[142] *Refugee Consortium* (n 124) [64].   [143] Ibid [63].   [144] Ibid [63], [66].   [145] Ibid [63].
[146] Ibid [44].   [147] Ibid [85].   [148] *Samow Mumin Mohamed* (n 121) [26].
[149] *Kituo Cha Sheria* [2013] (n 3) [64].

the bare minimum of protection from persecution and obscures the broader and richer notions of refuge reflected in *Kituo Cha Sheria*, such as the need to establish normalcy, heal from past trauma, create a new community and pursue education. It limits refuge's objectives to a narrow conception of its restorative function (re-establishing safety and security) and ignores its regenerative and palliative functions. It also severs the connections between rights in the Kenyan Constitution (in particular dignity and fair administrative action) and durable solutions for refugees. What is lost in this subsequent jurisprudence is a recognition of the ways in which everyday 'normalcy' is integral to integrating into the host community and establishing a sense of security and hope for the future.

In abandoning categorical reasoning and solely focussing on the petitioners' specific circumstances, Kenyan judges also skewed the nature of refuge from a remedy that addresses the difficulties associated with displacement to a commodity to be given to the most deserving or vulnerable. In *Refugee Consortium of Kenya*, the refugee petitioner had to establish vulnerabilities beyond refugeehood to obtain a court order enabling her to leave the camp. If she was not a single mother and could not have highlighted how her encampment infringed her children's rights, her case may not have been successful. In *Samow Mumin Mohamed*, the Court found that 'there is nothing to show that [the petitioners'] businesses will be disrupted' and stressed that, like all other refugees living in refugee camps in Kenya, they could apply for movement permits.[150] In making this determination, the Court implied that the petitioners' work is not consequential or prestigious enough that it would be disrupted by forced relocation to a refugee camp. Unlike the legal academic in *Kituo Cha Sheria* who could not continue his profession in the confines of a camp or the other petitioners who were 'productive residents' and 'contributing to the economy', the petitioners in *Samow Mumin Mohamed* did not meet these thresholds. This change indicates that Kenyan Courts are no longer inclined to make a blanket ruling that forced encampment directives are unconstitutional and a violation of international law. Instead, they are only willing to permit individual refugees to challenge their forced relocation based on their specific circumstances. In doing so, they require the refugee petitioners to establish that they contribute to the Kenyan economy in unique or exceptional ways and, thus, are exemplary refugees (or what Fiddian-Qasmiyeh refers to as 'super-refugee[s]')[151] who do not deserve to be relocated to a camp environment. Refuge is no longer understood to be a response to the vicissitudes of persecution and displacement, but a prize to be granted to the most meritorious refugees. This is an unhelpful decision for those who, because of factors such as age, gender, disability and family responsibilities, cannot become what is understood to be productive or exemplary refugees. It also ignores the situation of refugees confined to a camp environment and who have never had the opportunity to contribute to Kenyan society, which is the issue I turn to next.

3.4.3   An End to Encampment?

All of the cases in the previous sections concerned urban refugees challenging forced relocation to a refugee camp, but what about refugees in a camp environment who may have been living there for many years or who may have been born there and do not know

---

[150] *Samow Mumin Mohamed* (n 121) [26].
[151] Elena Fiddian-Qasmiyeh, 'Introduction' in Elena Fiddian-Qasmiyeh (ed), *Refuge in a Moving World: Tracing Refugee and Migrant Journeys Across Disciplines* (UCL Press, 2020) 1, 2.

any other home? In the cases examined so far, the Courts could not directly address this issue. A different type of protection from refuge challenge was made in *Coalition for Reform and Democracy v Kenya* (*'Coalition for Reform and Democracy'*).[152] One of the issues in this 2015 case was whether an amendment to Kenya's Refugee Act (2006) that provided that refugees living in one of Kenya's refugee camps shall 'not leave the designated refugee camp without the permission of the Refugee Camp Office'[153] violated refugees' right to freedom of movement. This case was an opportunity for the High Court of Kenya to consider the legality of forcing refugees residing in camps to remain there.

The Court's approach to determining this claim continued its trajectory of lost focus on the significance of refugeehood and the consequential dilution of the force of refugees' rights claims in the face of states constraining their mobility. The diminishing significance of refugeehood is evident in the Court's failure to consider the rights refugees are entitled to domestically, regionally and internationally. The Court acknowledged that refugees are entitled to freedom of movement under article 39 of the Kenyan Constitution.[154] However, it did not acknowledge that refugees are considered vulnerable persons within the meaning of the Kenyan Constitution and that the government has a special duty to address their needs. While the Court referred to the Refugee Convention and *Convention Governing the Specific Aspects of the Refugee Problems in Africa*,[155] it did so only with respect to provisions that confirm that refugees have a duty to conform to the host country's laws and regulations.[156] The Court did not consider the rights to freedom of movement and residence in those instruments, or other refugee-specific rights despite earlier precedent confirming that these rights are part of Kenyan law.[157]

Without reference to these additional rights, the petitioners' claim was a weak one. The Court dismissed the claim on the grounds that the 'right to enter, remain and reside anywhere in Kenya is constitutionally reserved to citizens and therefore there is no violation of the right to freedom of movement in requiring that refugees wishing to leave the camp obtain permission from the Camp Officer'.[158] It did not consider the greater freedom of movement rights refugees have pursuant to the Refugee Convention.

Without adopting a categorical approach and considering the irreducible experiences of refugeehood, the Court did not reflect on the importance of freedom of movement for refugees and its connection to other rights such as education and healthcare. This dilutes the force of refugee rights in contests against state interests and narrows ideas of refuge. The Court did not reflect on the significance of freedom of movement rights for refugees and justified the requirement to remain in a camp on the ground that it enabled the Kenyan government to 'protect and offer security to refugees' by ensuring the Camp Officer 'knows the whereabouts of each refugee', which is particularly important for ensuring national security.[159] This limits the

---

[152] [2015] eKLR (High Court of Kenya, Constitutional and Human Rights Division).

[153] The Refugee Act (2006) was amended by section 47 of the Security Laws (Amendment) Act (2014) by adding section 14(c), which applies only to those living in camps and requires them to remain there unless they have the refugee camp officer's permission to leave.

[154] *Coalition for Reform and Democracy* (n 152) [394].

[155] Convention Governing the Specific Aspects of the Refugee Problems in Africa, 10 September 1969, 1001 UNTS 45, in force 20 June 1974, preamble ('OAU Refugee Convention').

[156] Article 2 of the Refugee Convention and Article 3 of the OAU Refugee Convention, referred to in *Coalition for Reform and Democracy* (n 152) [398], [399].

[157] *Kituo Cha Sheria* [2013] (n 3) [32].   [158] *Coalition for Reform and Democracy* (n 152) [402].

[159] Ibid [402].

notion of refuge to offering protection and security to refugees and ignores broader ideas of refuge associated with rebuilding lives, regenerating futures and healing from trauma.

The approach taken by the High Court of Kenya in *Coalition for Reform and Democracy* was a missed opportunity for it to rule on the legality of encampment. If the Court adopted the same approach taken in *Kituo Cha Sheria*, it would have considered, with reference to domestic, regional and international human rights and refugee law, whether it is permissible to allow refugees to leave camps only with government permission. The categorical approach taken in the earlier decision would have prompted the Court to consider whether such restrictions were an infringement of refugees' rights in the context of their vulnerable position of having fled their homeland and needing to build a life for themselves in a foreign land.

Further, the trajectory of forced encampment jurisprudence in Kenya means that human rights arguments are more useful for refugees who have managed to leave a camp environment or avoid it altogether and to establish residence in an urban area. Under the precedent of *Kituo Cha Sheria*, urban refugees were able to have the first Directive quashed on the grounds that the sense of normalcy they had established would be disrupted if forced to live in a refugee camp. While the subsequent decisions are less powerful, they still provide grounds for urban refugees to point to some exceptional, individual grounds as to why their rights would be infringed by forced transfer to a refugee camp. The judgment in *Coalition for Reform and Democracy* indicated no human rights grounds that refugees living in a camp environment can raise to avoid being confined there. There are many reasons why refugees living in camps would face challenges in moving to an urban area, such as disability, youth, old age and family responsibilities. The decision of *Coalition for Reform and Democracy* compounds these challenges.

Finally, when human rights arguments against forced encampment atrophy, refuge becomes relative. In a twist to the battles between refugees and the government in Kenya's forced encampment saga, in 2017, the Kenyan National Commission on Human Rights lodged a petition in the High Court of Kenya contesting the closure of Dadaab Refugee Camp.[160] The Kenyan government had ordered the camp's closure along with the repatriation of all Somali refugees. The Court declared the decision to close Dadaab Refugee Camp null and void because it did not allow individual refugees to make representations about the closure and, thus, infringed the right to fair administrative action.[161] This legal challenge sheds a different light on Harrell-Bond's observation that 'refugee camps are not good for anyone' and '[e]veryone who can gets out of them as quickly as possible'.[162] The camp, which urban refugees petitioned against being transferred to and refugees in the camp fought for permission to leave, became a place that refugees and their advocates fought to keep open.

The battle recommenced in 2021 with the Kenyan government declaring that both Kakuma and Dadaab refugee camps will be closed by 30 June 2022, citing national security concerns. The closure has been challenged on the grounds that it violates refugee rights in domestic and international law. In April 2021, the High Court of Kenya issued a temporary stay order.[163] The matter had not proceeded to final judgment at the time of writing.

---

[160] *Kenya National Commission on Human Rights v Attorney General* [2017] eKLR. [161] Ibid 35.
[162] Harrell-Bond (n 1) 1.
[163] *Peter Solomon Gichira v The Attorney General et al* (Petition No E102 of 2021) The High Court of Kenya at Nairobi, 7 April 2021.

3.5   Conclusion

In this chapter, I have examined how Kenyan judges have approached and determined protection from refuge claims in the form of forced encampment litigation. I have shown that, when courts employ categorical or blended categorical and experiential reasoning, they engage with the concept of refuge in a purposive manner. I have suggested that, through the prism of human and refugee rights, judges engage with refuge's restorative, regenerative and palliative functions. They also use human rights law as a medium to recognise the nature of refuge as a remedy, legal status and process. Further, these approaches encompass the ways refuge must respond to refugees of different ages and genders as well as refugees with family responsibilities and disabilities. This type of reasoning also lends potency to human rights arguments when pitted against states' containment policies.

However, this legal victory for refugees in Kenya was short lived. In subsequent decisions, courts look for some type of additional factors beyond refugeehood before they can trigger the protection of human rights law. Refugeehood is given less emphasis and the protection from refuge litigant must establish why they are acutely vulnerable or otherwise exceptional or distinctive. Requiring refugees to establish that they are exceptional in some way dilutes the concept of refuge and diminishes the force of rights arguments in contests with state's justifications for containment policies. It enables only particular refugees to turn to courts to continue their quest for refuge and often does not assist those who face the greatest challenges in travelling in search of refuge.

This trajectory aligns with Douzinas' views on the role of the courts in human rights protection, especially his argument that human rights challenges can at best 'lead to small individual improvements', but ultimately 'reinforce rather than challenge established arrangements'.[164] However, there is one important point of distinction. Douzinas suggests that the only way human rights can 'reactivate a politics of resistance' is through 'the recognition of the absolute uniqueness of the other person and my moral duty to save and protect her'.[165] The analysis in this chapter indicates that identifying common aspects of refugeehood is the factor that can harness the power of human rights arguments, especially when pitted against states' containment mechanisms. When courts and other decision-making bodies ignore the relevance of refugeehood and concentrate on the uniqueness of the protection from refuge litigant, human rights arguments lose their potency in facilitating refugees' journeys in search of refuge.

---

[164] Costas Douzinas, *Human Rights and Empire: The Political Philosophy of Cosmopolitanism* (Routledge, 2007) 109–10.
[165] Ibid 348.

4

Using Human Rights Law to Travel in Search of Refuge in Europe

4.1   Introduction

'The conditions are so bad that describing them . . . cannot capture the squalor. You have to smell conditions like these and feel the squelch of mud mixed with urine and much else through your boots to appreciate the horror'.[1] This is evidence given to a UK tribunal about the refugee settlement in Calais, known as 'the Jungle'. In this Chapter, I follow the journeys of asylum seekers and refugees who travel to Europe and use human rights treaties in their attempts to leave or resist return to the Jungle and other places of ostensible refuge.

This chapter continues my examination of how adjudicative decision-makers determine protection from refuge claims grounded in human rights instruments. Some have been brought before UN treaty bodies. Most have been heard by the European Court of Human Rights (ECtHR) or domestic decision-making bodies. The rights available to asylum seekers and refugees in Europe to plead are more limited than in Kenya (discussed in Chapter 3). They cannot directly argue that the respective host state does not comply with the Refugee Convention. They raise a limited number of rights in the ECHR, ICCPR, CAT and CRC – rights that are not in the Refugee Convention and would be considered rudimentary rights when compared to the literature on refugee protection discussed in Chapter 2.

The other significant difference is that, unlike in Kenya where the central issue is whether a refugee can be forced to live in a camp in Kenyan territory, in the European context adjudicators must grapple with whether a refugee can be sent to another host state. In Section 4.2, I discuss this additional layer of complexity with reference to scholarship on states' re-bordering and externalisation tactics. Moving to the jurisprudence, in Section 4.3 I deepen the argument made in the previous chapter by highlighting that, when decision-makers adopt categorical reasoning, they use these generic rights, not specifically designed to address refugeehood, as a prism to develop a purposive understanding of refuge and give effect to its remedial nature. However, in Section 4.4 I show that, similar to Kenya, in the European context the focus on refugeehood has waned and there has been a shift to looking for the exemplary or exceptionally vulnerable refugee. Decision-makers now approach refuge as if it is a scarce commodity that must be distributed on a needs basis. While the judicial search for the exceptional refugee could have provided grounds to facilitate journeys for those who face the greatest challenges in travelling across borders, in Section 4.5 I argue that this has not occurred, due to decision-makers' notional consideration of factors such as gender, age and disability.

---

[1] *R (on the application of ZAT and Others) v Secretary of State for the Home Department* IJR [2016] UKUT 00061 (IAC) [5] ('*R v SSHD*').

4.2   The Role of Human Rights in Determining 'Whose Refugee'

Referring to the different standards in refugee protection across the globe and the disproportionate burden some states face in hosting refugees, Juss posits that 'the relevant ethical
question' is not 'Who is a refugee?' but 'Whose refugee?'[2] In European protection from
refuge claims, this becomes a legal question. Adjudicators have to determine whether, for
example, Germany can send a refugee family to Hungary or whether Italy can intercept
asylum seekers on the high seas and return them to Libya.

These legal challenges have arisen as a consequence of Europe's re-bordering and
externalisation policies. Briddick uses the term 're-bordering' to encompass both enforcement of borders between European states and 'physical re-bordering at Europe's external
borders' (such as interceptions at sea).[3] With respect to the former, EU member-states
seek to control refugees' movement through the Dublin System (adopted in 2003 and
recast in 2013),[4] with one of its objectives being to prevent refugees moving between EU
countries.[5]

The Dublin System allocates responsibility between member-states for hearing an
asylum seeker's claim, but in practice it also 'determines in which Member State the
refugee will have to make her home'.[6] The Dublin System produces 'the most severe
imbalances in the distribution of protection seekers' because it is not designed to be
a responsibility-sharing mechanism.[7] In determining the state that must hear
a person's asylum claim, it does not take into account member-states' varying capacities to provide protection and its structure effectively allocates responsibility to border
states.[8]

Externalisation refers to states' attempts to push migration control beyond their borders.
Most of the externalisation literature in the European context focuses on states employing
migration control tactics outside of European territory and onto the territory of non-European

---

[2] Satvinder Juss, *International Migration and Global Justice* (Ashgate, 2006) 199.

[3] Catherine Briddick, 'Some Other(ed) 'Refugees'?: Women Seeking Asylum under Refugee and Human
Rights Law' in Satvinder Juss (ed), *Research Handbook on International Refugee Law* (Edward Elgar, 2019)
281, 283.

[4] Regulation (EC) No 604/2013 of the European Parliament and of the Council of 29 June 2013 Establishing
the Criteria and Mechanisms for Determining the Member State Responsible for Examining an
Application for International Protection Lodged in One of the Member States by a Third-Country
National or a Stateless Person (Recast) [2013] OJ L180/31–180/59 ('Dublin III Regulation'). As noted in
Chapter 1, there was a proposal for its reform. However, in 2020, the European Commission announced
that the Dublin System would be abolished and the reform proposal withdrawn.

[5] Vincent Chetail, 'Looking Beyond the Rhetoric of the Refugee Crisis: The Failed Reform of the Common
European Asylum System' (2016) 5 *European Journal of Human Rights* 584, 598.

[6] Cathryn Costello, 'Courting Access to Asylum in Europe: Recent Supranational Jurisprudence Explored'
(2012) 12(2) *Human Rights Law Review* 287, 314.

[7] Francesco Maiani, 'The Dublin III Regulation: A New Legal Framework for a More Humane System?' in
Vincent Chetail, Philippe De Bruycker and Francesco Maiani (eds), *Reforming the Common European
Asylum System: The New European Refugee Law* (Brill, 2016) 101, 112.

[8] Madeline Garlick, 'The Dublin System, Solidarity and Individual Rights' in Vincent Chetail, Philippe De
Bruycker and Francesco Maiani (eds), *Reforming the Common European Asylum System: The New
European Refugee Law* (Brill, 2016) 156, 165–6. The Dublin System determines the state responsible for
hearing an asylum claim. The first factors to be considered are family unity and the best interests of
children: Dublin III Regulation arts 8–11. If these criteria are not applicable, the responsible state will be
the state that granted the asylum seeker residence or gave them permission to enter the EU legally or, if not
applicable, the state where the asylum seeker first entered the EU: Dublin III Regulation arts 1, 12.

states, in particular countries in Northern Africa.[9] Examples of externalisation policies include interceptions at sea, increased extraterritorial surveillance and the rise of '"contactless" control' (inducing transit countries to enhance migration control in order to decrease onward movement).[10] Gammeltoft-Hansen explains that externalisation policies 'seem constantly to push refugees back to sites closer and closer to the state of persecution, a development that ultimately threatens to undermine the very concept of refuge'.[11]

The use of re-bordering and externalisation is problematic from a refugee rights perspective. As discussed in Chapter 2, many of the rights in the Refugee Convention are not absolute but relative to the rights a host state provides to its citizens or certain non-nationals. Further, in practice there are significant discrepancies between the protection different states provide refugees. Thus, determining which state is responsible for a refugee raises the issue of whether the host state in question will provide protection and also 'the quality of this protection'.[12]

The leading sociolegal studies of litigation challenging re-bordering and externalisation in Europe are written from the perspective of how European human rights law is being used to develop migrant rights rather than refugee rights more specifically. Dembour's analysis of migrants' rights claims before the ECtHR analyses challenges to the Dublin System alongside other significant cases brought by migrants who have not sought international protection.[13] Baumgärtel's study involves applicants who have or have sought refugee or complementary protection.[14] He analyses the outcomes with respect to how the judgments have been received by migrant right defenders[15] and also develops a conception of vulnerability that can be deployed in future migrant rights cases.[16]

While Baumgärtel explains that he refrains from 'measuring judicial outcomes against abstractly defined standards',[17] I take a different approach. I analyse the jurisprudence with reference to standards and understandings of refugee protection discussed in Chapter 2. In the rest of the chapter, I draw on Dembour's and Baumgärtel's seminal publications, and others', in my analysis of the case law. However, I shift the focus to how European and international human rights law has been used to develop ideas of refuge, in particular the objectives and nature of refugee protection. I also consider these judicial approaches to protection from refuge claims from a gender perspective. As noted in Chapter 1, legal and sociolegal examinations of this case law do not take a feminist or intersectional approach.[18] Briddick has bemoaned the lack of gender analysis in externalisation and Dublin System scholarship.[19]

---

[9] See, e.g., Thomas Gammeltoft-Hansen, *Access to Asylum: International Refugee Law and the Globalisation of Migration Control* (Cambridge University Press, 2011); Maarten Den Heijer, *Europe and Extraterritorial Asylum* (Hart, 2012); Violeta Moreno-Lax and Mariagiulia Giuffré, 'The Rise of Consensual Containment: From "Contactless Control" to "Contactless Responsibility" for Forced Migration Flows' in Satvinder Juss (ed), *Research Handbook on International Refugee Law* (Edward Elgar, 2019) 82.

[10] Moreno-Lax and Giuffré (n 9) 84.   [11] Gammeltoft-Hansen (n 9) 236.   [12] Ibid 30.

[13] Marie-Bénédicte Dembour, *When Humans Become Migrants: Study of the European Court of Human Rights with an Inter-American Counterpoint* (Oxford University Press, 2015).

[14] Moritz Baumgärtel, *Demanding Rights: Europe's Supranational Courts and the Dilemma of Migrant Vulnerability* (Cambridge University Press, 2019).

[15] Ibid 7.   [16] Ibid 114–15, ch 7.   [17] Ibid 7.

[18] Ibid; Cathryn Costello, *The Human Rights of Migrants and Refugees in European Law* (Oxford University Press, 2015); Dembour (n 13) 29.

[19] Briddick (n 3) 284.

4.3 Human Rights as a Prism to Engage with the Concept of Refuge

There are strong similarities between the methods of reasoning adopted by the High Court of Kenya in *Kituo Cha Sheria v Attorney General* ('*Kituo Cha Sheria*')[20] (discussed in Chapter 3) and those deployed in early or initial European protection from refuge challenges. Decision-makers start their analysis by identifying what it means to be a refugee and, in particular, irreducible aspects of refugeehood. They then use generally applicable human rights as vehicles to respond to refugees' needs and predicaments. In this section, I show that this categorical method of reasoning is evident across international, supranational and domestic decision-making bodies determining protection from refuge claims in the European context. I highlight the ways it allows decision-makers to engage with the concept of refuge and lends strength to refugees' human rights arguments in the face of state interests. In Section 4.3.1, I discuss these themes with respect to the first successful challenge to a Dublin System transfer in the ECtHR. While this decision focussed on article 3 of the ECHR (an absolute right), in Section 4.3.2 I consider one of the few Dublin System challenges grounded solely on a qualified right: article 8 of the ECHR (right to private and family life). In Section 4.3.3, I analyse early or initial Dublin System challenges before UN treaty bodies. In Section 4.3.4, I examine the first challenge to externalisation policies heard by the ECtHR.

4.3.1 The European Court of Human Rights' Categorical Approach to a Dublin System Challenge

The first successful challenge to a Dublin System transfer was the 2011 ECtHR decision of *MSS v Belgium and Greece*.[21] In this case, an Afghani asylum seeker challenged his transfer from Belgium to Greece made pursuant to the Dublin System. This case has been dissected by a number of scholars[22] and Baumgärtel explains that '[a]ssessing the overall impact . . . in terms of law development is not easy, given the sheer number of legal issues raised in the proceedings and subsequent commentaries'.[23] Much of the scholarship focuses on the significance of the Court's approach to the burden of proof (the ECtHR lightened the applicant's burden of proof by accepting information provided by international organisations[24] and showing scepticism towards states' positions).[25] Another aspect of the judgment discussed heavily in the literature is how the Court employed the 'principle of refutability' (that a person can challenge the presumption that an EU member-state complies with its international obligations).[26]

To open the unexplored question of bringing *MSS v Belgium and Greece* into conversation with ideas of refuge, the most crucial aspect of the judgment is the Court's assessment of the applicant's submission that his experience of homelessness and poverty in Greece

---

[20] [2013] eKLR (High Court of Kenya, Constitutional and Human Rights Division).
[21] [2011] I Eur Court HR 255. The detention conditions in Greece were also raised in an earlier case, but were not considered by the ECtHR on the grounds that any claim with respect to the reception conditions and/or conditions of detention in Greece would first have to be pursued domestically: *KRS v. UK* (Application No 32733/08, 2 December 2008) 18.
[22] See, e.g., Baumgärtel (n 14) ch 3; Costello (n 6); Dembour (n 13) ch 12; Patricia Mallia, 'Case of *M.S. S. v. Belgium and Greece*: A Catalyst in the Re-Thinking of Dublin II Regulation' (2011) 30(3) *Refugee Survey Quarterly* 107; Violeta Moreno-Lax, 'Dismantling the Dublin System: *M.S.S. v. Belgium and Greece*' (2012) 14(1) *European Journal of Migration and Law* 1.
[23] Baumgärtel (n 14) 53.   [24] Dembour (n 13) 408.   [25] Ibid 409–10.
[26] Baumgärtel (n 14) 53; Dembour (n 13) 415, 419; Moreno-Lax (22) 6.

constituted inhuman and degrading treatment. There is no doubt as to the veracity of the applicant's claims with respect to his living conditions. The Court observed that the applicant 'spent months living in a state of the most extreme poverty, unable to cater for his most basic needs: food, hygiene and a place to live'.[27] However, difficult living conditions alone cannot constitute a breach of the ECHR's article 3. The Court referred to a previous decision in which it ruled that the ECHR does not oblige states to provide everyone in their jurisdiction with a home.[28] The Greek government's submissions stressed that to decide otherwise would 'open the doors to countless similar applications from homeless persons and place an undue positive obligation on the States in terms of welfare policy'.[29] Accordingly, the Court had to determine whether homelessness and extreme poverty amounted to a breach of article 3 for the particular applicant, recalling that the minimum level of severity for inhuman and degrading treatment is relative.[30]

In answering this question, the Court specifically focussed on the applicant's position as an asylum seeker. It stated that it attached 'considerable importance to the applicant's status as an asylum-seeker and, as such, a member of a particularly underprivileged and vulnerable population'.[31] In this part of its reasoning, the Court invoked the concept of 'group vulnerability'[32] that it has used for other groups such as ethnic minorities.[33] This was the first time the Court recognised asylum seekers to be a vulnerable group.[34] In doing so, the ECtHR in *MSS v Belgium and Greece* adopted a parallel approach to the High Court of Kenya in *Kituo Cha Sheria*. Although the High Court of Kenya referred to the concept of vulnerability in the Kenyan Constitution and the ECtHR drew on its own vulnerability jurisprudence, both used the concept of vulnerability to identify and reflect on irreducible aspects of refugeehood.

In explaining why being an asylum seeker made the applicant a member of a vulnerable group, the ECtHR referred to 'everything he had been through during his migration and the traumatic experiences he was likely to have endured previously'[35] and that the international community recognises that asylum seekers are in need of special protection.[36] Thus, according to the ECtHR, the applicant's vulnerability was grounded both in his experience as an asylum seeker and his membership of a group that international law treats as distinct

---

[27] *MSS v Belgium and Greece* (n 21) [254].
[28] *Chapman v UK* [2001] I Eur Court HR 41 cited in *MSS v Belgium and Greece* (n 21) [249].
[29] *MSS v Belgium and Greece* (n 21) [243].
[30] *Kuldla v Poland* [2000] XI Eur Court HR 197 cited in *MSS v Belgium and Greece* (n 21) [219].
[31] *MSS v Belgium and Greece* (n 21) [251].
[32] Lourdes Peroni and Alexandra Timmer, 'Vulnerable Groups: The Promise of an Emerging Concept in European Human Rights Law' (2013) 11(4) *International Journal of Constitutional Law* 1056, 1057. See also Yussef Al Tamimi, 'The Protection of Vulnerable Groups and Individuals by the European Court of Human Rights' (2016) 5 *European Journal of Human Rights* 561; Baumgärtel (n 14); Alexandra Timmer, 'A Quiet Revolution: Vulnerability in the European Court of Human Rights' in Martha Fineman and Anna Grear (eds), *Vulnerability: Reflections on a New Ethical Foundation for Law and Politics* (Ashgate, 2013) 147.
[33] *DH and Others v the Czech Republic* [2007] IV Eur Court HR 241 [182]. The Court has also described people living with HIV as a vulnerable minority: *Kiyutin v Russia* [2011] II Eur Court HR 29 [63].
[34] Costello (n 18) 188.   [35] *MSS v Belgium and Greece* (n 21) [232].
[36] Ibid [251]. Similar reasoning is apparent in relation to the applicant's submission that detention in Greece amounted to inhuman and degrading treatment. In relation to the conditions of detention, the Court emphasised that the cells were overcrowded, there was a lack of adequate ventilation, water and sanitation: [230]. The Court then stressed that the applicant's distress in relation to these abhorrent conditions was 'accentuated by the vulnerability inherent in his situation as an asylum-seeker': [233].

and deserving of a specific form of protection. The Court's use of the concept of vulnerability in *MSS v Belgium and Greece* has been analysed with respect to the development of
migrants' rights,[37] but it is important to remember that the Court did not find that the
applicant was vulnerable because he was a migrant but, instead, because he was an asylum
seeker. This is clear from the very first paragraph of the Court's judgment on the merits of
the article 3 argument, which emphasised that '[s]tates' legitimate concern to foil the
increasingly frequent attempts to circumvent immigration restrictions must not deprive
asylum-seekers of the protection afforded by' the Refugee Convention and ECHR.[38] While
Dembour suggests that one of the 'jurisprudential leaps'[39] the judgment took was 'implicitly
rejecting the relevance of the "well-established" principle of international law which grants
states the right to expel aliens (subject to certain exceptions)',[40] another perspective is that
the Court simply acknowledged a long-standing principle of international law: that states
owe a special type of protection to refugees.[41]

The idea of vulnerability is a contentious one in refugee and forced migration literature.
On the one hand, scholars recognise that a person who has travelled to a foreign land to seek
protection is in an inherently vulnerable position and that law and policy must take account
of this.[42] However, emphasising vulnerability leads to dehumanising depictions and understandings of refugees that downplay their agency.[43] Focussing on vulnerability can also
produce policy decisions that disempower refugees by, for example, causing them to be
reliant on aid or welfare.[44]

The ECtHRs' use of the notion of vulnerability has also proved controversial. Timmer
argues that *MSS v Belgium and Greece* 'represents an important step towards an embrace
of the vulnerable subject in asylum law'.[45] Timmer draws on Fineman's theory (discussed in Chapter 3) that every person is vulnerable. She defends the Court's recognition
of asylum seekers as a vulnerable group on the ground that 'while vulnerability is
universal, our experience of it is particular'.[46] Taking a different view, Baumgärtel
criticises the shift in *MSS v Belgium and Greece* from focusing on the applicant's
experience in Greece to recognising that as an asylum seeker he is a member of
a vulnerable group.[47] He says that by doing so the Court 'did not add to the reasoning
in this judgment; the analysis of [the] applicant's situation already provided sufficient

---

[37] Baumgärtel (n 14); Dembour (n 13).   [38] *MSS v Belgium and Greece* (n 21) [216].
[39] Dembour (n 13) 402.   [40] Ibid 403.
[41] For a discussion of this long-standing principle see Guy Goodwin-Gill and Jane McAdam, *The Refugee in
International Law* (Oxford University Press, 3rd ed, 2007) 201–5; 355–8.
[42] Richard Black, 'Livelihoods under Stress: A Case Study of Refugee Vulnerability in Greece' (1994) 7(4)
Journal of Refugee Studies 360, 362; Marcia Inhorn, *America's Arab Refugees: Vulnerability and Health on
the Margins* (Stanford University Press, 2018) 37; Astri Suhrke, 'Human Security and the Protection of
Refugees' in Edward Newman (ed), *Refugees and Forced Displacement: International Security, Human
Vulnerability, and the State* (United Nations University Press, 2002) 93, 106–7.
[43] Liisa Malkki, 'Speechless Emissaries: Refugees, Humanitarianism, and Dehistoricization' (1996) 11(3)
Cultural Anthropology 377, 378, 388; Evangelia Tastsoglou et al, '(En)Gendering Vulnerability:
Immigrant Service Providers' Perceptions of Needs, Policies, and Practices Related to Gender and
Women Refugee Claimants in Atlantic Canada' (2014) 30(2) *Refuge* 67, 69, 70.
[44] Alexander Betts and Paul Collier, *Refuge: Transforming a Broken Refugee System* (Allen Lane, 2017) 137;
Barbara Harrell-Bond, *Imposing Aid: Emergency Assistance to Refugees* (Oxford University Press, 1986);
Malkki (n 43) 388.
[45] Timmer (n 32) 153.   [46] Ibid 145.
[47] Moritz Baumgärtel, 'Facing the Challenge of Migrant Vulnerability in the European Court of Human
Rights' (2020) 38(1) *Netherlands Quarterly of Human Rights* 12, 21.

reasons to consider him vulnerable'.[48] Baumgärtel draws on this case and others to develop 'a *socio-contextual* perspective' of vulnerability 'that bases a finding of vulnerability on identifiable social processes of discrimination and exclusion rather than characteristics presumably inherent in groups and specific persons'.[49] Baumgärtel's analysis also draws on Fineman's theory of vulnerability; in particular, arguing that vulnerability is situational as opposed to inherent, Fineman eschews group and identity-based approaches to vulnerability.

Baumgärtel's development of a notion of vulnerability that highlights processes of discrimination and exclusion is an important step forward in understanding how courts can use legal concepts of vulnerability. The value of this approach can be seen in *MSS v Belgium and Greece* in the Court's determination of the argument that the applicant's homelessness and poverty amounted to a violation of article 3. The Court examined contested evidence from the perspective of the applicant's experience of marginalisation. For example, in response to Greece's argument that the applicant was issued with a pink card and hence able to undertake employment, the Court noted that access to the job market was 'riddled with administrative obstacles' which were hampered by the applicant's 'lack of command of the Greek language' and 'lack of any support network'.[50] In rebuffing Greece's argument that the applicant failed to register at the police headquarters within three days, the Court stated that the time limit was impossible to comply with.[51] This is because of the difficulties asylum seekers have in accessing the police headquarters and that the information provided to the applicant was ambiguous.[52]

Nevertheless, I argue that the recognition that the applicant was an asylum seeker and therefore a member of a vulnerable group did add something to the Court's reasoning. Baumgärtel acknowledges that Fineman's understanding of vulnerability, being universal, overlooks the needs of specific groups.[53] I would add that Fineman's theory does not sit well with the way in which international human rights law is structured. As discussed in the previous chapter, the existence of group-specific international human rights treaties indicates an acceptance that specific groups require a tailoring of the general human rights regime.[54] These categories, while they risk essentialisation, can be valuable because they draw together common experiences that lend strength to mobilisation for law reform efforts.[55] Indeed, the ECtHR has referenced international human rights instruments to justify recognising certain groups as vulnerable.[56] Eschewing group vulnerability for asylum seekers also does not align with a wealth of scholarship that, while acknowledging the similarities between refugees and migrants, insists that those who cannot return because they have lost the protection of their homeland (whether or not they come within the

[48] Ibid 22.   [49] Baumgärtel (n 14) 115.   [50] *MSS v Belgium and Greece* (n 21) [261].
[51] Ibid [306]–[309].   [52] Ibid [306]–[309].   [53] Baumgärtel (n 47) 15.
[54] Frédéric Mégret, 'The Disabilities Convention: Human Rights of Persons with Disabilities or Disability Rights?' (2008) 30(2) *Human Rights Quarterly* 494, 515. See also Jane McAdam and Tamara Wood, 'The Concept of "International Protection" in the Global Compacts on Refugees and Migration' (2021) 23(1) *Interventions: International Journal of Postcolonial Studies* 2, 8.
[55] Jaya Ramji-Nogales, 'Revisiting the Category "Women"' in Susan Harris Rimmer and Kate Ogg (eds), *Research Handbook of Feminist Engagement with International Law* (Edward Elgar, 2019) 240, 244.
[56] Al Tamimi (n 32) 571. For example, Al Tamimi discusses cases such as *Eremia v The Republic of Moldova*, 28 May 2013 (Application No. 3564/11), in which the ECtHR refers to the UN Declaration on the Elimination of Violence against Women (1993) in its discussion of why victims of domestic violence are vulnerable.

international or a regional refugee definition or entitled to complementary protection) should be treated separately in international law and need a specialised rights regime.[57]

Scholars recognise that the Court's treatment of the applicant's arguments with respect to homelessness and poverty was significant because the Court used article 3 and group vulnerability to recognise that states have positive obligations towards asylum seekers.[58] Taking this insight further, I argue that, by recognising that asylum seekers are a vulnerable group, the Court used the right to be free from inhuman and degrading treatment as a prism to develop a purposive understanding of refuge. The Court implicitly identified refuge's restorative and regenerative functions as well as the ways these relate to refuge's temporality. This can be observed in the grounds on which the Court found that the applicant's experience of poverty and homelessness amounted to inhuman and degrading treatment. The Court ruled that this was in violation of article 3 because Greece demonstrated complete indifference towards the applicant.[59] By having no regard for the applicant's plight, Greece showed 'a lack of respect for [the asylum seeker's] dignity',[60] caused him 'feelings of fear, anguish or inferiority capable of inducing desperation'[61] and placed him in a state of 'prolonged uncertainty'.[62] It was the applicant's abysmal living conditions, coupled with the host state's indifference, which meant the applicant had a 'total lack of any prospects of his situation improving' that 'attained the level of severity required to fall within the scope of Article 3 of the [ECHR]'.[63] The Court emphasised that if Greece 'examined the applicant's asylum request promptly, [it] could have substantially alleviated his suffering'.[64] The judgment in *MSS v Belgium and Greece*, in criticising Greece for not promptly examining the applicant's asylum claim, manifests an appreciation that one of the functions of refuge is to restore a person's bond with a nation-state. This cannot occur if the host state ignores refugees' asylum claims and treats them with complete apathy. Also reflected in this reasoning is the idea that asylum seekers and refugees need to be able to imagine and generate a future. This is evident in the Court's emphasis on the applicant's state of uncertainty and lack of any prospect of his situation improving.

Further, by focusing on the applicant as an asylum seeker and thus part of a vulnerable group, the ECtHR gives character to the nature of refuge. While article 3 of the ECHR confers a right, the Court used it in a similar way to which a remedy is often understood: a response to a wrong or harm. While scholars have argued that the concept of vulnerability

---

[57] See, e.g., Jean-François Durieux, 'Three Asylum Paradigms' (2013) 20(2) *International Journal on Minority and Group Rights* 147; Madeline Garlick and Claire Inder, 'Protection of Refugees and Migrants in the Era of the Global Compacts' (2021) 23(1) *Interventions: International Journal of Postcolonial Studies* 1, 8, 11; Colin Harvey, 'Is Humanity Enough? Refugees, Asylum Seekers and the Rights Regime' in Satvinder Juss and Colin Harvey (eds), *Contemporary Issues in Refugee Law* (Edward Elgar, 2013) 68; James Hathaway, *The Rights of Refugees under International Law* (Cambridge University Press, 2005) 121, 186 (see also James Hathaway, *The Rights of Refugees under International Law* (Cambridge University Press, 2nd ed, 2021)); Jane McAdam, *Complementary Protection in International Refugee Law* (Oxford University Press, 2007); McAdam and Wood (n 54).

[58] Baumgärtel (n 14) 54; Costello (n 18) 188–9; Dembour (n 13) 406; Timmer (n 32) 156.

[59] *MSS v Belgium and Greece* (n 21) [263].   [60] Ibid [263].   [61] Ibid [263].   [62] Ibid [263].

[63] Ibid [263].

[64] Ibid [262]. The Court did not dwell on the distinction between asylum seekers and refugees. As noted in Chapter 1, refugee status is declaratory as opposed to constitutive, meaning that a person is a refugee once they cross an international border, as long as their circumstances satisfy the criteria in the relevant refugee definition.

could be used to 'extend the protective scope' of article 3,[65] from an international refugee law perspective the Court used the notion of vulnerability in an even more significant way. With respect to asylum seekers' need for special protection, the Court referred to 'the existence of a broad consensus at the international and European level concerning this need for special protection, as evidenced by the [Refugee] Convention, the remit and the activities of the UNHCR and the standards set out in the Reception Directive'.[66] The Court did not and could not go as far as to bring all of these protection standards into the realm of article 3 of the ECHR. Rather, through the medium of article 3, the Court reasoned that host states cannot be apathetic or indifferent towards asylum seekers, but must respond with 'due regard' to their specific vulnerabilities.[67] Thus, the Court used article 3 of the ECHR not only as a right, but to facilitate a legal remedy being a state's obligation to respond appropriately to refugees it is responsible for.

In producing these ideas of refuge, the Court acknowledged that asylum seekers are vulnerable because of the position they are in – they have lost the protection of their country of origin or habitual residence and need to be able to foster a connection with a (sometimes unwelcoming) host state. This is a situational approach to vulnerability rather than one grounded in the belief that some people or groups have inherent characteristics that render them vulnerable.

This landmark judgment is significant from the perspective of the role of courts in facilitating refugee journeys. The Court explicitly recognised the tension between refugee protection and states' interests and explained why refugees' rights triumph. It acknowledged that Greece was confronted with 'considerable difficulties in coping with the increasing influx of migrants and asylum seekers', which was 'exacerbated' by the Dublin System.[68] However, it confirmed that this does not excuse Greece from its obligations under article 3 of the ECHR.[69] In Mallia's assessment of the decision, she argues that the Court 'makes clear that human rights supersede the interest – or necessity – of States in controlling irregular immigration'.[70] After *MSS v Belgium and Greece*, states stopped transferring asylum seekers to Greece even if Greece was the responsible member-state pursuant to the Dublin System.[71] In a later decision, the ECtHR referred back to *MSS v Belgium and Greece* in its ruling that Italy was in violation of the ECHR by transferring asylum seekers to Greece.[72] There have also been some domestic cases that have drawn on the reasoning in *MSS v Belgium and Greece* in their determinations that Dublin System transfers to other member-states would be in violation of article 3 of the ECHR.[73]

---

[65] Baumgärtel (n 47) 21; Peroni and Timmer (n 32) 1079.   [66] *MSS v Belgium and Greece* (n 21) [251].
[67] Ibid [263].   [68] Ibid [223].   [69] Ibid [223].   [70] Mallia (n 22) 126–7.
[71] Baumgärtel notes that the judgment resulted in suspensions of transfers to Greece but did not prompt legislative change at domestic levels in EU member-states: Baumgärtel (n 14) 79. The European Commission recommended that, due to improvements in conditions for asylum seekers in Greece, transfers could resume from March 2017: European Commission, 'Recommendation on the Conditions for Resuming Dublin Transfers of Asylum-Seekers to Greece' (Press Release, Memo/16/4250, 8 December 2016). As outlined in Section 4.4 of this chapter, there has been a shift in judicial approaches and courts are more willing to allow a transfer if the receiving state provides guarantees that the refugees will be treated in a manner compliant with EU law. In a 2020 decision, the Supreme Administrative Court of Finland ruled that, despite evidence of inadequate reception conditions in Greece, the refugee applicant could be transferred there because the Greek government had provided appropriate guarantees: *Applicant A v Finnish Immigration Authorities* Supreme Administrative Court, KHO: 4219: 2020, 13 November 2020.
[72] *Sharifi and Others v Italy and Greece* (Application No 16643/09, 21 October 2014).
[73] A German court explicitly drew on the reasoning in *MSS v Belgium and Greece* in its determination that asylum seekers could not be sent to Hungary pursuant to the Dublin System: Administrative Court of Oldenburg, 12th Chamber, Decision of 2 October 2015, 12 A 2572/15.

Later reflections with hindsight have been more nuanced. Dembour highlights that '[r]ather than coming across as a resounding victory for migrant rights, it can be read instead as showing how absolutely terrible conditions must be before the Court finds it within itself to intervene on issues related to migration'.[74] Nevertheless, she acknowledges that the case was 'remarkable' because it 'did not hesitate to bring into question in a most decisive way a central piece of the Common European Asylum System put in place by the European Union'.[75] Dembour suggests that the two national judges (Judge Tulkens for Belgium and Judge Rozakis for Greece), who had previously displayed pro-migrant attitudes, played a significant role in persuading other members of the bench.[76] Next, I examine a similar victory for unaccompanied child asylum seekers in Calais, but one grounded in different provisions of the ECHR.

4.3.2 Categorical Approaches to Qualified Rights in Challenging the Dublin System

The use of a categorical approach to inform the right to family life in article 8 of the ECHR is evident in a 2015 decision by the United Kingdom Upper Tribunal. The first four applicants in this case were living in the 'Jungle' outside Calais. Three were unaccompanied minors and one was a twenty-six-year-old who had significant mental health impairments. The other three applicants were their family members who were seeking asylum in the UK. Pursuant to the Dublin System, the first four applicants were required to lodge their protection applications in France. However, they relied on the right to family life to petition to be transferred to the UK and reunited with the last three applicants.

The Tribunal approached the dispute on the premise that the Dublin System and ECHR operate alongside each other.[77] Due to the fact that article 8 is a qualified right (meaning that it is subject to permissible interferences), the Tribunal reasoned that the question to be determined was whether there was a disproportionate interference with the asylum seekers' right to family life.[78] The applicants' asylum-seeking experience was central to the Tribunal's approach to this question. The Tribunal listed a number of 'factors in the proportionality equation' that 'tip the balance in favour of the [a]pplicants'.[79] In addition to youth, one factor was the psychological damage they experienced as refugees: the Tribunal stressed that the applicants had 'all fled the war in Syria, claiming to have suffered extreme trauma there'.[80] Other determinants were the disruption and difficulties of displacement, especially with respect to family unity.[81] Also, the Tribunal placed weight on the fact that the first four applicants mistrusted the French authorities due to deficiencies in the French asylum system and would suffer 'mentally painful and debilitating fear, anxiety and uncertainty' if 'swift entry to the United Kingdom cannot be achieved'.[82]

Through the aforementioned reasoning, the United Kingdom Upper Tribunal employed the right to family life in the ECHR to invoke restorative, regenerative and palliative functions of refuge with particular sensitivity to age and disability. The Tribunal demonstrated an understanding that family reunification is an important aspect of restoring a normal life, in particular

---

[74] Marie-Bénédicte Dembour, 'An Anthropological Approach to *M.S.S. v Belgium and Greece*' in Damien Gonzalez-Salzberg and Loveday Hodson (eds), *Research Methods for International Human Rights Law* (Routledge, 2020) 227, 243.
[75] Dembour (n 13) 25.   [76] Ibid 419–20; Dembour (n 74) 239.   [77] *R v SSHD* (n 1).   [78] Ibid [51].
[79] Ibid [55].   [80] Ibid [17].   [81] Ibid [55].   [82] Ibid [55].

for unaccompanied minors and those with poor mental health. Also, it recognised that being able to have security in a brighter future is an essential component of refuge with its emphasis on the need to prevent further 'fear, anxiety and uncertainty' caused by the first four applicants' mistrust of the French asylum system.[83] Finally, the Tribunal's focus on the pain and trauma experienced by the asylum seekers has resonance with the idea that one role of refuge is to provide a space in which to address the trauma associated with persecution.

Similar to the High Court of Kenya in *Kituo Cha Sheria*, the United Kingdom Upper Tribunal displayed what Motz refers to as 'disability-sensitive' reasoning in refugee law decision-making – outlined in the previous chapter as one that aligns with the way the CRPD positions disability.[84] The CRPD's approach to disability is that impairments can lead to a disability, but disabilities result from the interactions between people with these impairments and various barriers in their environments. The Tribunal described the fourth applicant as having a 'mental disability'.[85] He had been diagnosed with a psychiatric disorder and post-traumatic stress disorder. The Tribunal did not dwell on the fourth applicant's medical conditions but instead emphasised the difficult circumstances in which he was living in Calais and the importance of family unity for his conditions (he was completely dependent on his younger brother who was with him in Calais but needed the additional care and support that could be offered by his siblings in the UK). This reflects a human rights-based, as opposed to a medical, approach to disability – the focus remained on the fourth applicant's human rights and how he could meaningfully realise them as opposed to how his conditions could be best treated with drugs or medical care.

The Tribunal acknowledged that the Dublin System and ECHR 'sometimes tug in different directions'.[86] The Tribunal was careful to emphasise that neither 'has any inherent value or status giving one precedence over the other'.[87] However, the applicants succeeded in establishing a disproportionate interference with their right to family life and this enabled them to use court processes to continue their journey in search of refuge across the English Channel. This is an important outcome because it evidences the preparedness of adjudicative decision-making bodies to use qualified rights to override state interests.

This decision of the United Kingdom Upper Tribunal is also significant in light of the restrictive approach to article 8 taken by the ECtHR. Dembour's detailed study of the Court's approach to migrants' rights claims indicates that, in cases involving article 8, the Court 'has reached verdicts of violation in only a handful of family reunion cases'.[88] Similarly, Desmond argues that the ECtHR in its application of article 8 has reduced 'its scope of protection' for migrants.[89]

The four young asylum seekers were transferred to the UK after the Tribunal's ruling.[90] Starfield's analysis of the case as a form of strategic litigation highlights how lawyers and

---

[83] Ibid [55].

[84] Stephanie Motz, 'The Persecution of Disabled Persons and the Duty of Reasonable Accommodation' in Céline Bauloz, Meltem Ineli-Ciger, Sarah Singer and Vladislava Stoyanova (eds), *Seeking Asylum in the European Union: Selected Protection Issues Raised by the Second Phase of the Common European Asylum System* (Brill, 2015) 141 ('The Persecution of Disabled Persons'). See also Stephanie Motz, *The Refugee Status of Persons with Disabilities* (Brill, 2021).

[85] *R v SSHD* (n 1) [6], [55].   [86] Ibid [50].   [87] Ibid [50].   [88] Dembour (n 13) 3.

[89] Alan Desmond, 'The Private Life of Family Matters: Curtailing Human Rights Protection for Migrants under Article 8 of the ECHR?' (2018) 29(1) *The European Journal of International Law* 261, 262.

[90] Gina Starfield, 'Forging Strategic Partnerships: How Civil Organisers and Lawyers Helped Unaccompanied Children Cross the English Channel and Reunite with Family Members' (RSC Working Paper Series 133, 19 October 2020).

civil society actors worked together to bring many children in France to the UK to reunite with family members.[91] Next, I show that UN treaty bodies have delivered similar victories to asylum seekers resisting the Dublin System.

4.3.3   Categorical Approaches to Dublin System Challenges before UN Treaty Bodies

A categorical approach to protection from refuge claims challenging the Dublin System is also evident in UN treaty body views.[92] In a 2015 view, the UN Human Rights Committee considered a communication made by Jasin, a Somalian refugee, and her children (*Jasin v Denmark*).[93] Jasin, who arrived in Italy when her first child was a year old, was granted subsidiary protection. Italy initially gave her accommodation, but later evicted her and did not offer any assistance in finding housing or work. She had no option but to live on the street. She became pregnant with her second child and Italy did not provide any medical care during the pregnancy and birth. Jasin travelled to Denmark, but Denmark attempted to return her to Italy pursuant to the Dublin System. Jasin and her children argued before the Committee that this would be a breach of article 7 of the ICCPR (no one shall be subjected to torture or to cruel, inhuman or degrading treatment or punishment). Similar to the categorical reasoning adopted by the ECtHR, the Human Rights Committee focussed on the authors' need for protection. It explained that its view with respect to a breach of article 7 of the ICCPR must be informed by 'the unique status of the author and her children as asylum seekers entitled to subsidiary protection'.[94]

Akin to the High Court of Kenya in *Kituo Cha Sheria*, the UN Human Rights Committee walked a fine line between recognising that there are experiences common to all refugees but that the ways these are experienced differ with respect to factors such as age and gender. The Committee stressed that Denmark did not have assurances that Italy would receive 'the author and her children in conditions adapted to the *children's age* and the *family's vulnerable status*, which would enable them to *remain in Italy*'.[95] This reflects the restorative objectives (that a host state must establish a bond with the refugee) and temporality of refuge (that this must lead to an enduring relationship between the refugee and the host state), but also indicates that refuge must be adapted in an appropriate way for young children and a single female-headed family. It also provides a counterpoint to the legitimate concerns from some scholars that group-based vulnerability reasoning can result in stereotyping and stigmatisation.[96] The UN Human Rights Committee determined that Denmark deporting Jasin and her children to Italy would be a violation or their article 7 ICCPR rights

---

[91] Ibid.

[92] For a comprehensive examination of *non-refoulement* decisions by UN treaty bodies see Başak Çalı, Cathryn Costello and Stewart Cunningham, 'Hard Protection through Soft Courts? Non-Refoulement before the United Nations Treaty Bodies' (2020) 21(3) *German Law Review* 355. Most concern return to a person's country of origin or habitual residence and are thus outside the scope of this book. See also European Legal Network on Asylum, *Note on Asylum and the UN Treaty System* (March 2021) <www.ecre.org/wp-content/uploads/2021/03/Legal-Note-8.pdf>.

[93] Human Rights Committee, *Views: Communication No 2360/2014*, UN Doc CCPR/C/114/D/2360/2014 (25 September 2015) ('*Jasin v Denmark*').

[94] Ibid [1].   [95] Ibid [8.9] (emphasis added).

[96] See, e.g., Baumgärtel (n 47) 17; Peroni and Timmer (n 32) 1071.

(torture and cruel, inhuman or degrading treatment or punishment) and only the dissenting member expressed concerns about the decision's effect on the Dublin System.[97]

Similarly, the UN Committee against Torture in a decision as to whether an Eritrean asylum seeker could be sent from Switzerland to Italy pursuant to the Dublin System said that Switzerland had to consider 'his specific vulnerability as an asylum seeker and victim of torture'.[98] The Committee was of the view that transfer to Italy would be a violation of the right to be free from torture. Crucial to its decision was that there were no guarantees that the asylum seeker would have rehabilitation services in Italy and separation from his family in Switzerland would remove him from a stable social environment.[99] The Committee displayed an awareness of the fact that those who have experienced the trauma of persecution need to be with family to cope with these experiences, reflecting an understanding that refuge has a palliative function.

The UN Committee on the Rights of the Child determined its first case concerning externalised border control in *DD v Spain*.[100] The complaint concerned a child who fled war in Mali and entered Morocco as an asylum seeker. He tried to enter Melilla, Spain's territorial enclave in Morocco, but Spanish authorities apprehended him and returned him to Morocco. The Committee concluded that Spain's summary deportation was a violation of articles 3 (best interests of the child), 20 (special protection and assistance to children deprived of their family environment) and 37(a) (no child shall be subject to torture or other cruel, inhuman or degrading treatment or punishment) of the CRC. That DD was an unaccompanied asylum seeker was central to the Committee's reasoning. The Committee highlighted Spain's lack of identification process, absence of procedures whereby DD could object to his deportation, failure to provide special protection and assistance to DD and undertake a best interest assessment, and the unavailability of legal or translation assistance prior to deportation. The Committee's focus on procedural protections is significant in the context of unaccompanied minors. The decision has parallels with literature that stresses the need for robust procedural protections for child refugees due to the challenges they face in navigating asylum systems.[101]

In summary, while McAdam and Hathaway correctly highlight that general human rights instruments do not address refugee-specific concerns, when decision-makers employ categorical reasoning they shape these rights in a way that responds to refugees' predicaments. In particular, by identifying irreducible experiences of refugeehood, decision-makers use rights in generic human rights instruments to conceptualise the objectives and nature of refuge and tailor this to take into account factors such as age, gender and disability. Next, I show a similar pattern of judicial reasoning in the context of a challenge to externalisation policies but one that indicates a shift towards a less protection-sensitive outlook.

---

[97] The dissenting member said that finding for the author and her children on the grounds outlined by the majority would 'unduly widen the ambit of article 7 and make it applicable to the situation of thousands of poor and destitute people in the world, especially those who want to move from the South to the North': *Jasin v Denmark* (n 93) Appendix I [1].

[98] Committee against Torture, *Views: Communication No 742/2016*, UN Doc CAT/C/64/D/742/2016 (3 September 2018) ('*AN v Switzerland*') [8.6].

[99] Ibid [8.8]–[8.10].

[100] Human Rights Committee, *Views: Communication No 4/2016*, UN Doc CRC/C/80/D/4/2016 (12 February 2019).

[101] Jacqueline Bhabha, 'Seeking Asylum Alone: Treatment of Separated and Trafficked Children in Need of Refugee Protection' (2004) 42(1) *International Migration* 141.

4.3.4 A Categorical Approach to the First Challenge to Externalisation before the European Court of Human Rights

The ECtHR handed down its first judgment on an externalisation practice in *Hirsi Jamaa v Italy*.[102] This case was brought by 24 Somalian and Eritrean asylum seekers who had been part of a group of approximately 200 people who left Libya by boat with the aim of reaching Italy. Italy intercepted the vessel and returned it to Libya pursuant to an agreement between the two countries. After confirming that the applicants were under Italy's jurisdiction and, therefore, entitled to the rights in the ECHR,[103] one issue was whether Italy breached article 3 by transferring the applicants to Libya on account of the conditions in Libya and the risk that Libya would return them to Somalia and Eritrea. The Court was also asked to rule on whether the applicants' return to Libya was a collective expulsion in the meaning of article 4 of Protocol 4 to the ECHR.

This was an eagerly anticipated judgment. The aspect most heavily discussed is the Court's ruling on jurisdiction. In particular, Judge Pinto de Albuquerque's concurring opinion has been celebrated for its symbolic overturning of the ruling by the US Supreme Court in *Sale v Haitian Centers Council Inc*[104] that article 33 of the Refugee Convention (*non-refoulement*) does not operate extraterritorially.[105] Scholars have also recognised that the judgment is significant because it acknowledges state responsibility for migrants at sea[106] and rules that states cannot evade human rights obligations through bilateral agreements.[107]

While most analyses of the judgment view it as progressive from a human rights perspective, others have reservations.[108] Some scholars argue that the Court's ruling on jurisdiction would not apply if the facts were different and Italy were acting by 'proxy' and assisting Libya to intercept asylum seeker vessels[109] (a practice Italy now adopts and one being challenged at the time of writing).[110]

What has not yet been part of the conversation is the extent to which the ECtHR in *Hirsi Jamaa v Italy* engages with ideas of refuge through the ECHR. While some judge *Hirsi Jamaa v Italy* as a step back from *MSS v Belgium and Greece*, when viewed from the perspective of the Court drawing links between the ECHR and notions of refuge protection, this is not the case. Central to the Court's approach to its decision was that the applicants were seeking protection as refugees. Thus, the Court adopted a categorical approach akin to its earlier judgment in *MSS v Belgium and Greece*. This can be seen in the majority judgment, which focussed on the experience of refugees in Libya. For example,

---

[102] [2012] II Eur Court HR 97 ('*Hirsi Jamaa v Italy*').   [103] Ibid [82].   [104] 509 US 155, 133 (1993).
[105] Baumgärtel (n 14) 87–9; Itamar Mann, 'Dialectic of Transnationalism: Unauthorized Migration and Human Rights' (2013) 54(2) *Harvard International Law Journal* 315, 362 ('Dialectic of Transnationalism'). Although see Mann's later critique: Itamar Mann, 'Maritime Legal Black Holes: Migration and Rightlessness in International Law' (2018) 29(2) *The European Journal of International Law* 347, 357.
[106] Costello (n 18) 242; Dembour (n 13) 21; Maarten Den Heijer, 'Reflections on *Refoulement* and Collective Expulsion in the *Hirsi* Case' (2013) 25(2) *International Journal of Refugee Law* 265.
[107] Mann, 'Dialectic of Transnationalism' (n 105) 362.   [108] Baumgärtel (n 14) 90.
[109] Thomas Gammeltoft-Hansen, 'International Refugee Law and Policy: The Case of Deterrence Policies' (2014) 27(4) *Journal of Refugee Studies* 574, 588; Mann, 'Dialectic of Transnationalism' (n 105) 366.
[110] *SS and Others v Italy* (Application No 21660/18). See discussion in Violeta Moreno-Lax 'The Architecture of Functional Jurisdiction: Unpacking Contactless Control—On Public Powers, S.S. and Others v. Italy, and the "Operational Model"' (2020) 21(3) *German Law Review* 385.

the majority stressed that refugees in Libya were 'subjected to particularly precarious living conditions' and 'vulnerable to xenophobic and racist acts'.[111] The Court not only focussed on the experiences of refugees in Libya but also intimated that refugees are entitled to a special form of protection. The majority noted that during the relevant period Libya did not have any rules regarding refugee protection and made 'no distinction between irregular migrants and asylum seekers'.[112] With respect to whether conditions in Libya constituted inhuman and degrading treatment and Italy was in breach of article 3 for sending them there, the Court stressed that Italy should have been aware[113] that activities by the UNHCR office in Tripoli 'were never recognised in any way by the Libyan government'[114] and 'that the refugee status granted by the UNHCR did not guarantee the persons concerned any kind of protection in Libya'.[115] Judge Albuquerque, in the opening line of his concurring judgment, puts the issue more bluntly: '[t]he *Hirsi* case is about the international protection of refugees'.[116]

Through this focus on the experience of refugees in Libya, refugees' entitlement to special protection and the need for refugee status assessment systems, the ECtHR deepened its understanding of refuge's restorative objectives in *Hirsi Jamaa v Italy*. Its reasoning reflects an understanding that the restorative aspect of refuge is not only about re-establishing the bond between a refugee and a nation-state; it also should enable refugees to lead a normal life in the host community. This is seen in the Court's observation that the applicants were 'destined to occupy a marginal and isolated position in Libyan society', because they were not given any form of special protection.[117] Further, the Court extended its thinking with respect to the nature of refuge; a host state must not only take action with respect to asylum seekers and refugees within its territory, but this response or remedy must also manifest in some form of legal status. The Court conveyed this idea through its emphasis on Libya's lack of special protection for refugees and its refusal to recognise the UNHCR's activities with respect to designation of refugee status.[118]

Gammeltoft-Hansen warns that extraterritorialisation risks resulting in 'what could be termed "protection lite", understood as the presence of formal protection, but with a lower degree of certainty about the scope and/or level of rights afforded'.[119] While this certainly occurs in many externalisation contexts, it is important to note that the ECtHR in *Hirsi Jamaa v Italy* didn't offer a minimalist or 'protection lite' approach to refuge. Judge Pinto de Albuquerque stated that the case opened up important questions about the 'intrinsic link' between refugee and human rights law.[120] As noted earlier, the majority made explicit connections between article 3 of the ECHR and the Refugee Convention and channelled important concepts of refugee protection through the prism of European human rights law.

Nevertheless, the significance of *Hirsi Jamaa v Italy* for asylum seeker journeys is less clear. Similar to its earlier judgment in *MSS v Belgium and Greece*, the Court acknowledged the tension between state interests and human rights claims but emphasised that human rights prevail. The Court noted that 'states which form the external borders of the European

---

[111] *Hirsi Jamaa v Italy* (n 102) [125].   [112] Ibid [125].   [113] Ibid [131].   [114] Ibid [130].
[115] Ibid [130].   [116] Ibid 167.
[117] Ibid [125]. A similar position was taken in a German decision regarding the transfer of asylum seekers to Malta. The Court determined that it would raise a real risk of inhuman and degrading treatment and one reason for the decision was that Malta does not provide special protection to asylum seekers and refugees: Hannover Administrative Court, 5 November 2015, No 10 A 5157/15.
[118] *Hirsi Jamaa v Italy* (n 102) [130].   [119] Gammeltoft-Hansen (n 9) 30.
[120] *Hirsi Jamaa v Italy* (n 102) 167.

Union are currently experiencing difficulties in coping with the increasing influx of migrants and asylum-seekers'[121] and stressed that it does 'not underestimate the burden and pressure this situation places on the States concerned, which are all the greater in the present context of the economic crisis'.[122] Despite this recognition, the Court ruled that these concerns 'cannot absolve a state of its obligations' under article 3 of the ECHR.[123] Dembour highlights that the verdict 'puts into question the very idea and practice of intercepting irregular migrants in the high seas and summarily returning them'.[124]

However, Dembour[125] and Baumgärtel[126] criticise the ECtHR for the remedy granted in *Hirsi Jamaa v Italy* (ordering Italy to seek assurances that the applicants not be subject to treatment contrary to article 3 and not be arbitrarily repatriated as opposed to ordering that they be returned to Italy). Disagreeing with the majority on this point, Judge Pinto de Albuquerque wrote that Italy has 'a positive obligation to provide the applicants with practical and effective access to an asylum procedure in Italy'.[127] Dembour suggests that the remedy was 'a concession to state interests in a judgment which otherwise reminds states in no uncertain terms that their obligations under the Convention are [not] negotiable'.[128] There was little in the way of a meaningful outcome for most of the applicants, all but six of whom had lost contact with their lawyers and thus did not receive the compensation they were awarded.[129] Italy suspended the practice of pushbacks to Libya after the judgment but still provides support to Libya with respect to Libya's interception of migrants and asylum seekers attempting to reach Europe by boat.[130]

Does this remedy take away from the Court's understandings of refuge? It does in the sense that Libya's complete disregard for refugees, noted by the Court throughout the judgment, could not be remedied by diplomatic assurances. The relief granted indicates that, while the Court outlined strong ideas of refugee protection, it was not prepared to encroach on state interests by delivering the applicants a meaningful remedy. However, by the time the case was heard, the applicants had already been returned to Libya and their lawyers had lost contact with most of them.[131] In outlining the remedy to be provided, the majority said, '[h]aving *regard to the circumstances of the case*, the Court considers that the Italian Government must take all possible steps to obtain assurances from the Libyan authorities that the applicants will not be subjected to treatment incompatible with Article 3 of the Convention or arbitrarily repatriated'.[132] This leaves open the question whether the Court would have granted a different remedy if the lawyers had managed to stay in contact with their clients. Indeed, in a case dealing with a very similar factual scenario, an Italian court ruled that Italy was obliged not only to compensate fourteen Eritrean asylum seekers it had intercepted and returned to Libya but also to permit them to enter Italy to apply for protection.[133] The key difference in this case was that lawyers were in touch with each of the asylum seekers.

---

[121] Ibid [122].   [122] Ibid [122].   [123] Ibid [122].

[124] Marie-Bénédicte Dembour, 'Interception at Sea: Illegal as Currently Practiced – Hirsi and Others v. Italy' (1 March 2012) Strasbourg Observers <https://strasbourgobservers.com/2012/03/01/interception-at-sea-illegal-as-currently-practiced-hirsi-and-others-v-italy/#more-1441>.

[125] Marie-Bénédicte Dembour, 'Hirsi (Part II): Another Side of the Judgment' (2 March 2012) Strasbourg Observers <https://strasbourgobservers.com/2012/03/02/hirsi-part-ii-another-side-to-the-judgment/#more-1444>.

[126] Baumgärtel (n 14) 90.   [127] *Hirsi Jamaa v Italy* (n 102) 186.   [128] Dembour (n 125).

[129] Baumgärtel (n 14) 92.   [130] Moreno-Lax (n 110) 387.   [131] *Hirsi Jamaa v Italy* (n 102) 110.

[132] Ibid [211] (emphasis added).

[133] Sentence No. 22917/2019, First Civil Section of the Rome Court, 28 November 2019.

Nevertheless, a sanguine perspective on what the ECtHR may have done in *Hirsi Jamaa v Italy* if the circumstances were different is probably misplaced. As will be outlined next, judicial examinations of protection from refuge claims in the European context have shifted to approaches that are less protection-sensitive and offer paltry understandings of refuge. The robust judgment in *Hirsi Jamaa v Italy* coupled with a feeble remedy may be best understood as a foreshadowing of this about-face.

4.4   Judicial Disengagement with Refuge

The decisions discussed in the previous sections, in particular the Dublin System jurisprudence, may provide grounds for optimism with respect to the force of human rights arguments to enable refugees to continue their journey to find a genuine place of refuge. Asylum seekers and refugees continue to successfully use the ECHR to resist a Dublin System transfer in situations of chain *refoulement* (where a person is sent to a third country and there is a real risk that the third country may expel them to a nation-state where their life or freedom would be threatened or they may face torture or inhuman and degrading treatment or punishment).[134] The ECtHR has also found in favour of asylum seekers in a chain *refoulement* case not involving the Dublin System.[135]

However, in this section, I show that the ways decision-makers approach protection from refuge challenges, where the issue is not chain *refoulement* but the adequacy of reception conditions, has shifted. There are some cases where decision-makers approach these legal challenges in a manner akin to the categorical approach first adopted by the ECtHR in *MSS v Belgium and Greece*.[136] Also, it is important to note that, in decisions subsequent to those

---

[134] See, e.g., Belgium, Council for Alien Law Litigation, 25 August 2016, No 173 581 (an asylum seeker in Belgium successfully challenged his Dublin System from Belgium to Austria and crucial to the decision was the Belgian government had not taken into account the impact of Austria's moratorium on the processing of asylum applications); Bordeaux Administrative Court of Appeal, Third Chamber No 16BX00997 (27 September 2016) (an asylum seeker successfully challenged his Dublin System Transfer from France to Hungary on the grounds that his asylum claim would not be considered in Hungary); *Ibrahimi and Abasi v Secretary of State for the Home Department* [2016] EWCH 2049 (two Iranian asylum seekers successfully challenged their Dublin System transfer from the UK to Hungary on the grounds that their asylum claim would not be heard in Hungary and there was a real risk they would be returned to Iran); Administrative Court of Madgeburg (Germany) 2 B 92/20 MD, 24 March 2020 (the Court ruled that Germany could not return the asylum seeker to Bulgaria pursuant to the Dublin System because Bulgaria would not undertake a serious examination of his asylum application, thus there was a real risk that the applicant would be returned to his home country); Administrative Court of Munich (Germany), M 11 S 19.50722 and M 11 S 19.50759, 17 July 2019 (the Court declared that the asylum seeker could not be sent from Germany to Greece pursuant to the Dublin System because there was a risk that Greece would send him to Turkey).

[135] *MK and Others v Poland* (Application Nos 40503/17, 42902/17 and 43643/17, 23 July 2020). Chechen asylum seekers were attempting to enter Poland from its border with Belarus. The Court ruled that Poland was in breach of article 3 of the ECHR because the applicants did not have a genuine possibility of applying for international protection in Belarus and there was a real risk Belarus would return them to Chechnya: [185]–[186]. The Court also found breaches of article 13 of the ECHR and article 4 of Protocol Number 4 to the ECHR.

[136] Of particular note is a French decision regarding the transfer of an asylum seeker to Italy: Rennes Administrative Tribunal, 5 January 2018, Application No 1705747. The Tribunal ruled that a Sudanese asylum seeker could not be transferred to Italy. The Tribunal reasoned that the conditions in Italy would be distressing and his distress would be accentuated by his vulnerability as an asylum seeker. Just before this book went to press, a German court ruled that two asylum seekers could not be returned to Greece pursuant

discussed earlier, the Committee against Torture and Committee on the Rights of the Child have upheld the rights of refugees resisting a Dublin System transfer.[137]Çalı, Costello and Cunningham suggest that these two treaty bodies, having 'a single-issue focus', are able to 'challenge the logic of migration control and operate with less deferential standards'.[138] But, in most of the more recent jurisprudence, the significance of being a person in need of international protection is lost and decision-makers look for an additional vulnerability beyond refugeehood.

In Section 4.4.1, I highlight the diminishing focus on refugeehood in human rights challenges involving the Dublin System. I show that, once the significance of refugeehood fades, decision-makers consider whether the applicant is a 'peculiarly vulnerable' refugee. In Section 4.4.2, I look at recent challenges to externalisation practices and highlight that there is a focus on finding the 'deserving' refugee. In Section 4.4.3, I explain that these shifts change the nature of refuge from a legal remedy and status to a commodity. What I mean by this is that decision-makers are treating refuge in a similar way to how welfare is often conceived – as a limited resource that must be apportioned to the most needy and deserving. I discuss how this change obscures refuge's remedial nature, promulgates impoverished understandings of refuge and renders human rights arguments less potent against states' interests in restricting refugees' mobility.

4.4.1   From Vulnerable Refugees to the 'Peculiarly Vulnerable' Refugee

The move away from a categorical approach to protection from refuge decisions involving the Dublin System is evident in the ECtHR 2014 decision of *Tarakhel v Switzerland*.[139] This case concerned a family of Afghani asylum seekers (parents and six children) who sought asylum in Italy before travelling to Switzerland. Switzerland attempted to return the family to Italy pursuant to the Dublin System, but the family resisted. They claimed they would be at risk of homelessness and gave evidence that the number of asylum seekers in Italy far outstripped the number of places available in asylum seeker accommodation.[140] Even when accommodation was available, the evidence attested to 'lack of privacy, insalubrious conditions and [widespread] violence'.[141]

The Court's decoupling of the relevance of refugees' specific predicaments from the decision as to what constitutes inhuman and degrading treatment is apparent in its comparison of the conditions in Italy and Greece. While the Court noted that asylum

---

to the Dublin System because they could not meet their basic needs in Greece: Higher Administrative Court of North Rhine-Westphalia, 21 January 2021, ECLI:DE:OVGNRW:2021:0121.11A1564.20A.00.

[137] Committee against Torture, *Views: Communication No 758/2016*, UN Doc CAT/C/65/D/758/2016 (8 February 2019); Committee on the Rights of the Child, *Views: Communication No 56/2018*, UN Doc CRC/C/85/D/56/2018 (30 October 2020) ('*VA v Switzerland*'). In *VA v Switzerland*, the Committee on the Rights of the Child concluded that Switzerland's decision to send a family to Italy pursuant to the Dublin System was in violation of article 3 (best interests of the child) and article 12 (right to be heard) of the CRC. While the Committee declared the complaint under article 22 (protection and humanitarian assistance for child asylum seekers) admissible, it did not consider the complaint on the merits. This may have been a missed opportunity for the Committee to provide guidance on the interpretation and scope of article 22: Ellen Desmet and Sara Lembrechts, 'Communication 56/2018: V.A. v Switzerland' (Case Note 2021/1) Leiden Children's Rights Observatory <www.childrensrightsobservatory.nl/case-notes/casenote2021-1>.

[138] Çalı, Costello, and Cunningham (n 92) 383.

[139] [2014] VI Eur Court HR 195 ('*Tarakhel v Switzerland*').   [140] Ibid [108]–[110].   [141] Ibid [111].

seekers are a vulnerable group requiring special protection,[142] this did not inform its reasoning. Unlike its earlier decision in *MSS v Belgium and Greece*, the Court did not consider whether the risk of homelessness and insalubrious and unsafe conditions in reception centres would be inhuman and degrading for asylum seekers, recalling that the minimal severity is relative. Rather, the Court used the conditions in Greece (as described in *MSS v Belgium and Greece*) as a litmus test for conditions that act as a complete bar to all Dublin System transfers. The Court reasoned that, while the conditions in Italy are problematic, they did not compare to Greece, where there are 'fewer than 1,000 places in reception centres to accommodate tens of thousands of asylum seekers and that the conditions of the most extreme poverty described by the applicant existed on a large scale'.[143] On these grounds, the Court ruled that the conditions in Italy could not act as a bar to all transfers to that country and, therefore, transfers to Italy had be considered on a case-by-case basis.[144]

Another example of the waning relevance of refugeehood and the reference to conditions in Greece as a litmus test for what constitutes inhuman and degrading treatment can be found in the United Kingdom High Court of Justice's 2014 decision of *R (Tabrizagh) v Secretary of State for the Home Department*.[145] This case concerned six male asylum seekers resisting a Dublin System transfer to Italy. Two had experienced homelessness, destitution and violence in Italy. The Court did not take into account their situation as asylum seekers in its consideration as to whether the conditions in Italy presented a real risk of inhuman and degrading treatment. Rather, similar to the ECtHR in *Tarakhel v Switzerland*, the United Kingdom High Court of Justice used the conditions in Greece as the relevant threshold. While there was no up-to-date evidence given to the Court regarding the accommodation available to asylum seekers in Italy, the Court was satisfied that the numbers 'exceed the 1000 spaces which were available in Greece for the "tens of thousands" of asylum seekers at the time of *MSS*'.[146]

When the focus on refugeehood declines, decision-makers fixate on finding the exceptional refugee. In *Tarakhel v Switzerland*, the distinguishing factor was that the applicants were a family with six children. The Court ruled that Switzerland would be in breach of article 3 if it returned the family to Italy, because it did not have 'sufficient assurances that ... the applicants would be taken charge of in a manner adapted to the age of the children'.[147] However, in *R (Tabrizagh) v SSHD*, the applicants could not point to any additional risk factors to resist their transfer to Italy. The High Court of Justice ruled that a transfer to Italy did not present an article 3 risk and, in coming to this conclusion, a significant factor was that the claimants were young, single men[148] and none had any individual vulnerabilities that could create an article 3 risk.[149] A similar approach was taken by the ECtHR in *AME v The Netherlands*,[150] which concerned a Dublin transfer of a Somali asylum seeker to Italy. The Court held that the transfer would not be in violation of article 3

---

[142] Ibid [118].   [143] Ibid [114].   [144] Ibid [114]–[115].
[145] [2014] EWHC 1914 (Admin) ('*R v Tabrizagh v SSHD*'). This case was decided subsequent to *EM (Eritrea) v Secretary of State for the Home Department* [2014] UKSC 12 concerning the transfer of asylum seekers to Italy in which the United Kingdom Supreme Court held that there was no requirement to establish a *systemic* deficiency. The Court of Justice of the European Union has now clarified that even when there are not systemic deficiencies in the asylum system of an EU member-state, a transfer cannot occur if there is evidence that a transfer would result in a real risk that a particular asylum seeker would be subject to inhuman or degrading treatment: *CK v Supreme Court of the Republic of Slovenia* (C 578/16, 16 February 2017), [92], [96].
[146] *R (Tabrizagh) v SSHD* (n 145) [71].   [147] *Tarakhel v Switzerland* (n 139) [121].
[148] *R (Tabrizagh) v SSHD* (n 145) [179].   [149] Ibid [179], [182], [184], [186], [187].
[150] (Application No 51428/10, 13 January 2015) ('*AME v The Netherlands*').

because '[u]nlike the applicants in the case of *Tarakhel* . . . who were a family with six minor children, the applicant is an able young man with no dependents'.[151]

This pattern of shifting focus from refugeehood to requiring some additional form of acute vulnerability is also evident in Human Rights Committee views. Just a year after the decision of *Jasin v Denmark*, the Committee considered a similar complaint in *RAA and ZM v Denmark*, but adopted different reasoning.[152] The complaint concerned a married Syrian couple expecting a baby. Both had been granted refugee status in Bulgaria, but, due to fears for their safety, left and sought protection in Denmark. Denmark arranged for their return to Bulgaria pursuant to the Dublin System. The Committee did not place any significance on the authors' refugee status. To trigger article 7 of the ICCPR, they had to establish that their situation was exceptional in some way. The Committee concluded that, 'in these particular circumstances',[153] returning the couple to Bulgaria would amount to a breach of article 7. Crucial to this decision was that the couple were 'in a particularly vulnerable situation', because they would soon have a child, would be victims of racially motivated violence, would not be able to provide for themselves and the male author had a heart condition for which he would not receive appropriate treatment in Bulgaria.[154]

The reasons why the Human Rights Committee changed its approach may be gleaned from the dissenting members who were concerned that article 7 of the ICCPR was being extended 'beyond breaking point'.[155] They explained that:

> [w]ith the possible exceptions of those individuals who face *special hardships* due to their *particular situation of vulnerability* which renders their plight *exceptionally harsh* and irreparable in nature, non-availability of social assistance or delays in access to medical services do not in themselves constitute grounds for non-refoulement.[156]

While this is a dissenting opinion, the Committee's switch from an expansive to a much narrower approach in just over a year perhaps indicates a realisation that its initial approach would apply to almost all asylum seekers resisting a Dublin System transfer. Accordingly, they changed their emphasis in a way that prioritises refugees with 'special hardships' or in a 'particular situation of vulnerability'. In subsequent views, the Human Rights Committee again focussed on the authors' 'special vulnerability' beyond refugeehood, including single mothers, children with significant medical conditions and unaccompanied minors.[157] While each of these complaints have been successful, they have rested on the applicants establishing a vulnerability beyond refugeehood.

Similar concerns are evident in the United Kingdom Court of Appeal's reversal of the Upper Tribunal's decision regarding the use of the right to family life to petition for a transfer from France to the UK in 2016. The Court of Appeal stated that the Tribunal 'set too low a hurdle for permitting [the Dublin] process to be displaced by Article 8 considerations'.[158]

---

[151] Ibid [34].
[152] Human Rights Committee, *Views: Communication No 2608/2015*, UN Doc CCPR/C/118/D/2608/2015 (29 December 2016) ('*RAA and ZM v Denmark*').
[153] Ibid [7.9].   [154] Ibid [7.8].   [155] Ibid Annex [3].   [156] Ibid Annex [3] (emphasis added).
[157] Human Rights Committee, *Views: Communication No 2470/2014*, UN Doc CCPR/C/120/D/2470/2014 (9 October 2017); Human Rights Committee, *Views: Communication No 2512/2014*, UN Doc CCPR/C/119/D/2512/2014 (10 April 2017) [8.9]; Human Rights Committee, *Views: Communication No 2681/2015*, UN Doc CCPR/C/119/D/2681/2015 [7.9]; Human Rights Committee, *Views: Communication No 2770/2016*, UN Doc CCPR/C/121/D/2770/2016.
[158] *Secretary of State for the Home Department v ZAT* [2016] EWCA Civ 810 [92] ('*SSHD v ZAT*'). While *SSHD v ZAT* was grounded in article 8 of the ECHR, a qualified right, the ECtHR, in a subsequent and separate case, ruled that France's treatment of unaccompanied minors in the Jungle amounted to

The dilution of refugeehood's significance and search for some type of exceptionality is evident in the Court's insistence that only in an 'especially compelling case' can the right to family life override the Dublin System.[159] The Court stressed that all asylum seekers, including unaccompanied minors, must first make their application for asylum in the country in which they are located, and only once they can show that the system in that country is not working for them should they turn to the UK.[160] The Court acknowledged that there would be exceptions to this, but they would be extreme and rare cases.[161] The example the Court gave is a baby 'left behind in France when the door of a lorry bound for England closed after his mother got onto the lorry'.[162] The Court referred to an earlier judgment delivered by Lord Justice Laws to explain that the underlying rationale for this approach was because the Dublin System's purpose would be 'critically undermined' if 'it were seen as establishing little more than a presumption as to which State should deal with the claim'.[163] The UK and France have now entered into an agreement to prevent refugee crossings at the English Channel.[164]

This search for the exceptional asylum seeker or refugee is best encapsulated in the phrase 'peculiarly vulnerable', formulated by the United Kingdom Court of Appeal in its 2016 decision of *NA (Sudan) and MR (Iran) v Secretary of State for the Home Department* ('*NA (Sudan)*').[165] The case concerned a Sudanese and an Iranian asylum seeker resisting a Dublin System transfer to Italy. The Court acknowledged that all refugees are vulnerable 'simply by reason of the fact that they have had to leave their homes, in circumstances typically of great stress and often danger, and find themselves trying to make a new life, for an indefinite period and perhaps permanently, in a new country'.[166] However, certain refugees such as unaccompanied minors and pregnant women face additional difficulties and Lord Justice Underhill said, 'I will refer to such persons as "peculiarly vulnerable"'.[167] The United Kingdom Court of Appeal has also acknowledged that some asylum seekers have 'increased vulnerability'.[168] A similar concept has arisen in Dutch jurisprudence where courts have referred to child refugees as being 'extra vulnerable'.[169] In Denmark, there is the notion of extreme or particular vulnerability.[170]

---

a violation of article 3 of the ECHR, an absolute right: *Khan v France* (Application No12267/16 28, February 2019). The implications of the latter decision for the type of application made in *SSHD v ZAT* is an important question for future research.

[159] *SSHD v ZAT* (n 158) [8].   [160] Ibid [95].   [161] Ibid [95].   [162] Ibid [95].

[163] *R (CK (Afghanistan)) v Secretary of State for the Home Department* [2016] EWCA Civ 166 [31] cited in *SSHD v ZAT* (n 158) [92].

[164] 'UK and France Sign Deal to Make Channel Migrant Crossings "Unviable"' *The Guardian* (online 29 November 2020) <www.theguardian.com/uk-news/2020/nov/28/uk-and-france-sign-deal-to-make-channel-migrant-crossings-unviable?mc_cid=814c1ebeb1&mc_eid=677b225ed4>.

[165] [2016] EWCA Civ 1060 ('*NA (Sudan)*').   [166] Ibid [45].

[167] Ibid [45]. His Honour was referring to article 21 of Directive 2013/33/EU of the European Parliament and Council of 26 June 2013 Laying Down Standards for the Reception of Applicants for International Protection (Recast) [2013] OJ L 180/96-105/32, which provides that states are required to 'take into account the specific situation of vulnerable persons such as minors, unaccompanied minors, disabled people, elderly people, pregnant women, single parents with minor children, victims of human trafficking, persons with serious illnesses, persons with mental disorders and persons who have been subjected to torture, rape or other serious forms of psychological, physical or sexual violence'.

[168] *The Queen on the Application of: 1) HK (Iraq) HH (Iran) SK (Afghanistan) v SSHD* [2017] EWCA Civ 1871 [49] ('*HK, HH, SK v SSHD*').

[169] Court of the Hague, 18 July 2016, NL16.1221; Administrative Jurisdiction Division of the Council of State, 9 December 2016, ECLI:RVS:2016:3291.

[170] Refugee Appeal's Board Decision (Denmark) of 20 November 2017 (accepting that a transfer to Italy would not ordinarily be in breach of article 3 of the ECHR except in circumstances where the applicants were extremely vulnerable due to factors such as gender and age); Refugee Appeal's Board Decision

This trend of searching for peculiar, extreme or extra vulnerability that is emerging across protection from refuge claims in the European context reflects Timmer's observation that the ECtHR has developed a notion of 'compounded vulnerability', meaning people are vulnerable for a combination of reasons.[171] It also represents a change in the ways decision-makers understand vulnerability in protection from refuge scenarios. As discussed earlier, in *MSS v Belgium and Greece*, the ECtHR drew on the concept of vulnerability to highlight that asylum seekers and refugees are vulnerable because of their experiences (trying to eke out an existence in a hostile host country) and because the international community recognises that they are a group in need of special protection.[172] The Court recognised that vulnerability is a result of the position refugees are in (having lost the protection of their homeland and facing challenges in establishing a connection with a host state), rather than any innate or immutable qualities. This approach focuses on how legal, economic and cultural structures can produce vulnerability. However, in the move towards 'peculiar vulnerability' jurisprudence, decision-makers have shifted their focus to whether an individual is vulnerable due to personal factors such as health conditions and gender. This draws attention to the asylum seeker or refugee applicant's personal circumstances and obscures the ways in which host states produce vulnerability through, for example, not providing adequate housing or delays in conducting refugee status assessments. It means that decision-makers are more focussed on whether the refugee is exceptionally vulnerable in some way rather than examining the conditions in the place of resisted refuge. Next, I consider how European jurisprudence on externalisation has gone through a similar trajectory.

4.4.2   From Vulnerable Refugees to the 'Good' Refugee

In 2020, the ECtHR handed down its decision in *ND and NT v Spain*.[173] This was the first time the Court considered a challenge to externalisation policies since its 2012 decision in *Hirsi Jamaa v Italy*. *ND and NT v Spain* concerned two men who attempted to enter Melilla – Spain's enclave in Morocco. There are four land border crossings located along the fenced perimeter. The two applicants had attempted to enter the Spanish enclave by scaling the fence. While both managed to enter Melilla, Spanish officials immediately removed them to Moroccan territory without any identification procedure or opportunity to explain their personal circumstances. Both men eventually made their way to Spain. The first applicant applied for international protection but was refused, and the second applicant did not make an asylum claim. Nevertheless, the Court analysed the applicants' main argument (that their treatment amounted to collective expulsion within the meaning of article 4 of Protocol 4 to the ECHR) with reference to those intending to claim asylum.

This case can, in some ways, be seen as a reinforcement of refugee rights. The Court referred back to its earlier jurisprudence, including *Hirsi Jamaa v Italy*, to confirm that expulsions at the border fell within Spain's jurisdiction and hence triggered its ECHR obligations.[174] The judgment confirmed that 'expulsion' encompasses push backs and non-admission at the border,[175] and that article 4 of Protocol Number 4 requires that every

(Denmark) of 17 April 2018 (accepting that a transfer to Greece would not ordinarily be in breach of article 3 of the ECHR except in circumstances where the applicants were particularly vulnerable due to factors such as gender and age).
[171] Timmer (n 32) 153.   [172] *MSS v Belgium and Greece* (n 21) [230], [232], [233], [251].
[173] (Application Nos 8675/15 and 8697/15, 13 February 2020) ('*ND and NT v Spain*').
[174] Ibid [110]–[111].   [175] Ibid [187].

person has 'a genuine and effective possibility of submitting arguments against his or her expulsion'.[176] The Court also drew connections between article 4 of Protocol 4 and the Refugee Convention.[177]

However, the Court applied a principle outlined in earlier case law that there is no violation of article 4 of Protocol Number 4 if the applicant's own conduct was the reason for the lack of an individual decision on expulsion.[178] The applicants were ultimately unsuccessful because the Court deemed that there were no cogent reasons for them not attempting to seek asylum from Spain in an authorised manner such as at the land borders between Morocco and the Spanish enclave and nearby Spanish embassies.[179]

The difference between *ND and NT v Spain* and earlier ECtHR protection from refuge decisions, in particular *MSS v Belgium and Greece* and *Hirsi Jamaa v Italy*, is that the Court did not put itself in the place of an asylum seeker in assessing the evidence. As already outlined, in *MSS v Belgium and Greece*, the Court outlined why, reflecting on the experiences and position of asylum seekers in Greece, the applicant could not have complied with the formalities Greece imposed on him. In *ND and NT v Spain*, the Court did not adopt the same approach in assessing why the applicants did not attempt to claim protection at a land border or nearby embassy. This information was available from the UNHCR's and Council of Europe's Commissioner for Human Rights' interventions. Both interveners submitted that sub-Saharan Africans were prevented from reaching the land border crossings.[180] It may be true that Spain was not responsible for this state of affairs[181] but the relevant question was whether there were cogent reasons for the applicants not attempting to use these other procedures. The Court made no attempt to understand why, from the perspective of asylum seekers, there were valid reasons for not attempting a land border crossing. Further, the Court did not question whether the applicants had access to information about other ways to apply for asylum (such as in nearby embassies) and whether the information was clear and comprehensible.

In making no attempt to view the situation from the perspective of an asylum seeker, the Court framed the situation as a binary of rational choice and deviancy.[182] By this I mean that, similar to the construct of the 'reasonable person' in the common law, the Court's expectation was that the applicants would make the rational and lawful choice when

---

[176] Ibid [198].   [177] Ibid [188]   [178] Ibid [200].

[179] Ibid [213–222], [227]–[228], [231]. However, see *MN and Others v Belgium* (Application No 3599/18, 5 March 2020) in which the ECtHR ruled that a Syrian family that travelled to the Belgium embassy in Lebanon did not come within Belgium's jurisdiction: [125]. This case is outside the scope of this book. It is not a protection from refuge case because the applicants were seeking protection from their country of origin, returned to Syria after lodging their visa application and raised no issues with respect to protection in Lebanon (see [10]). In ruling against the applicants on jurisdiction, the Court may have shut the door on future claims in which refugees who are not safe in their host country attempt to trigger protection obligations under the ECHR by lodging visa applications in embassies of European countries. For a discussion, see Moritz Baumgärtel, 'Reaching the Dead End: M.N. and Others and the Question of Humanitarian Visas' (7 May 2020) Strasbourg Observers <https://strasbourgobservers.com/2020/05/07/reaching-the-dead-end-m-n-and-others-and-the-question-of-humanitarian-visas/>. The Court of Justice of the European Union has also determined a case with a very similar factual scenario, which is briefly discussed in Chapter 5: *X and X v État belge* (C-638/16 PPU, 7 March 2017).

[180] *ND and NT v Spain* (n 173) [155].   [181] The Court in *ND and NT v Spain* (n 173) stressed this: [221].

[182] In making this point I borrow from Pickering's analysis of Australian refugee policy in which she argues that Australia's border protection laws construct refugees in a similar way to the 'rational man' in liberal philosophy who has full control over his actions and will mould his behaviour in response to criminal sanctions: Sharon Pickering, *Refugees and State Crime* (Federation Press, 2005) 90.

deciding the method they used to claim asylum. By failing to engage with the reasons why asylum seekers may not follow what states deem to be legitimate methods for claiming asylum, this judgment frames asylum seeking in a manner that echoes states' border control narratives.

A similar approach can be observed in *Asady and Others v Slovakia*.[183] In this 2020 decision, the ECtHR drew on *ND and NT v Spain* in ruling that there had been no breach of article 4 of Protocol Number 4 when Slovakia returned the applicants, nineteen Afghanis, to Ukraine. The key issue was whether the applicants had a genuine and effective opportunity to submit arguments against their expulsion.[184] The applicants were interviewed by Slovakian authorities but there was conflicting evidence as to whether the applicants claimed asylum in these interviews. The Court ruled that the ten-minute interviews carried out by police officers late at night and in the early hours of the morning without the applicants having access to legal advice constituted a genuine and effective opportunity to submit arguments against their expulsion.[185] Similar to *ND and NT v Spain*, the Court did not put itself in the position of the applicants in order to understand why they may not have mentioned a claim for asylum in the interview. The reasons were outlined in the applicants' submissions, in particular that they did not have access to legal assistance or the UNHCR, did not have any information about asylum[186] and 'were in a vulnerable position and unable to collect evidence regarding the exact course of events'.[187] These arguments mirror studies of the reasons why many asylum seekers do not mention persecution or claim protection in an initial interview.[188] In *Asady and Others v Slovakia*, the applicants were expected to conform to what a good refugee would do, which is to clearly articulate an asylum claim at the first opportunity. Next, I explain the consequences of this judicial disengagement with the experiences of asylum seeking.

4.4.3   Fragmented and Rudimentary Refuge

Scholars have already identified the backlash with respect to judicial treatment of asylum seekers' human rights claims in the European context and have attributed it to the higher number of asylum seekers in Europe as a result of the Syrian conflict.[189] What remains unidentified and unexamined is the shift towards identifying the 'peculiarly vulnerable' or 'good' refugee. I suggest that this has transformed judicial conceptualisations of the nature

---

[183] (Application No 24917/15, 24 March 2020) ('*Asady and others v Slovakia*'). Also see *MS v Slovakia and Ukraine* (Application No 17189/11, 11 June 2020), in which the Court ruled, among other issues, that the applicant's argument that Slovakia was in breach of articles 3 and 13 of the ECHR by returning him to the Ukraine was inadmissible: [91]. There was contested evidence as to whether the applicant, an Afghani asylum seeker, requested international protection from the Slovakian authorities. The Court held that the applicant was 'unable to establish to the required standard of proof that the applicant brought any of his personal concerns as to the risk of return to Ukraine or Afghanistan to the attention of the Slovakian authorities, even though he had an opportunity to do so': [89].

[184] *Asady and others v Slovakia* (n 183) [65].   [185] Ibid [71].   [186] Ibid [48].   [187] Ibid [50].

[188] See, e.g., Diana Bögner, Chris Brewin and Jane Herlihy, 'Refugees' Experience of Home Office Interviews: A Qualitative Study on the Disclosure of Sensitive Personal Information' (2010) 36(3) *Journal of Ethnic and Migration Studies* 519; Philip Spinhoven, Tammy Bean and Liesbeth Eurelings-Bontekoe, 'Inconsistencies in the Self-Report of Traumatic Experiences by Unaccompanied Refugee Minors' (2006) 19(5) *Journal of Traumatic Stress* 663.

[189] Cathryn Costello and Itamar Mann, 'Border Justice: Migration and Accountability for Human Rights Violations' (2020) 21 *German Law Journal* 311, 320.

of refuge from a remedy and provision of a legal status to a commodity. Similar to the 'hallmark of the welfare state' where benefits are extended to 'the most vulnerable',[190] decision-makers have approached refuge as if it is a scarce resource that they should apportion on a needs basis and only to those who follow the proper procedures.

While it is well accepted that factors such as gender, age, family responsibilities and disability exacerbate protection risks, conceiving of refuge as a commodity to be distributed to the neediest is at odds with the idea of refuge in refugee law. Hathaway explains that, in formulating the refugee definition, the Refugee Convention's drafters 'were at pains to carefully limit the beneficiary class' and excluded 'persons who have yet to leave their own country, who cannot link their predicament to civil or political status, who already benefit from surrogate national or international protection, or who are found not to deserve protection'.[191] However, outside of these exclusions, refugees should be 'conceived as a generic class, all members of which are *equally worthy of protection*'.[192]

Expecting refugees to claim asylum in the 'right' way is also antithetical to the Refugee Convention. The drafters acknowledged that refugees are often not in a position to comply with legal requirements for entry.[193] Article 31(1) of the Refugee Convention provides that states shall not impose penalties on refugees on account of their illegal entry and presence. Denying a refugee access to an asylum procedure on account of not having used the proper channels for entry can be considered a penalty and may be in breach of the Refugee Convention.[194] While article 31(1) requires refugees to present themselves without delay to authorities and show good cause for their illegal entry or presence, there is no requirement that they immediately claim asylum. Hathaway argues that entrusting determination of asylum claims to officials such as border guards or police officers may be in violation of *non-refoulement*.[195] They are often not properly trained in asylum claims and may not carry out their duties thoroughly and reliably. They may resort to formalistic approaches such as whether the person uses precise words or phrases such as 'asylum' or 'international protection'.

What has also been lost in the aforementioned changes in adjudicative reasoning is the use of human rights law as a medium through which to elucidate refuge's objectives. This is most starkly seen in the adoption of the conditions in Greece as a litmus test for conditions that place a complete bar on Dublin System transfers. At no stage in its judgment in *MSS v Belgium and Greece* did the ECtHR specify that, to trigger article 3 protection, asylum seekers must establish that there is manifestly inadequate housing available in the prospective host state. Rather, the Court considered whether the particular situation in which the applicant found himself (being homeless with no means of providing for himself) amounted to inhuman and degrading treatment and the applicant's position as an asylum seeker was crucial to the Court's decision. This categorical reasoning enabled the Court to adopt a purposive approach to refuge through the prism of article 3 and engage with its restorative and regenerative functions. However, in later decisions when there is no longer a focus on refugeehood, courts ask whether the conditions in the host country are comparable to Greece. This neuters the potential for decision-makers to use human rights instruments to adopt a purposive approach to refuge. While there is a recognition in many domestic

[190] Yeheskel Hasenfeld and Eve Garrow, 'Non-Profit Human Service Organizations, Social Rights, and Advocacy in a Neoliberal Welfare State' (2012) 86(2) *Social Service Review* 295.
[191] Hathaway (2005) (n 57) 448.   [192] Ibid 239 (emphasis added).   [193] Ibid 405–6.   [194] Ibid 408–12.
[195] Ibid 319–20.

decisions that whether a transfer would be in breach of article 3 of the ECHR is a two-stage test (first, whether the conditions impose a general ban on all transfers and, if not, whether the applicant's special circumstances would raise a real risk of exposure to inhuman and degrading treatment),[196] decision-makers rarely consider the vulnerabilities associated with refugeehood like the ECtHR did in *MSS v Belgium and Greece*. This means that there is no longer an engagement with refuge's restorative, regenerative and palliative functions.

As a result, the idea of refuge reflected in these later decisions is a rudimentary one. By using the conditions in Greece as the relevant comparator, the ECtHR and domestic courts have set the threshold for what is deemed to be inadequate refuge as 'the most extreme poverty . . . on a large scale' and being left 'without any means of subsistence'.[197] The ECtHR has never used the right to be free from inhuman and degrading treatment as a platform to evaluate whether a host state complies with all of its obligations towards refugees. Nevertheless, homelessness, extreme poverty and having absolutely no means of subsistence are very high thresholds for what can be deemed an inadequate protection environment for refugees and asylum seekers. The reduction in the standard for what is understood to constitute adequate refuge is also evident in the Human Rights Committee's jurisprudence. In its 2015 view (*Jasin v Denmark*), the Committee suggested that article 7 of the ICCPR could be triggered when the prospective host state does not comply with its international protection obligations to refugees. However, in its 2016 view (*RAA and ZM v Denmark*), the Committee narrowed the circumstances to situations where refugees cannot provide for themselves or will not be protected from physical violence.[198]

The loss of a purposive approach fractures and truncates the concept of refuge. In earlier jurisprudence, there is consideration of refuge's temporality and the ways it should enable refugees to build a better future and heal from past trauma. In later decisions, there is no consideration of a refugee's future and past. For example, in *Tarakhel v Switzerland*, the ECtHR limited its focus to the conditions the asylum-seeking family would face on arrival or shortly after arrival.[199] It was satisfied that Italy would immediately take charge of them and concentrated only on the conditions in Italian reception centres. It did not consider the situation the family would be in once they left the centre. This is despite evidence that the situation for refugees in Italy often significantly deteriorates after they are forced to leave reception centres.[200] They are not provided with accommodation or any assistance with entry into the workforce and many become homeless.[201] This preludes a consideration of the enduring relationship between the prospective host state and refugee. By focussing only on the circumstances immediately on arrival, the ECtHR also partially removed the place of refuge (Italy) from the judicial lens. Further, by declaring that Switzerland was in breach of article 3 for not having obtained guarantees from Italy that the family would be kept

---

[196] See *HK, HH, SK v SSHD* (n 168) [45]–[51]; Federal Constitutional Court of Germany, 29 August 2017, 2 BVR 863/17.

[197] *Tarakhel v Switzerland* (n 139) [117]. See also *Khaled v Secretary of State for the Home Department No 1* [2016] EWHC 857 [116] ('*Khaled v SSHD No 1*') in which the United Kingdom High Court of Justice stated that, with respect to lack of social security and access to employment, the relevant standard for a breach of article 3 was that established in *MSS v Belgium and Greece* (n 21), where 'asylum seekers are left without any form of support' and live in a 'situation of extreme poverty'.

[198] *RAA and ZM v Denmark* (n 152) [7.8].   [199] *Tarakhel v Switzerland* (n 139) [80].

[200] Médecins Sans Frontières, *Informal Settlements: Social Marginality, Obstacles to Access to Healthcare and Basic Needs for Migrants, Asylum Seekers and Refugees* (2018) 10–11 <www.msf.org/sites/msf.org/files/out_of_sight_def.pdf>.

[201] Ibid 14.

together and taken charge of in a manner adapted to the age of the children,[202] the Court indicated that transfers would be acceptable if guarantees were obtained. Thus, Switzerland only temporarily suspended transfers until Italy provided the requisite guarantees.[203] In subsequent cases, courts have relied on bilateral guarantees to declare a transfer is compatible with human rights obligations despite evidence of serious problems in the receiving state's asylum system.[204]

Another example of how a lack of a purposive approach obscures consideration of refugees' futures and a full examination of the place of refuge is seen in the United Kingdom Court of Appeal's judgment in NA (Sudan). The Court was satisfied that the applicant, who had been raped and rendered homeless in Italy, could return without a real risk of inhuman and degrading treatment. This was because she would be assisted by NGOs in the airport on her return to Italy that would assist in finding her accommodation.[205] Limiting the enquiry in this manner is problematic, because a refugee relies on the host state's surrogate protection until they find a durable solution and the host state's obligations to the refugee should increase the longer the refugee remains in the host state.[206] By only examining the situation immediately on or shortly after arrival, hope for a more promising future is diminished and the place of refuge remains largely out of judicial view.

In addition, concentrating on NGO assistance without consideration of the protection the Italian state would provide diminishes judicial understandings of refuge. As noted in Chapter 2, there is scholarship on the important roles NGOs play in refugee protection, but a recognition that it is states that owe protection obligations and they cannot delegate these duties to international organisations and NGOs.[207] By focussing on NGO assistance, the Court positions refuge not as a state duty or obligation but rather an act of discretion and benevolence.

A further example of how refuge's temporality is curtailed can be observed in the United Kingdom Court of Appeal's reversal of the Upper Tribunal's decision on the right to family life.[208] The Court of Appeal obscured refuge's palliative function through its insistence that article 8 of the ECHR can only be successfully invoked in rare circumstances such as a child being left behind when the door of a lorry closes just before it departs.[209] This displaced the Tribunal's focus on the ways family reunification can address the pain and suffering associated with persecution and displacement and severed consideration of the ways refuge should provide a space to heal from past trauma.

The shift in decision-makers' conceptualisation of refuge diminishes human rights law's potency with respect to challenging states' interests in constraining refugees' movements. What is apparent in the jurisprudence's trajectory is that human rights law first proved somewhat robust in circumventing the Dublin System and externalisation practices.

---

[202] Tarakhel v Switzerland (n 139) 52.   [203] Baumgärtel (n 14) 66.

[204] See, e.g., Applicant A v Finnish Immigration Authorities, Supreme Administrative Court, KHO: 4219: 2020, 13 November 2020.

[205] NA (Sudan) (n 165) [213]–[219].   [206] Hathaway (2005) (n 57) 154.

[207] Michelle Foster, 'Protection Elsewhere: The Legal Implications of Requiring Refugees to Seek Protection in Another State' (2007) 28 Michigan Journal of International Law 223, 237. Schultz accepts that non-state actors can provide protection but only in circumstances where they essentially have the powers and responsibility of a state: Jessica Schultz, The Internal Protection Alternative in Refugee Law (Brill, 2019) 210.

[208] SSHD v ZAT (n 158).   [209] Ibid [95].

However, decision-making bodies have now reined in the force of human rights law and only permit it to impinge on states' interests in limited and exceptional circumstances. It means that only those whom decision-makers deem to be 'peculiarly vulnerable' or 'compliant' refugees can use court processes to continue their search for refuge. Nevertheless, the 'peculiarly vulnerable' development in the jurisprudence may provide a space in which women, parents, children and refugees with disabilities are successfully able to use human rights law in protection from refuge challenges. This is the question I turn to next.

4.5   The Peculiarly Vulnerable Refugee

There are some domestic decisions where a person was able to successfully challenge a transfer on the grounds that they were peculiarly or extra vulnerable due to factors associated with gender,[210] age[211] or having a disability or serious health condition.[212] However, many decision-makers in the European context do not approach questions of gender and intersectionality in a thoughtful or sophisticated manner. In Section 4.5.1, I show that, in some cases, decision-makers simply do not consider the ways factors such as age, gender and disability can exacerbate protection risks. In Section 4.5.2, I argue that, in cases where decision-makers do turn their minds to these questions, they often do so in a perfunctory way. This further diminishes the potential to use human rights law to engage with the concept of refuge and enable refugees from more marginalised backgrounds to continue their journeys.

---

[210]   See Refugee Appeals Board (Denmark) Decision of 30 November 2017. The Board accepted that, while the reception conditions in Italy did not generally present a real risk of inhuman and degrading treatment, the applicant was extremely vulnerable because she was a single mother with two young children, suffered from post-traumatic stress disorder and had previously stayed in Italy, where she was homeless and a victim of sexual assault. The Board ruled that, due to her particular circumstances, it would be a violation or article 3 of the ECHR to send her to Italy. See also Administrative Tribunal of Toulouse, 9 November 2018, No 1805185, in which the Tribunal determined that a single female asylum seeker could not be transferred to Italy pursuant to the Dublin System. That she had previously been a victim of a prostitution network in Italy was crucial to the decision.

[211]   Migration Court of Appeal (Sweden), 1 July 2016, UM 1859–16 (the Court held that the reception conditions in Hungary do not amount to a violation of article 3 of the ECHR but two of the asylum seeking applicants in the case were children and it was not in their best interests to send them to Hungary pursuant to the Dublin System); Court of the Hague, 16 October 2015, JV 2015/343 (the Court was not satisfied that sending asylum seekers to Hungary would amount to a violation of article 3 of the ECHR but the applicant was successful in this case because she had two young children and there was no guarantee from Hungary that they would not be placed in overcrowded accommodation with unacceptable living conditions).

[212]   Braunschweig Administrative Court decision of 12 October 2016, 5 A 332/15 (a male asylum seeker successfully challenged a Dublin System transfer from Germany to Italy on the grounds that it would be a violation or article 3 ECHR – the fact that he was suffering from tuberculosis and Hepatitis B was crucial to the decision); Constitutional Court of Austria decision of 23 September 2016, E 1200/2016-12 (a male asylum seeker successfully challenged a Dublin System transfer from Austria to Italy on the grounds that it would be a violation of article 3 of the ECHR – crucial to the Court's reasoning was that the applicant was not a young and healthy man but a 58-year-old suffering from Parkinson's disease); Administrative Court of Nantes, 24 July 2015, No 1506136 (the Court ruled that the applicant could not be transferred to Italy and part of the judgment refers to the applicant having contracted Hepatitis B and that he had previously been required to live in unsanitary conditions in Italy).

4.5.1   Gender-blind Decisions

There are a number of instances where the ECtHR wholly ignores gender in its assessment as to whether a transfer pursuant to the Dublin System would be in breach of article 3 of the ECHR. For example, in 2013, the Court considered a case brought by a Somali woman granted refugee status in Italy.[213] She became pregnant while in Italy after being raped. She travelled to the Netherlands and had another child there. She resisted being transferred to Italy on the grounds that it would be a breach of article 3, but the Court ruled her case inadmissible on the grounds that it was manifestly ill-founded.[214] In 2015, the Court handed down a judgment in a case concerning an Eritrean woman who sought asylum in Italy and was granted residence, but 'was not provided with (money for) food or medical assistance, and was forced to live on the street'.[215] She travelled to the Netherlands in 2009, became pregnant and was subsequently diagnosed with HIV. The Court held that transferring the applicant and her five-year-old daughter to Italy would not be in breach of article 3 of the ECHR.

In neither of these cases did the Court consider whether Italy had adequate protection policies for single mothers or those who have previously experienced sexual violence or have a significant health condition. Further, in ignoring the risks of sexual violence for female asylum seekers, the ECtHR disregarded its own jurisprudence. The Court has held on a number of occasions that rape can amount to inhuman and degrading treatment[216] and torture,[217] and failure by the relevant authorities to investigate properly allegations of sexual violence can amount to a breach of article 3 of the ECHR.[218] In addition, in these and other cases regarding the transfer of families with children to Italy, the ECtHR held that it was satisfied that appropriate accommodation would be provided without enquiring as to the children's needs.[219]

Similarly, in a 2019 view concerning a Syrian asylum seeker family resisting a Dublin System transfer from Austria to Bulgaria, the Human Rights Committee found the complaint inadmissible without considering the mother's health condition and the children's best interests.[220] The Committee decided that the complaint was inadmissible because the authors could not substantiate their claims that the reception conditions in Bulgaria were incompatible with article 7 of the ICCPR.[221] The dissenting member said that the Committee failed to take into account the mother's health condition (she was suffering

---

[213] *Samsam Mohammed Hussein v The Netherlands and Italy* (Application No 27725/10, 2 April 2013) ('*Samsam Mohammed Hussein v The Netherlands and Italy*').

[214] The reason is that she was given subsidiary protection in Italy and access to reception facilities. Dembour highlights that this is arguably no different from the applicant in *MSS v Belgium and Greece* (n 21) who was in possession of a pink card in Greece and thus theoretically entitled to benefits and services granted to refugees in Greece: Dembour (n 13) 423.

[215] *ATH v The Netherlands* (Application No 54000/11, 10 December 2015) [4] ('*ATH v The Netherlands*').

[216] *Cyprus v Turkey* (1982) 4 EHRR 482; *E v UK* (Application No 33218/96, 26 November 2002) [89].

[217] *Aydin v Turkey* (1998) 25 EHRR 251.

[218] See, e.g., *IG v Moldova* (Application No 53519/07, 15 May 2012); *MA v Slovenia* (Application No 3400/07, 15 January 2015); *PM v Bulgaria* (Application No 49669/07, 24 January 2012); *SZ v Bulgaria* (Application No 29263/12, 3 March 2015).

[219] *ATH v The Netherlands* (n 215); *SMH v The Netherlands* (Application No 5868/13, 9 June 2016); *Samsam Mohammed Hussein v The Netherlands and Italy* (n 213).

[220] Human Rights Committee, *Views: Communication No 2956/2017*, UN Doc CCPR/C/127/D/2956/2017 (16 December 2019).

[221] Ibid [11].

from depression due to her experiences on the journey from her homeland to Austria) and the children's best interests (they did not receive adequate food or healthcare in Bulgaria and had no access to education).[222] Nevertheless, there are cases where decision-makers have explicitly considered gender and other intersectional factors and I turn to this next.

4.5.2 Notional Consideration of Gender, Childhood and Disability

In cases where decision-makers do take account of gender, age and disability, most do so only superficially. One example is the United Kingdom Court of Appeal's judgment in *NA (Sudan)*. The Court accepted that NA was 'peculiarly vulnerable' because she was raped while in Italy, had an overwhelming fear of being returned to the country in which she had been the victim of sexual violence, had no family to provide support and no ability to seek other forms of support.[223] However, it concluded that the assistance provided by NGOs at the airport would alleviate these vulnerabilities without enquiring into the nature and level of assistance that they would provide beyond assistance with finding accommodation.[224]

With respect to children's protection from refuge claims, the ECtHR in *Tarakhel v Switzerland* acknowledged that children are 'extremely vulnerable' and 'have specific needs that are related in particular to their age and lack of independence, but also to their asylum-seeker status'.[225] It also referred to obligations in the CRC to take appropriate measures to ensure that children seeking asylum receive appropriate attention.[226] Costello and Mouzourakis argue that the Court had the opportunity to develop this point further by referring to the principle of best interests of the child but declined to do so.[227] However, in cases involving minors post-*Tarakhel v Switzerland*, the Court has taken a much more cursory approach to children's protection needs. In a case that concerned an adult Eritrean refugee with children resisting return to Italy, the ECtHR noted that her status as a single parent meant that she belonged to a 'particularly underprivileged and vulnerable population group in need of special protection'.[228] The Court held that returning her to Italy would not expose her to a real risk of inhuman and degrading treatment, because she would have 'access to the available resources in Italy for an asylum-seeking single mother with a minor child'.[229] However, there was no examination of whether these resources would be adequate and appropriate for her children. In particular, there was no consideration of the children's ages or genders or any other factors that may be relevant to determining whether the resources available were appropriate.

Further, when considering additional vulnerabilities, decision-makers often fail to take into account the ways they intersect with a person's position as an asylum seeker or refugee. This is apparent in *AS v Switzerland*,[230] a case brought by a Syrian asylum seeker who resisted Switzerland's attempt to transfer him to Italy pursuant to the Dublin System. He

---

[222] Ibid.   [223] *NA (Sudan)* (n 165) [213].   [224] Ibid [213]–[219].
[225] *Tarakhel v Switzerland* (n 139) [99].   [226] Ibid [99].
[227] Cathryn Costello and Minos Mouzourakis, 'Reflections on Reading Tarakhel: Is "How Bad Is Bad Enough" Good Enough?' (2014) 10 *Asiel en Migrantenrecht* 404, 408.
[228] *JA v The Netherlands* (Application No 21459/14, 26 November 2015) [28].   [229] Ibid [32].
[230] (Application No 39350/13, 30 June 2015) ('*AS v Switzerland*'). Also see *AM v Switzerland* (Application No 37466/13, 3 November 2015), which concerned the transfer of an asylum seeker from Switzerland to Italy. He claimed that he suffered from post-traumatic stress disorder and would be at risk of suicide if returned to Italy. The Court deemed the case inadmissible on the grounds that the facts were indistinguishable from *AS v Switzerland*.

suffered from significant mental and physical health conditions caused by the torture and trauma he experienced in Syria and, therefore, could be considered to have a disability. The applicant had two sisters in Switzerland and submitted that by being able to spend time with them he had 'regained a certain emotional stability in his life'.[231] He argued that, if forced to return to Italy, he would have no family to care for him and this would aggravate his mental health problems.

This case involved not only Dublin System jurisprudence but also case law relating to breaches of article 3 of the ECHR in situations of the expulsion of seriously ill persons.[232] In his submissions, the applicant attempted to highlight the intersections between his health conditions and his situation as an asylum seeker. He drew specifically on the reasoning in *MSS v Belgium and Greece* and argued that, as an asylum seeker, he belonged to 'a particularly vulnerable group in need of special protection'.[233] The ECtHR acknowledged that, in *MSS v Belgium and Greece*, 'considerable importance' was attached to 'the applicant's status as an asylum-seeker and, as such, a member of a particularly underprivileged and vulnerable population group in need of special protection'.[234] However, the Court stressed that the expulsion of a seriously ill person would only breach article 3 in rare cases[235] and the applicant's case did 'not disclose very exceptional circumstances'.[236] In coming to this conclusion, the Court did not consider the intersections between having a disability and being an asylum seeker; in particular, that his mental and physical health conditions were caused by the persecution he suffered in Syria.

Further, in justifying the high threshold in healthcare cases, the Court did not demonstrate an appreciation of the distinction between expelling a person to their home country and expelling an asylum seeker to an alternative place of refuge; the Court even used the phrase 'country of origin'. The Court explained that '[a]dvances in medical science, together with social and economic differences between countries, entail that the level of treatment available in the Contracting State and the *country of origin* may vary considerably', but 'Article 3 does not place an obligation on the Contracting State to alleviate such disparities through the provision of free and unlimited health care to all aliens without a right to stay within its jurisdiction'.[237]

---

[231] *AS v Switzerland* (n 230) [7].

[232] *N v UK* [2008] III Eur Court HR 227 ('*N v UK*'); *D v the UK* [1997] 24 EHRR 423 ('*D v UK*').

[233] *AS v Switzerland* (n 230) [18].   [234] Ibid [29].

[235] *N v UK* (n 232); *D v the UK* (n 232). The ECtHR has subsequently clarified its approach to when expulsion of seriously ill persons will expose a person to inhuman and degrading treatment within the meaning of article 3 of the ECHR. It still adopts the test established in *N v UK* (n 232) that article 3 will only be triggered by expulsion of seriously ill persons in exceptional circumstances but has clarified that this includes not only imminent risk of death but also situations where the applicant 'would face a real risk, on account of the absence of appropriate treatment in the receiving country or the lack of access to such treatment, of being exposed to serious, rapid and irreversible decline in his or her state of health resulting in intense suffering or a significant reduction of life expectancy': *Paposhvili v Belgium* (Application No. 41738/10, 13 December 2016) [183]. See *AM (Zimbabwe) and Hamzeh Mamoun Naji Abu Nowar v Secretary of State for the Home Department* [2018] EWCA Civ 64 [39] in which the England and Wales Court of Appeal stated that *Paposhvili* 'only intended to make a very modest extension of the protection under Article 3 in medical cases'.

[236] *AS v Switzerland* (n 230) [51].

[237] Ibid [31] (emphasis added). Another example is the United Kingdom High Court of Justice's decision in *Khaled v SSHD No 1* (n 197) in which five male asylum seekers unsuccessfully challenged their Dublin System transfer from the UK to Bulgaria. The Court dismissed the argument that the transfer would be a violation of article 3 of the ECHR for three of the applicants who had been victims of torture on the

In dismissing the applicant's argument that removal to Italy would be a violation of article 8 of the ECHR, the Court drew on its previous jurisprudence that, for article 8 to be triggered between adult siblings, the applicants need to demonstrate additional elements of dependence.[238] It also referred to previous jurisprudence which provides that only in exceptional circumstances will article 8 prevent removal when the family life was created at a time the applicant knew their immigration status was precarious.[239] The Court did not consider whether the applicant as an asylum seeker with significant health conditions could demonstrate 'additional elements of dependence' on his sisters or exceptional circumstances. The Court ruled that Switzerland's interest in controlling immigration outweighed the applicant's interests in establishing family life in Switzerland.[240]

With respect to the applicant's physical and mental impairments, the Court's reasoning is more akin to what Motz describes as a medical as opposed to a social and human rights-based approach to judicial reasoning on disabilities in the refugee context (focussing on correcting the impairment through medical treatment as opposed to changing structural barriers that prevent persons with disabilities from leading full and rewarding lives).[241] The Court focussed on the medical treatment the applicant needed and highlighted that this would be available in Italy.[242] The applicant's submissions, however, did not stress the lack of medical care in Italy but instead the crucial role his sisters played in his recovery.[243] The Court did not consider, in the context of article 3 or article 8, the significance of the care his sisters provided and that by being removed to Italy he would no longer benefit from their support.[244] This frames persons with disabilities as predominately being in need of drugs to treat their conditions. It fails to recognise that having a disability is not having a physical, mental, intellectual or sensory impairment, but rather disability arises out of interactions between these impairments and various barriers imposed by legal, physical and social environments.[245]

Not only do decision-makers' desultory approaches to the ways age, gender and disability exacerbate protection risks make it more difficult for refugees to draw on human rights law to challenge Dublin System transfers, they further disengage decision-makers from the concept of refuge. These cases presented an opportunity for the respective courts to delineate ideas about the function and nature of refuge for children, single parents, those who have experienced sexual violence and people with disabilities. Unlike in decisions discussed earlier in this chapter, where decision-makers considered the ways these factors interact with irreducible experiences of refugeehood, in these judgments there is no or only nominal consideration of these intersections. For example, the Court's failure in *A S v*

---

grounds that there was evidence that asylum seekers in Bulgaria were entitled to the same healthcare as Bulgarian nationals: [122]. This was upheld on appeal: *HK, HH, SK v SSHD* (n 168). For another example of a cursory consideration of arguments relating to an asylum seeker's mental health conditions and previous experiences of torture see *Pour, Hisari and Ghulama v SSHD* [2016] EWHC 401 [187]–[196].

[238] *FN v UK* (Application No 3202/09, 17 September 2013) cited in *AS v Switzerland* (n 230) at [49].

[239] *Jeunesse v The Netherlands* (Application No 12738/10, 4 December 2012) cited in *AS v Switzerland* (n 230) at [48].

[240] *AS v Switzerland* (n 230) [50]. The Court took a similar approach in a subsequent case concerning a Dublin System transfer of two asylum seekers from Switzerland to Italy: *ZH and RH v Switzerland* (Application No 60119/12, 8 December 2015).

[241] Motz 'The Persecution of Disabled Persons' (n 84) 141.   [242] *AS v Switzerland* (n 230) [36].

[243] Ibid [18]–[20], [41].   [244] Ibid [36], [51].

[245] This is the definition of disability in article 1 of the CRPD.

Switzerland to recognise the compounding effect of being an asylum seeker on a person's mental health condition means that there was no consideration of refuge's palliative function: that it should provide a space in which refugees can heal from past trauma and that this is often facilitated through family reunification.

4.6 Conclusion

This chapter continued my analysis of how decision-makers determine protection from refuge claims grounded in human rights arguments by examining claims made in the European context and drawing comparisons with Kenyan jurisprudence. In Chapters 3 and 4, looking across international, supranational and domestic decision-making bodies and claims based in international, regional and domestic human rights and refugee law, I have identified three different judicial approaches: categorical, blended categorical and experiential, and exceptionality reasoning. When decision-makers employ categorical or blended categorical and experiential reasoning, they engage with the concept of refuge in a purposive manner. I have suggested that, through the prism of human and refugee rights, decision-makers engage with refuge's restorative, regenerative and palliative functions. They also use human rights law as a medium to recognise the nature of refuge as a remedy, legal status and process. Further, these approaches encompass the ways refuge must respond to refugees of different ages and genders as well as refugees with family responsibilities and disabilities. This type of reasoning also lends potency to human rights arguments when pitted against states' containment policies. They provide human rights grounds for large numbers of refugees to be able to continue their quests for refuge.

However, I have also argued that these decision-making bodies have shifted to finding the exemplary or exceptional refugee. Refugeehood is given less emphasis and the protection from refuge litigant often must establish why they are 'good' refugees or acutely vulnerable. Understandings of vulnerability have transitioned from structural (how host states' policies produce vulnerability) to personal (the traits an individual has that may render them vulnerable). This narrows the concept of refuge to minimalist ideas of refugee protection and truncates refuge's temporality – in particular, the way it addresses refugees' future and past. It usurps refuge's remedial nature and transforms it into a commodity to be given to the most vulnerable or a reward to be bestowed on the most deserving. This approach thwarts the potential for human and refugee rights to dismantle containment policies, because it assesses the application of such policies to individual refugees on a case-by-case basis.

The case law's trajectory indicates a shift from a human rights approach to protection from refuge scenarios to one more focussed on containment (albeit still cloaked in human rights language). My analysis indicates that these challenges are most powerful when decision-makers conceptualise the figure of the refugee as a metaphysical one based on the irreducible experiences of refugeehood. The refugee litigant's individual circumstances can inform this abstract notion of refugeehood, but only to demonstrate the particular ways their rights would be infringed – not to make distinctions between refugees based on concepts such as vulnerability or self-sufficiency. Requiring refugees to establish that they are exceptional in some way dilutes the concept of refuge and diminishes the force of rights arguments in contests with state's justifications for containment policies. It enables only particular refugees to turn to courts to continue their quest for refuge and often does not assist those who face the greatest challenges in travelling in search of sanctuary.

5

Direct Challenges to Regional Containment Instruments

5.1 Introduction

'The journey was worth it. I'm happy I'm here. To go back, I lose my life'.[1] Seidu Mohammed, a Ghanaian refugee, spoke these words after he had all of his fingers amputated. He had walked across the border from the US to Canada in December 2016 in freezing conditions, suffered severe frostbite and almost died. The US had refused to hear his asylum claim and he crossed into Canada in a remote area to avoid the operation of an agreement between the two countries pursuant to which Canada could have returned him to the US.[2] In this chapter, I examine legal challenges to this and other bilateral or regional containment instruments. All of the refugee litigants are, similar to Seidu Mohammad, trying to escape from one country to another in their search for refuge, but in doing so confront state mechanisms designed to prevent or disrupt these journeys. However, unlike the refugee litigants in Chapter 4, the protection from refuge claimants discussed in this chapter are directly challenging these instruments' validity or operation.

This chapter provides different insights on the questions posed in this book. In the previous two chapters, I investigated how decision-makers approach protection from refuge claims grounded in human and refugee rights. The arguments that refugee litigants plead in the cases discussed in this chapter are more wide-ranging. Human and refugee rights are present, but they are not the focal point. The arguments the litigants raise traverse many areas of domestic, regional and international law, and courts must assess which aspects of these bodies of law are relevant in determining the claim. Another contentious issue is whether these legal frameworks permit courts to pass judgment on another state's laws and policies. The third difference is that, unlike the previous two chapters where decision-makers consider the objectives of refuge, in these cases judges are grappling with the standard of refuge other countries must meet. There are analyses of the Australian, Canadian, EU, Libyan and Papua New Guinean jurisprudence discussed in this chapter.[3]

---

[1] Austin Grabish, Canadian Broadcasting Commission, 'Frostbitten Refugee Will Lose Fingers, Toe after 7-Hour Trek to Cross US-Canada Border', *CBS News* (online 12 January 2017) <www.cbc.ca/news/canada/manitoba/refugees-frostbite-manitoba-1.3930146>.

[2] For a discussion of the increase in such border crossings, see Mireille Paquet and Robert Schertzer, 'Irregular Border Crossings and Asylum Seekers in Canada: A Complex Intergovernmental Problem' (Study 80, Institute for Research and Public Policy, November 2020).

[3] See, e.g., Majd Achour and Thomas Spijkerboer, 'The Libyan Litigation about the 2017 Memorandum of Understanding between Italy and Libya' (2 June 2020) EU Immigration and Asylum Law and Policy <http://eumigrationlawblog.eu/the-libyan-litigation-about-the-2017-memorandum-of-understanding-between-italy-and-libya/>; Efrat Arbel, 'Shifting Borders and the Boundaries of Rights: Examining the Safe Third Country Agreement between Canada and the United States' (2013) 25(1) *International Journal of Refugee Law* 65; Azadeh Dastyari and Maria O'Sullivan, 'Not for Export: The Failure of Australia's

The examination here is unique in that it comparatively tracks the thresholds of effective protection being set across these jurisdictions, the judicial approaches that produce them and the gendered consequences.

Because of the above noted differences between the jurisprudence in this and the previous chapters, the role of juridical and geographic boundaries is more salient in these cases. Thus, I commence this chapter, in Section 5.2, by discussing scholarship on the relationship between law and borders, particularly in refugee contexts, which will guide the analysis of the case law. I then examine, in Sections 5.3 and 5.4, the ways judges position juridical borders in conceptualising the threshold and nature of refuge and determining a regional containment instruments' legality. In Section 5.5, I consider whether judges' manoeuvring of borders facilitates or frustrates refugees' (or particular refugees') journeys in search of refuge.

I argue that, when first presented with these challenges, courts in most jurisdictions set a threshold for adequate refuge along a continuum of robust to minimal protection. It is when courts consider the significance of refugeehood and expand their juridical borders that they establish a high threshold for effective protection and disrupt the continuation of containment laws. However, in subsequent cases, courts ignore the salience of refugee status and retract their juridical borders. This means that there is no longer a minimum standard of refuge set in these protection elsewhere cases and refugees become trapped in the resisted place of refuge, unable to continue their journey except in exceptional or extraordinary circumstances.

5.2   Borders and Boundaries

States are increasingly implementing bilateral or regional instruments designed to disrupt refugee journeys.[4] Australia has an offshore processing regime whereby it has entered into agreements with Malaysia, Nauru and Papua New Guinea to send refugees to these countries. Canada and the US have entered into the Agreement between the Government of Canada and the Government of the United States of America for Cooperation in the Examination of Refugee Status Claims from Nationals of Third Countries ('Canada–US Agreement').[5] Pursuant to the Canada–US Agreement, asylum seekers who first arrive in the US are barred from pursuing a claim for refugee protection in Canada, and those who first arrive in Canada cannot lodge an asylum claim in the US. The Canada–US Agreement only applies at a Canada–US land border port of entry. If an asylum seeker makes a refugee

---

Extraterritorial Processing Regime in Papua New Guinea and the Decision of the PNG Supreme Court in Namah' (2016) 42(2) *Monash University Law Review* 308; Michelle Foster, 'The Implications of the Failed "Malaysian Solution": The Australian High Court and Refugee Responsibility Sharing at International Law' (2012) 13 *Melbourne Journal of International Law* 395; Itamar Mann, 'Dialectic of Transnationalism: Unauthorized Migration and Human Rights' (2013) 54(2) *Harvard International Law Journal* 315; Thomas Spijkerboer, 'Bifurcation of People, Bifurcation of Law: Externalization of Migration Policy before the EU Court of Justice' (2018) 31(2) *Journal of Refugee Studies* 216; Tamara Wood and Jane McAdam, 'Australian Asylum Policy all at Sea: An Analysis of *Plaintiff M70/2011 v Minister for Immigration and Citizenship* and the Australia–Malaysia Arrangement' (2012) 61 *International and Comparative Law Quarterly* 274.

[4] Thomas Gammeltoft-Hansen, *Access to Asylum: International Refugee Law and the Globalisation of Migration Control* (Cambridge University Press, 2011) 2.

[5] Signed 5 December 2002, TIAS 04–1229, in force 29 December 2004.

claim at a land border port of entry, they can be summarily turned back, subject to some exceptions.[6] The EU has the Dublin System (discussed in Chapter 4) that determines which member-state is responsible for examining a person's asylum claim. There has also been an agreement with respect to sending asylum seekers in the Greek Islands to Turkey in exchange for European states resettling refugees in Turkey to Europe (Europe–Turkey Agreement). In this chapter, I examine court challenges to each of these containment instruments. I also briefly discuss a decision by the Court of Appeal in Tripoli with respect to an agreement Italy has entered into with Libya, an agreement designed to prevent asylum seekers from reaching Italian shores. As noted in Chapter 1, I do not consider US safe third-country agreements with Guatemala, Honduras and El Salvador (entered into by the Trump Administration). At the time of writing, the Biden Administration had initiated the process of terminating these agreements.

In all of the legal challenges considered in this chapter, there are tensions between law and borders. Questions arise regarding the extent to which international law is relevant or the decision must be determined solely with respect to supranational or domestic law. Another controversy is the extent to which these legal frameworks permit decision-makers to pass judgment on conditions of refugee protection in other nation-states.

The relationship between law and borders is a perennial theme in refugee and migration law scholarship. As discussed in Chapter 4, there is a growing focus on externalisation: tactics states use to push migration control beyond their borders. Externalisation informs some of the protection from refuge contests examined in this chapter, such as challenges to Australia's offshore processing policy. However, not all of the aforementioned containment agreements neatly fit in to an externalisation context. The Canada–US Agreement is more about border control than either nation externalising its border.

What is constant across each of the legal challenges examined in this chapter is the idea of the multiplication and malleability of borders. Kesby argues that states do not have a single, distinct border, but many borders that strategically include or exclude people in different locations.[7] Shachar draws a distinction between states' geographic and juridical borders and highlights the ways juridical borders shift.[8] She argues that:

> The firm borderlines drawn in the world atlas do not necessarily coincide with those adhered to, indeed created through, immigration law and policy. Instead, we increasingly witness a border that is in flux: at once more open and more closed than in the past ... the location of the border is shifting – at times penetrating into the interior, in other circumstances extending beyond the edge of the territory.[9]

While Shachar focusses on how the legislature and executive expand and shift state borders, courts also engage in moving, enlarging and retracting legal boundaries. They do this when they consider the relevance of international law and foreign jurisprudence as well as the extent to which they examine and pass judgment on other states' laws and policies. With respect to the relationship between decision-makers and juridical borders, Slaughter

---

[6] The exceptions relate to family reunification, unaccompanied minors and document holders, and there is also a public interest exception: ibid arts 4(2), 6.

[7] Alison Kesby, 'The Shifting and Multiple Border in International Law' (2007) 27(1) *Oxford Journal of Legal Studies* 101, 112–13.

[8] Ayelet Shachar, 'The Shifting Border of Immigration Regulation' (2009) 30(3) *Michigan Journal of International Law* 809, 810.

[9] Ibid 810.

analyses 'transjudicial communication' – courts around the world having a global conversation.[10] Transjudicial communication can be vertical, which involves domestic courts drawing on decisions by international bodies.[11] It can also be horizontal, whereby judges in domestic, supranational or international courts refer to each other's jurisprudence.[12] She suggests that such 'judicial globalization'[13] may lead to increased protection of human rights[14] and 'the gradual construction of a global legal system'.[15]

Refugee law scholars draw on Slaughter's idea of transjudicial communication to assess the extent to which decision-makers engage in comparative jurisprudence. Many share Slaughter's view that it is a positive phenomenon for the development of common understandings of international rights and obligations. Lambert highlights that 'refugee law provides tremendous opportunity in terms of seeking a greater transnational judicial role'.[16] This is because it has 'evolved mostly under the influence of judges'.[17] However, her study of transjudicial communication among courts in EU member-states conducted with Goodwin-Gill indicates that 'judges rarely *use* each other's decisions', and 'the extent of this problem is remarkable'.[18] Goodwin-Gill argues that, in refugee law decisions, judges 'ought to have some regard to relevant case law from the jurisdictions of other states party to the Convention'.[19] Beyond the EU and with respect to the refugee definition in the Refugee Convention, Hathaway and Foster argue that decision-makers engage in transjudicial communication and 'the result has been a rich comparative jurisprudence concerning the key terms of the refugee definition, which shows a determined effort to engage with the international and comparative nature of the refugee definition'.[20] In contrast, Mann is more sceptical about the claim that transnationalism in courts can increase rights protection in refugee contexts.[21] In Section 5.3, I draw on these ideas of multiple shifting borders and transjudicial communication in analysing the first judicial responses to challenges to regional containment instruments in Australia, Canada and the EU.

5.3 Setting a Threshold for Adequate Protection: The Role of Borders in Judicial Reasoning

In this section, I consider the different ways courts, in what were the first challenges to regional containment instruments, manoeuvred their juridical borders in determining two

---

[10] Anne-Marie Slaughter, *A New World Order* (Princeton University Press, 2004) 66.   [11] Ibid 67.
[12] Ibid 67.   [13] Ibid 66.
[14] Anne-Marie Slaughter, 'A Typology of Transjudicial Communication' (1994) 29(1) *University of Richmond Law Review* 99, 135.
[15] Slaughter (n 10) 67.
[16] Hélène Lambert, 'Transnational Law, Judges and Refugees in the European Union' in Guy Goodwin-Gill and Hélène Lambert (eds), *The Limits of Transnational Law: Refugee Law, Policy Harmonization and Judicial Dialogue in the European Union* (Cambridge University Press, 2010) 1, 4.
[17] Ibid 4.   [18] Ibid 8 (emphasis in original).
[19] Guy Goodwin-Gill, 'The Search for One, True Meaning . . . ' in Guy Goodwin-Gill and Hélène Lambert (eds), *The Limits of Transnational Law: Refugee Law, Policy Harmonization and Judicial Dialogue in the European Union* (Cambridge University Press, 2010) 204.
[20] James Hathaway and Michelle Foster, *The Law of Refugee Status* (Cambridge Univesity Press, 2nd ed, 2014) 4–5.
[21] Mann (n 3) 318.

questions. In Section 5.3.1, I examine the threshold they set with respect to what level of protection a third country (where the refugee may be sent or is already) must guarantee. In Section 5.3.2, I discuss the extent to which they expanded their judicial gaze across borders and were willing to pass judgment on a foreign state's law and policy. The analysis indicates that adopting categorical reasoning by focussing on refugeehood or refugee status, an idea established in Chapters 3 and 4, carries over into protection from refuge challenges where the litigants are directly challenging a regional containment instrument.

5.3.1   *Refuge Beyond* Non-refoulement?

When courts in Australia, Canada and the EU first determined challenges to a regional containment instrument's legality or operation, they each set a standard of effective protection – a level of protection that must be guaranteed for refugees to be transferred to or remain in a third country. However, each set markedly different standards for adequate refuge. The High Court of Australia in *Plaintiff M70/2011 v Minister for Immigration and Citizenship and Plaintiff M106/2011 v Minister for Immigration and Citizenship* ('*Plaintiff M70*')[22] set a high water mark for refugee protection.[23] While not going as far as stipulating a precise standard, the decision provides that the rights and protections in the Refugee Convention (not just the protection against *refoulement*) are relevant when determining the minimum standard for adequate protection. In *Canadian Council for Refugees v Canada* ('*Canadian Council for Refugees*'),[24] the Federal Court of Canada, at first instance, set the standard much lower at protection from *refoulement*. The Court of Justice of the European Union (CJEU) in *NS v Secretary of State for the Home Department and ME v Refugee Applications Commissioner, Minister for Justice, Equality and Law Reform* ('*NS and ME*')[25] established a similarly low standard, but one further removed from international refugee law: the right to not be subjected to inhuman or degrading treatment. While each Court is interpreting legal instruments from its own jurisdiction, next I suggest, taking each case in turn, that the different standards relate to the ways the courts position their juridical borders and the significance they place on refugee status.

5.3.1.1   A High Standard of Refugee Protection
in the Oceanic Region

The High Court of Australia's decision in *Plaintiff M70* was the first in a series of cases that challenged Australia's offshore processing regime. Two asylum seeker plaintiffs, who were in Australian territory but whom the Australian government planned to transfer to Malaysia, instigated the case in Australia's final appellate court. Australia entered into the Arrangement between the Government of Australia and the Government of Malaysia on Transfer and Resettlement[26] ('Malaysia Agreement') pursuant to section 198A(1) of Australia's Migration Act 1958 (Cth) ('Migration Act'). Section 198A(1) has subsequently been removed, but, pursuant to the wording at the time, it provided that an asylum seeker may be taken to another country if the Minister for Immigration has made a declaration that the third country satisfied the criteria in s198A(3)(a):

---

[22] (2011) 244 CLR 144.   [23] Foster (n 3) 418.   [24] [2007] FC 1261.   [25] [2011] ECR I 13905.
[26] Signed 25 July 2011.

(i) provides access, for persons seeking asylum, to effective procedures for assessing their need for protection;
(ii) provides protection for persons seeking asylum, pending determination of their refugee status;
(iii) provides protection for persons given refugee status, pending their voluntary repatriation to their country of origin or resettlement in another country; and
(iv) meets the relevant human rights standards in providing that protection.

The plaintiffs argued that the Minister's declaration with respect to Malaysia was made *ultra vires*. This argument was based on the plaintiffs' submission that the aforementioned criteria were jurisdictional facts. This meant that these criteria would have to be objectively satisfied before the Minister could make a valid declaration. The lead majority (Justices Gummow, Hayne, Crennan and Bell), as well as Justice Kiefel in a concurring opinion, accepted this argument.[27] This finding allowed the High Court of Australia to then consider whether the Malaysia Agreement satisfied the aforementioned criteria.

While the High Court of Australia's approach to whether the Malaysia Agreement was consistent with the relevant criteria was essentially one of domestic statutory construction,[28] its reasoning has resonance with categorical approaches to elucidating refuge. The categorical reasoning is subtler than the decisions considered in Chapters 3 and 4, but is nevertheless detectable and consequential to the outcome of the decision. The lead majority in *Plaintiff M70* referred to the special position refugees occupy in international law through a process of textual legislative interpretation. The plaintiffs submitted that the word 'protection' in the aforementioned provision was 'a legal term of art to describe the rights to be accorded to a person who is, or claims to be, a refugee under the Refugee Convention'.[29] In line with this submission,[30] the lead majority reasoned that the word 'protection' 'must be understood as referring to access and protections of the kinds that Australia undertook to provide by signing the [Refugee] Convention'.[31] Their Honours explained that 'this is most clearly evident from consideration of the requirement . . . that the country in question "provides protection to persons *who are given refugee status*"'.[32] Taking a slightly different approach by drawing on principles of statutory interpretation,[33] Justice Kiefel stated that a construction of section 198A that 'closely accords with the fulfilment of Australia's Convention obligations . . . is to be preferred to one which does not'.[34] Chief Justice French confirmed that the provision 'must be understood in the context of relevant principles of international law concerning the movement of persons from state to state'.[35]

All of these approaches place significance on the fact that the plaintiffs were seeking recognition of their refugee status. This provided the Court with a bridge to consider what

---

[27] *Plaintiff M70* (n 22) [109].   [28] Wood and McAdam (n 3) 287.
[29] *Plaintiff M70* (n 22) [63] (French CJ).
[30] The lead majority 'largely agreed' with this submission: Wood and McAdam (n 3) 295.
[31] *Plaintiff M70* (n 22) [118].   [32] Ibid [119] (emphasis in original).
[33] When there is ambiguity in domestic legislation that implements an international treaty, Australian courts aim to interpret the legislation consistently with these international obligations: *Minister for Immigration and Ethnic Affairs v Teoh* (1995) 183 CLR 273, 287. This rule of statutory construction is discussed in Justice Kiefel's judgment in *Plaintiff M70* (n 22) [247]. This principle of interpretation is also used in other jurisdictions. See, e.g., the Canadian decision of *National Corn Growers Assn v Canada (Import Tribunal)* [1990] 2 SCR 1324, 1371.
[34] *Plaintiff M70* (n 22) [246].   [35] Ibid [91].

type of rights refugees are entitled to in international law. At this juncture, the High Court of Australia blended categorical reasoning with a rights-based approach to the meaning of section 198A(3)(a) of the Migration Act. In doing so, the Court extended its juridical border vertically to take into account international law on refugee protection. Each of the majority judges was satisfied that the word 'protection' in the Migration Act encompassed Australia's Refugee Convention obligation of *non-refoulement*.[36] However, the lead majority went further and stated that the concept of 'protection' and the criteria in section 198A(3)(a) of the Migration Act were a 'reflex of obligations Australia undertook when it became signatory to the [Refugee] Convention'.[37] Thus, the word 'protection' referred to the 'provision of *protections of all of the kinds* which parties to the [Refugee Convention] are bound to provide to such persons. Those protections include, but are not limited to, protection against refoulement'.[38] Their Honours listed some of these other obligations such as freedom of religion, access to the courts and work and education rights.[39] Justice Kiefel added that the reference to 'relevant human rights standards' in the Migration Act encompasses 'standards required by international law'.[40]

Extending its juridical borders vertically to take into account international law also led the Court to characterise the nature of refuge as a duty. The lead majority classified the protections in the Refugee Convention as 'obligations' undertaken by signatory states[41] and stressed that nation-states 'are *bound* to accord to those who have been determined to be refugees the rights that are specified in' the Refugee Convention.[42] Accordingly, the lead majority reasoned that reference to 'protection' in the Migration Act must be 'construed as references to provision of access or protection *in accordance with an obligation to do so*'.[43] This means that, in transferring refugees to a third country, the prospective third country must have a legal obligation to accord the relevant protections to refugees and reference to what occurs in practice is not sufficient.

In establishing a high standard for adequate refugee protection, Australia's final appellate court did not engage in what Slaughter refers to as horizontal transjudicial communication. It did not consider protection elsewhere cases from other jurisdictions, but was guided directly by the Refugee Convention. Next, in discussing the first instance decision in the 2007 challenge to the Canada–US Agreement, I show that the Federal Court of Canada took a different approach.

5.3.1.2   A Lower Standard for Protection for Refugees Crossing the Canada–US Border

In *Canadian Council for Refugees*, a number of applicants, most of them refugee advocacy organisations, challenged the Canada–US Agreement. The asylum-seeking applicant was 'John Doe', a Colombian man living in the US whose asylum claim was not entertained because of the US's one-year time bar.[44] Due to the lack of protection available to him in the US, he wanted to seek refugee protection in Canada. He had not attempted to enter Canada, because Canada would have denied him entry pursuant to the Canada–US Agreement. The

---

[36] Ibid [63] (French CJ), [117] (Gummow, Hayne, Crennan and Bell JJ), [240] (Kiefel J).
[37] Ibid [118] (Gummow, Hayne, Crennan and Bell JJ).   [38] Ibid [119] (emphasis added).
[39] Ibid [117], [119].   [40] Ibid [240].   [41] Ibid [117].   [42] Ibid [117] (emphasis added).
[43] Ibid [135] (emphasis added).
[44] In the US, those who do not file their application for asylum within a year of arriving are barred from claiming asylum: Immigration and Nationality Act 1952 8 USC § 1158(2)(B). There are some limited discretionary exceptions: Aliens and Nationality 8 CFR § 208.4(a).

applicants grounded their challenge in many different aspects of domestic and international law. They sought a declaration that Canada's decision to declare the US a safe third country was unlawful pursuant to administrative law principles, the Canadian Charter of Rights and Freedoms ('Canadian Charter'),[45] the Refugee Convention and CAT.

While transjudicial communication may, in some contexts, strengthen human rights protection, when decision-makers engage in horizontal transjudicial communication but disregard the significance of refugeehood, this can result in bare minimum protections travelling across national frontiers. In determining the appropriate standard of protection, the Federal Court of Canada did not place significance on John Doe being a person seeking recognition of his refugee status. Unlike the High Court of Australia in *Plaintiff M70*, the Court was not guided by the rights in the Refugee Convention. Instead, Justice Phelan referred to UK and Council of Europe jurisprudence 'for comparative purposes' and to 'establish international norms'.[46] However, His Honour did this without questioning whether the approach adopted in those jurisdictions is consistent with the Refugee Convention. Justice Phelan's examination of UK and European Court of Human Rights (ECtHR) case law led His Honour to conclude that, when assessing the validity of a protection elsewhere agreement under international law, the only relevant consideration is *non-refoulement* and not the broader panoply of refugee rights.[47]

Without focussing on John Doe being a person seeking refugee protection, the Federal Court of Canada was misguided in its selection of comparative sources. In particular, when referring to Council of Europe jurisprudence, Justice Phelan did not take into account that the ECtHR does not have jurisdiction to consider the Refugee Convention.[48] There were other sources available to the Federal Court of Canada to suggest that it was required to consider whether the US respects the rights in the Refugee Convention. For example, at the time UNHCR materials defined effective protection to include *non-refoulement*, but also 'accession to and compliance with the 1951 Convention and/or 1967 Protocol . . . unless the destination country can demonstrate that the third State has developed a practice akin to the 1951 Convention and/or its 1967 Protocol'.[49] Another available source was the Michigan Guidelines on Protection Elsewhere,[50] which stipulate that 'effective protection' means not only *non-refoulement* but compliance with all of the obligations outlined in the Refugee Convention.[51] Also, expert evidence given to the Court by two leading refugee law scholars indicated that rights beyond *non-refoulement* should be considered in determining protection elsewhere decisions.[52]

Further, by setting the standard of refugee protection through selective horizontal transjudicial communication, the Court did not consider international law in interpreting

---

[45] Canada Act 1982 c 11, sch B pt I.   [46] *Canadian Council for Refugees* (n 24) [110].

[47] Ibid [118], [125].

[48] The ECtHR' jurisdiction is limited to matters concerning the interpretation of the ECHR: ECHR art 32(1).

[49] UNHCR, *Summary Conclusions on the Concept of 'Effective Protection' in the Context of Secondary Movements of Refugees and Asylum Seekers (Lisbon Expert Roundtable, 9–10 December 2002)* (February 2003) [15(e)] <www.unhcr.org/en-au/protection/globalconsult/3e5f323d7/lisbon-expert-roundtable-summary-conclusions-concept-effective-protection.html>.

[50] Fourth Colloquium on Challenges in Refugee Law, 'The Michigan Guidelines on Protection Elsewhere' (2007) 28(2) *Michigan Journal of International Law* 207.

[51] Ibid [8].

[52] Affidavits of Professors James Hathaway and Kay Hailbronner. See Michelle Foster, 'Responsibility Sharing or Shifting: "Safe" Third Countries and International Law' (2008) 25(2) *Refuge* 64, 67.

its domestic legislation. Canada entered into the Canada–US Agreement pursuant to the Immigration and Refugee Protection Act SC 2001 ('Immigration and Refugee Protection Act'). While the relevant sections of the legislation predominantly focus on whether the prospective third country complies with its *non-refoulement* obligations,[53] there was nevertheless an opportunity for the Court to refer to international law to set a higher threshold for refugee protection. In particular, the Immigration and Refugee Protection Act provides that, in deciding to designate a country as a safe third country, the executive must consider the country's policies and practices with respect to the Refugee Convention[54] and its human rights record.[55] Unlike the High Court of Australia in *Plaintiff M70*, the Federal Court of Canada did not extend its juridical border vertically to encompass Canada's international law obligations when interpreting domestic legislation, thus missing an opportunity to bring a broader set of refugee rights into the frame of judicial consideration in setting the standard for adequate refuge. In the next section, I suggest that the CJEU took a similar approach in determining minimum levels of effective protection.

5.3.1.3   Missed Opportunities in Setting the Standard for Refugee Protection in the EU

Akin to the approach taken by the Federal Court of Canada in *Canadian Council of Churches*, in the first direct challenge to a regional refugee containment instrument in the EU, *NS and ME*, the CJEU failed to place any significance on refugeehood. It also engaged in selective transjudicial communication and circumscribed international law's relevance.

The case arose from questions referred by the Court of Appeal of England and Wales and High Court of Ireland. One of the questions was whether, when transferring an asylum seeker to another EU state pursuant to the Dublin System, the transferring state should consider whether the asylum seeker's fundamental human rights would be observed. (At the time the case was heard, the Dublin II Regulation was in force.[56] The Dublin Regulation has since been recast and is known as the Dublin III Regulation.)[57] This question arose because the Court of Appeal of England and Wales and High Court of Ireland were hearing cases in which asylum seekers were resisting Dublin System transfers to Greece. This question is distinct from the arguments raised in the cases discussed in Chapter 4. It does not concern asylum seekers using rights available under the ECHR to resist a Dublin System transfer. Rather, the question asks whether and when rights under EU law, in particular, the *Charter of Fundamental Rights of the European Union* ('EU Charter'),[58] may prohibit transfers under the Dublin System. Unlike the cases considered in Chapter 4, this case was a direct challenge to the Dublin System's operation.

The CJEU in *NS and ME* had the opportunity to articulate a high standard of refugee protection. In particular, there was flexibility as to what it could deem to be a 'fundamental

---

[53] Immigration and Refugee Protection Act s101(e).   [54] Ibid s102(2)(b).   [55] Ibid s102(2)(c).

[56] Regulation (EC) 343/2003 of 18 February 2003 Establishing the Criteria and Mechanisms for Determining the Member State Responsible for Examining an Asylum Application Lodged in one of the Member States by a Third-Country National [2003] OJ L50.

[57] Regulation (EC) 604/2013 of 29 June 2013 Establishing the Criteria and Mechanisms for Determining the Member State Responsible for Examining an Application for International Protection Lodged in one of the Member States by a Third-Country National or a Stateless Person (Recast) [2013] OJ L 180/31–180/59.

[58] Charter of Fundamental Rights of the European Union, 7 December 2000, [2012] OJ C 326/321, in force 1 December 2009.

right'. The rights the parties highlighted were articles 1 (human dignity), 4 (prohibition of torture and inhuman and degrading treatment or punishment), 18 (right to asylum), 19(2) (prohibition of removal where there is a serious risk of being subjected to the death penalty, torture or other inhuman or degrading treatment or punishment) and 47 (right to an effective remedy and a fair trial) of the EU Charter. Also referenced were a number of EU Directives on minimum standards for asylum seekers and refugees.[59] Many of these sources of EU law make direct reference to the Refugee Convention. For example, article 18 of the EU Charter provides that 'the right to asylum shall be guaranteed with due respect for the rules of the [Refugee Convention]'. The preambles to all of the EU Directives the parties referred to[60] state that the Common European Asylum System is designed to achieve the 'full and inclusive application of the [Refugee Convention]'. The UNHCR intervened and argued that a transfer should be precluded when there is a 'real risk of a breach of fundamental rights, including (but not limited to) serious breaches of the minimum standards laid out in the EU Asylum Directives'.[61] The UNHCR also insisted that the Dublin System, being secondary EU legislation, 'must be read as subject to fundamental rights, not the other way around'.[62] Advocate General Trstenjak concluded that 'the transfer of asylum-seekers to a Member State in which there is a serious risk of violation of the asylum-seekers' fundamental rights is incompatible with the [EU Charter]'.[63]

However, the CJEU adopted a much narrower approach. It described the purpose of the Common European Asylum System as 'full and inclusive application of the [Refugee] Convention'[64] and acknowledged that article 18 of the EU Charter requires that 'the rules of the [Refugee Convention] are to be respected'.[65] Nevertheless, the Court held that, when transferring an asylum seeker pursuant to the Dublin System, the sending state only has to consider whether they will be subject to inhuman or degrading treatment within the meaning of article four of the EU Charter.[66] In coming to this position, the CJEU did not consider the

---

[59] Directive 2003/9/EC of 27 January 2003 Laying Down Minimum Standards for the Reception of Asylum Seekers [2003] OJ L 31/18 (this has subsequently been recast: Directive 2013/33/EU of the European Parliament and Council of 26 June 2013 Laying Down Standards for the Reception of Applicants for International Protection (Recast) [2013] OJ L 180/96); Directive 2004/83/EC of 29 April 2004 on Minimum Standards for the Qualification and Status of Third Country Nationals or Stateless Persons as Refugees or as Persons Who Otherwise Need International Protection and the Content of the Protection Granted [2004] OJ L 304/12 (this has subsequently been recast: Directive 2011/95/EU of the European Parliament and of the Council of 13 December 2011 on Standards for the Qualification of Third-Country Nationals or Stateless Persons as Beneficiaries of International Protection, for a Uniform Status for Refugees or for Persons Eligible for Subsidiary Protection, and for the Content of the Protection Granted (Recast) [2011] OJ L 337/9); Directive 2005/85/EC of 1 December 2005 on Minimum Standards on Procedures in Member States for Granting and Withdrawing Refugee Status [2005] OJ L 326/13 (this has subsequently been recast: Directive 2013/32/EU of the European Parliament and of the Council of 26 June 2013 on Common Procedures for Granting and Withdrawing International Protection (Recast) [2013] OJ L 180/60–180/95.

[60] See note 59.

[61] UNHCR, *UNHCR Intervention before the Court of Justice of the European Union in Joined Cases of N S and M E and Others* (28 June 2011) [14].

[62] Ibid [5].

[63] Opinion of Advocate General Trstenjak in *NS v Secretary of State for the Home Department and ME v Refugee Applications Commissioner, Minister for Justice, Equality and Law Reform*, C-411/10 and C-493/10, 22 September 2011 [116].

[64] *NS and ME* (n 25) [7].   [65] Ibid [75].

[66] Specifically, the Court held that the only grounds upon which an EU member-state is prevented from transferring an asylum seeker to the responsible member-state is '[w]here they cannot be unaware that

significance of refugeehood and the protections refugees are entitled to under EU and international law. Rather, the starting point was the need to preserve the continued operation and integrity of the Dublin System. The Court reasoned that, if minor breaches of the EU Charter or relevant EU Directives prevent a member-state from transferring an asylum seeker, the objective of the Common European Asylum System (to provide a speedy determination of the responsible member-state) will be undermined. The Court stressed that: 'At issue here is the raison d'être of the European Union and the creation of an area of freedom, security and justice and, in particular, the Common European Asylum System, based on mutual confidence and a presumption of compliance, by other Member States, with European Union law and, in particular, fundamental rights'.[67] This low standard for refugee protection is also arrived at through selective transjudicial communication. The CJEU handed down its judgment in *NS and ME* not long after the ECtHR judgment of *MSS v Belgium and Greece*[68] (discussed in Chapter 4) and referred to that decision.[69] However, in *MSS v Belgium and Greece*, the asylum seeker litigant specifically pleaded article 3 of the ECHR (equivalent to article 4 of the EU Charter). The ECtHR was restricted in its ability to consider other legal instruments, in particular, the Refugee Convention and relevant EU Directives, to set a higher threshold for refugee protection. This is because its jurisdiction is limited to matters concerning the interpretation of the ECHR.[70] Conversely, the CJEU in *NS and ME* had the opportunity to delineate a more comprehensive standard for refugee protection by reference to the spectrum of rights in the EU Charter and relevant EU Directives, all of which reference the Refugee Convention. As Costello explains:

> The referring national courts in [*NS and ME*] invited the [CJEU] to go further than the ECHR, and explore the Charter's additional protections. However, the Court declined, instead focusing only on Article 4 of the [EU Charter] (Article 3 ECHR). There are many legally innovative paths not taken. . . . The judgment is strikingly economical, in that the [CJEU] traces a path already worn by [the ECtHR].[71]

As a consequence of the Court's approach to the questions posed, protection from refuge litigants in the EU are caught in a region that regards EU law as supreme, does not entertain arguments grounded in broader international law and refers to Council of Europe jurisprudence in a way that has the effect of lowering protection standards. Thus, these cases are arbitrated in a European enclave in which the potential for refugees to invoke international refugee law to challenge transfer decisions and continue their journeys in search of refuge has been restrained.

---

systemic deficiencies in the asylum procedure and in the reception conditions of asylum seekers in that Member State amount to substantial grounds for believing that the asylum seeker would face a real risk of being subjected to inhuman or degrading treatment within the meaning of Article 4 of the Charter': ibid [94]. As noted in Chapter 4, the CJEU has since clarified that, even when there are not systemic deficiencies in the asylum system of an EU member-state, a transfer cannot occur if there is evidence that it would result in a real risk that an asylum seeker would be subject to inhuman or degrading treatment: *CK v Supreme Court of the Republic of Slovenia* (C 578/16, 16 February 2017), [92], [96] ('*CK v Supreme Court of the Republic of Slovenia*'). The Court's departure from the systemic deficiency test may be due to criticism of that test by the UK Supreme Court and ECtHR: *R (EM (Eritrea)) v Secretary of State for the Home Department* [2014] UKSC 12; *Tarakhel v Switzerland* [2014] VI Eur Court HR 195.
[67] *NS and ME* (n 25) [83].   [68] [2011] I Eur Court HR 255.   [69] *NS and ME* (n 25) [88]–[90], [112].
[70] As noted in note 48, the ECtHR's jurisdiction is limited to matters concerning the interpretation of the ECHR.
[71] Cathryn Costello, 'Courting Access to Asylum in Europe: Recent Supranational Jurisprudence Explored' (2012) 12(2) *Human Rights Law Review* 287, 333.

The prospect for a higher standard for refugee protection is evident in some domestic decisions in which courts have been willing to refuse transfers on grounds other than article 4 of the EU Charter. For example, in a case concerning transfer of an asylum seeker to Malta, the German Minden Administrative Court held that, due to serious shortcomings in the reception conditions in Malta, it could no longer be assumed that asylum seekers are treated in accordance with the EU Charter, ECHR and Refugee Convention.[72] Nevertheless, the test set down by the CJEU in *NS and ME* is the one codified in the recast Dublin III Regulation. The Court has, in subsequent cases, strengthened protections with respect to detention associated with Dublin transfers,[73] procedural aspects of the Dublin System[74] and time limits associated with transfers.[75] But it has confirmed that the relevant threshold of protection is conditions that preclude inhuman or degrading treatment.[76] With respect to when living conditions can pose a risk of inhuman and degrading treatment, the Court has stressed that this will only occur when the asylum seeker faces 'a situation of extreme material poverty that does not allow him [or her or them] to meet his [or her or their] most basic needs'.[77]

There was also a missed opportunity in *NS and ME* to characterise the nature of refuge as incorporating international solidarity. The Dublin Regulations refer to solidarity,[78] and solidarity is part of EU law.[79] The notion of solidarity has been marginal in EU decisions on refugee transfers.[80] In fact, the Court has only used the principle of solidarity to support rather than disrupt agreements regarding member-state responsibility for refugees.[81]

---

[72] Minden Administrative Court decision of 12 January 2015, 1 L 551/14.A.

[73] *Mohammad Khir Amayry v Migrationsverket* (C-60/16, 13 September 2017); *Policie ČR, Krajské ředitelství policie Ústeckého kraje, odbor cizinecké policie v Salah Al Chodor, Ajlin Al Chodor, Ajvar Al Chodor* (C-528/15, 15 March 2017).

[74] *Bundesrepublik Deutschland v Kaveh Puid* (C-4/11, 14 November 2013); *George Karim v Migrationsverket* (C-155/15, 7 June 2016); *Mehrdad Ghezelbash v Staatssecretaris van Veiligheid en Justitie* (C-63/15, 7 June 2016); *Shamso Abdullahi v Bundesasylamt* (C-394/12, 10 December 2013); *Halaf v Darzhavna agentsia za bezhantsite pri Ministerskia savet* (C-528/11, 30 May 2013).

[75] *A H v Préfet du Pas-de Calais* (C-647/16, 31 May 2018); *Bundesrepublik Deutschland v Aziz Hasan* (C-360/16, 25 January 2018); *Majid Shiri v Bundesamt für Fremdenwesen und As X* (C-201/16, 25 October 2017); *Tsegezab Mengesteab v Bundesrepublik Deutschland* (C-670/16, 26 July 2017); *X and X v Staatssecretaris van Veiligheid en Justitie* (C-47/17 and C-48/17, 13 November 2018).

[76] *CK v Supreme Court of the Republic of Slovenia* (n 66) [65]; *AS v Slovenian Republic* (C-646/16, 26 July 2017) [101] ('*AS v Slovenian Republic*'); *Bashar Ibrahim et al v Bundesrepublik Deutschland* (C-297/17, C-318/17, C-319/17 and C-438/17, 19 March 2019) [90] ('*Bashar Ibrahim v Bundesrepublik Deutschland*').

[77] *Abubacarr Jawo v Bundesrepublik Deutschland* (C-163/17, 19 March 2019) [92] ('*Abubacarr Jawo v Bundesrepublik Deutschland*'); *Bashar Ibrahim v Bundesrepublik Deutschland* (n 76) [90].

[78] There is one reference to solidarity in the preamble to Dublin II (n 56) and 9 references to solidarity in Dublin III (n 57).

[79] Article 80 in Chapter Two of the Treaty on the Functioning of the European Union provides: 'The policies of the Union set out in this Chapter and their implementation shall be governed by the principle of solidarity and fair sharing of responsibility, including its financial implications, between the Member States. Whenever necessary, the Union acts adopted pursuant to this Chapter shall contain appropriate measures to give effect to this principle'. For a discussion of the principle of solidarity in EU law see, e.g., Eleni Karageorgiou, 'The Distribution of Asylum Responsibilities in the EU: Dublin, Partnerships with Third Countries and the Question of Solidarity' (2019) 88(3) *Nordic Journal of International Law* 315.

[80] Luisa Freier De Ferrari, Eleni Karageorgiou and Kate Ogg, 'Evolving Safe Third Country Law and Practice' in Cathryn Costello, Michelle Foster and Jane McAdam (eds), *Oxford Handbook on Refugee Law* (Oxford University Press, 2021) 518, 522.

[81] The Court drew on principle of solidarity in ruling that, even in situations of increasing numbers of refugees, the first entry criterion in the Dublin III Regulation still applies: *AS v Slovenian Republic* (n 76)

A comparison between Australian, Canadian and EU jurisprudence indicates that, in establishing a threshold for adequate refuge in protection from refuge challenges, a higher standard is set when courts consider refugees' special position in international law and extend their juridical border vertically to encompass the rights in the Refugee Convention. In each of the aforementioned cases, the courts had the opportunity to do this pursuant to the legal instruments pleaded, but only the High Court of Australia did so. Conversely, the Federal Court of Canada and the CJEU engaged in selective horizontal transjudicial communication without placing significance on refugee status and set much lower standards for adequate refuge. While courts in Australia, Canada and the EU have set different thresholds for adequate protection, next I examine where these courts position their juridical borders in determining whether the third country meets these standards.

5.3.2   Manoeuvring Juridical Borders in Protection Elsewhere Challenges

While the courts in each of these seminal cases had to set a threshold for effective protection, another question they had to determine was the extent to which they could pass judgment on conditions of refuge beyond their borders. When courts expand their juridical borders in response to this issue, and in particular when they align them with that of the legislature and executive, they undermine containment instruments. In doing so, they not only deliver protection from refuge victories, they can also produce decisions of particular significance for refugees who face additional challenges in their journeys in search of refuge due to factors such as gender, youth and sexuality.

5.3.2.1   Alignment of Australia's Juridical Borders

Not only did the High Court of Australia in *Plaintiff M70* set a high standard for refugee protection, it also interpreted the Migration Act in a way that permitted an assessment of Malaysia's law and practice. In particular, in characterising refuge as a duty owed to refugees by nation-states, the Court conducted an examination of Malaysia's legal obligations towards refugees. Thus, in *Plaintiff M70*, the High Court of Australia brought its juridical borders in line with those of the executive and the legislature.

The Court found that Malaysia had no obligation to provide refugees with the protections in the Refugee Convention.[82] The Court highlighted that Malaysia was not a signatory to the Refugee Convention and had not made a 'legally binding arrangement with Australia obliging it to accord the protections required by those instruments'.[83] Also, the Court stressed that Malaysia did not provide for refugee status in its domestic law and did not undertake any activities with respect to refugee registration, but instead left these tasks to the UNHCR. On these grounds, the lead majority ruled that the Minister made the declaration under the Migration Act without power and the refugee plaintiffs could not be transferred to Malaysia.[84] In her judgment, Justice Kiefel added that the state itself must undertake refugee status assessments and cannot defer the obligation to the UNHCR.[85] The Court also indicated that, in addition to assessing legal obligations, there should also be an

---

[88]. The Court has also referred to the principle of solidarity in dismissing Poland, Hungary and the Czech Republic's objections to provisional measures for relocation of refugees within Europe in response to the high numbers entering Greece and Italy as a result of the Syrian conflict: *Commission v Poland, Hungary and the Czech Republic* (C-715/17, C-718/17 and C-719/17, 2 April 2020).

[82] *Plaintiff M70* (n 22) [135].   [83] Ibid [135].   [84] Ibid [148].   [85] Ibid [242].

examination of the third country's practices.[86] Chief Justice French emphasised that '[c]onstitutional guarantees, protective domestic laws and international obligations are not always reflected in the practice of states'.[87]

The High Court of Australia declined to answer the question of whether it would be in the second plaintiff's (an unaccompanied minor) best interests to transfer him to Malaysia. Nevertheless, in referring to the Refugee Convention to determine the appropriate standard for protection and examining Malaysia's treatment of refugees in law and practice, the case provides strong guidance on refugee children's rights. At a number of points in the judgment, the Court referenced the rights to education in the Refugee Convention and, in particular, the obligation to accord refugees the same treatment as is accorded to nationals with respect to elementary education.[88] Chief Justice French stated that one of the 'salient' findings of the Department of Foreign Affairs' assessment of Malaysia's treatment of refugees is that lack of official status impedes access to formal education.[89] The right to education is particularly important for refugee children, and the approach taken by the High Court of Australia indicates that it is a necessary consideration in cases where refugees are resisting transfer to a third country. Next, I show that expansion of juridical borders in response to the 2007 challenge to the Canada–US Agreement helped to produce a gender-sensitive judgment.

5.3.2.2   Extending the Reach of Judicial Borders in Canada

While the Federal Court of Canada set a much lower standard for adequate refuge, when examining whether the US complied with the principle of *non-refoulement* as the 'minimum recognized standard',[90] the Court aligned its juridical borders with those of the legislature and executive. To determine if the Governor in Council acted reasonably in concluding that the US complied with its *non-refoulement* obligations, the Court conducted a thorough investigation of US refugee law and policy. This assessment included consideration of US legislation and case law, expert evidence and UNHCR commentary. Justice Phelan held that the US did not comply with its *non-refoulement* obligations under the Refugee Convention,[91] because of its one-year bar,[92] exclusion of people from refugee status for reasons impermissible by the Refugee Convention[93] and equivocal approach to gender claims.[94] Further, Justice Phelan found that the US did not comply with its *non-refoulement* obligations under CAT, because there was no absolute bar on deportation to a country where a person faces a real risk of torture.[95] Thus, even though Justice Phelan set a bare minimum standard for refugee protection, His Honour's judgment provided a protection from refuge victory: the Court declared the Canada–US Agreement *ultra vires*, and this provided grounds for refugees in the US to travel to Canada in search of refuge. This is largely due to the Federal Court of Canada expanding its juridical border to enable it to assess and pass judgment on US refugee law and policy.

Another way in which the Federal Court of Canada manoeuvered juridical borders to reach across the geographic border was through Justice Phelan's approach to the Canadian

---

[86] Ibid [67] (French CJ), [112] (Gummow, Hayne, Crennan and Bell JJ), [245] (Kiefel J).   [87] Ibid [67].
[88] Ibid [117], [119].   [89] Ibid [28].   [90] *Canadian Council for Refugees* (n 24) [136].   [91] Ibid [154].
[92] If an asylum seeker cannot make a claim for refugee status due to the one-year bar, they can only apply for withholding status or protection under the CAT, which imposes a higher threshold than the test for 'well-founded fear of persecution' under the Refugee Convention. This higher threshold means that some refugees are at a real risk of *refoulement*: ibid [154].
[93] Ibid [191].   [94] Ibid [206].   [95] Ibid [256]–[262].

Charter. The applicants pleaded that the Canada–US Agreement violated sections 7 and 15 of the Charter (the right to life, liberty and security of the person and the right to equality). While John Doe, the asylum seeker applicant, was not within Canadian territory, Justice Phelan found that the rights in the Canadian Charter extended to him. Justice Phelan reasoned that, if John Doe had approached the Canadian border, the Charter would apply to him. However, if he did in fact approach the border, he would have been denied entry into Canada and returned to US authorities. On this basis, Justice Phelan explained that:

> it would be pointless to force a claimant in the US to approach Canada, and then be sent back to US custody in order to prove that this would in fact happen. Given other findings by this Court as to the operation of the US system, that individual could be exposed to the very harm at issue before the Court.[96]

Through this reasoning, the Court set up a 'legal fiction – imagining John Doe as having approached the border without requiring to do so'.[97] This legal fiction enabled the Court to shift the border and bring John Doe 'within the fold of constitutional protection'.[98] The Court held that the Canada–US Agreement offended section 7 of the Canadian Charter because refugees' lives, liberty and security were put at risk because the US did not comply with its *non-refoulement* obligations in the Refugee Convention and CAT.[99] The right to equality was also violated because the Canada–US Agreement 'discriminates against and exposes people to risk [of *refoulement*] based solely on the method of arrival in Canada, a wholly irrelevant Charter consideration'.[100] These breaches could not be justified pursuant to section 1 of the Canadian Charter.[101] The Court's manoeuvring of juridical borders is significant in the context of refugees' journeys in search of refuge. John Doe did not have to make the arduous and risky journey to the Canadian border to trigger Canada's domestic human rights law in making his protection from refuge claim.

   The Federal Court of Canada's extension of its juridical borders enabled consideration of the relationship among gender, sexuality and *non-refoulement*. One argument the applicants raised was that the US equivocal approach to gender claims created a *refoulement* risk for female refugees, especially those basing their claim on family violence.[102] Another argument was that the one-year time bar disadvantaged female refugees and those making sexual orientation claims, because they were more likely to file for asylum outside the one-year period.[103] This is because they most likely would not know that the refugee definition can encompass claims grounded in sexual orientation and family violence, and in any event they would be reticent to disclose the details necessary to make a protection claim on these grounds.[104] The Court assessed the gendered operation of US refugee law[105] and agreed that these aspects of US refugee law created a *refoulement* risk for female refugees and refugees making sexuality claims.[106] These findings formed part of the Court's decision that the

---

[96] Ibid [48].   [97] Arbel (n 3) 81.   [98] Ibid 80.   [99] *Canadian Council for Refugees* (n 24) [285].
[100] Ibid [333].   [101] Ibid [337].
[102] The applicants argued that US law on the relationship between gender and particular social group was 'in a state of flux' and this created *refoulement* risks, especially for women basing their claims on domestic violence: ibid [198]. The US had issued proposed guidelines confirming that identification of an immutable or fundamental trait was the only necessary factor in establishing a particular social group and gender was considered an immutable or fundamental trait: [199]. However, at the time of judgment, the guidelines were not finalised and there was no authoritative case law confirming the position in the guidelines: [203].
[103] Ibid [162].   [104] Ibid [162]–[163].   [105] Ibid [162]–[164], [197]–[216].   [106] Ibid [164], [206].

executive's determination that the US complies with its *non-refoulement* obligations was unreasonable.[107]

By extending the Canadian Charter's reach across the geographic border and finding the Canada–US Agreement inconsistent with the Canadian Charter, the Federal Court of Canada's decision was of particular value for refugees who would face the greatest impediments in travelling to the Canadian border. As discussed in Chapter 2, it is well established that female refugees, children and refugees with care responsibilities and disabilities are less likely to be able to make these arduous journeys. Also, by removing the necessity to present at the border to trigger Canadian Charter protection, the Federal Court of Canada's decision defuses the risk of being subject to immigration detention. Arbel explains that when asylum seekers and refugees in the US come to the Canadian border, they are often summarily returned to the US and immediately placed in immigration detention.[108] While immigration detention conditions in the US are problematic for people of all genders,[109] female refugees who are rejected at Canada's border with the US 'are more likely to be detained under worse conditions of confinement'.[110] This is because, while men are transferred to a dedicated immigration detention facility, women are 'more likely to be held in mixed-purpose facilities or local jails, sometimes under questionable conditions of confinement'.[111] Because they are not in dedicated immigration detention facilities, they are not given appropriate assistance to advance their asylum claim and may simply 'fall off the radar'.[112] Next, I highlight that the CJEU has been more reticent to expand juridical borders in Dublin System jurisprudence.

5.3.2.3   The Conundrum of Borders and Refugee Protection in the EU

It may seem incongruous to examine the role of borders in EU protection elsewhere decisions. The EU is a 'community committed to the removal of internal borders'.[113] It has a supranational agreement on standards for refugee protection, a regional responsibility-sharing agreement and a regional human rights instrument, questions or disputes about which can be referred to the CJEU. This may suggest that borders, either geographic or juridical, diminish in significance.

Nevertheless, unlike the High Court of Australia in *Plaintiff M70* and the Federal Court of Canada in *Canadian Council for Refugees*, which undertook rigorous examinations of Malaysian and US refugee law and policy respectively, the CJEU in *NS and ME* indicated that EU member-states should be cautious in passing judgment on other member-states' law and practice. The CJEU does not determine factual disputes, so did not rule on whether the UK and Ireland could transfer the asylum seekers to Greece. Nevertheless, it stressed that there must be a presumption (albeit a rebuttable one) that all EU member-states comply with the requirements of the EU Charter, Refugee Convention and ECHR.[114] This is because the Common European Asylum System 'was conceived in a context making it possible to assume that all the participating states . . . observe fundamental rights, including the rights based on the [Refugee Convention], and on the ECHR'.[115]

---

[107] Ibid [237]–[240].
[108] Efrat Arbel, 'Gendered Border Crossings' in Efrat Arbel, Catherine Dauvergne and Jenni Millbank (eds), *Gender in Refugee Law: From the Margins to the Centre* (Routledge, 2014) 243, 254.
[109] Ibid 254–6. [110] Ibid 256. [111] Ibid 256. [112] Ibid 256. [113] Goodwin-Gill (n 19) 205.
[114] *NS and ME* (n 25) [80]. [115] Ibid [78].

Thus, there is discernible discomfort with respect to juridical borders penetrating geo-graphic borders in the CJEU's decision in *NS and ME*. The Court's guidance is that domestic courts can consider conditions of refuge in other EU member-states, but the asylum seeker resisting a transfer must rebut the presumption of compliance.[116] As a result of the presumption of compliance, the geographic borders of individual EU states became salient. This makes it more difficult for refugees to turn to courts in EU member-states to continue their quests to find refuge. In the next section, I show that, as a result of subsequent decisions across all three regions, refugees are less able to use litigation to navigate geographic and juridical borders in search of refuge.

5.4   Misaligned Borders

In the cases already discussed, where some content was given to the standard of refuge, the courts framed the matter in a way that enabled decision-makers to consider and pass judgment on the conditions of refuge in a foreign country (with courts in Australia and Canada doing this to a much greater extent than the CJEU). However, in subsequent cases, courts in each of these jurisdictions have retracted their judicial lens to avoid having to cast judgment on the allegedly inadequate place of refuge. Next, I outline these changes, taking each region in turn, and highlight how this manoeuvring of juridical borders has meant that the idea that there is a standard for adequate refuge in protection elsewhere scenarios has disappeared from jurisprudence.

5.4.1   Asymmetrical Borders and Judicial Dissonance in the Oceanic Region

While the High Court of Australia in the 2011 decision of *Plaintiff M70* extended its juridical borders to be in line with the executive and legislative branches of government, in subsequent decisions these juridical borders have been retracted. The outcome of these legal developments, from the perspective of effective protection, is that the High Court of Australia has shifted from a high standard for adequate refuge guided by the rights in the Refugee Convention to an approach whereby no standard for adequate protection is set. Further, while in *Plaintiff M70* the Court positioned refuge as an international obligation, as a result of subsequent legal developments, the idea of refuge promulgated is one of discre-tion that states can assign to third countries without judicial oversight.

This is partly due to amendments to domestic legislation. In 2012, in response to the High Court of Australia's decision in *Plaintiff M70*, the Australian parliament removed section 198A from the Migration Act and inserted new sections 198AA to 198AH.[117] These provisions give the Minister for Immigration the power to designate a third country as a 'regional processing centre'.[118] The only condition for the exercise of this power is that the Minister thinks that it is in the national interest.[119] The reforms specifically provide that 'the

---

[116] For an example of the application of the presumption of compliance, see Netherlands, Court of The Hague, NL20.15181, NL20.15183, NL20.15188 and NL20.15194, 19 October 2020, ECLI:NL: RBDHA:2020:10437. The applicants, a refugee family from Syria, had international protection in Bulgaria and then travelled to the Netherlands. The Court held that it must presume that Bulgaria complies with its obligations and the burden of proof lay with the applicants to prove otherwise.

[117] Migration Legislation Amendment (Regional Processing and Other Measures) Act 2012 (Cth).

[118] Migration Act s198AB(1).   [119] Ibid s198AB(2).

designation of a country to be a regional processing country need not be determined by reference to the international obligations or domestic law of that country'.[120] These reforms indicate that, by grounding its decision on the word 'protection' in the Migration Act and relying on principles of statutory interpretation, the High Court of Australia in *Plaintiff M70* exposed 'enforcement vacuums'[121] and provided 'a blueprint for another offshore processing framework'.[122]

The situation created by the amendments to the Migration Act has resonance with Kesby's observations that states have multiple borders that 'strategically include or exclude people in different locations'.[123] In particular, while the executive's juridical border can extend outwards to contemplate transferring asylum seekers to other countries, the judiciary's juridical border cannot similarly extend to examine refugee law and policy in those countries. Pursuant to these amendments, Nauru and Papua New Guinea have been designated as regional processing centres. Asylum seekers have been sent to Nauru and Papua New Guinea since August 2012, but Australia retains a significant degree of control of the asylum seekers and the facilities in which they are accommodated.[124] Thus, Australia has expanded its juridical border outside of its territory and into the territory of other nation-states. At the same time, the Migration Act restricts the Australian judiciary's ability to look to international law and Papua New Guinea's and Nauru's law and practice in arbitrating the legality of Australia's offshore processing regime.

These misaligned borders are evident in *Plaintiff S156/2013 v Minister for Immigration and Border Protection* ('*Plaintiff S156*'),[125] a 2014 case brought by an Iranian asylum seeker detained in Papua New Guinea. The High Court of Australia was asked to determine, inter alia, whether the Minister had validly designated Papua New Guinea as a regional processing country.[126] The asylum seeker argued that the Minister was obliged to take into account factors such as Australia's and Papua New Guinea's international law obligations, Papua New Guinea's domestic law and practice and the conditions in which asylum seekers were being detained. In a unanimous judgment, the Court rejected this submission on the grounds that section 198AB(2) of the Migration Act provides that the only condition for the minister's exercise of power is that he or she 'thinks that it is in the national interest' which is 'largely a political question'.[127]

But the retraction of the High Court of Australia's juridical borders in offshore processing cases subsequent to *Plaintiff M70* cannot be explained solely with reference to these legislative changes. The High Court of Australia has also limited the reach of constitutional protections. This occurred in its 2016 decision in *Plaintiff M68/2015 v Minister for Immigration and Border Protection* ('*Plaintiff M68*').[128] This case was initiated by a Bangladeshi asylum seeker transferred to and detained on Nauru, but sent back to Australia for medical treatment. She sought an injunction against the minister and officers

---

[120] Ibid s198AA(d).   [121] Mann (n 3) 373.   [122] Ibid 370.   [123] Kesby (n 7) 112–13.

[124] Human Rights Committee, *Concluding Observations on the Sixth Period Report of Australia*, UN Doc CCPR/C/AUS/CO/6 (9 November 2017) [35]; Senate Select Committee on the Recent Allegations Relating to Conditions and Circumstances at the Regional Processing Centre in Nauru, Parliament of Australia, *Taking Responsibility: Conditions and Circumstances at Australia's Regional Processing Centre in Nauru* (2015) 121.

[125] (2014) 254 CLR 28.

[126] The plaintiff also argued that ss198AB and 198AD of the Migration Act are not supported by section 51 of the Australian Constitution (the aliens power), but the High Court rejected this submission: ibid [38].

[127] Ibid [40].   [128] (2016) 257 CLR 42.

of the Commonwealth of Australia and a writ of prohibition preventing them from removing her to Nauru if she were to be detained there. After she filed the proceedings, Nauru
introduced 'open centre arrangements', whereby asylum seekers would not be detained, but
would be granted permission to leave between certain hours. Therefore, the plaintiff would
not be detained if sent back to Nauru as long as Nauru continued with its open centre
arrangements. The Court was satisfied that the plaintiff had standing to bring the claim,
because it would 'determine the question whether the Commonwealth is at liberty to repeat
that conduct if things change on Nauru and it is proposed, once again, to detain the plaintiff
at the centre'.[129] The issue the High Court determined was whether the plaintiff was entitled
to a declaration that the conduct of the Commonwealth in relation to her past detention was
unlawful. In answering this question, the High Court of Australia restrained the reach of
constitutional limits on the Commonwealth's executive power to detain. The majority
(Chief Justice French and Justices Kiefel and Nettle with Justice Keane concurring) held
that these protections would not apply to the plaintiff once Australia transfers her to
Nauruan authorities.[130]

The High Court of Australia not only limited the reach of constitutional protections but
also drew a sharp boundary between the actions of the governments of Australia and Nauru.
It found that the plaintiff was detained by Australia for the purposes of removing her to
Nauru,[131] but, thereafter, she would be detained by Nauru.[132] The majority created a clear
demarcation of responsibility, despite the facts that the processing centres in Nauru were
established at Australia's request, Australia funds the operation of the centres, Australia
deploys contractors to carry out the running of the centres and Australian government staff
are present at the centres.[133]

This creation of a neat juridical boundary is also apparent in the Court's assessment of the
plaintiff's argument that her detention would be invalid under article 5(1) of the
Constitution of the Republic of Nauru[134] and that sections 198AHA(2) and 198AHA(5) of
the Migration Act 'should not be construed as referring to detention which is unlawful
under the law of the country where the detention is occurring'.[135] The majority found that
the authority given in section 198AHA is not qualified by the requirement that Nauruan
laws 'be construed as valid according to the Constitution of Nauru'.[136] It also stressed that it
is not for the High Court of Australia to examine the constitutional validity of another
state's laws.[137] Justice Keane explained that section 198AHA(2) is not 'conditional upon
a judgment by the domestic courts of this country as to the validity of the laws of Nauru'[138]
and highlighted that 'considerations of international comity and judicial restraint militate
strongly against' such a construction.[139]

The creation of a sharp boundary between Australia and Nauru has created a situation of
multiple and misaligned borders that enables Australia and Nauru to remain unaccountable

[129] Ibid [23] (French CJ, Kiefel and Nettle JJ).
[130] Ibid [41] (French CJ, Kiefel and Nettle JJ), [238]–[241] (Keane J).
[131] Ibid [31] (French CJ, Kiefel and Nettle JJ), [239] (Keane J).
[132] Ibid [32] (French CJ, Kiefel and Nettle JJ), [239] (Keane J).   [133] Senate Select Committee (n 124) 13.
[134] Article 5(1) of the Constitution of the Republic of Nauru states that a person shall not be deprived of
their personal liberty except as authorised by law for the purposes specified in that article. In 2013,
asylum seekers in Nauru unsuccessfully challenged their detention under article 5: *AG & Ors v Secretary
for Justice* [2013] NRSC 10.
[135] *Plaintiff M68* (n 128) [47].   [136] Ibid [52] (French CJ, Kiefel and Nettle JJ).
[137] Ibid [48] (French CJ, Kiefel and Nettle JJ).   [138] Ibid [248].   [139] Ibid [250].

for their actions. In the Memorandum of Understanding between Nauru and Australia, Australia accepts some responsibility for those transferred to Nauru with respect to their detention, assessment of refugee status, deportation or settlement in Nauru or a third country. A Senate Committee report in 2015 concluded that, due to Australia's involvement with the setting up and running of the centre, Australia has obligations under international and domestic law in relation to the care of asylum seekers in the centre and holds joint obligations with Nauru in respect to the asylum seekers' human rights.[140] In making this assessment, the Committee's views are in line with the principle that a state carries its human rights obligations with it when acting extraterritorially.[141] The Committee further stated that 'Australia's purported reliance on the sovereign and legal system on Nauru in the face of allegations of human rights abuses and serious crimes at the [Regional Processing Centre] is a cynical and unjustifiable attempt to avoid accountability for a situation created by this country'.[142] The High Court of Australia in *Plaintiff M68* had an opportunity to recognise that Australia was acting extraterritorially in Nauru and that its obligations should extend with it across borders. However, due to the juridical boundary drawn by the majority judges, Australia can continue to operate in Nauru without the limitations placed on it by the Australian Constitution and the Court's oversight. Also, Nauru's treatment of refugees and asylum seekers remains outside the judicial lens, because of the High Court of Australia's unwillingness to pass judgment on Nauru's refugee law and policy.

Plaintiff M68 provided an opportunity to advance the Courts' conceptualisation of refuge with respect to considerations of gender. While there has been criticism of the conditions all refugees in Nauru and Papua New Guinea are subject to,[143] there is particular concern about women. There have been reports of sexual violence and unsafe conditions for women refugees in Nauru.[144] However, by retracting its juridical border, the High Court of Australia has removed judicial scrutiny of these injustices in refugees' legal challenges to be transferred permanently to or remain in Australia.

The retraction of juridical borders gives rise to disharmony between courts in different countries, which imposes greater difficulties for refugees wanting to cross international borders in their searches for refuge. This is evident in a failed attempt by asylum seekers on Manus Island to secure a transfer to Australia through successive litigation in the Supreme Court of Papua New Guinea and the High Court of Australia. In the 2016 decision of *Belden Norman Namah v Hon Rimbink Pato, Minister for Foreign Affairs and Immigration* ('*Belden Norman Namah*'),[145] asylum seekers challenged the legality of their detention before the Supreme Court of Papua New Guinea. The Court stated that the asylum seekers on Manus Island were 'forcefully brought into [Papua New Guinea]'[146] and acknowledged that the

---

[140] Senate Select Committee (n 124) 121.

[141] *Legal Consequences of the Construction of a Wall in the Occupied Palestinian Territory (Advisory Opinion)* [2004] 1CJ Rep 136 [109]; Human Rights Committee, *General Comment No 23: Article 27 (Rights of Minorities)*, UN DOC CCPR/C/21/Rev.1/Add.5 (8 April 1994) [4].

[142] Senate Select Committee (n 124) 122.

[143] See, e.g., Australian Human Rights Commission, *Asylum Seekers, Refugees and Human Rights: Snapshot Report (Second Edition)* (2017) <https://humanrights.gov.au/our-work/asylum-seekers-and-refugees/publications/asylum-seekers-refugees-and-human-rights-0>; Human Rights Council, *Report of the Working Group on the Universal Periodic Review: Australia*, UN Doc A/HRC/31/14 (13 January 2016).

[144] Senate Select Committee (n 124) 99; Wendy Bacon et al, *Protection Denied, Abuse Condoned: Women on Nauru at Risk* (June 2016) <https://static1.squarespace.com/static/5624aa24e4b0bca6fa63ec33/t/5754f2f327d4bd54e0327996/1465185083858/Women_on_Nauru_WEB.pdf>.

[145] [2016] PJSC 13.   [146] Ibid [20].

litigation's ultimate aim was to secure their removal from the Manus Detention Centre and transfer to Australia.[147] The Court found that the asylum seekers' detention was in violation of the right to liberty in section 42 of the Constitution of Papua New Guinea. In coming to this conclusion, the Court engaged in categorical and rights-based reasoning. It placed emphasis on the fact that those in the Manus Detention Centre were seeking recognition of their refugee status and discussed Papua New Guinea's international obligations as a signatory to the Refugee Convention.[148] The Court also referred to the UNHCR's detention guidelines and noted that the UNHCR had reported that the conditions in the Manus Detention Centre 'lack some of the basic conditions and standards required'.[149] The Court ruled that Papua New Guinea's Memorandum of Understanding with Australia was unconstitutional and invalid.[150] It ordered Australia and Papua New Guinea to take all steps necessary to cease and prevent the continued detention of the asylum seekers at the Manus Detention Centre.[151]

While the asylum seekers' challenge to the bilateral agreement between Papua New Guinea and Australia was successful in the Supreme Court of Papua New Guinea, they could not secure a transfer to Australia without a similar victory in the Australian courts. Four months after the Supreme Court of Papua New Guinea handed down its judgment in *Belden Norman Namah*, an Iranian asylum seeker held in the Manus Detention Centre challenged the validity of the Memorandum of Understanding between the two countries before the High Court of Australia in *Plaintiff S195/2016 v Minister for Immigration and Border Protection* ('*Plaintiff S195*').[152] One issue the Court addressed was whether Australia's entry into the Memorandum of Understanding with Papua New Guinea was beyond the power of the Commonwealth of Australia[153] by reason of the Supreme Court of Papua New Guinea's decision in *Belden Norman Namah*. One argument the plaintiff advanced was that 'the Constitution denies to the Commonwealth any legislative or executive power to authorise or take part in activity in another country which is unlawful according to the domestic law of that country'.[154] In its short judgment, the High Court of Australia referred to this proposition as 'novel and sweeping'[155] and stated that:

> neither the legislative nor the executive power of the Commonwealth is constitutionally limited by any need to conform to international law. Equally there should be no doubt that neither the legislative nor the executive power of the Commonwealth is constitutionally limited by any need to conform to the domestic law of another country.[156]

These two decisions are indicative of the dissonance that can occur between domestic courts when juridical borders are misaligned and the consequences for refugees' quests for refuge. The Supreme Court of Papua New Guinea stretched its juridical border more broadly than the Australian High Court. While it based its decision on the right to liberty in the Constitution of Papua New Guinea, it also took into account Papua New Guinea's international law obligations such as those under the Refugee Convention and made an order directed to Australia. Conversely, the High Court of Australia referred exclusively to Australian domestic law and ignored the Supreme Court of Papua New Guinea's decision in *Belden Norman Namah*. This incongruity is partly due to Australia's lack of a federal Bill

---

[147] Ibid [39].   [148] Ibid [67].   [149] Ibid [27], [66], [68].   [150] Ibid [39].   [151] Ibid [72].
[152] (2017) 346 ALR 181. The High Court of Australia noted that the plaintiff asserted that he is a refugee but Papua New Guinea rejected his claim to refugee status: [1].
[153] As conferred by section 61 of the Australian Constitution and section 198AHA of the Migration Act.
[154] *Plaintiff S195* (n 152) [19].   [155] Ibid [19].   [156] Ibid [20].

of Rights or Human Rights Act as well as the absence of a regional human rights regime in the South Pacific. This gives rise to a situation where asylum seekers are trapped within a place of unsafe and inadequate refuge, unable to wield legal arguments to continue their journey to find genuine sanctuary. The prospect of transnational public law litigation[157] did not eventuate. Next, I examine similar developments for asylum seekers in the US without adequate protection wanting to cross into Canada.

5.4.2 Malleable and Misaligned Borders in North America

A situation of multiple and asymmetrical borders exists with respect to the Canada–US Agreement, but was not brought about by legislative change. In 2008, the Federal Court of Appeal overturned Justice Phelan's judgment and restored the validity of the Canada–US Agreement.[158] In doing so, the Federal Court of Appeal adopted a different interpretation of the Immigration and Refugee Protection Act, and one that limits judicial oversight of the Governor in Council's decisions. The Federal Court of Appeal held that Justice Phelan erred in ruling that US compliance with the Refugee Convention and CAT was a condition precedent to the Governor in Council exercising delegated authority.[159] Rather, the only requirement was that the Governor in Council considered the factors outlined in the relevant sections of the Immigration and Refugee Protection Act and, 'acting in good faith', designated the US as a country that complied with its *non-refoulement* obligations and was 'respectful of human rights'.[160] Thus, while the first instance decision set the standard only at the protection from *refoulement*, the appeal decision removed this baseline level of protection.

By adopting a different interpretation of the Immigration and Refugee Protection Act, the Federal Court of Appeal retracted the juridical boundary in a way that does not permit consideration and assessment of refugee law and policy in the US. This creates multiple and misaligned borders similar to those in the Australian context: the executive's juridical border extends horizontally to take into account the law and practice of other states, but the judiciary's juridical border does not have the same reach.

Another way in which the 2008 appeal decision retracted juridical borders was through restraining the reach of constitutional protections. While the 2007 Federal Court of Canada judgment extended the Canadian Charter's reach beyond Canada's geographic borders and into US territory, the Federal Court of Appeal limited its application to those at or within Canada's geographic borders. The Federal Court of Appeal held that the rights in the Canadian Charter were not triggered, because 'John Doe never presented himself at the Canadian border'.[161] The Court stated that the Federal Court's 'conclusion that John Doe should nevertheless be considered as having come to the border and as having been denied entry runs directly against the established principle that Charter challenges cannot be mounted on the basis of hypothetical situations'.[162] The consequence for refugees in the US wanting to have recourse to Canadian courts to continue their journey in search of refuge is that they now have to make the journey to the Canadian border.

While the motivations behind judicial approaches to protection for refuge claims are outside this book's scope, one reason why the Federal Court of Appeal reversed the

---

[157] Harold Hongju Koh, 'Transnational Public Law Litigation' (1991) 100 *Yale Law Journal* 2347.
[158] *Canada v Canadian Council for Refugees* [2008] FCA 229 ('*Canada v Canadian Council for Refugees*').
[159] Ibid [80].   [160] Ibid [80].   [161] Ibid [102].   [162] Ibid [102].

approach taken by the Federal Court may be due to a reticence to pass judgment on US law, especially given the diplomatic ties and geographic proximity of Canada and the US. However, if the asylum seeker is in Canada's territory and makes such a claim, Canadian courts usually have no choice but to assess the allegations. Such is the case when those subject to the death penalty in the US cross the border into Canada and resist extradition.[163] Conversely, for protection from refuge litigants outside Canada's territory such as John Doe, juridical borders remain malleable and can be manoeuvred by decision-makers to short-circuit claims involving an assessment of another state's human rights compliance. Thus, John Doe and other protection from refuge claimants in his position wanting to cross international borders in search of refuge are made acutely aware of the 'persistent impact of sovereignty',[164] as opposed to the prospect of a transnational legal order.

By requiring refugees in the US to present at the Canadian border to trigger Canadian Charter protections, the Federal Court of Appeal's decision disadvantages female refugees and places them at heightened risk. Due to factors such as care responsibilities or lack of financial independence, female asylum seekers are less likely to be in a position to make the journey to Canada's border with the US. Those who do and are summarily returned face the prospect of being detained, not in dedicated immigration detention centres, but in remote and mixed-purpose jail facilities.[165]

This is precisely what occurred when the Canada–US Agreement was challenged again in 2020 in the Federal Court of Canada. There were four refugee applicants. The first three were a refugee family (a mother and two daughters) from El Salvador who feared gang violence if returned to their homeland. They were in the US but travelled to the Canadian border to seek asylum there. The family were granted a stay of their removal to the US pending judicial review of their challenge to the Canada–US Agreement. The fourth was a woman from Ethiopia who had lived in the US for a number of years but was ineligible for asylum. She arrived at the Canadian border and claimed asylum but was returned to the US and immediately detained.

The applicants argued that the Immigration and Refugee Protection Act requires a continuing review of Canada's designation of the US as a safe third country and obligates the Minister to form an opinion that the designation should be maintained. The applicants provided evidence attesting to the US not being a safe third country, including information about immigration detention, the risk of *refoulement* due to aspects of US asylum law, including the one-year bar, border policies designed to deter 'illegal' immigration such as detention and separation of families, and that US asylum jurisprudence makes it difficult for applicants who fear gang violence and gender-based persecution to be considered refugees.

However, Justice McDonald of the Federal Court found that she was bound by the 2008 Federal Court of Appeal decision.[166] In dismissing the argument, Her Honour stressed that the 2008 judgment held that the Immigration and Refugee Protection Act does not require actual compliance with the Refugee Convention or CAT for a state to be designated as a safe

163 See, e.g., *United States v Burns* [2001] SCR 283.
164 Antonio Cassese, 'A Plea for a Global Community Grounded in a Core of Human Rights' in Antonia Cassese (ed), *Realizing Utopia: The Future of International Law* (Oxford University Press, 2012) 136, 138.
165 Arbel (n 108) 256.
166 *The Canadian Council for Refugees et al v The Minister of Immigration, Refugees and Citizenship and the Minister of Public Safety and Emergency Preparedness* [2020] FC 770 [80] ('*Canadian Council for Refugees et al 2020*').

third country.[167] Thus, the 2020 decision on the Canada–US Agreement maintained the situation of multiple and misaligned borders produced by the 2008 judgment of the Federal Court of Appeal: the executive and legislature can expand their juridical borders by entering into an agreement with the US and designating it as a safe third country, but the Canadian judiciary cannot consider or pass judgment on US asylum law and policy, in particular its compliance with international law.

The 2020 challenge to the Canada–US Agreement was successful in the Federal Court of Canada with respect to Canadian Charter arguments. The applicants argued that the Agreement, by exposing them to US immigration detention, was a violation of section 7 of the Charter (the right the life, liberty and security of the person). In finding that there had been a violation, the Court used section 7 of the Canadian Charter as a prism to engage with ideas of refugee protection, similar to the seminal judgments discussed in Chapters 3 and 4. The Court found that, due to the challenges in advancing asylum claims while in immigration detention (lack of access to lawyers and necessary documents), there is a risk of *refoulement*.[168] Further, the Court held that those returned to the US pursuant to the Agreement 'are detained without regard to their circumstances, moral blameworthiness, or their actions',[169] which is 'grossly disproportional to the administrative benefits of the [Canada–US Agreement]'.[170] Her Honour emphasised that '[t]he penalization of the simple act of making a refugee claim is not in keeping with the spirit or the intention of the [Canada–US Agreement] or the foundational *Conventions* upon which it was built'.[171] This reasoning has parallels with the obligation in article 31(1) of the Refugee Convention not to penalise those who have crossed a border without authorisation if they did so for the purpose of seeking asylum.

Nevertheless, the judgment only slightly expanded the Court's juridical borders, and certainly not to the same extent that was achieved in Justice Phelan's 2007 decision. The applicants could only trigger the protections in the Canadian Charter because they had 'been physically present in Canada'.[172] Unlike the 2007 judgment, the 2020 decision did not extend the Canadian Charter's reach extraterritorially so that it could apply to asylum seekers in the US who wanted to claim protection in Canada but could not make the journey to the border. Further, only a small aspect of US asylum practice was considered by the Court. Justice McDonald stated that breaches of human rights by other nation-states are only justiciable under the Canadian Charter if 'there is a sufficient causal connection between our government's participation and the deprivation'.[173] In this case, the connection was Canadian officials being 'involved in the physical handing over of claimants to US officials'.[174] Thus, the only aspect of US asylum practice the Court considered was detention of asylum seekers after they had been returned to the US pursuant to the Canada–US Agreement. Justice McDonald emphasised that '[a]lthough the US system has been subject to much debate and criticism, a comparison of the two systems is not the role of this Court, nor is it the role of this Court to pass judgment on the US asylum system. The narrow focus here is the consequences that flow when a refugee claimant is returned to the US'.[175]

The applicants also argued that the Canadian–US Agreement is in violation of section 15 of the Canadian Charter because of its disproportionate impact on women. However, the Federal Court declined to consider the argument because of the Court's conclusion that the

[167] Ibid [76].   [168] Ibid [106].   [169] Ibid [135].   [170] Ibid [136].
[171] Ibid [139] (emphasis in original). Her Honour was referring to the Refugee Convention and CAT.
[172] Ibid [87].   [173] Ibid [100].   [174] Ibid [101].   [175] Ibid [138].

Agreement is in violation of section 7 of the Canadian Charter.[176] This was a missed opportunity for the Court to examine the gender bias in the US refugee regime. From the narrow approach to the section 7 argument (only considering immigration detention once returned to US authorities) it may be inferred that Justice McDonald was reluctant to determine the section 15 argument because it may have required Her Honour to pass judgment on broader aspects of US asylum law and policy.

The Federal Court of Canada's decision was overturned on appeal.[177] The Federal Court of Appeal held that the applicants did not properly constitute their Charter challenge because they focussed on Canada's initial designation of the US as a safe third country in 2004 and did not include argument with respect to the subsequent administrative reviews of that decision.[178] Thus, the applicants did not provide enough evidence for the courts to adequately assess whether the legislative scheme as a whole (including subsequent administrative reviews undertaken pursuant to the Immigration and Refugee Protection Act) infringes Charter rights.

The appeal decision indicates an even greater reticence to pass judgment on US asylum law and policy and that it will be exceptionally difficult to instigate any future challenge to the Canada–US Agreement. The Federal Court of Appeal not only dismissed the applicants' case but also provided 'guidance [to] those advancing section 7 claims in the area in the future'.[179] The guidance indicated that an exceptionally high evidentiary threshold will be required. Future challenges must provide not only affidavit evidence from asylum seekers and immigration officials but also 'the opinion of experts testifying on system-wide phenomena, the content of United States laws and its effects'.[180] There must be evidence that detention is mandatory as opposed to discretionary[181] and that unacceptable detention conditions such as solitary confinement are 'widespread and regular'.[182] Future applicants arguing that US detention conditions are cruel and unusual must provide stronger evidence than media reports, which are often 'hearsay upon hearsay'.[183] On this point, the Court explained that 'Charter cases with wide implications should not depend on what one finds in a newspaper'.[184] Finally, the Federal Court of Appeal emphasised that the Canadian Charter only applies to 'Canadian state action'[185] and will 'respond to the removal of individuals to foreign legal systems and administrations only where they will suffer effects that are so deplorable they "shock the conscience" of Canadians'.[186] The Court indicated that the applicants produced 'evidence of individual cases of substandard treatment but nothing that rises to the very high level required by the "shocks the conscience" standard'.[187] In the next section, I show that asylum seekers in Europe similarly face a situation in which courts are reluctant to adjudicate the merits of a challenge to a protection elsewhere agreement.

5.4.3   Dissonant Juridical Borders in Europe

The pattern of narrowing of the judicial gaze, removing the threshold for effective protection and creating multiple and misaligned juridical borders, observed in Oceania and North America, is also apparent in Europe. After *NS and ME*, the next opportunity for the CJEU to

---

[176] Ibid [154].
[177] *The Minister of Citizenship and Immigration and The Minister of Public Safety and Emergency Preparedness v The Canadian Council for Refugees et al* [2021] FCA 72.
[178] Ibid [90].   [179] Ibid [132].   [180] Ibid [139].   [181] Ibid [139]–[140].   [182] Ibid [142].
[183] Ibid [150].   [184] Ibid [150].   [185] Ibid [154].   [186] Ibid [158].   [187] Ibid [161].

rule on a protection elsewhere arrangement was the 2017 case concerning the Europe–Turkey Agreement. The Agreement involves asylum seekers on Greek Islands being sent to Turkey and, in exchange, EU member-states agreeing to resettle some Syrian refugees living in Turkey. The case was brought due to concerns about the lack of protection in Turkey. While Turkey is a party to the Refugee Convention, it has maintained the geographical limitation, meaning it is only obliged to consider as refugees those individuals who have fled from events taking place in Europe.[188] Thus, its Refugee Convention obligations would not extend to those being sent to Turkey pursuant to the Europe–Turkey Agreement, most of whom were fleeing the Syrian conflict.

This case was an opportunity for the CJEU to set a high standard for effective protection. As outlined earlier, the reason why the Court set a low bar in *NS and ME* was due to the need to preserve the integrity of the Dublin System. Thus, the Court's view was that there must be a presumption of compliance with respect to fundamental rights between EU member-states. However, this is not applicable to a challenge to the EU–Turkey Agreement, with Turkey not being a member of the EU. Thus, it was open to the Court to refer to rights in the EU Charter, including the right to asylum in article 18 (which the Court had previously acknowledged requires 'the rules of the [Refugee Convention] to be respected'),[189] in ruling on the Agreement's legality.

The Court held that it did not have jurisdiction to hear the case and, thus, did not consider any of the substantive allegations. The Europe–Turkey Agreement was published by way of a press release on the Council of the European Union's website. Nevertheless, the Council denied that it, or any other EU body, authored the statement.[190] Instead, it argued that the statement was issued by individual EU member-states.[191] As part of this argument, the Council stressed that, while there was a meeting between the Council of the European Union and Turkey on 17 March 2016, there was a separate meeting between heads of state or government of EU member-states and Turkey on 18 March 2016. The Council alleged that the statement was the result of the latter meeting.[192] The Court accepted this argument and stated that the words 'Members of the European Council' in the press release 'must be understood as references to the Heads of State or Government of the European Union'.[193] It held that it did 'not have jurisdiction to rule on the lawfulness of an international agreement concluded by the Member States'.[194] The Court declined to determine whether the agreement was legally binding.[195]

The Court's decision has been described as 'hyper-formalistic',[196] 'steeped in factual detail'[197] and 'legally unpersuasive'.[198] The main critique is that the Court did not acknowledge that EU member-states would not have had the power to conclude an agreement

---

[188] Article 1B(1) of the Refugee Convention allowed states to elect to apply the Convention to 'events occurring in Europe before 1 January 1951' or 'events occurring in Europe or elsewhere before 1951'. Article 1(2) of the 1967 Protocol Relating to the Status of Refugees removed the temporal limit. Article 1(3) of the Protocol removed the geographic limitation with an exception for those states that had made declarations limiting their obligations to 'events occurring in Europe'.

[189] *NS and ME* (n 25) [7].   [190] *NF v European Council* (Case T-192/16, 28 February 2017) [37].

[191] Ibid [38].   [192] Ibid [38].   [193] Ibid [69].   [194] Ibid [73].   [195] Ibid [71].

[196] Violeta Moreno-Lax, 'The Migration Partnership Framework and the EU-Turkey Deal: Lessons for the Global Compact on Migration Process?' in Thomas Gammeltoft-Hansen et al (eds), *What is a Compact? Migrants' Rights and State Responsibilities Regarding the Design of the UN Global Compact for Safe, Orderly and Regular Migration* (Raoul Wallenberg Institute of Human Rights and Humanitarian Law, 2017) 27, 31.

[197] Spijkerboer (n 3) 225.   [198] Freier De Ferrari, Karageorgiou and Ogg (n 80) 524.

covering matters (such as border control and asylum) already regulated by EU law.[199] Some scholars go further and highlight that the Court could have invalidated the agreement on these grounds.[200] The other major criticism is that the Court ignored evidence which indicated that the European Council had in fact adopted the agreement. For instance, EU institutions have been involved in implementing the agreement[201] and EU actors, including the President of the European Council, have described it as an EU agreement.[202] The decision was appealed but the appeal was held to be inadmissible because the appellants did not state the grounds of appeal 'with the requisite degree of precision'.[203]

With respect to why the Court approached the case in this manner, Spijkerboer suggests that the Court wanted to 'steer free of the substantive issues of this case'.[204] This is because if it held that it had jurisdiction, it would have to determine that the EU–Turkey Agreement was not in compliance with refugee protection standards or, alternatively, it would have had to interpret these standards narrowly.[205] The first option would have caused political controversy and the second would not be in refugees' best interests.[206] (In a decision handed down just a week later concerning a Syrian family claiming asylum in a Belgium embassy, a case outside this book's scope, the Court similarly avoided controversy by declining jurisdiction).[207]

---

[199] Sergio Carrera, Leonhard den Hertog and Marco Stefan, 'It wasn't Me! The Luxembourg Court Orders on the EU-Turkey Refugee Deal' (Paper No 2017-15, CEPS Policy Insights, April 2017) 8; Moreno-Lax (n 196) 31; Spijkerboer (n 3) 225.

[200] Carrera, den Hertog and Stefan (n 199) 8.   [201] Ibid 2.   [202] Spijkerboer (n 3) 221.

[203] *NF, NG, NM* (C-208/17 P to C-210/17 P, 12 September 2018).

[204] Spijkerboer (n 3) 224. See also Iris Goldner Lang, 'Towards "Judicial Passivism" in EU Migration and Asylum Law?' in Tamara Capeta, Iris Goldner Lang, Tamara Perišin (eds), *The Changing European Union: A Critical View on the Role of Law and Courts* (Hart, 2020).

[205] Spijkerboer (n 3) 224.   [206] Ibid 224.

[207] *X and X v État belge* (C-638/16 PPU, 7 March 2017). The Court had to determine whether a Syrian family's application for a visa for humanitarian purposes in the Belgian embassy in Lebanon triggered obligations under the European Charter, the ECHR and Refugee Convention: [28]. The family returned to Syria after lodging the visa application and framed their argument with respect to feared persecution in Syria and their inability to claim protection in neighbouring countries due to border closures: [20] (see also the framing of the applicant's case in Opinion of Advocate General Mengozzi in *X and X v État belge*, C-638/16 PPU, 7 February 2017 [32]). The applicants did not raise issues with respect to the quality of protection in Lebanon or other neighbouring countries; hence, the case is outside this book's scope. Nevertheless, legal advice provided to the applicants highlighted the lack of adequate protection in Lebanon: Thomas Spijkerboer, Evelien Brouwer and Yussef Al Tamimi, 'Advice in Case C-638/16 PPU on Prejudicial Questions Concerning Humanitarian Visa' (5 January 2017) [4.3]–[4.4] <www.refworld.org/docid/5874ee484.html>. The Advocate General (in an opinion not followed by the Grand Chamber) considered not only the conditions in Syria but also those in Lebanon and the precarious nature of the journey to Europe: Opinion of Advocate General Mengozzi in *X and X v État belge*, C-638/16 PPU, 7 February 2017 [145]–[155]. In any event, the outcome of the litigation is consistent with the argument in this chapter. The Court had an opportunity to set a high standard for refuge by determining that, when a person applies for a short-term visa under the EU's Visa Code, EU member-states must respect the rights in the EU Charter, ECHR and Refugee Convention. The Advocate General held that because the applicants applied for a short-term visa under the Visa Code, the Court had jurisdiction to determine the case ([49]–[54]), and when adopting a decision on such visa applications member-states must comply with articles 4 and 18 of the EU Charter, which, in the Advocate General's view, are equivalent to article 3 of the ECHR and article 33 of the Refugee Convention: [106]–[107]. However, the Grand Chamber determined that the Court did not have jurisdiction because, while the applicants formally applied for a short-term visa under the Visa Code, they intended to apply for longer-term humanitarian visas, which are not regulated by the Visa Code or any other aspect of EU Law: [42]–[45]. For a discussion, see Spijkerboer (n 3) 225–7.

As a result of the Court constricting its judicial lens by declaring it lacked jurisdiction, no guidance was given as to what constitutes an appropriate standard of effective protection. As noted earlier, if the Court made a ruling on the substantive issues in dispute, it could have set a high standard for the protection that needs to be in place before a refugee can be transferred to a third country outside the EU. However, as Moreno-Lax opines '[n]o regard was had to the non-refoulement protections, the right to asylum, the prohibition of collective expulsion, or the freedom to leave any country including one's own inscribed in international and EU law'.[208]

Not only did the CJEU retract its juridical border, the decision resulted in the production of multiple and misaligned juridical borders, similar to those created by Australian and Canadian courts. By holding that the agreement was not the product of EU institutions but was entered into by EU member-states, and not declaring it invalid on this basis, the Court did two things. First, it contracted its own legal reach with respect to hearing and determining the substantive allegations in the case, most of which concerned inadequate refugee protection. Second, it allowed EU member-states to continue implementation of the EU–Turkey Agreement unconstrained by checks and balances imposed by EU law.[209] As a result, refugees in Europe are subject to the EU–Turkey Agreement but, at the same time, not protected by any of the rights in the EU Charter. It is a further example of Mann's observation that 'courts have been active players in a process that reduces the accountability of executive branches for human rights violations'.[210]

In addition, the decision has given rise to a situation of judicial dissonance akin to the discordance in the Oceanic region created through challenges to offshore processing in different jurisdictions. Giuffré highlights the irony that, prior to the CJEU's decision on the EU–Turkey Agreement, the ECtHR had ruled in a handful of cases that Turkey's treatment of refugees is in violation of a number of rights, including inhuman and degrading treatment and liberty.[211] Because the CJEU washed its hands of the EU–Turkey Agreement, individual refugees on Greek Islands resisting transfer to Turkey will have to frame their case with reference to rights in the Council of Europe's ECHR. They will have to exhaust all domestic remedies before they can bring their case to the ECtHR, which will determine each challenge on a case-by-case basis. Lack of access to legal assistance and interpreters for refugees on the Greek Islands[212] raises a number of significant obstacles to a successful challenge.[213]

A similar situation has been produced by the Court of Appeal in Tripoli in a 2020 ruling that it does not have jurisdiction to determine a claim regarding the validity of a Memorandum of Understanding with Italy whereby Italy provides support to Libya to prevent refugees reaching its shores.[214] The Court ruled that it did not have jurisdiction because the Memorandum is

---

[208] Moreno-Lax (n 196) 31.   [209] Carrera, den Hertog and Stefan (n 199) 2, 9.   [210] Mann (n 3) 320.

[211] Mariagiulia Giuffré, *The Readmission of Asylum Seekers under International Law* (Hart, 2020) 170. Giuffré cites *Abdolkhani and Karimnia v Turkey* (Application No 30471/08, 22 September 2009) and *SA v Turkey* (Application No 74535/10, 15 December 2015).

[212] Gisti/Migreurope, *Inferno at the Greece-Turkey Border* (April 2020) 45 <www.gisti.org/IMG/pdf/report_samos_2020.pdf>.

[213] Neylon discusses how instruments such as the EU–Turkey Agreement produce 'a series of precarious legal statuses, under which refugees and asylum seekers are constantly at threat of removal': Anne Neylon, 'Producing Precariousness: "Safety Elsewhere" and the Removal of International Protection Status Under EU Law' (2019) 21 *European Journal of Migration Law* 1, 2.

[214] For a discussion of the Memorandum of Understanding, see Violeta Moreno-Lax, 'The Architecture of Functional Jurisdiction: Unpacking Contactless Control—On Public Powers, S.S. and Others v. Italy, and the "Operational Model"' (2020) 21(3) *German Law Review* 385, 390–6.

a sovereign act and the Court's jurisdiction is limited to administrative acts.[215] The Court, by declining jurisdiction, has 'mirrored' the position taken by the CJEU, most probably to avoid political controversy.[216] It may potentially give rise to judicial dissonance, with the ECtHR soon to decide whether Italy's actions under the agreement are in violation of the ECHR.[217] In the next section, I consider which, if any, asylum seekers and refugees can navigate these multiple and misaligned borders in their search for a place of refuge.

5.5   The Trapped Refugee

As a result of the ways judges manoeuvre juridical borders in challenges to containment agreements, are particular refugees more likely to be successful in using courts in their searches for refuge? In Chapters 3 and 4, I argued that refugees have to be viewed as acutely vulnerable or exemplary to succeed in protection from refuge claims grounded in human rights law. There are echoes of this story in Dublin System jurisprudence. But the multiple and mismatching borders present in the cases examined in this chapter add another dynamic. Scholars have argued that refugees challenging bilateral or regional containment instruments are outside the scope of law[218] or in a state of liminality.[219] Next, taking each region in turn, I argue that a more accurate understanding is that they are often trapped between misaligned borders, unable to wield legal arguments to continue their journey to find genuine sanctuary except in extreme and exceptional circumstances.

5.5.1   Navigating Borders and Bifurcation in Europe

With respect to the Dublin System, asylum seekers who are deemed particularly vulnerable are in a stronger position to draw on EU law to resist a transfer. This is similar to the pattern observed in Chapters 3 and 4. While the threshold of protection remains as preclusion of inhuman and degrading treatment, in 2017, the CJEU provided guidance on transfers of people with serious health conditions. The case concerned a woman who had recently given birth and was experiencing severe psychiatric problems. The Court indicated that, if asylum seekers will not be provided with appropriate medical care in the receiving state, or conditions in the receiving state may exacerbate the condition, this may amount to inhuman and degrading treatment.[220] Further, in exceptional cases, the transfer itself, notwithstanding the conditions in the receiving state, may present a risk of the person suffering inhuman and degrading treatment.[221] The asylum seeker must provide proof of the 'particular seriousness of his [or her or their] state of health and the significant and irreversible consequences to which his [or her or their] transfer might lead'.[222] A similar approach has been taken in a decision by the Netherlands Council of State.[223]

---

[215] I am grateful to Majd Achour for the English translation of the case, see Achour and Spijkerboer (n 3).
[216] Ibid.
[217] As noted in Chapter 4, a case has been lodged in the ECtHR but had not been determined at the time of writing: *SS and Others v Italy* (Application No 21660/18). See discussion in Moreno-Lax (n 214).
[218] Emma Larking, *Refugees and the Myth of Human Rights: Life Outside the Pale of Law* (Ashgate, 2014) 120; Spijkerboer (n 3) 232.
[219] Arbel (n 3) 83.   [220] *CK v Supreme Court of the Republic of Slovenia* (n 66) [68].
[221] Ibid [73]–[74].   [222] Ibid [75].
[223] *Applicant v Secretary for Justice and Security* NL19.2855 and NL19.2857, 15 July 2019. The case concerned a Dublin System transfer of a mother and daughter to Greece. The Court noted that it had,

The notion of particular or extreme vulnerability has also arisen in cases regarding living conditions in the responsible member-state. In 2019, the CJEU held that, when a person would be transferred to a member-state that provides no subsistence allowance but would not be treated differently to that state's nationals, article 4 will only be triggered when the person will 'because of his or her particular vulnerability' be subject 'a situation of extreme material poverty'.[224] On the same day, in a case concerning the transfer of an asylum seeker from Germany to Italy, the Court held that Italy's lack of support and integration programmes for refugees does not present a real risk of being subjected to inhuman or degrading treatment.[225] The Court did, however, stress that an asylum seeker 'may be able to demonstrate the existence of exceptional circumstances' or a 'particular vulnerability' that would mean they would be facing 'a situation of extreme material poverty' if they were transferred to the responsible state pursuant to the Dublin System.[226]

The CJEU has also acknowledged that extreme and exceptional circumstances may give rise to conditions that present a risk of inhuman or degrading treatment. In a case concerning increased numbers of refugees entering Croatia as a result of the Syrian conflict, the Court indicated that there may be risk of inhuman and degrading treatment 'following the arrival of an unusually large number of third-country nationals seeking international protection'.[227] However, in this case it held that increased numbers of refugees from Syria entering Europe in 2015 did not overwhelm Croatia's asylum system to the extent that there was such a risk.

There are also some additional protections for children and family unity. The CJEU has held that, when an unaccompanied minor has submitted applications for international protection in more than one member-state, the principle of the best interests of the child dictates that the member-state responsible for examining the application is the one in which the unaccompanied minor is present.[228] The Court explained that '[s]ince unaccompanied minors form a category of particularly vulnerable persons, it is important not to prolong more than is strictly necessary the procedure for determining the Member State responsible, which means that, as a rule, unaccompanied minors should not be transferred to another Member State'.[229] However, the Court has also determined that the principle of the best interests of the child does not oblige an EU member-state to examine a child's application for international protection for which it is not responsible.[230] In these circumstances, a child and their family can be transferred to the member-state responsible. The CJEU has also considered provisions of the Dublin II Regulation that require family unity in circumstances of familial dependency.[231]

---

in prior cases, approved transfers to Greece on the ground that its reception conditions had significantly improved and were in line with its human rights obligations. However, in this case, the daughter had significant mental health conditions. The Court ordered the State Secretary to reassess the case with due regard to the daughter's vulnerability and determine whether, given her medical conditions, she would be exposed to inhuman or degrading treatment if sent to Greece.

[224] *Bashar Ibrahim v Bundesrepublik Deutschland* (n 76) [93]. This was followed by the Dutch Council of State with respect to an asylum seeker with significant mental health concerns resisting transfer to Greece: Ruling 202006266/1/V3, 28 January 2021, ECLI:NL:RVS:2021:179.

[225] *Abubacarr Jawo v Bundesrepublik Deutschland* (n 77) [96].   [226] Ibid [95].

[227] *AS v Slovenian Republic* (n 76) [101].

[228] *The Queen on the application of MA, BT, DA v Secretary of State for the Home Department* (C-648/11, 6 June 2013).

[229] Ibid [55].   [230] *MA and Others v Ireland* (C-661/17, 23 January 2019) [71].

[231] *K v Bundesasylamt* (C-245/11, 6 November 2012). The Court was considering the dependency clause in Dublin II (n 56) (article 15). The dependency clause in Dublin III (n 57) is article 16.

With respect to those subject to the EU–Turkey Agreement, there is an additional layer of complexity. Because the CJEU determined it did not have jurisdiction, asylum seekers subject to the agreement are not protected by EU human rights law. Spijkerboer astutely observes that this represents a bifurcation of EU human rights law: the Court 'reserv[ed] European law for Europeans'[232] and placed refugees 'outside the scope of European law'.[233] However, Spijkerboer was only referring to EU law. As noted earlier, refugees subject to the EU–Turkey Agreement are still protected by Council of Europe human rights law (the ECHR in particular). A refugee in Greece subject to a transfer to Turkey pursuant to the Agreement could rely on the ECHR to resist the transfer. An asylum seeker in Turkey could bring an action under the ECHR with respect to the conditions in Turkey and petition for return to Europe.[234] As outlined in Chapter 4, such an argument is unlikely to succeed unless the refugee can establish they are peculiarly vulnerable in some way. Nevertheless, this is a situation of multiple but overlapping legal systems. While those subject to the EU–Turkey Agreement are beyond the scope of EU human rights law, they at least still have the protection of Council of Europe law.

A similar situation exists for those challenging the Memorandum of Understanding between Italy and Libya. While Libyan litigation has been unsuccessful, those who are subject to the Memorandum can still challenge it in the ECtHR. Indeed, as noted earlier, such a case is pending.[235] Next, I argue that, for refugees challenging bilateral containment instruments in North America and Oceania, no such safety net exists.

5.5.2   State of Exception or State of Exceptionality in North America?

In the Canadian context, Arbel argues that refugees in the US wanting to cross into Canada in search of refuge are in a state of liminality.[236] She explains that after the Federal Court of Appeal's 2008 decision, in which it upheld the Canada–US Agreement, the asylum seeker applicant, John Doe, was '[s]tripped of recourse to effective legal action under the Canadian law, and suspended between two conflicting directives, his predicament is that of liminality: he is still subject *to* the law, but left bereft *by* it'.[237] She notes that this 'is in many ways reminiscent of the "state of exception" as discussed by Agamben'.[238] As discussed earlier, the 2020 challenge to the Canada–US Agreement does not change the position of asylum seekers, such as John Doe, within US territory who do not have adequate protection and wish to cross into Canada to claim asylum there. The reason the applicants could bring the 2020 challenge was because, unlike John Doe, they had approached the Canadian border.

Conceiving of John Doe, or any asylum seeker in the US wanting to enter Canada to seek protection, as a person suspended in a liminal state misses an essential dynamic in the scenario. Perhaps it can be said that John Doe and other asylum seekers in the US are in a state of exception: they are subject to US asylum laws, but also abandoned by them because of deficiencies in US refugee law such as the one-year bar. However, their attempt to trigger Canadian legal protections and continue their journey in search of refuge there provides additional layers of complexity obscured by an Agambenian framework, which focusses on

[232] Spijkerboer (n 3) 233.   [233] Ibid 232.
[234] The ECtHR may be reticent to grant return as a remedy. See discussion of *Hirsi Jamaa v Italy* [2012] II Eur Court HR 97 in Chapter 4.
[235] *SS and Others v Italy* (n 217).   [236] Arbel (n 3) 83.   [237] Ibid 83.   [238] Ibid 83.

the relationship between the sovereign and the individual[239] and does not contemplate situations where a refugee is in one place of refuge, but wants to escape to another. These missing dynamics are evident in Arbel's analysis. She describes John Doe as in an 'impossible bind', because he is required to present at the Canadian border to trigger the Canadian Charter, but the Canada–US Agreement prevents him from doing so.[240] This is not quite accurate. It is true that the 2008 Federal Court of Appeal decision and 2020 Federal Court judgment required asylum seekers to present at the Canadian border to trigger Charter protection, but there is nothing in the Canada–US Agreement to prevent them from doing this. It may be very difficult in a practical sense for asylum seekers in the US to reach the Canadian border, and they may be taking great risks in making the journey, but they are not legally prevented from travelling to the border.

Therefore, it is not correct to say that John Doe and asylum seekers in his position are bound by the law but left bereft by it. According to the 2008 Federal Court of Appeal and 2020 Federal Court judgments, asylum seekers in US territory are not subject to the Canadian Charter. Similarly, while asylum seekers in the US are subject to the Canada–US Agreement, they are not left bereft by it. They are able to challenge the Agreement in Canadian courts. Canadian courts have entertained arguments regarding the validity of the executive's designation of the US as a safe third country. Asylum seekers are not required to be within Canadian territory or present at the border for Canadian courts to hear this argument.

Further, the 2008 Federal Court of Appeal left open the possibility of asylum seekers in the US mounting a claim under the Canadian Charter by presenting at the border and triggering the Canadian Charter's protection.[241] While Mann suggests that '[h]igh-minded judicial opinions ... become guidelines explaining how not to be held responsible for human rights violations',[242] in its 2008 decision, the Canadian Federal Court of Appeal did the opposite: it highlighted a pathway for asylum seekers and their advocates to pursue in future litigation. This was the invitation taken up by the applicants in the 2020 challenge to the Canada–US Agreement who instigated legal proceedings after having approached the Canadian border.

A more complete way to understand the predicament of asylum seekers in the US wanting to seek refuge in Canada is that they are in a country that does not provide them with adequate refuge, but they are trapped there, unable to trigger Canada's legal protections to continue their journey to find sanctuary. They are trapped because Canadian courts have retracted the judiciary's borders by refusing to review the decision to designate the US as a safe third country, and by requiring asylum seekers to present at the border to trigger protections in the Canadian Charter.

The only option is to travel to the border to enliven Canadian Charter protections or cross into Canada in a way that avoids the operation of the Canada–US Agreement through a remote border region or by air travel. Both options are risky and would be impossible for the majority of asylum seekers and refugees in the US, many of whom would not have the finances or physical ability to make the journey. Those with care responsibilities or disabilities that affect their mobility are less likely to be able to cross successfully from the US into Canada. Further, by presenting at the border to trigger the protection of the Canadian Charter, asylum seekers risk being summarily returned to the US, placed in immigration detention and possibly deported. This is what occurred to the fourth applicant in the 2020

[239] Giorgio Agamben, *State of Exception*, tr Kevin Attell (University of Chicago Press, 2005) 1–2.
[240] Arbel (n 3) 83.   [241] *Canada v Canadian Council for Refugees* (n 158) [103].   [242] Mann (n 3) 373.

challenge to the Canada–US Agreement. After Canada returned her to US authorities, she was imprisoned in the same facility as people with criminal convictions, placed in solitary confinement, forced to endure freezing conditions and not provided with adequate food. The 2021 decision of the Federal Court of Canada indicated that even treatment of this nature would not provide grounds for a successful Charter challenge to the Canada–US Agreement.[243] For asylum seekers in the US, continuing the journey to Canada to find refuge requires extraordinary – for some, impossible – feats of bravery. Next, I show that those subject to Australia's offshore processing regime are similarly trapped between multiple and misaligned borders with the intervention of exceptional and extraordinary circumstances their only hope.

5.5.3   Beyond the Pale of Law or Trapped between Dissonant Legal Systems in the Oceanic Region?

Which refugees have been able to resist or escape offshore processing centres in Nauru and Papua New Guinea and what role does the placement of cartographic and juridical borders play in their attempts to secure a place of refuge? Drawing on Arendt's theory of the right to have rights, Larking argues that refugees in Nauru and Papua New Guinea subject to Australia's offshore processing regime cannot 'be considered to exist within the privileged pale of law'.[244] This is because, unlike citizens, permanent residents or lawful visitors, they are not the bearers of 'a constituted legal personality'.[245] While they are 'occasionally subjects of pity, compassion and "humanitarian concern"', they are 'never full subjects of justice, law and rights'.[246]

When the High Court of Australia first retracted its juridical borders in *Plaintiff S156*, it was possible to conceptualise asylum seekers in the Manus Island detention centre as being beyond the pale of law. They were not full subjects of justice, law and rights, because the High Court of Australia did not entertain their arguments regarding their treatment in Papua New Guinea and instead deferred to what the Minister of Immigration believed to be in the national interest. One could also say that these asylum seekers were suspended in a state of liminality: they were subject to Australian law (the Migration Act stated that they can be transferred to an offshore territory and the Memorandum of Agreement between Australia and Nauru provided for their transfer), but were left bereft by it (Australian courts would not examine complaints about the transfer or conditions in which they are detained).

Nevertheless, if we rest the analysis at this point, we are missing an important element: that the asylum seekers were in Papua New Guinea's territory and, therefore, beneficiaries of Papua New Guinea's human rights protections. In their protection from refuge challenge before the Supreme Court of Papua New Guinea (*Belden Norman Namah*), the asylum seekers had a constituted legal personality. They were not objects of humanitarian concern or pity, but full bearers of rights. They were also not in a state of liminality, because, while they were subject to Papua New Guinean law, they were not left bereft by it. Rather, they were able to use the human rights protections in Papua New Guinea's Constitution to argue successfully against their confinement in the Manus Island detention centre.

---

[243] *The Minister of Citizenship and Immigration and The Minister of Public Safety and Emergency Preparedness v The Canadian Council for Refugees et al* (n 177) [161].
[244] Larking (n 218) 120.　　[245] Ibid 135.　　[246] Ibid 135.

However, due to misaligned juridical borders, asylum seekers in Papua New Guinea were only able to trigger human rights law to obtain a partial victory, the closing of the Manus Detention Centre. They could not use legal processes to secure their ultimate aim, which was transfer to Australia. They were not beyond the pale of law or in a liminal state, but were trapped within multiple and misaligned juridical borders, unable to use courts to escape from a place of inadequate refuge and continue their journeys in search of genuine sanctuary. Thus, in the South Pacific region at least, the prospect of a transnational jurisprudence that bolsters human rights protection remains far off.

The only way asylum seekers and refugees can escape their entrapment and continue their searches for refuge in the South Pacific region is by virtue of extraordinary circumstances. This is evident in the aftermath of the High Court of Australia's decision in *Plaintiff M68*. As a result of this judgment, asylum seekers and refugees in Nauru or in Australian territory awaiting transfer to Nauru are trapped within multiple and misaligned juridical borders. The Australian government can transfer them to Nauru and cooperate in their detention or containment in open processing centres through its extraterritorial expansion of its juridical borders. However, they cannot challenge their detention or the conditions they are subject to before Australian courts. They are able to challenge their detention under the Constitution of Nauru, and have done so once but unsuccessfully.[247] However, given the High Court of Australia's decision in *Plaintiff S195/2016*, even a successful challenge in Nauru is unlikely to result in the asylum seekers being transferred to Australia. Nevertheless, the Minister for Immigration permitted the asylum seeker litigant in *Plaintiff M68* to remain in Australian territory. Her story 'triggered an outpouring of public support' for asylum seekers in specific situations[248] and inspired the 'Let Them Stay' campaign.[249] It may have been the fact that M68 was a mother to a child born in Australia that stirred a compassionate response from the Australian public.[250] As a result of this grassroots campaign, she and other asylum seekers understood to have special protection needs such as children, cancer patients, those identified as a suicide risk and victims of sexual assault have been permitted to stay in Australia.[251] However, they only have permission to stay on a temporary basis and at the minister's discretion.[252]

In addition to extra-legal grounds for a transfer, refugees in Nauru and Papua New Guinea have initiated cases against the Minister for Immigration in Australian courts seeking to be transferred from offshore processing facilities. The refugees have to ground their pleading in tort law (they alleged a breach of the minister's duty of care), because there is no public law cause of action available to them that would secure a transfer to Australia.[253]

---

[247] As already noted (n 134), in 2013, asylum seekers in Nauru unsuccessfully challenged their detention under article 5 of the Constitution of the Republic of Nauru (right to liberty). A further action was lodged in the Supreme Court of Nauru in 2016, but no decision has been handed down: Jane Lee, 'Asylum Seekers: Nauru's Top Court May be Forced to Decide Whether Detention is Lawful', *Sydney Morning Herald* (online 18 August 2016) <www.smh.com.au/national/asylum-seekers-naurus-top-court-may-be-forced-to-decide-whether-detention-is-lawful-20160818-gqvm5i.html>.

[248] Madeline Gleeson, *Offshore: Behind the Wire at Manus and Nauru* (University of New South Wales Press, 2016) 5.

[249] Law Institute of Victoria, 'Let Them Stay Campaign a Success' (2016) 90(5) *Law Institute Journal* 26.

[250] Kate Ogg, 'Sexing the Leviathan: When Feminisms and Crimmigration Meet' in Peter Billings (ed), *Crimmigration in Australia: Law, Politics and Society* (Springer, 2019) 63, 79.

[251] Gleeson (n 248).   [252] Ogg (n 250) 79–80.

[253] For a discussion of other contexts in which tort law has been used in Australia as a proxy to address refugee rights, see Gabrielle Holly, 'Challenges to Australia's Offshore Detention Regime and the Limits of Strategic Tort Litigation' (2020) 21(3) *German Law Journal* 549.

The relief sought in these claims has been granted only in exceptional circumstances and only to access medical care. For example, in two interlocutory matters, the Federal Court of Australia ordered transfers of child asylum seekers on Nauru who had attempted suicide so that they could receive specialist mental healthcare.[254]

The case that gave rise to the possibility of temporary transfer on medical grounds was *Plaintiff S99/2016 v Minister for Immigration and Border Protection ('Plaintiff S99').*[255] S99 was raped in Nauru after having an epileptic fit and becoming unconscious. She fell pregnant and wanted to terminate the pregnancy. This case epitomises the multiple legal borders to which refugees in offshore processing facilities are subject. As I have argued elsewhere, S99:

> arrived in Christmas Island, part of Australia's sovereign territory but excised from Australia's migration zone. She was then sent to Nauru and placed in an immigration detention centre established at Australia's request, funded by Australia, and staffed by Australian Government employees and contractors employed by the Australian Government. When released from detention, Nauru issued her with a visa but she lived in accommodation funded by the Australian Government. She was the victim of a criminal act over which Nauru has jurisdiction to investigate and prosecute but in relation to which the Australian authorities did not provide her with protection. After realising that she was pregnant she could have been brought to Australia as a 'transitory person' if her circumstances were exceptional. The Minister did not deem her circumstances exceptional but 'assumed responsibility' for her and arranged for her to be taken to PNG to undergo surgery. While in PNG, S99 contested this decision in the Australian court system pleading Australian tort law.[256]

S99's legal challenge also indicates the ways in which these manifold legal boundaries are gendered. People of all genders are subject to overlapping legal jurisdictions inherent in externalisation agreements but S99's reproductive capacity and disability meant that these borders were personalised.[257] She could not terminate the pregnancy in Nauru because Nauru criminalises abortion. That Papua New Guinea also criminalises abortion and does not have the medical facilities to perform the surgery on a person with S99's medical conditions was crucial to the Federal Court's decision to issue an injunction.

This case and those following it indicate that there must be exceptional circumstances before the very limited protection offered by tort law can be triggered. In *Plaintiff S99*, it was not the fact that she was subject to a brutal criminal act that gave rise to a successful legal challenge, but that she became pregnant, wanted to terminate the pregnancy and the Minister for Immigration assumed responsibility for her accessing the necessary medical procedures.[258] Subsequent legal challenges in which refugees are seeking medical transfer, the majority of which are still ongoing,[259] indicate that they must be moribund or in extremis before tort law will secure a temporary transfer from offshore processing

---

[254] *AYX18 v Minister for Home Affairs* [2018] FCA 283 (6 March 2018); *FRX17 as Litigation Representative for FRM17 v Minister for Immigration and Border Protection* [2018] FCA 63 (9 February 2018).

[255] [2016] FCA 483.   [256] Ogg (n 250) 73–4.

[257] Ibid 77. In making this argument, I draw on Pickering's idea of personalised borders: Sharon Pickering, *Women, Borders and Violence: Current Issues in Asylum, Migration and Trafficking* (Springer, 2010).

[258] *Plaintiff S99* (n 255) [258]–[263].

[259] For a summary of over sixty medical transfer cases, see Andrew and Renata Kaldor Centre for International Refugee Law, *Medical Transfer Proceedings* <www.kaldorcentre.unsw.edu.au/medical-transfer-proceedings>.

facilities.[260] This litigation prompted the Parliament of Australia in 2019 to pass legislation permitting temporary transfers if the refugee had been assessed by doctors as requiring urgent medical treatment.[261] This legislation was later repealed. Most of those transferred pursuant to court proceedings or the legislation remain in some form of detention.[262] Tort litigation, while securing vital and lifesaving medical transfers for some, has not been successful in dismantling Australia's offshore processing system.[263]

When trapped between multiple and misaligned juridical borders and without the ability to escape through some form of exceptional or extraordinary circumstances, refuge becomes relative. The judicial dissonance in the saga of challenges to Australia's offshore processing regime has given rise to a situation in which refugees on Manus Island, who launched litigation in the Supreme Court of Papua New Guinea to have the Manus Detention Centre closed, later petitioned for it to remain open. After the judgment in *Beldon Norman Namah*, the Papua New Guinean government started closing down the Manus Detention Centre, but the Australian government insisted that it would not bring any refugees from the centre to Australia.[264] Many of the refugees in the Manus Detention Centre were afraid of leaving the centre because they felt they would not be safe in the Manus Island community.[265] They argued for the Manus Detention Centre to be kept open, but the Supreme Court of Papua New Guinea dismissed the action.[266] Thus, similar to the trajectory of forced encampment jurisprudence in Kenya (Chapter 3), what asylum seekers on Manus Island saw as an unacceptable and inadequate place of refuge became the only space of protection available to them and they fought to keep it open.

5.6 Conclusion

In this chapter, I set out to build on my analysis of decision-maker approaches to protection from refuge cases. In Chapters 3 and Chapter 4, I examined how decision-makers determine protection from refuge challenges grounded in human and refugee rights. In this chapter, I investigated protection from refuge claims in which these rights are part of a broader range of legal arguments. Four patterns emerge across these chapters. First, decision-makers adopt robust ideas of refuge when they adopt categorical reasoning by interpreting legal instruments with reference to experiences common to refugeehood or refugees' position in international law. When the High Court of Australia adopted this approach in *Plaintiff M70*, it set a high standard for refuge and characterised it as a duty. Second, in most initial or

---

[260] Kate Ogg, 'Destination Australia: Journeys of the Moribund' in Steven Bender and Veronica Fynn Bruey (eds), *Deadly Voyage: Migrant Journeys Across the Globe* (Lexington Books, 2019) 87.

[261] Home Affairs Legislation Amendment (Miscellaneous Measures) Act 2019 (Cth) sch 6. See discussion in Ogg (n 260).

[262] Refugee Council of Australia, *Offshore Processing Statistics* (1 March 2021) <www.refugeecouncil.org.au /operation-sovereign-borders-offshore-detention-statistics/5/>.

[263] Holly (n 253) 569–70.

[264] Lizzie Dearden, 'Australia to Close Manus Island Refugee Processing Centre after Papua New Guinea Rules Detention Illegal', *Independent* (online 17 August 2016) <www.independent.co.uk/news/world/ australasia/australia-to-close-manus-island-refugee-processing-centre-papua-new-guinea-rules- detention-illegal-a7195106.html>.

[265] Liam Fox, 'Manus Island Detention Centre to Permanently Close Today, 600 Men Refusing to Leave', *ABC News* (online 31 October 2017) <www.abc.net.au/news/2017-10-31/manus-island-detention- centre-to-close-at-5pm-today/9102768>.

[266] *Boochani v Independent State of Papua New Guinea* [2017] PGSC 28 (7 November 2017).

early cases, decision-makers approach protection from refuge challenges in a way that disrupts containment agreements, but subsequent decisions ensure their continuation. Third, as part of this change, decision-makers excise or partially excise the place of refuge from the judicial lens. Fourth, once this shift occurs, the refugee or asylum seeker must be exceptional in some way or be the beneficiary of extraordinary circumstances to continue their journeys in search of refuge.

The additional element of complexity in the cases I examined in this chapter is the role of borders in judicial decision-making. The analysis indicated that taking account of refugees' special position and invoking international law may set higher thresholds for adequate refuge as opposed to referring to comparative jurisprudence. Thus, lack of horizontal transjudicial communication should not always be viewed as a 'problem'.[267] I am not suggesting that transjudicial communication is inherently problematic or should be discouraged. In some contexts, it has enabled courts in different jurisdictions to reach 'correct and authoritative' interpretations of many aspects of refugee law.[268] However, an understanding of refugeehood and refugees' status in international law must guide decision-makers in their use of comparative jurisprudence in protection from refuge contexts.

Once decision-makers determine the threshold for adequate refuge, they must be willing and able to extend their juridical boundaries across geographic borders. In the protection from refuge decisions examined in this chapter, decision-makers excise consideration of the place of refuge through retracting their juridical borders. These decisions give rise to a situation where borders' salience is simultaneously diminished and enhanced to the detriment of refugees: governments extend their juridical borders extraterritorially to transfer or keep refugees in third countries, but courts retract their juridical borders to avoid passing judgment on sites of refuge in other nation-states.

These multiple and misaligned borders trap refugees in inadequate places of refuge and make it impossible for them to continue their journeys in search of genuine sanctuary except in exceptional or extraordinary circumstances. However, the protection provided in these atypical circumstances is less secure, often being achieved extra-legally, or through transfers for temporary periods only. Through this process, the idea of a standard for adequate refuge dissipates and the nature of refuge morphs from a duty to a discretion. Due to the changes in the ways courts approach these protection from refuge challenges, their answer to the 'essential question' of '"Whose refugee?" is all too easily answered by a curt "Not mine"'.[269]

---

[267] Hélène Lambert refers to the lack of transjudicial communication in refugee decisions in the EU as a 'problem': Lambert (n 16) 8.
[268] Hathaway and Foster (n 20) 4.
[269] Jean-François Durieux, 'Three Asylum Paradigms' (2013) 20(2) *International Journal on Minority and Group Rights* 147, 172.

6

Seeking Refuge as a Palestinian Refugee

6.1 Introduction

Palestinian refugees are the second largest refugee group in the world[1] and constitute the longest-standing protracted refugee group.[2] They were also the only group of refugees excluded from the Refugee Convention when it was drafted. The majority of Palestinian refugees live in the Middle East region and receive protection and assistance from UNRWA. While Palestinian refugees have worked hard to rebuild their communities in exile,[3] many feel they have a bleak existence. Samar, a twenty-year-old living in a Palestinian refugee camp in Lebanon, declares, 'We have no rights and no future. We have a lot of problems; We can't work freely, we cannot own a house, we cannot move around. We are treated as if we are not human'.[4]

The difficulties Palestinian refugees face are partly due to ongoing hostilities,[5] discrimination and lack of rights in host countries,[6] and UNRWA's difficult financial circumstances. UNRWA has experienced financial stress for a number of years with a significant mismatch between its mandated activities and UN member-state financial contributions.[7] In 2015, UNRWA had to suspend basic education, health and welfare services.[8] UNRWA's financial crisis was exacerbated by the Trump Administration's 2018 decision to stop funding it (the US was UNRWA's largest donor)[9] and the United Arab Emirates' suspension of

---

[1] The most recent figures are that there are 5.6 million refugees under UNRWA's mandate and 20.4 million refugees under UNHCR's mandate, totalling 26 million refugees globally: UNHCR, *Global Trends: Forced Displacement in 2019* (18 June 2020) 2 <www.unhcr.org/en-au/statistics/unhcrstats/5ee200e37/unhcr-global-trends-2019.html>. This means that Palestinian refugees account for approximately one out of every five refugees in the world. They were the largest group of refugees until recently when the numbers of Syrian refugees reached a reported 6.6 million, making Syrians the largest group of refugees in the world: ibid 3.

[2] Susan Akram, 'Palestinian Refugees and their Legal Status' (2002) 31(3) *Journal of Palestinian Studies* 36.

[3] See Nadya Hajj, *Protection Amid Chaos: The Creation of Property Rights in Palestinian Refugee Camps* (Columbia University Press, 2016).

[4] Clancy Chassay and Duncan Campbell, 'Middle East: Life Inside the Palestinian Refugee Camps in Lebanon', *The Guardian* (online 30 May 2007) <www.theguardian.com/world/2007/may/29/syria.israelandthepalestinians>.

[5] Itamar Mann, 'The New Palestinian Refugees', *EJIL: Talk! Blog of the European Journal of International Law* (19 May 2021) <www.ejiltalk.org/the-new-palestinian-refugees/>.

[6] Akram (n 2); Francesca Albanese and Lex Takkenberg, *Palestinian Refugees in International Law* (Oxford University Press, 2020) ch IV.

[7] Kate Ogg, 'International Solidarity and Palestinian Refugees: Lessons for the Future Directions of Refugee Law' (2020) *Human Rights Law Review* (advance).

[8] Nisreen El-Shamayleh, 'UNRWA Funds Crisis Worries Palestinian Refugees', *Aljazeera* (online 5 August 2015) <www.aljazeera.com/blogs/middleeast/2015/08/unrwa-funds-crisis-worries-palestinian-refugees-150805155300792.html>; UNRWA, 'Lack of Funds Forces UNRWA to Suspend Cash Assistance for Housing Palestinian Refugees from Syria in Lebanon' (Press Release, 22 May 2015).

[9] In 2018, the US cut 300 million dollars in funding to UNRWA, the 'largest ever reduction in funding UNRWA has faced', and UNRWA had to discontinue cash for work activities, food assistance

funding in 2020.[10] In November 2020, UNRWA said it had run out of funds to pay staff and provide critical services due to systemic underfunding and additional costs associated with COVID-19.[11] In 2021, the Biden Administration resumed US funding for UNRWA but at a lower rate than previous levels.[12]

Some Palestinian refugees search for better protection conditions.[13] These journeys are particularly difficult and precarious for Palestinian refugees, many of whom are stateless.[14] In their quest to find refuge further abroad, Palestinian refugees confront article 1D: the Refugee Convention's only 'contingent inclusion' clause.[15] Depending on how decision-makers approach these claims, and, in particular, where they set the scope of refuge, Palestinian refugees will continue to be contained in the UNRWA region or will have a pathway to secure refugee protection further abroad.

Human rights arguments are relevant to these article 1D cases and borders play a role in their determination. But the other conspicuous aspect of this jurisprudence is decision-makers' concern about the Refugee Convention providing a gateway for large numbers of people to migrate to the Global North. To guide my exploration of judicial approaches to these claims, I draw on scholarship that employs critical race theory, postcolonial theory and third-world approaches to international law ('TWAIL') to expose how the Refugee Convention acts to contain those in need of protection in the Global South.[16]

I commence this chapter, in Section 6.2, by outlining the already-noted literature. In Section 6.3, I discuss how it applies to Palestinian refugees' unique status under the Refugee

---

programmes, community mental health programmes and mobile health clinics: UNRWA, 'UNRWA Statement on Implications of Funding Shortfall on Emergency Services in the OPT' (Press Release, 26 July 2018). The US later stopped funding UNRWA altogether. See discussion in Ogg (n 7).

[10] The UAE suspended funding in 2020 and did not resume funding in 2021 due to allegations of financial mismanagement by UNRWA: 'UAE Halts Funding to UN Palestinian Agency in "Reset" of Aid Programme', *Reuters* (online 8 February 2021) <https://news.trust.org/item/20210208153818-1fpqb>.

[11] 'UN Agency for Palestine Refugees Runs out of Money as COVID-19 Spreads', *UN News* (online 10 November 2020) <https://news.un.org/en/story/2020/11/1077332?mc_cid=28ebc11940& mc_eid=677b225ed4>.

[12] Matt Spetalnick, Patricia Zengerle and Jonathan Landay, 'U.S. to Restore More than $200 million in Aid to Palestinians', *Reuters* (online 8 April 2021) <www.reuters.com/article/us-palestinians-usa-exclusive /exclusive-u-s-to-restore-more-than-200-million-in-aid-to-palestinians-sources-idUSKBN2BU23M? mc_cid=99422c12e3&mc_eid=677b225ed4>.

[13] Albanese and Takkenberg (n 6) consider journeys made to Europe, the Americas, Asia-Pacific and Africa: ch V.

[14] Ibid 149–65. Statelessness is defined as 'a person who is not considered as a national by any State under the operation of its law': Convention Relating to the Status of Stateless Persons, 28 September 1954, 360 UNTS 117, in force 6 June 1960 art 1 ('1954 Statelessness Convention'). Many Palestinian refugees fit within this definition. Jordan is the only country in which UNRWA operates that has granted collective citizenship to Palestinian refugees: Akram (n 2) 51. However, article 1(2)(i) of the 1954 Statelessness Convention contains an exclusion clause similar to article 1D of the Refugee Convention.

[15] Akram (n 2) 39; Guy Goodwin-Gill and Susan Akram, 'Brief *Amicus Curiae* on the Status of Palestinian Refugees under International Law' (2000) 11 *Palestine Yearbook of International Law* 187, 191; Mutaz Qafisheh and Valentina Azarov, 'Article 1D' in Andreas Zimmermann, Jonas Dörschner and Felix Machts (eds), *The 1951 Convention Relating to the Status of Refugees and its 1967 Protocol: A Commentary* (Oxford University Press, 2011) [25].

[16] Achiume encourages scholars to use critical race theory and TWAIL to develop a 'more sustained conceptual, theoretical and doctrinal engagement with how [refugee] law mediates racial equality for refugees': Tendayi Achiume, 'Race, Refugees and International Law' in Cathryn Costello, Michelle Foster and Jane McAdam (eds), *The Oxford Handbook of International Refugee Law* (Oxford University Press, 2021) 43, 58.

SEEKING REFUGE AS A PALESTINIAN REFUGEE

Convention. In Sections 6.4 and 6.5, I examine how decision-makers determine the scope and nature of refuge for Palestinians. I argue that particular approaches have come close to setting a broad scope of refuge for Palestinian refugees and characterising the nature of refuge as right as well as a duty. But, in most cases, decision-makers determine these protection from refuge claims in a way that narrows and truncates the scope of refuge for Palestinian refugees and inhibits Palestinian refugees' ability to find a place of refuge outside the UNRWA region. This jurisprudence creates additional barriers for female Palestinian refugees. Nevertheless, some recent decisions provide grounds for a more protection-sensitive approach to Palestinian refugees' journeys in search of refuge.

6.2   The Refugee Convention as a Containment Mechanism

Approximately 85 per cent of the world's refugees are hosted in what the UNHCR refers to as 'developing' countries.[17] This is predominantly because these host states share borders with or are close to countries producing large numbers of refugees. Refugees seek safety in these nearby countries and, while some do not want to travel any further, those who do face a number of barriers in reaching places of refuge further afield. In reflecting on this problem, the UN Secretary-General explains that '[s]tronger solidarity with refugee-hosting countries in the [G]lobal South is absolutely a must'.[18] In this chapter, as noted, I draw on scholars who employ critical race, postcolonial and TWAIL perspectives to illuminate how refugee law compounds these inequities.

Providing one of the first critical race analyses of refugee law, Tuitt argues that the creation of refugee law and refugee definitions in the first half of the twentieth century[19] served as a type of containment mechanism in the sense that this new area of international law restricted, rather than facilitated, movement across international borders.[20] International refugee law's 'supposed positive benefit' is the principle of *non-refoulement*.[21] However, Tuitt writes that we can only conceive of refugee law granting such a benefit if before its emergence migrants 'were confronted with closed state borders'.[22] Tuitt argues that this is 'manifestly not the case'[23] because the emergence of international refugee law in the early twentieth century coincided with the withdrawal of open borders.[24] Thus, the creation of refugee categories did not empower those in need of protection 'to move more freely than they had been in the days before the introduction of refugee status'.[25] Further, the position of those who do not fit within refugee definitions 'became qualitatively worse', because they had been stripped of the benefit of 'free and unfettered' movement.[26] In sum, the creation of international refugee law was not prompted by a desire to extend a benefit to the included category of refugees, but to remove a benefit previously enjoyed by the excluded category (those who do not meet refugee definitions).[27]

---

[17] UNHCR (n 1) 2.
[18] António Guterres, UN Secretary-General, 'Press Conference by Secretary-General António Guterres at United Nations Headquarters' (Press Conference, SG/SM/18580, 20 June 2017).
[19] For discussion of the international instruments pertaining to and defining refugees in the first half of the twentieth century prior to the adoption of the Refugee Convention in 1951, see Guy Goodwin-Gill and Jane McAdam, *The Refugee in International Law* (Oxford University Press, 3rd ed, 2007) 16–20.
[20] Patricia Tuitt, 'Defining the Refugee by Race: The European Response to "New" Asylum Seekers' in Paddy Ireland and Per Laleng (eds), *The Critical Lawyers' Handbook 2* (Pluto Press, 1997) 96.
[21] Ibid 98.   [22] Ibid 98.   [23] Ibid 98.
[24] James Hathaway, *The Law of Refugee Status* (Butterworths, 1991) 1, cited in ibid 98.
[25] Tuitt (n 20) 98.   [26] Ibid 99.   [27] Ibid 97.

Tuitt contends that the definition of a refugee in the Refugee Convention perpetuates the inequities between the Global North and the Global South with respect to responsibility for refugees. This is because the refugee definition has a Western 'ideological slant'.[28] In particular, the persecution requirement includes as refugees those who can prove that they are the victim of harms 'thought to emanate from culpable acts',[29] but excludes those subjected to indiscriminate violence or targeted by non-state actors.[30] (This concern has now been partly addressed by subsequent jurisprudence and legal reforms.[31])

Tuitt also argues that the alienage requirement[32] disadvantages those who cannot travel to make a claim for international protection, especially women and children.[33] Tuitt explains that, while 'movement', particularly journeying across borders, is refugees' 'signifier', 'territorial boundaries, cultural perceptions, age and disability all conspire to curtail movement ... and constantly to withhold the "official" designation "refugee" from those most deserving or it'.[34] Deepening this critique, Kyriakides highlights the irony that, while a person must cross an international border to be a refugee, '[t]he performative expectations of contemporary refuge construct refugees as involuntary, non-wilful objects shaped and moved by forces of conflict'.[35] He explains that, through the notion of the involuntary refugee, '[t]he West (self) is constructed as active (masculine), knowledgeable, and moral; the East (other) as passive (feminine), to be led by Western virtue'.[36]

Similar to Tuitt, Mayblin also examines the history of the Refugee Convention's creation but does so specifically from a postcolonial perspective.[37] Mayblin exposes the colonial forces at play through her analysis of the *travaux préparatoires* and other historical records. She focuses in particular on article 1B of the Refugee Convention, which allowed states to declare whether they would apply the Convention to those displaced as a result of 'events occurring in Europe before 1 January 1951' or 'events occurring in Europe or elsewhere before 1 January 1951'.[38] Mayblin argues that European states and the US were aware of

---

[28] Ibid 100.   [29] Ibid 101.   [30] Ibid 101.

[31] It is now accepted in many jurisdictions that a person will have a well-founded fear of persecution if targeted by non-state actors and the state cannot or will not protect them: see, e.g., *Minister for Immigration and Multicultural Affairs v Khawar* (2002) 210 CLR 1 [29]–[31] (Gleeson CJ), [112]–[114] (Kirby J) ('*Khawar*'); Directive 2011/95/EU of the European Parliament and of the Council of 13 December on Standards for the Qualification of Third Country Nationals or Stateless Persons as Beneficiaries of International Protection, for a Uniform Status for Refugees or for Persons Eligible for Subsidiary Protection, and for the Content of the Protection Granted (Recast) [2011] OJ L 337/9–337/26, art 6(c) ('Directive 2011/95/EU'). There is also protection for people fleeing indiscriminate harm: Directive 2011/95/EU arts 2(f), 15(b)–(c) provide protection to those who, if returned to their country of origin, would face a real risk of torture, or inhuman or degrading treatment, or punishment, or a serious and individual threat to their life or person by reason of indiscriminate violence in situations of international or internal armed conflict.

[32] To qualify as a refugee, a person must be 'outside the country of his [or her or their] nationality' or 'not having a nationality' is 'outside the country of his [or her or their] former habitual residence': Refugee Convention art 1A(2).

[33] Patricia Tuitt, 'Rethinking the Refugee Concept' in Frances Nicholson and Patrick Twomey (eds), *Refugee Rights and Realities: Evolving International Concepts and Regimes* (Cambridge University Press, 1999) 106, 116.

[34] Ibid 116.   [35] Christopher Kyriakides, 'The Racialised Refugee Regime' (2019) 35(1) *Refuge* 3.

[36] Ibid 5.

[37] Lucy Mayblin, *Asylum after Empire: Colonial Legacies in the Politics of Asylum Seeking* (Rowman & Littlefield, 2017) ch 6.

[38] The 1967 Protocol relating to the Status of Refugees removed both the temporal and geographic restrictions to the refugee definition so that the Refugee Convention would have universal application.

refugee-producing situations outside of Europe and were 'willing to provide significant financial aid to alleviate these situations but nevertheless saw them as external to the Refugee Conventions [sic]. As custodians of the world, it was in some sense their responsibility to protect "the children of the Earth" especially if this could be done in situ'.[39]

Critical race, postcolonial and TWAIL scholarship also informs how the Refugee Convention has been interpreted and applied, in particular in the post-Cold War era. Tuitt highlights that, even in situations where the Refugee Convention should respond to refugees from the Global South, Western states have interpreted it in a way that denies international protection to those from that part of the world. She argues that many of what were seen as the 'new' asylum seekers from Asia and Africa who came to the Global North in larger numbers during the 1990s would have fit within the refugee definition.[40] However, Western states did not consider them to be refugees and 'continued to perceive the majority of these refugees according to their excluded status'.[41]

Similarly, Chimni, who provides the most well-known TWAIL analysis of refugee law, contends that Western states disavowed the Refugee Convention as anachronistic once the Cold War ended and 'refugees no longer possessed ideological or geopolitical value'.[42] The 'new' refugees were not politically valuable to Western states, because they were no longer people fleeing communist regimes but 'individuals fleeing the Third World'.[43] Global North states created a 'myth of difference'[44] by claiming that the 'new' asylum seekers coming from developing countries were 'economic migrants rather than political refugees'.[45] (Subsequent to Chimni's scholarship, there is now some jurisprudence that responds to this critique.[46])

With respect to refugee status assessments, Tuitt and Chimni argue that decision-makers restrict the Refugee Convention's responsiveness to claimants from lower-income countries through purported objectivism.[47] This is a process whereby decision-makers undertake an assessment of concepts such as reasonableness, safety or well-founded fear that is supposedly objective, but is 'tainted with local perceptions and thus fails to be context specific'.[48] Chimni and Tuitt contend that 'objectivism' eclipses the refugee's voice and prioritises the state's subjective views over the refugee's experiences.[49]

---

[39] Mayblin (n 37) 144.

[40] Tuitt argues that they were not new refugees, but only new to Western states: Patricia Tuitt, *False Images: The Law's Construction of the Refugee* (Pluto Press, 1996) 69–71.

[41] Tuitt (n 20) 103.

[42] B.S. Chimni, 'From Resettlement to Involuntary Repatriation: Towards a Critical History of Durable Solutions to Refugee Problems' (2004) 23(3) *Refugee Survey Quarterly* 55, 58.

[43] Ibid 58.

[44] B.S. Chimni, 'The Geopolitics of Refugee Studies: A View from the South' (1998) 11(4) *Journal of Refugee Studies* 350, 351.

[45] Ibid 356. Chimni (n 42) also argues that this shift gave rise to Western states supporting repatriation as the preferred durable solution. He suggests that, due to this change in preference, states are able to use the Refugee Convention as a containment mechanism through the operation of the cessation clause (article 1C): (n 42) 61–3.

[46] Many jurisdictions recognise that discriminatory denial of economic and social rights can constitute a well-founded fear of persecution: see, e.g., *RRT Case No N94/04178* (Refugee Review Tribunal, 10 June 1994); *Chen Shi Hai v Minister for Immigration and Multicultural Affairs* (2000) 170 ALR 553 [31] ('*Chen Shi Hai*'); *BG (Fiji)* [2012] NZIPT 800091 [90] ('*BG (Fiji)*'); *MK (Lesbians) Albania v Secretary of State for the Home Department CG* [2009] UKAIT 00036 [353] ('*MK (Lesbians)*'); Michelle Foster, *International Refugee Law and Socio-Economic Rights: Refuge From Deprivation* (Cambridge University Press, 2007).

[47] Chimni (n 42) 62; Tuitt (n 40) 85.   [48] Tuitt (n 40) 85.   [49] Chimni (n 42) 61–2; Tuitt (n 40) ch 5.

Mayblin argues that the colonial forces at play in the creation of the Refugee Convention are reproduced in contemporary refugee law and policy.[50] For example, UK welfare policy is designed to maintain 'asylum seekers in a situation of poverty'[51] and in conditions 'thought unacceptable for citizens'.[52] This resonates with many of the Refugee Convention's drafters' belief that 'higher level[s] of protection [should be] reserved for the non-colonised peoples of the world'.[53] Mayblin explains that refugee law ascribes 'differential value to the lives of human beings'[54] and a postcolonial perspective is essential in explaining this 'exclusionary impulse'.[55]

Taking up and deepening these critiques, Achiume writes about '[x]enophobic anxiety' in refugee law and policy.[56] She explains that xenophobic anxiety can be 'attributable to political bodies or entities such as nation-states that enact policies prohibiting the territorial admission of refugees of specific national origin'.[57] Xenophobic anxiety is predicated by a 'perceive[d] loss of control' over territory and associated implications for the polity.[58] It is 'responsive to actual and perceived shifts in the distribution of state sovereignty, and is in some respects a backlash that seeks to reconsolidate sovereignty in the state'.[59]

Achiume argues that 'international law and policy on involuntary migration are seemingly themselves part of the problem of xenophobia' and she focusses in particular on law (or lack thereof) on responsibility-sharing.[60] She observes that 'disproportionate refugee responsibility sharing can drive refugees to take dangerous chaotic journeys in order to survive'.[61] With respect to the Syrian conflict, Achiume explains that:

> Syrian refugees reportedly chose to return to Syria and risk death in conflict, rather than face starvation in regional host countries. … More generally, early research identified regional conditions of scarcity and livelihood precariousness as drivers of Syrian refugee movements from the Middle East and North Africa onward to Europe. In this case, there is a sense in which shortcomings in the international law governing refugee responsibility sharing can be seen as a 'push factor' contributing to the movement of refugees from the Middle East to Europe, thereby creating conditions that go on to ratchet up anxiety about resulting refugee 'floods'.[62]

The aforementioned scholarship, in critiquing refugee law and policy as mechanisms that contain those in need of protection in the Global South, does not consider Palestinian refugees' specific situation. The only express reference to Palestinian refugees is in Chimni's critical assessment of durable solutions, in which he does not include Palestinians among the refugees in the developing world trying to seek a place of refuge in the Global North.[63] Instead, he classifies them as wanting 'to return to their country of origin'.[64] While Palestinian refugees agitate for the right to return,[65] those who do not feel they have a place of genuine refuge and travel to states that are signatory to the Refugee Convention confront the application of article 1D. Article 1D excludes Palestinian refugees from the Refugee Convention, but also grants ipso facto refugee status if UN

---

[50] Mayblin (n 37) 146, 172–3.   [51] Ibid 173.   [52] Ibid 172.   [53] Ibid 172.   [54] Ibid 26.   [55] Ibid 25.
[56] Tendayi Achiume, 'Governing Xenophobia' (2018) 51(2) *Vanderbilt Journal of Transnational Law* 333, 370.
[57] Ibid 370.   [58] Ibid 371.   [59] Ibid 371.   [60] Ibid 341.   [61] Ibid 384.   [62] Ibid 384–5.
[63] Chimni (n 42) 73.   [64] Ibid 73.
[65] Akram (n 2) 41; John Quigley, 'Displaced Palestinians and the Right to Return' (1998) 39(1) *Harvard International Law Journal* 171. See Mann (n 5) for discussion of the political implications of Palestinian refugees leaving an UNRWA area and claiming protection under the Refugee Convention.

protection or assistance ceases for any reason. In the next section, I explore debates on interpretations of article 1D.

6.3   Article 1D as a Containment Mechanism

There are a number of detailed examinations of the circumstances surrounding article 1D's drafting and states' disparate interpretations of its meaning and application.[66] Of relevance to this chapter is whether article 1D can be considered a mechanism that contains Palestinian refugees in the UNRWA region and frustrates their attempts to seek protection elsewhere. In this section, I position article 1D's drafting history and courts' and scholars' differing interpretations against the backdrop of critical race, postcolonial and TWAIL scholarship to illuminate and orient article 1D's containing effects.

When the Refugee Convention was being drafted, the overwhelming majority of Palestinian refugees were receiving protection and assistance from UNRWA and the now non-operational UN Conciliation Commission for Palestine ('UNCCP').[67] Arab nations took the view that Palestinian refugees should not be part of the Refugee Convention, because the UN was responsible for Palestinians' situation and, thus, bore direct responsibility for them.[68] They also stressed that Palestinian refugees should be repatriated and the drafters assumed that an early solution would be achieved.[69] The exclusion of Palestinian refugees from the Refugee Convention was also supported by Western states because they were reticent to accept 'a new, large group of refugees'.[70] Therefore, as a result of an 'uneasy and ironic conformity',[71] Arab and Western nations agreed that Palestinian refugees should be excluded from the Refugee Convention and continue to be assisted by UNRWA and UNCCP in the Middle East region.

Mayblin's postcolonial analysis of the Refugee Convention's drafting does not neatly map on to the drafters' decisions on article 1D. Palestinians were formerly British colonial subjects, and prior to that, subjects of the Ottoman empire. The decision to exclude them could be seen as part of the colonial desire to protect non-European refugees in situ. However, as part of the negotiations the Egyptian delegate suggested that, while Palestinian refugees should be excluded from the Refugee Convention, they should automatically receive the benefits of the Refugee Convention if UN protection or assistance ceased without Palestinian refugees' position being definitively settled.[72] The drafters agreed

---

[66] Akram (n 2) 40–3; Goodwin-Gill and McAdam (n 19) 151–7; James Hathaway and Michelle Foster, *The Law of Refugee Status* (Cambridge University Press, 2nd ed, 2014) 509–21; Qafisheh and Azarov (n 15).

[67] The UNCCP still exists and reports annually to the UNGA, but has been inactive since the mid-1960s: Terry Rempel, 'From Beneficiary to Stakeholder: An Overview of UNRWA's Approach to Refugee Participation' in Sari Hanafi, Leila Hilal and Lex Takkenberg (eds), *UNRWA and Palestinian Refugees: From Relief Works to Human Development* (Routledge, 2014) 145.

[68] Mostafa Bey, Egyptian Representative, UNGA, *UN Conference of Plenipotentiaries on the Status of Refugees and Stateless Persons: Summary Record of the Twenty-Ninth Meeting*, UN Doc A/CONF.2/SR.29 (28 November 1951). For further discussion, see Akram (n 2) 40; Albanese and Takkenberg (n 6) 80; Goodwin-Gill and Akram (n 15) 201–2.

[69] Bey (n 68) 16; Goodwin-Gill and McAdam (n 19) 153.

[70] Mr Rochefort, French representative, UNGA, *UN Conference of Plenipotentiaries on the Status of Refugees and Stateless Persons: Summary Record of the Nineteenth Meeting*, UN Doc A/CONF.2/SR.19 (26 November 1951) 11. See also Mr Warren, US representative, ibid.

[71] *Amer Mohamed El-Ali v Secretary of State for the Home Department* [2003] EWCA Civ 1103 [16] ('*El-Ali*').

[72] Bey (n 68) 6.

with this proposal on the grounds that it would ensure that Palestinian refugees receive continuity of international protection.[73] As a result of this compromise, article 1D provides:

> This Convention shall not apply to persons who are at present receiving from organs or agencies of the United Nations other than the United Nations High Commissioner for Refugees protection or assistance.
>
> When such protection or assistance has ceased for any reason, without the position of such persons being definitively settled in accordance with the relevant resolutions adopted by the General Assembly of the United Nations, these persons shall ipso facto be entitled to the benefits of this Convention.

Thus, article 1D's first paragraph excludes Palestinian refugees from the Refugee Convention's ambit,[74] but its second paragraph provides that they are ipso facto entitled to the benefits of the Refugee Convention if their UN protection and assistance ceases for any reason.

Applying Tuitt's ideas to article 1D's drafting history indicates that it is both a containment mechanism for Palestinian refugees (in the sense that it confines them to the UNRWA region) and a provision that frees Palestinian refugees from the Refugee Convention's containing effects. Article 1D disenfranchises Palestinian refugees to a far greater extent than other refugees. The benefit of free movement is removed, they cannot access the 'supposed benefit' of *non-refoulement* and to receive protection and assistance they must remain in an UNRWA area of operation (Jordan, Lebanon, Syria, the Gaza Strip and the West Bank). However, article 1D's second paragraph liberates Palestinian refugees from the refugee definition's Western ideological slant: they are automatically accepted as part of the 'included' category and can journey to a country signatory to the Refugee Convention and receive the benefits of refugee protection without having to satisfy the refugee definition.[75]

Nevertheless, article 1D is a clause 'pregnant with ambiguity',[76] and where the balance between containment and liberation from containment lies in Palestinian refugees' quests for refuge depends on the manner in which it is interpreted. One of the main debates on article 1D is whether it should have a 'historically bounded' interpretation (it applies only to those receiving UN protection and assistance when the Refugee Convention was drafted in 1951) or a 'continuative' interpretation (it also applies to their descendants and Palestinians displaced as a result of subsequent hostilities).[77] If the former interpretation is adopted, the group of Palestinian refugees excluded from the Refugee Convention will get smaller over time and article 1D will eventually become redundant.[78] This was the approach taken by the Court of Appeal of England and Wales in *Amer Mohamed Eli-Ali v Secretary of State for the Home Department*.[79] The Court held that article 1D only applies to Palestinian refugees in receipt of UN protection or assistance in 1951.[80] The Federal Court of Australia took

---

[73] Albanese and Takkenberg (n 6) 83; Goodwin-Gill and McAdam (n 19) 154.

[74] While it does not mention Palestinian refugees specifically, it is well accepted that article 1D applies to Palestinians who were displaced as a result of the creation of Israel: El-Ali (n 71) [22]; Goodwin-Gill and McAdam (n 19) 151–2; Hathaway and Foster (n 66) 510; UNHCR, *Guidelines on International Protection No 13: Applicability of Article 1D of the 1951 Convention Relating to the Status of Refugees to Palestinian Refugees*, UN Doc HCR/GIP/16/12 (December 2017) 1–5.

[75] The UNHCR (n 74) states that 'ipso facto' means that the Palestinian refugee is entitled to the rights in the Refugee Convention as long as articles 1C, 1E and 1F of the Refugee Convention do not apply: [29]–[31].

[76] *Minister for Immigration and Multicultural Affairs v WABQ* (2002) 197 ALR 35 [18] ('*WABQ*').

[77] Hathaway and Foster (n 66) 513.   [78] *El-Ali* (n 71) [24].   [79] Ibid.

[80] Ibid [28]. The Court reasoned that a continuative interpretation of article 1D is inconsistent with its plain language: 'at present' cannot be read to mean those who later receive assistance or those who are now

a similar position in *Minister for Immigration and Multicultural Affairs v WABQ*.[81] Hathaway and Foster support this 'historically bounded' interpretation of article 1D.[82] They explain that '[t]he ultimate demise of Art. 1(D) exclusion is, in our view, a result that is not only legally correct, but also deeply principled, as it will restore Palestinians to the position of all other groups who are entitled to protection as refugees so long as they meet the requirements of the refugee definition'.[83] With respect to the Refugee Convention's constraining effect on Palestinian refugees' searches for refuge, Australian and UK courts as well as Hathaway and Foster reach a balanced position. Palestinian refugees not in receipt of UN protection and assistance in 1951 (the majority alive today) do not need to remain in an UNRWA area of operation to receive protection and assistance. They can, like all persons in need of protection, make the journey to a state party to the Refugee Convention. Nevertheless, to obtain refugee protection, they must satisfy the refugee definition and be subject to its constraining effects. Further, Hathaway and Foster, in advocating for this position on both legal and ethical grounds, provide a counterpoint to Chimni's criticism that refugee law scholars analyse the Refugee Convention in a political vacuum.[84]

Other jurisdictions have adopted a different interpretation. The Court of Justice of the European Union's (CJEU) position is that article 1D applies to anyone who is presently entitled to UNRWA's protection and assistance as long as they have availed themselves of that protection.[85] The New Zealand Immigration and Protection Tribunal similarly rejected a historically bounded interpretation of article 1D.[86] The Tribunal ruled that article 1D

receiving assistance: [33]. Further, the ipso facto entitlement to the benefits of the Refugee Convention confers on Palestinian refugees 'highly preferential and special treatment' and, therefore, 'the class of persons caught by the first sentence should be identified and fixed by reference to a particular date': [36]. In relation to the meaning of 'ceased for any reason', the Court determined that this refers to UNRWA ceasing to function as an institution because the drafters did not intend for article 1D's inclusionary paragraph to apply 'piecemeal and haphazardly': [47]. The Court acknowledged that UNRWA's protection or assistance can cease for an individual Palestinian refugee, but only in exceptional circumstances such as where the refugee would be prevented from returning to UNRWA's area of operations: [48].

81 *WABQ* (n 76) [69], [162]–[163]. At [69], the Court was satisfied that the drafters intended that article 1D was only to apply to Palestinian refugees. However, if article 1D had continuative effect, then it would apply to any refugee population where the UN set up alternative agencies for protection, which would be antithetical to the drafters' intent. Further, article 1D was intended to be a 'temporary measure' applied until a permanent solution could be found and the drafters did not contemplate that the situation would become 'so intractable'. The Court also held that article 1D's second paragraph does not apply on a case-by-case basis. The Court reasoned that the prospect of an individual Palestinian refugee being ipso facto entitled to the benefits of the Refugee Convention by simply leaving UNRWA's area of operation is inconsistent with the *travaux préparatoires*, which indicate that European states were concerned about the prospect of 'a flood of Palestinian refugees'. Also, article 1D was never intended to give Palestinian refugees the choice between special UN protection or assistance and protection as Convention refugees.

82 Hathaway and Foster (n 66) 513–14. They highlight that the Refugee Convention was drafted simultaneously with the UNHCR Statute, which uses the language 'continues to receive from other organs or agencies of the United Nations protection or assistance'. However, the Refugee Convention's drafters rejected the language 'continue to receive' and adopted 'at present receiving', which indicates a historically bounded interpretation is to be preferred: 514.

83 Ibid 515.   84 Chimni (n 42) 353.

85 *Bolbol v Bevándorlási és Állampolgársági Hivatal* [2010] ECR I-05572 [51]. In 2012, the UK accepted that it was bound by this decision: *Said (Article 1D: Interpretation) v Secretary of State for the Home Department* [2012] UKUT 00413.

86 *AD (Palestine)* [2015] NZIPT 800693-695 [133], [148] ('*AD (Palestine)*'). In relation to Hathaway and Foster's argument regarding the different language between the Refugee Convention and UNHCR

continues to apply to all Palestinian refugees entitled to receive UN protection and assistance.[87] It based its conclusion on a reading of article 1D in its historical context,[88] the drafters' intentions[89] and article 1D's object and purpose, which the Tribunal said is to ensure that Palestinian refugees continue to receive protection as a special class and 'avoid overlapping agency competence for the protection of Palestinian refugees'.[90] These EU and Aotearoa/New Zealand decisions are consistent with the UNHCR's position that article 1D applies to Palestinian refugees displaced from Israel in 1948 and subsequent hostilities and their descendants.[91] Similarly, Goodwin-Gill and McAdam argue that article 1D should be interpreted as 'persons who were and/or are now receiving protection and assistance'.[92] This is based on a purposive approach to article 1D: its objective is to ensure that Palestinians are treated as a special and distinct group of refugees and not merged into the general refugee problem.[93]

As a consequence of this continuative interpretation of article 1D, Palestinian refugees continue to be excluded from the Refugee Convention and must remain in the UNRWA region if they want international protection and assistance. The justifications for this interpretation, in particular, that it preserves Palestinian refugees' special treatment, can be seen through the lens of Achiume's scholarship on disproportionate responsibility sharing. Reference to a special protection regime for Palestinian refugees ignores the fact that UNRWA, due to financial difficulties,[94] has long struggled to offer the protection and assistance it is mandated to provide.[95] It also disregards that UNRWA's financial difficulties are largely due to higher-income countries' persistent underfunding.[96] Palestinian refugees who choose to leave an UNRWA area may do so for myriad reasons. But the extent to which substandard living conditions and lack of healthcare, education and employment are motivating factors should not be understood without reference to the international community's failed commitment to provide adequate funding for their protection and assistance.[97]

Nevertheless, pursuant to Europe's and Aotearoa/New Zealand's interpretation of article 1D, Palestinian refugees retain ipso facto entitlement to the benefits of the Refugee Convention in the event that UN protection or assistance ceases for any reason. Therefore, the crucial question is: what is the scope of UN protection and assistance and what factors determine that Palestinian refugees are not in receipt of either? This question

---

Statute discussed earlier (n 82), the Tribunal stated that these instruments 'did not proceed entirely in tandem, with the Refugee Convention being subjected to further review at the Conference of Plenipotentiaries' and 'the difference in language may reflect no more than this': [139]. Also, the Tribunal reasoned that the proposition that the drafters were only prepared to give automatic refugee status to a narrowly defined and ascertainable group of refugees is inconsistent with the fact that, while the Refugee Convention was being drafted, 'the actual beneficiary class scope of UNRWA assistance was uncertain and in a state of flux': [141]. Finally, the Tribunal highlighted that the drafting materials indicate that the treatment of Palestinians as a *sui generis* class of refugees would continue until a definitive solution could be achieved: [143].

[87] Ibid [154].   [88] Ibid [144].   [89] Ibid [147].   [90] Ibid [159].   [91] UNHCR (n 74) [8].
[92] Goodwin-Gill and McAdam (n 19) 157.   [93] Ibid 158.
[94] The New Zealand Immigration and Protection Tribunal discussed UNRWA's difficult financial circumstances in the context of determining when protection and assistance can be deemed to have ceased: *AD (Palestine)* (n 86) [168]–[172].
[95] See above (n 8) and (n 9).   [96] Ogg (n 7).
[97] Kate Ogg, 'Backlashes against International Commitments and Organisations: Asylum as Restorative Justice' (2021) 38(1) *Australian Yearbook of International Law* 230.

has received much less attention than the well-established debate on whether article 1D should have a historically bounded or continuative interpretation. It is also the question that arises in protection from refuge claims made by Palestinian refugees. When Palestinian refugees seek ipso facto entitlement to the benefits of the Refugee Convention, they must establish that the situation they faced in, for example, a Palestinian refugee camp in Lebanon was such that UN protection and assistance can be deemed to have ceased. Thus, through the prism of article 1D, they are seeking protection from a place that is, notionally at least, providing refuge to thousands of other Palestinian refugees.

Depending on the approach decision-makers take to these protection from refuge claims, article 1D's second paragraph can provide a mechanism for large numbers of Palestinian refugees to claim ipso facto refugee status in Europe or Aotearoa/New Zealand, or it can establish grounds for only a few Palestinian refugees in specific circumstances to do so, perpetuating the containment of most Palestinian refugees in the UNRWA region. Next, I examine Aotearoa/New Zealand and European jurisprudence on this question.

6.4 A Broad Scope of Refuge for Palestinian Refugees

In examining the scope of refuge set in these decisions, two ideas established in previous chapters carry over: the importance of categorical reasoning and the risks of transjudicial communication in diluting the concept of refuge. At a point in the 2015 Aotearoa/New Zealand decision of *AD (Palestine)*,[98] the New Zealand Immigration and Protection Tribunal espoused a broad understanding of the protections available to Palestinian refugees under international law. In doing so, the Tribunal adopted a blended categorical and rights-based approach similar to the reasoning the High Court of Australia employed in *Plaintiff M70/2011 v Minister for Immigration and Citizenship and Plaintiff M106/2011 v Minister for Immigration and Citizenship ('Plaintiff M70')*.[99] As discussed in Chapter 5, in *Plaintiff M70*, the lead majority placed significance on the plaintiffs being persons seeking recognition of their refugee status and referred to the rights in the Refugee Convention. In *AD (Palestine)*, the New Zealand Immigration and Protection Tribunal focussed on Palestinian refugeehood and then considered the protections to which Palestinian refugees are entitled. The Tribunal outlined who is a Palestinian refugee and reviewed UNRWA's 'working definition' from 1948 onwards.[100] It then examined the meaning of the word 'protection' in the specific context of Palestinian refugees.[101]

Through this process, the New Zealand Immigration and Protection Tribunal delineated a wide ambit of protection. Referencing Bartholomeusz's[102] work on UNRWA's 'multidimensional' and 'individualised protection activity',[103] the Tribunal referred to the UN's 'endorsement of UNRWA performing protection-related activities in relevant UN General Assembly resolutions, often with direct reference to applicable international human rights treaties'.[104] In particular, it discussed *Operations of the United Nations Relief and Works Agency for Palestinian Refugees in the Near East*,[105] in which the UN General Assembly

---

[98] *AD (Palestine)* (n 86).   [99] (2011) 244 CLR 144.   [100] *AD (Palestine)* (n 86) [106]–[110].
[101] Ibid [113]–[116].
[102] Lance Bartholomeusz, 'The Mandate of UNRWA at Sixty' (2009) 28(2–3) *Refugee Survey Quarterly* 452 cited in *AD (Palestine)* (n 86) [114].
[103] *AD (Palestine)* (n 86) [114].   [104] Ibid [114].
[105] GA Res 69/88, UN Doc A/RES/69/88 (16 December 2014).

encourages UNRWA to 'continue making progress in addressing the needs of rights of children, women and persons with disabilities'[106] in accordance with the CRC, CEDAW and CRPD. By setting the scope of protection and assistance for Palestinian refugees with reference to UNRWA's mandates and the human rights instruments in those mandates, the Tribunal adopted a broad understanding of what refuge encompasses for Palestinian refugees. It also acknowledged that this scope of refuge is a malleable one that differs according to factors such as age, gender and disability.

Further, by invoking these legal instruments, the Tribunal positioned the nature of refuge for Palestinian refugees as a right and a duty. The Tribunal did not characterise UNRWA's humanitarian assistance as an act of charity, discretion or political benevolence, but as a *right* Palestinian refugees are entitled to under international law. The Tribunal classified the humanitarian assistance UNRWA provides as having 'an inherent protection element'.[107] It based this on the rights in ICESCR 'not merely being aspirational in nature' but 'fully fledged *rights* with both *duty bearers and beneficiaries*'.[108] Therefore, 'UNRWA's provision of education and health services and activities . . . directly and necessarily involves the protection of the *right* of Palestinian refugees to the highest standard of health and education under articles 12 and 13 of ICESCR'.[109]

Recognising UNRWA's humanitarian assistance as a right is particularly important in the context of economic, social and cultural rights. ICESCR stipulates that developing countries may determine the extent to which they guarantee economic rights to non-nationals.[110] This clause would apply to most Palestinian refugees who are not nationals in their country of refuge (Jordan is the only UNRWA region country that permits Palestinian refugees to acquire citizenship).[111] By referring to ICESCR through UN General Assembly resolutions that inform UNRWA's mandate, the New Zealand Immigration and Protection Tribunal situated the humanitarian assistance Palestinian refugees are entitled to as a right that the UN, through UNRWA, has a duty to address.

The importance of a blended categorical and rights-based approach, as opposed to rights-based reasoning alone, can be seen by comparing the Tribunal's understanding of protection with the UNHCR's approach. In its guidelines on article 1D,[112] the UNHCR does not define the phrase 'protection and assistance'. Accordingly, it does not consider the nature and extent of protection and assistance Palestinian refugees are entitled to under international law. Instead, in considering when article 1D's inclusionary paragraph is triggered, the UNHCR moves directly to when protection and assistance can 'cease for any reason'.[113] The UNHCR's position is that UNRWA's protection or assistance may cease if a Palestinian refugee faces a threat to their life, physical security or liberty, or other serious protection concerns such as 'sexual or gender-based violence, torture, inhuman or degrading treatment or punishment, human trafficking and exploitation, forced recruitment, severe discrimination, or arbitrary arrest or detention', or there is a situation of 'civil unrest, widespread insecurity or events seriously disturbing public order'.[114] While the UNHCR includes

---

[106] Ibid [14].   [107] *AD (Palestine)* (n 86) [116].   [108] Ibid [116] (emphasis added).   [109] Ibid [116].

[110] ICESCR art 2(3). Edwards argues that article 2(3) ought to be interpreted narrowly and in many circumstances will not permit a lower-income country to limit the extent to which it guarantees economic rights to refugees in its territory: Alice Edwards, 'Human Rights, Refugees, and the Right "To Enjoy" Asylum' (2005) 17(2) *International Journal of Refugee Law* 293, 324–5.

[111] Akram (n 2) 51.   [112] UNHCR (n 74).   [113] Ibid 8.

[114] Ibid 10–11. The UNHCR also stipulates that protection and assistance ceases if UNRWA's mandate is terminated, if UNRWA discontinues its protection and assistance for all Palestinian refugees or if

human rights concepts in its guidelines on article 1D's contingent inclusion clause, it is not guided by Palestinian refugees' specific situation. The reference to harms such as torture and civil unrest, while not exhaustive, is much narrower than the New Zealand Immigration and Protection Tribunal's approach which was to refer to the protection and assistance UNRWA is mandated to provide, including provisions of socio-economic rights such as health and education.

Applying Tuitt's ideas on the Refugee Convention as a containment mechanism on top of this analysis suggests that the New Zealand Immigration and Protection Tribunal's understanding of refuge (at the aforementioned part of its judgment) is a powerful one for Palestinian refugees. As noted earlier, Palestinian refugees were triply disenfranchised through article 1D: they no longer had the benefit of free movement, but they were also prohibited from accessing the 'supposed positive benefit' of *non-refoulement*, and to receive protection and assistance they had to remain in an UNRWA region. By defining the ambit of protection and assistance with reference to UNRWA's mandate, it could be said that, once this special protection and assistance ceases for any reason (e.g. UNRWA cannot provide access to education due to funding difficulties), Palestinian refugees are entitled to the benefits of the Refugee Convention on an ipso facto basis. This liberates Palestinian refugees from the containment imposed by article 1D's first paragraph (interpreted by the Tribunal as having continuative effect) as well as the containing effects of the refugee definition in article 1A(2) of the Refugee Convention. It provides grounds for large numbers of Palestinian refugees to leave the UNRWA region, if they wish and if they are able, and travel in search of refuge elsewhere.

However, while the New Zealand Immigration and Protection Tribunal recognised that protection and assistance for Palestinian refugees must be understood with reference to UNRWA's evolving mandate, it moved away from this position in determining when article 1D's inclusionary paragraph is triggered. In obiter, the Tribunal acknowledged that 'in principle' if UNRWA's funding deficits rendered it unable to provide protection and assistance, article 1D's second paragraph could be triggered.[115] However, the judgment instead focussed on the difference between a voluntary and involuntary decision to leave an UNRWA area of operation.[116] The Tribunal discussed the 'degree of compulsion which must exist in order for the second paragraph of article 1D to apply'[117] and stated that, to ipso facto obtain the benefits of the Refugee Convention, the Palestinian refugee must have left the UNRWA region involuntarily,[118] or, in other words, it must have been a 'forced departure'.[119]

Where did these ideas of compulsion and involuntariness derive from? They do not sit well with article 1D's text, which refers to UN protection and assistance ceasing 'for any reason'. They also do not align with the Tribunal's reasoning that all Palestinian refugees are beneficiaries of UNRWA's protection and assistance mandate. Ideas of compulsion and involuntary departure creep into the judgment through the Tribunal's reference to the CJEU's 2012 decision in *Mostafa Abed El Karem El Kott*.[120] In this case, the CJEU had to determine the same question as the New Zealand Immigration and Protection Tribunal:

a refugee faces practical, legal or safety barriers in re-availing themselves of UNRWA's protection: ibid 9–12.
[115] *AD (Palestine)* (n 86) [172].   [116] Ibid [173]–[180].   [117] Ibid [180].   [118] Ibid [186].
[119] Ibid [186].
[120] *Mostafa Abed El Karem El Kott v Bevándorlási és Állampolgársági Hivatal* (C-364/11, 19 December 2012) ('*Mostafa Abed El Karem*').

when does UN protection and assistance cease for Palestinian refugees? In its approach to this question, the CJEU did not consider the meaning of the term 'protection and assistance' and, in particular, what it may encompass for Palestinian refugees. It did not refer to UNRWA's mandate or international law for guidance. Instead, the Court focussed on when protection and assistance can be deemed to have ceased. The Court held that this will occur if UNRWA ceases to exist, an event or events occur that make it impossible for UNRWA to carry out its mission or a Palestinian refugee involuntarily leaves an UNRWA area of operation.[121] With respect to the third point, the Court explained that a 'voluntary decision to leave' cannot amount to cessation of protection or assistance,[122] but being 'forced to leave for reasons unconnected with that person's will' may indicate that UNRWA's protection or assistance has ceased.[123] The New Zealand Immigration and Protection Tribunal engaged in horizontal transjudicial communication and brought the EU's test of involuntariness and forced migration into Aotearoa/New Zealand jurisprudence.

Most European jurisprudence focusses on whether the Palestinian refugee bringing an article 1D claim left an UNRWA region involuntarily (as opposed to whether UNRWA can carry out its mission). Further, the concept of involuntary departure is also applied in what can be described as something akin to an internal relocation or safe third-country test in article 1D jurisprudence.[124] The CJEU held in a subsequent 2018 case that a Palestinian refugee is excluded from the benefits of the Refugee Convention if they are a 'beneficiary of effective protection or assistance from [UNRWA] in a third country that is not the territory in which he or she habitually resides but which forms part of the area of operations of [UNRWA]' and that third country agrees to readmit them, recognises UNRWA's protection and assistance, supports the principle of *non-refoulement* and will allow the person to stay in safety and dignified living conditions.[125] The Court explained that in such circumstances the Palestinian refugee 'cannot be regarded . . . as having been forced, by reason of circumstances beyond his or her control, to leave UNRWA's area of operations'.[126] In a later case, the CJEU ruled that departure cannot be considered involuntary if a Palestinian refugee leaves an UNRWA field of operation where they had protection and assistance and travels to a second UNRWA field where their personal safety is at risk and they do not have UNRWA protection and assistance.[127]

Despite the conundrum of 'forced migration' being heavily discussed in refugee studies literature,[128] it has never been a question that refugee law judges have been required to

---

[121] Ibid [58].   [122] Ibid [59].

[123] Ibid [59]. The Court confirmed this test in *Serin Alheto v Zamestnik-predsedatel na Darzhavna agenstsia zia bezhantsite* (C-585/16, 25 July 2018) [86] ('*Serin Alheto*').

[124] I have argued elsewhere that an internal relocation test for Palestinian refugees is inconsistent with article 1D's text and the principle of continuity of international protection for Palestinian refugees: Kate Ogg, 'New Directions in Article 1D Jurisprudence: Greater Barriers for Palestinian Refugees Seeking the Benefits of the Refugee Convention' in Satvinder Juss (ed), *The Research Handbook on International Refugee Law* (Edward Elgar, 2019) 358, 369–70. For another critical discussion, see Albanese and Takkenberg (n 6) 120–1.

[125] *Serin Alheto* (n 123) [143].   [126] Ibid [134].

[127] *Bundesrepublik Deutschland v XT* (C-507/19, 13 January 2021) [72], [80].

[128] See, e.g., Kathy Burrell, *Moving Lives: Narratives of Nation and Migration among Europeans in Post-War Britain* (Ashgate, 2006); Stephen Castles, 'Towards a Sociology of Forced Migration and Social Transformation' (2003) 37 *Sociology* 13; Dawn Chatty and Philip Mafleet, 'Conceptual Problems in Forced Migration' (2013) 32(2) *Refugee Survey Quarterly* 1; B.S. Chimni, 'The Birth of a "Discipline": From Refugee to

grapple with when interpreting the Refugee Convention.[129] This is because the refugee definition in the Refugee Convention is prospective. Article 1A(2) of the Refugee Convention asks whether a person would have a well-founded fear of persecution if returned to their country of nationality or habitual residence. At no point must a decision-maker enquire as to whether a person's departure from their homeland was voluntary or forced. The CJEU's requirement of involuntariness or compulsion in article 1D cases, adopted by the New Zealand Immigration and Protection Tribunal, introduced such a consideration into the Refugee Convention for the first time. Next, I describe how, by insisting on involuntary departure, decision-makers in the EU and Aotearoa/New Zealand truncate the scope of refuge for Palestinian refugees and make it almost impossible for them to seek protection outside the UNRWA region except for in exceptional situations.

6.5   From Rights Protection to Mere Survival: The Involuntary Refugee

Here, I first discuss, in Section 6.5.1, how the involuntariness requirement limits the content of refuge to physical survival. In Section 6.5.2, I highlight the ways in which it reproduces the racialised dichotomy of 'genuine refugees' versus 'economic migrants' in the article 1D context. I then expose, in Section 6.5.3, how this leads to gendered protection gaps.

6.5.1   Refuge as Physical Survival

The phrase 'forced migration' is widely considered to be a misnomer, because crossing a border is inherently an exhibition of agency.[130] Nevertheless, if one accepts that a person can be 'forced to leave for reasons unconnected with that person's will',[131] then the circumstances giving rise to that involuntary departure must be exceptional or extreme. This is reflected in the CJEU's judgment in *Mostafa Abed El Karem El Kott*. The Court indicated that departure will be deemed involuntary when UNRWA cannot guarantee the living conditions 'commensurate with [its] mission' *and* the Palestinian refugee's personal safety is threatened.[132] Threats to life and security of the person are serious human rights issues covered by the ICCPR[133] and, of relevance to the CJEU, the *Charter of Fundamental Rights of the European Union*.[134] However, by insisting that departure be involuntary and,

---

Forced Migration Studies' (2009) 22 *Journal of Refugee Studies* 11; Finn Stepputat and Ninna Nyberg Sørensen, 'Sociology and Forced Migration' in Elena Fiddian-Qasmiyeh et al (eds), *Oxford Handbook of Refugee and Forced Migration Studies* (Oxford University Press, 2014) 86; David Turton, 'Conceptualising Forced Migration' (Working Paper 12/2003, Refugee Studies Centre Working Paper Series, 2003).

[129] African refugee law includes a reference to compulsion. Article 1(2) of the Convention Governing the Specific Aspects of the Refugee Problems in Africa, 10 September 1969, 1001 UNTS 45, in force 20 June 1974 provides that 'The term "refugee" shall also apply to every person who, owing to external aggression, occupation, foreign domination or events seriously disturbing public order in either part or the whole of his [or her or their] country of origin or nationality, is compelled to leave his [or her or their] place of habitual residence in order to seek refuge in another place outside his [or her or their] country of origin or nationality'.

[130] See, e.g., Burrell (n 128) 24; Castles (n 128) 13, 30; Chatty and Mafleet (n 128) 10–11; Chimni (n 128) 12; Stepputat and Sørensen (n 128) 88; Turton (n 128) 10.

[131] *Mostafa Abed El Karem* (n 120) [59].

[132] Ibid [63]. The Court confirmed this test in *Serin Alheto* (n 123) [86].   [133] Arts 6 and 9.

[134] 7 December 2000, [2012] OJ C 326/321, in force 1 December 2009 arts 2 and 6.

therefore, predicated by extraordinary circumstances, the CJEU prioritised protection of these rights above others. Albanese and Takkenberg assert that the most important rights for Palestinian refugees' day-to-day lives are education, employment, healthcare, housing, freedom of movement, family unity and a secure legal status.[135] Rights to housing may be covered by the 'living conditions' test but rights such as education, employment, healthcare, freedom of movement, family unity and legal status would most probably not come within the living conditions and personal safety tests unless these tests were interpreted broadly.[136]

This test for when article 1D can be triggered also narrows the scope of refuge for Palestinian refugees. UNRWA's protection and assistance mandate is much wider than merely ensuring basic living conditions and protecting physical security. While UNRWA's mandate includes 'basic subsistence support',[137] it also encompasses education and social services and human development programmes.[138] Also, while UNRWA's mandate includes undertaking effective measures to guarantee Palestinian refugees' safety and security,[139] it also extends to addressing their human rights more broadly.[140] By focussing only on living conditions and personal safety, the ambit of refuge is limited to physical survival. This curtails the wider-ranging aspects of refuge for Palestinian refugees such as gaining an education and building a career in exile. It also restricts decision-makers' assessment of the place of refuge: by limiting consideration of the UNRWA area of operation to the circumstances leading up to departure, other aspects of life in, for example, a Palestinian refugee camp are obscured.

The test developed in Aotearoa/New Zealand imposes additional hurdles for Palestinian refugees wanting to trigger article 1D's inclusionary paragraph. The New Zealand Immigration and Protection Tribunal stated that the circumstances leading to an involuntary departure 'must have some enduring quality and be of a sufficiently serious character so as to perpetuate the claimant's refugee-like character'.[141] The Tribunal adopted this test even though it agreed that, by virtue of the phrase 'ipso facto' in article 1D's inclusionary paragraph, Palestinian refugees seeking the benefits of the Refugee Convention are not required to satisfy the refuge definition in article 1A(2).[142] While the Tribunal did not specify what circumstances would perpetuate a refugee-like character, the application of the test to the facts indicates that Palestinian refugees have to demonstrate discriminatory denial of human rights. The Tribunal first summarised evidence about the general circumstances in Gaza, including high unemployment,[143] poverty,[144] lack of infrastructure,[145] civil unrest,[146] high levels of violence[147] and restrictions on freedom of movement.[148] The Tribunal also noted that UNRWA was facing 'its most serious financial crisis ever'.[149] However, these circumstances were not sufficient for the claimants to establish that

---

[135] Albanese and Takkenberg (n 6) 376–95.

[136] Albanese and Takkenberg advocate for a broad reading of these legal tests: ibid 117.

[137] Reference to basic subsistence support is made in UNRWA's 2008–2009 Programme Budget subsequently approved by a UNGA resolution: see UNRWA, *Report of the Commissioner-General of (UNRWA), Programme Budget, 2008–2009*, UN GAOR, UN Doc A/62/13/Add.1 (6 August 2007) [72]. UNGA's approval of the budget specifically mandates all activities contained in the budget: Bartholomeusz (n 102) 462.

[138] Albanese and Takkenberg (n 6) also critique the Court for focussing too narrowly on living conditions: 116–7.

[139] *United Nations Relief and Works Agency for Palestinians in the Near East*, GA Res 37/120, UN Doc A/RES/37/120 (16 December 1982) part (J) [1].

[140] Ibid part (J) [1].   [141] *AD (Palestine)* (n 86) [186].   [142] Ibid [183].   [143] Ibid [219], [222].

[144] Ibid [219], [222].   [145] Ibid [219], [220], [222].   [146] Ibid [221].   [147] Ibid [222].   [148] Ibid [219].

[149] Ibid [223].

UNRWA's protection and assistance had ceased. The Palestinian refugees in this case were Christians and the Tribunal considered the situation for Christians in Gaza, particularly discrimination in employment[150] and risks to physical security when publicly practising their religion.[151] It was 'the cumulative effect of these matters' that satisfied the Tribunal that UNRWA's protection and assistance had ceased.[152] Accordingly, the Palestinian refugees in this case were only successful because they could establish, in addition to the general conditions in Gaza, discrimination on religious grounds.

Aotearoa/New Zealand's fault-based conception of involuntary departure further narrows decision-makers' approach to the scope of refuge for Palestinian refugees. While the Tribunal acknowledged the difficult living conditions in Gaza, the Tribunal was only satisfied that the Palestinian refugees 'felt *compelled* to leave Gaza ... because of *fears for their safety* if they were to practice their religion'.[153] The Tribunal's focus on physical safety and religious discrimination renders most of UNRWA's broad protection and assistance mandate, especially with respect to education, healthcare, infrastructure and business development, irrelevant to article 1D decisions. It suggests that Palestinian refugees, who travel outside an UNRWA region because they are poor, cannot access adequate healthcare or feel they have no future because of lack of education and employment prospects, have not been *forced* to leave due to direct discrimination and attacks. Instead, they exercise choice and cannot trigger the inclusionary paragraph in article 1D.

6.5.2   Involuntary Flight: A Neocolonial and Racialised Oxymoron?

Insisting that Palestinian refugees establish involuntary flight magnifies and complicates an already existing injustice in the international refugee regime. Tuitt observes that to trigger refugee protection a person has to cross an international border, but such movement does not mean that their needs are any greater or their claim to international protection is any stronger than those who remain inside territorial boundaries.[154] Rather, the alienage requirement exists due to the international legal prohibition of interference with another state's territorial integrity[155] and is a 'practical impediment to the expansion of refugee law'.[156] Palestinian refugees making protection from refuge claims not only have to make the journey to a country signatory to the Refugee Convention (a practical impediment for many Palestinian refugees) but also have to establish that this journey was an involuntary one. This creates an evidentiary paradox for Palestinian refugees: the inclusionary aspect of article 1D can only be triggered by leaving an UNRWA field of operation, an act that is inherently an exhibition of agency, yet to obtain the benefits of the Refugee Convention Palestinian refugees must prove that departure was involuntary.[157] This incongruity obscures the difficult and often distressing choices that must be made when leaving a home (albeit for Palestinian refugees, a temporary one), family and community in search of refuge in unfamiliar territory.

The stories decision-makers favour when determining whether flight was involuntary echo Chimni's and Tuitt's observations on Western states' reactions to the 'new' asylum seekers. Chimni and Tuitt explain that, when larger numbers of refugees from the Global South started to arrive in Global North countries, they were perceived as 'bogus' refugees pursuing a better life and were distinguished from 'authentic' refugees fleeing political

---

[150] Ibid [224].   [151] Ibid [225]–[229].   [152] Ibid [234].   [153] Ibid [230].   [154] Tuitt (n 40) 67.
[155] Ibid 67.   [156] Ibid 67.   [157] Ogg (n 124) 368.

strife.[158] Neither the CJEU nor the New Zealand Immigration and Protection Tribunal is satisfied that poverty, poor access to healthcare and lack of education and employment prospects are enough to prompt a Palestinian refugee to flee against their will. Rather, according to their decisions, forced departure is predicated by something more than dire humanitarian circumstances. The CJEU focussed on threats to personal safety and the New Zealand Immigration and Protection Tribunal emphasised discriminatory denial of human rights. In doing so, these decisions reproduce, in the article 1D context, the distinction between the genuine refugee fleeing political and religious persecution and the fraudulent economic migrant. These approaches to article 1D indicate that a Palestinian refugee for whom UN protection and assistance has ceased because they do not have the means to survive or access to education or employment may be considered an object of humanitarian concern, but not a person entitled to the benefits of the Refugee Convention. This status is reserved for those who have been the victim of some form of targeted or discriminatory harm.

In addition, the New Zealand Immigration and Protection Tribunal's approach to article 1D's inclusionary paragraph has parallels with Tuitt's critique that the definition of a refugee in the Refugee Convention's article 1A(2) has a Western ideological slant due to its insistence on establishing fault. By requiring evidence of something beyond the general living conditions in Gaza and looking to religious discrimination, the Tribunal imported the idea of culpability into article 1D's second paragraph. It ensured that article 1D's inclusionary paragraph cannot be triggered by factors such as poverty or generalised violence, which are seen as 'harms of less discriminating origin',[159] but that Palestinian refugees must establish a harm that is personally directed towards them for illegitimate reasons.

While Tuitt critiques the idea of culpability in the refugee definition, she acknowledges that this 'conception of fault' is embedded in the Refugee Convention's text and is, therefore, not pillorying refugee law judges.[160] However, the New Zealand Immigration and Protection Tribunal inserted the idea of culpability into article 1D with no textual basis for doing so. The need to demonstrate discriminatory denial of human rights when seeking confirmation of refugee status under article 1A(2) is consistent with the text, context and purpose of the Refugee Convention,[161] but this is not the case for the inclusionary paragraph in article 1D. The ordinary meaning of the words 'when such protection or assistance has *ceased for any reason*' indicates that a Palestinian refugee should not have to establish that protection and assistance have ceased for reasons of, for example, their religion or political opinion. Also, the purpose of article 1D's second paragraph is to ensure the continuity of international protection for Palestinian refugees. This is defeated if the inclusionary paragraph can only be triggered by Palestinian refugees who can establish that denial of their fundamental human rights has a discriminatory element.

The 'forced migration' paradox, and the ways decision-makers arbitrate the distinction between voluntary and involuntary transnational movements, also obscures how Global North states are implicated in Palestinian refugees' journeys. Kyriakides explains that '[i]n

---

[158] Tuitt (n 40) 70; Chimni (n 42) 351.   [159] Tuitt (n 20) 101.   [160] Ibid 100.

[161] Hathaway argues that the requirement that a refugee have a well-founded fear of being persecuted for reasons of one of the enumerated grounds is justified. While two people may fear deprivation of fundamental human rights, if one fears it for reasons of, for example, their political opinion, that person is more likely to be socially marginalised and less likely to be able to obtain state protection: James Hathaway, 'Is Refugee Status Really Elitist? An Answer to the Ethical Challenge' in Jean Yves Carlier and Dirk Vanheule (eds), *Europe and Refugees: A Challenge?* (Kluwer Law International, 1997) 79, 86.

the cultural script of refuge, refugees are victims who "deserve" rescue; receiving societies are saviours who provide it'.[162] Thus, refugees are often positioned as 'involuntary, non-wilful objects' so that they are not seen as 'a threat to the receiving state'.[163] Achiume posits that xenophobic anxiety is often predicated by a 'perceive[d] loss of control over the territory' and often triggers laws and policies that 'reconsolidate sovereignty in the state'.[164] Achiume also highlights that what is often described in the media as 'floods' or 'waves' of refugees reaching Global North shores is often predicated by Western states' lack of international cooperation. Drawing on these ideas, the creation of the 'forced migration' test in article 1D jurisprudence is not only a way of limiting the application of article 1D's contingent inclusion paragraph. It is also an assertion of sovereignty – in response to what are understood as large numbers of refugees (in particular in the European context), Global North states are choosing which refugees they wish to welcome. In accepting only those whose journeys were 'involuntary', European and Aotearoa/New Zealand decision-makers position their nations as saviours of those few who had no choice in leaving but also as protecting their borders and their polity from the thousands who did have a choice. The way decision-makers construct involuntary flight masks Global North states' responsibility for Palestinian refugees' plight. As noted earlier, UNRWA's inability to carry out its protection and assistance mandate is in large part due to Western states' persistent underfunding. By requiring something greater than inadequate living conditions and focussing on physical insecurity (in Europe) and discrimination (in Aotearoa/New Zealand), the trigger for involuntary flight is characterised as an incident or series of incidents that manifest in the refugee's habitual residence. The transnational causes of poverty and instability remain outside the judicial purview.

Finally, the approach to article 1D in Europe and Aotearoa/New Zealand reproduces the colonial attitudes Mayblin observes were in force during the Refugee Convention's drafting. By insisting that article 1D continues to operate and then interpreting the inclusionary paragraph so that it can be triggered only in extreme or exceptional circumstances, decision-makers are accepting that Palestinian refugees are best protected in situ. The adoption of legal tests that sidestep considerations of UNRWA's underfunding and do not respond to situations where a person's basic needs are not met mirrors attitudes exhibited during the Convention's creation that there are differing levels of humanity.

6.5.3   Gendered Understandings of Involuntariness

Drawing on Tuitt and Chimni's critique of objectivism, decision-makers have applied their own assessment of whether the departure was involuntary, and the refugee's assessment of the reasons for their flight is rendered redundant. When determining whether targeted or discriminatory harm triggers involuntary flight, decision-makers have favoured harms that emanate in the public sphere and can be considered politically motivated. This limits the ability for female Palestinian refugees to use article 1D to find refuge outside the UNRWA area. These approaches have resonance with Tuitt's observation that refugee status assessment procedures are 'geared towards eliciting evidence of political involvement' and do not encourage evidence of other kinds of harms that may, for example, indicate gender persecution.[165]

---

[162] Kyriakides (n 35) 5.   [163] Ibid 5.   [164] Achiume (n 56) 371.

[165] Tuitt (n 40) 44–5. Since Tuitt's publication, decision-makers have interpreted the Refugee Convention's article 1A(2) in a manner that makes it more responsive to gender-based violence. For example, it is now

Favouring narratives based on politically motivated harm in the public sphere can be seen in a number of European article 1D cases decided subsequent to *Mostafa Abed El Karem El Kott*. In Hungarian case, a male Palestinian refugee was able to trigger the inclusionary clause in article 1D, but only after proving that he had suffered several physical assaults.[166] In a Belgian decision, a male Palestinian refugee gave evidence that, while working as a photo journalist in Gaza, he was injured by live fire from the Israeli army and received threats from both the Israeli army and Hamas.[167] The Belgian Council for Alien Law Litigation found that, due to these attacks and threats, he left Gaza for reasons independent of his will. The Council noted that he should not be required to retreat from informing the public about the human rights violations occurring in Gaza to avoid these threats to his life.

While the Council accepted that a person injured by live fire or physical assaults is compelled against his will to leave an UNRWA field of operation, the same result was not reached with respect to a woman subject to forced marriage. In a case concerning a stateless Palestinian refugee who had spent most of her life in Lebanon's Burj el-Shemali Camp,[168] the Belgian Council for Alien Law Litigation confirmed that article 1D's inclusionary paragraph would only be triggered if the asylum seeker personally found herself in grave danger and UNRWA was unable to offer her living conditions that meet the objectives with which it is tasked.[169] The Council acknowledged the harsh living conditions in the camp, but found that the applicant was not personally in grave danger. Accordingly, the Council concluded that the applicant did not leave Lebanon for reasons beyond her control or against her will. In this case, the Belgian Council for Alien Law Litigation inserted its assessment for what constitutes a feeling of grave danger, prompting involuntary departure and determined that forced marriage is not serious enough to be compelled to leave against one's will.

This decision can also be critiqued on the ground that forced marriage raises the prospect of sexual intercourse without consent, which is a threat to personal security in line with the test in *Mostafa Abed El Karem El Kott*. Further, UNRWA is responsible for addressing women's human rights in accordance with the CEDAW, which includes prohibition of forced marriage.[170] By not being able to protect her from forced marriage, UNRWA was not providing her the protection it is mandated to provide. However, she was unable to trigger the inclusionary paragraph in article 1D because she could not satisfy the Belgian authorities that she was personally in grave danger. Thus, the involuntary departure approach truncates the scope for the protection and assistance for Palestinian refugees in a way that has particularly problematic consequences for those facing gendered harms such as forced marriage.

Both the right to physical security and prohibition of forced marriage are protected by international human rights law and covered by UNRWA's mandate. However, it is perhaps easier to persuade a decision-maker that potentially lethal physical harm occurring in a public space would lead to involuntary departure than the prospect of forced marriage,

---

accepted in a number of jurisdictions that those fleeing family violence can be refugees within the meaning of article 1A(2): see, e.g., *Islam v Secretary of State for the Home Department; R v Immigration Appeal Tribunal ex parte Shah* [1999] 2 All ER 545; *Khawar* (n 31).

[166] *KKF v Bevándorlási és Állampolgársági Hivatal* 15.K30.590/2013/5 (Budapest Administrative and Labour Court, 21 March 2013).

[167] Belgium, Council for Alien Law Litigation, 7 August 2015, No 150535.

[168] Belgium, Council for Alien Law Litigation, 2 May 2013, No 102283.   [169] Ibid.

[170] CEDAW art 16(1)(b).

which involves unknown future harms that would most probably occur behind closed doors. It indicates that the element of compulsion, introduced in the EU and Aotearoa/ New Zealand, may mean that only those who can demonstrate dramatic and heroic narratives can make use of the inclusionary clause in article 1D in their searches for refuge beyond the UNRWA region. This analysis has parallels with Spijkerboer's examination of decision-makers' construction of gender in refugee status assessments. While the refugee definition in the Refugee Convention does not require adjudicators to determine flight motives or whether acts were voluntary or involuntary, Spijkerboer's study indicates that these questions emerged in interviews with those seeking recognition of their refugee status. He highlights that, with respect to female applicants, 'involuntary acts are considered non-political because they apparently lack the motivation which makes an act political', whereas '[a]cts construed as voluntary and purely a matter of free choice, such as having a child, are somehow construed as not relevant'.[171] When attributing flight motives, decision-makers assume that female asylum seekers are 'motivated by factors other than politics when their acts can be perceived emotional, personal . . . '.[172] Further, actions that take place in what is construed as the private realm are deemed irrelevant.[173] Nevertheless, recent jurisprudence indicates a shift towards a more gender- and protection-sensitive approach to article 1D, and I turn to this next.

6.6   A Pathway to Protection?

In 2019, the New Zealand Immigration and Protection Tribunal had another opportunity to consider when the inclusionary paragraph in article 1D can be triggered. While the 2015 decision of *AD (Palestine)* acknowledged in obiter that UNRWA's lack of funding could be grounds for the application of article 1D's second paragraph, the 2019 decision of *AE (Lebanon)* took this one step further. The case concerned a Palestinian refugee from Lebanon who was a qualified engineer. He could not find employment in Lebanon or establish a successful business due to discrimination against Palestinian refugees. He had a number of health issues and was often unable to pay for medical treatment. The Tribunal found that UN protection and assistance had ceased for him and he was ipso facto entitled to refugee protection in Aotearoa/New Zealand.

The Tribunal stressed that it is necessary to consider a person's personal circumstances when determining whether protection and assistance has ceased.[174] While this may suggest that the Tribunal adopted a similar approach to the aforementioned jurisprudence in that it required some form of exceptional and extreme harm, the types of circumstances the Tribunal highlighted would be shared by many Palestinian refugees in Lebanon. The Tribunal noted that:

> UNRWA is experiencing a dire funding shortfall such that it cannot fund any secondary or tertiary medical treatment for Palestine refugees. Even basic primary health services have been impacted by the funding crisis with replacement of medical personnel being delayed and services being cut. Nor does UNRWA have sufficient funds to provide

---

[171]   Thomas Spijkerboer, *Gender and Refugee Status* (Ashgate, 2000) 77.   [172]   Ibid 88.   [173]   Ibid 92.

[174]   *AE (Lebanon)* [2019] NZIPT 801588 [51]. See also *AQ (Jordan)* [2019] NZIPT concerning Palestinian refugees born in the West Bank and displaced to Jordan. The Tribunal held that UNRWA protection and assistance had ceased because they would not be able to return to the West Bank: [99].

financial or basic needs support, even for all of those who fall within the criteria of living in 'abject poverty'.[175]

The Tribunal then stated that the aforementioned circumstances 'would apply to the applicant'.[176] This is because the applicant previously relied on his brother for financial support but his brother could no longer provide it, and the applicant could not access work or establish a business due to discrimination against Palestinian refugees in Lebanon. The Tribunal reasoned that:

> [o]n that basis, the appellant will not be able to access, either privately or through UNRWA, financial assistance sufficient to provide the necessities of life, nor any assist-ance to pay for his ongoing medication and, possibly, hospitalisation costs. For the appellant, with his particular medical presentation, a lack of sufficient medical care may well result in significant cardiac issues or stroke.[177]

While the Tribunal highlighted his medical conditions, this was not critical to the Tribunal's decision. The Tribunal concluded that '[f]or the reasons given, in particular the inability of UNRWA to guarantee access to even the most basic living allowance and adequate medical services, the Tribunal finds that for the purpose of Article 1D(2), the assistance of UNRWA to which the appellant is entitled has de facto ceased'.[178]

The aforementioned reasoning could be applied to most Palestinian refugees in Lebanon. The Tribunal accepted that Palestinian refugees in Lebanon have difficulty accessing employment due to discrimination. Many would rely on family members for financial support but the Tribunal accepted that this was precarious, especially with challenges facing Lebanon's economy.[179] UNRWA's financial difficulties and its inability to provide adequate medical care, the necessities of life and education affect all Palestinians under UNRWA's care.

Similarly, in a 2020 decision, the Amsterdam District Court accepted that UN protection and assistance had ceased for a Palestinian refugee from Gaza because UNRWA could not provide for daily necessities due to financial difficulties and could not protect against physical insecurity due to the ongoing hostilities.[180] The Court emphasised that many people in Gaza live below the poverty line, there is significant unemployment, children live in appalling conditions in refugee camps, there are challenges with respect to providing secondary education due to shortages in teachers and materials, there is a lack of basic hospital and medical care and there is no adequate response to COVID-19. In a 2020 decision, the Administrative Court of International Protection in Cyprus ruled that UNRWA protection and assistance had ceased because the applicant would not receive protection against ongoing hostilities.[181]

By shifting the focus from involuntary flight prompted by extreme or exceptional circumstances to UNRWA's inability to provide for basic necessities and protect against ongoing hostilities, this jurisprudence provides a pathway for many Palestinians to trigger article 1D's inclusionary clause. It has the potential to transition article 1D from a containment clause (requiring Palestinians to remain in situ to receive protection and assistance) to enabling Palestinian refugees to leave an UNRWA region and seek refugee

---

[175] *AE (Lebanon)* (n 174) [81].   [176] Ibid [82].   [177] Ibid [85].   [178] Ibid [86].   [179] Ibid [84].
[180] *Rechtbank Den Haag* Amsterdam District Court (24 August 2020). Mann (n 5) states that the Belgian Council for Alien Law Litigation took a similar approach in February and March 2021.
[181] *AB v The Republic of Cyprus* (Reg. No 1118/18, 5 June 2020), Administrative Court of International Protection (Cyprus).

protection elsewhere. By accepting that Palestinian refugees are entitled to have access to education and employment, be protected from ongoing hostilities and be provided with adequate food, water, shelter and healthcare, this jurisprudence moves away from what Mayblin observes in historical and contemporary refugee law and policy as an acceptance of differing levels of humanity.

The case law also indicates that refugee law judges can acknowledge and respond meaningfully to the lack of international cooperation in the global refugee regime. The decision-makers in these cases did not go as far as to acknowledge that Western countries are largely to blame for UNRWA's financial difficulties. Thus, the judgments do not reflect Achiume's insights that these refugees' journeys were made necessary due to Global North states' lack of responsibility sharing. That refuge can have a restorative function or act as a form of corrective justice is not taken up by these decision-makers. Nevertheless, the decision-makers based their decisions on UNRWA's inability to provide adequate protection and assistance.

The reasoning in these decisions also indicates the potential for age- and gender-sensitive approaches to article 1D. The Aotearoa/New Zealand and Dutch decisions highlighted lack of primary and secondary education opportunities for Palestinian refugees, even though it was not relevant to the applicants in those cases because they were adults. Also, while there are often greater challenges for female and non-binary Palestinians with respect to international travel, the move away from the involuntary flight test and greater focus on UNRWA's inability to provide protection and assistance means that there is greater potential for them to trigger article 1D's inclusionary clause.

There is a risk that this approach can be seen as imposing Western superiority. As a parallel to Macklin's observation that in their approach to gender-based persecution Western adjudicators position Global North states as progressive and free from such concerns, these approaches to article 1D could risk positioning Western countries as free from poverty and deprivation. Indeed, Spijkerboer argues that 'each refugee from an underdeveloped country presents a failure of the Third World'.[182]

Soon, there will be additional opportunities for courts in Europe to again consider protection obligations towards Palestinian refugees. A request for a preliminary ruling has been lodged with the CJEU concerning whether a Palestinian family left Lebanon for 'objective reasons beyond their control and independent of their volition' (one of the family members is a 13-year-old boy with a significant disability and the family alleges that UNRWA cannot fulfil its mandate with respect to children with disabilities).[183] A case has also been submitted to the European Court of Human Rights concerning a Palestinian refugee excluded from the Refugee Convention by virtue of article 1D but claiming that returning him to the Ein El-Hilweh Refugee Camp in Lebanon would be a violation of article 3 of the ECHR.[184] Neither case had been determined at the time of writing.

6.7 Conclusion

This chapter built on the analysis undertaken in the previous case studies. Despite the legal differences between the protection from refuge claims studied in this and previous chapters,

---

[182] Spijkerboer (n 171) 199.
[183] *NB and AB v The Secretary of State for the Home Department* (First Tier Tribunal, Immigration and Asylum Chamber, PA/07865/2019 and PA/07864/2019, 29 July 2020) [98], [131].
[184] *HA v UK* (Application No 30919/20) lodged 22 July 2020.

there are a number of similarities. First, this chapter indicated that, when decision-makers take a categorical approach by reflecting on the nature of refugeehood (in this case, Palestinian refugeehood), they engage with the concept of refuge and give it a broad and rich meaning. Second, in an effort to limit the legal grounds on which a refugee can seek a different place of refuge, decision-makers partially excise the place of refuge from consideration and focus on the particular protection from refuge claimant and why their circumstances may be exceptional. This produces minimalist understandings of refuge, ensures the continuation of containment mechanisms and inhibits refugees' ability to use courts and other decision-making bodies in their searches for refuge.

The additional factor present in the Palestinian case study is that these protection from refuge claims are grounded in the Refugee Convention and trigger states' concerns that it provides a pathway for refugees to shift their place of refuge from the Global South to the Global North. Most EU and Aotearoa/New Zealand approaches to these protection from refuge claims entrench article 1D as a containment mechanism. Pursuant to these decisions, Palestinian refugees continue to be excluded from the Refugee Convention because article 1D is deemed to have continuative effect, but can only trigger the inclusionary second paragraph in limited and exceptional situations. As a consequence, many Palestinian refugees not enjoying the breadth of protection or assistance that UNRWA is mandated to provide will also not be able to secure a place of refuge in other parts of the world. This is particularly significant in the current European context, where many of those seeking protection due to the Syrian civil war are Palestinians refugees.[185] While the Hungarian Helsinki Committee, a human rights NGO, views the CJEU's decision in *Mostafa Abed El Karem El Kott* as a landmark victory that 'opens the way for tens of thousands of Palestinian refugees to be recognized as refugees in [EU] countries',[186] I suggest that it significantly restricts the circumstances in which Palestinian refugees can obtain international protection pursuant to article 1D of the Refugee Convention.

Through these approaches to article 1D's second paragraph, most EU and New Aotearoa/Zealand jurisprudence only rescues Palestinian refugees who resemble Cold War-inspired, Western notions of a refugee. The legal tests prioritise those who have been specifically targeted with a form of harm manifesting in the public sphere, but disregard those subject to gender-based violence or whose needs emanate from less discriminating circumstances such as hunger, poverty and idleness due to lack of education and employment. As a consequence, these forms of suffering remain an 'extensive unattended moral arena which states seek strategically to avoid'.[187] This is acutely problematic in the Palestinian context. Palestinian refugees were excluded from the Refugee Convention partly because they were seen as a special group of refugees who deserved a unique protection regime, but states agreed to grant them ipso facto refugee status once their UN protection and assistance ceased for any reason. UNRWA has been facing a funding crisis for a number of years, and, in response to funding cuts, the head of UNRWA, Pierre Krähenbühl, in an open letter to UNRWA staff stressed that Palestinian refugees 'cannot

---

[185] Euro-Mediterranean Human Rights Monitor, *Palestinian Syrians: Displaced Again* (2018) <https://euromedmonitor.org/en/palestinians-in-syria>.

[186] The Hungarian Helsinki Committee, *European Court of Justice Delivers Milestone Judgment on Asylum Claims by Palestinians* (13 January 2013) <www.helsinki.hu/en/important-european-judgment-concerning-fleeing-palestinians/>.

[187] Tuitt (n 40) 155.

be simply wished away'.[188] Yet, through most article 1D cases in the EU and Aotearoa/ New Zealand, decision-makers are washing their hands of this significant humanitarian problem. In most cases, the benefits of the Refugee Convention are only available to Palestinians whose circumstances are deemed to mimic the archetypal political refugee. The rest remain the responsibility of an underfunded and overstretched agency struggling to fulfil its protection and assistance mandate.

The 2019 and 2020 jurisprudence from these jurisdictions does, however, indicate that a more protection-sensitive approach, and one cognisant of the broader political contexts underlying refugee journeys and the importance of international cooperation, is possible.

---

[188] Pierre Krähenbühl, cited in Jeffrey Heller, 'UNRWA Chief Defends Refugee Criteria for Millions of Palestinians', *Reuters* (online 3 September 2018) <www.reuters.com/article/us-usa-palestinians-unrwa /unrwa-chief-defends-refugee-criteria-for-millions-of-palestinians-idUSKCN1LJ179?mc_cid=16 df1d1fb4&mc_eid=677b225ed4>.

Resisting the Prospect of Refuge in an IDP Camp

7.1 Introduction

After visiting IDP camps in Nigeria in 2016, Chaloka Beyani, the UN Special Rapporteur on the Human Rights of Internally Displaced People, reflected, 'camps should offer protection for those in need yet I am alarmed to learn that many are in fact the settings for violence, exploitation and abuse of the most vulnerable'.[1] In this chapter, I examine decision-makers' responses to cases in which putative refugees are resisting the prospect of seeking refuge in an IDP camp.

As noted in Chapter 1, a putative refugee is a person outside their country of origin or habitual residence, who has a well-founded fear of being persecuted for reasons of race, religion, nationality, membership of a particular social group or political opinion. Decision-makers may consider if the putative refugee can relocate to another part of their homeland in which they will have protection (the internal protection alternative (IPA) inquiry). In some cases, the putative refugee has argued that, if they internally relocated, they would have no option but to live in an IDP camp. Most of these claims have arisen in the UK but there is one case from Aotearoa/New Zealand.[2]

In this chapter, I continue the previous chapter's examination of how decision-makers approach protection from refuge claims grounded in the Refugee Convention and that give rise to a concern that the Convention is being used as a pathway for migration from the Global South to the Global North.[3] Unlike in Chapter 6, the protection from refuge claimants in the cases examined in this chapter are not yet recognised refugees. Rather,

---

[1] Chaloka Beyani, *End of Mission Statement by the United Nations Special Rapporteur on the Human Rights of Internally Displaced Persons, Mr Chaloka Beyani, on His Visit to Nigeria, 23 to 26 August 2016* (22 January 2016) <https://ohchr.org/EN/NewsEvents/Pages/DisplayNews.aspx?NewsID=20427>.

[2] As noted in Chapter 1, I conducted an extensive search of internal protection case law in Australia, Canada, Aotearoa/New Zealand, the US and EU member-states on LexisNexis, Westlaw and Refworld. The UK and Aotearoa/New Zealand are the only jurisdictions in which the question of relocation to an IDP camp has arisen in cases where protection under the Refugee Convention is being sought. The issue of internal relocation to an IDP camp has arisen in some decisions in which the individuals bringing the case are not entitled to refugee protection. In Chapter 1, I outlined why these decisions are outside this book's scope.

[3] These concerns are reflected in a United Kingdom House of Lords (now the United Kingdom Supreme Court) judgment in which the Court stressed that the Refugee Convention's function is 'not to procure a general levelling-up of living standards around the world, desirable though of course that is': *Secretary of State for the Home Department v AH (Sudan)* [2008] 1 AC 678 [5] ('*SSHD v AH (Sudan)*'). Mathew argues that IPA case law is part of the larger phenomenon of states containing refugee movements and, in particular, constricting the situations in which refugees can move from lower- to higher-income countries: Penelope Mathew, 'The Shifting Boundaries and Content of Protection: The Internal Protection Alternative Revisited' in Satvinder Juss (ed), *The Ashgate Research Companion to Migration Law, Theory and Policy* (Ashgate, 2013) 189, 205–6.

they are both putative refugees and prospective IDPs. Thus, I begin this chapter, in Section 7.2, by revisiting Tuitt's scholarship and outlining her ideas on why it is the IDP, as opposed to the refugee who is 'the figure that is most promising of a new political consciousness'.[4] I then use her ideas to explore how decision-makers conceptualise the scope and nature of refuge, respond to the conflict between a person's need for refuge and states' desires to control their borders, and whether, as a result, particular refugees are more likely to be able to secure a place of refuge in the Global North.

I argue that, when these types of claims started to arise in the early 2000s, decision-makers approached them with an ethic of international cooperation and in a manner that delineated a broad scope of refuge. However, from 2006, decision-makers narrowed the scope of refuge, ideas of international cooperation were lost and putative refugees had to prove that they were exceptional in some way to secure protection in the Global North. This has frustrated journeys in search of refuge for people of all genders and compounded the inequities between higher- and lower-income countries in relation to caring for those in need of protection.

7.2   IDPs: Neglected in Refugee Law and Scholarship

In her early scholarship on the Refugee Convention as a containment mechanism, Tuitt argues that there are many different notions of who is a refugee,[5] but the definition in the Refugee Convention has become the dominant understanding.[6] This definition 'captures only a tiny portion of the whole corpus of meanings within the notion of refugee'.[7] In particular, Tuitt emphasises that the alienage requirement (that you have to be outside your homeland to be a refugee) 'clearly helps to contain refugees'.[8] Further, she argues that by requiring refugees to cross an international border, refugee law '[c]onsciously . . . separates the strong from the weak', because many of those in need of international protection cannot leave their homeland due to factors such as age, gender and disability.[9] Therefore, IDPs are 'not only disenfranchised within their state of origin or domicile, but disenfranchised from the law'.[10] Additionally, the alienage requirement has resulted in refugees being 'conceived of as a *moving entity*'[11] and that movement is seen as 'synonymous with humanitarian need and suffering'.[12]

In later scholarship, Tuitt expands on these ideas and argues that scholars have neglected the figure of the IDP in scholarship on rightlessness[13] and bare life.[14] She contests the idea that it is the refugee who is 'the classic instance of the rightless person'.[15] Tuitt explains that

---

[4] Patricia Tuitt, 'Refugees, Nations, Laws and the Territorialization of Violence' in Peter Fitzpatrick and Patricia Tuitt (eds), *Critical Beings: Law, Nation and the Global Subject* (Ashgate, 2004) 37, 48.

[5] Patricia Tuitt, *False Images: The Law's Construction of the Refugee* (Pluto Press, 1996) 14.

[6] Ibid 14–15.

[7] Ibid 16. See Orchard's argument that during the drafting of the Refugee Convention there was support for a more expansive refugee definition that could have encompassed IDPs but the US acted to narrow the Convention's definition of a refugee to those outside their own state: Phil Orchard, *Protecting the Internally Displaced: Rhetoric and Reality* (Routledge, 2019) 79.

[8] Tuitt (n 5) 12.   [9] Ibid 13.   [10] Ibid 14.

[11] Patricia Tuitt, 'Rethinking the Refugee Concept' in Frances Nicholson and Patrick Twomey (eds), *Refugee Rights and Realities: Evolving International Concepts and Regimes* (Cambridge University Press, 1999) 107 (emphasis in original).

[12] Tuitt (n 5) 14.   [13] Tuitt (n 4) 37.   [14] Ibid 37.   [15] Ibid 38.

the refugee does not challenge the idea of the 'nexus of state, territory and identity', but is the 'tangible product of a legal imagination that is all too wedded to the territorially bound nation'.[16] Conversely, the IDP, being 'neither meaningfully within, nor formally outside, the nation-state',[17] threatens the idea of the territorially bounded state and indicates that 'there can be no fixed or impermeable border separating the inside of a nation and its outside'.[18] Thus, it is the IDP, rather than the refugee who can 'radically disrupt the comforting image of secure, stable, bounded nations'.[19] While there have been developments on IDP rights since Tuitt's writings,[20] with Cantor going so far as to argue that IDP law is emerging 'as a distinct field of law',[21] this does not take away from Tuitt's central thesis. It remains the case that, by virtue of the fact that IDPs have not crossed an international border, they cannot access refugee protection.

In the following sections, I draw on Tuitt's ideas on the figure of the IDP in dissecting protection from refuge claims involving the question of whether a person with a well-founded fear of persecution can have protection in an IDP camp. Some scholars suggest that it is possible to consider all putative refugees undergoing an IPA assessment as prospective IDPs, whether or not they face the prospect of life in an IDP camp once they internally relocate.[22] Indeed, most IDPs do not live in camp settings,[23] and sometimes find themselves in more precarious situations, partly because they are less able to access humanitarian services.[24] Nevertheless, I focus on IPA jurisprudence concerning IDP camps because in these cases, similar to previous chapters, refuge as a place and a concept collide: the putative refugee is resisting the prospect of seeking refuge in an IDP camp, a place intended to provide refuge to significant numbers of people displaced from their homes. As will be seen in the next section, the fact that an IDP camp is supposed to be a place of protection is significant in the context of determining the nature and scope of refuge for putative refugees.

7.3   Real and Meaningful Refuge

In this section, I highlight that, in UK cases in the early 2000s and the one Aotearoa/New Zealand case to consider this issue, decision-makers took a categorical approach to these protection from refuge claims. They understood refuge as a state responsibility and, most importantly, as a global endeavour that must be informed by an ethic of international solidarity. This jurisprudence also delineates a broad scope of refuge, encompassing an array of rights and protection beyond mere survival.

---

[16] Ibid 47.   [17] Ibid 46.   [18] Ibid 47.   [19] Ibid 51.

[20] In 2009, the African Union adopted the Convention for the Protection and Assistance of Internally Displaced Persons in Africa, 23 October 2009, 49 ILM 86, in force 6 December 2012. Twenty-seven countries now have national laws or policies relating to internal displacement: The Internal Displacement Monitoring Centre, *IDP Laws and Policies: A Mapping Tool* (2018) <www.internal-displacement.org/law-and-policy/>.

[21] David Cantor, '"The IDP in International Law"? Developments, Debates and Prospects' (2018) 30(2) *International Journal of Refugee Law* 191, 192.

[22] Jessica Schultz, *The Internal Protection Alternative in Refugee Law* (Brill, 2019) 7.

[23] Brookings-LSE, 'Under the Radar: Internally Displaced Persons in Non-Camp Settings' (October 2013) 1 <www.brookings.edu/wp-content/uploads/2016/06/Under-the-radarIDPs-outside-of-camps-Oct-2013.pdf>.

[24] Ibid 5.

The protection from refuge litigants in these cases are not IDPs in the precise sense that Tuitt discusses. Rather, they are people who have managed to leave their homeland to seek international protection. However, the figure of the IDP looms large in these decisions and, in particular, decision-makers' approaches to the nature and ambit of refuge. In UK jurisprudence from 2002 to 2005 and a 2008 Aotearoa/New Zealand case, decision-makers positioned the protection from refuge litigant as a prospective IDP. Decision-makers examined the situation for IDPs in the country of origin, in particular, their specific needs and whether the relevant authorities had capacity to provide protection to them. Similar to the pattern identified in previous chapters, this is an example of categorical reasoning – decision-makers started their analysis by focussing on the predicaments faced by IDPs. For example, in a decision concerning whether an Afghani putative refugee could internally relocate to Kabul, the New Zealand Refugee Status Appeals Authority considered evidence about the challenges IDPs in Kabul face. The Authority noted that 'the current upswing in the insurgency since 2006 has increased the numbers of [IDPs] coming to Kabul which, in turn, has placed strain on the city's capacity to provide them with basic levels of social welfare'.[25] The Refugee Status Appeals Authority cited a report by the Afghan Independent Human Rights Commission, which stated that 'a lack of basic economic and social rights is the primary cause of ongoing displacement and the main obstacle to durable integration of [IDPs]'.[26] After considering this evidence, the Authority concluded that the 'likelihood that the appellant would end up in an IDP camp in Kabul is all too real. In no way does this provide *meaningful* protection to him'.[27]

Similarly, in one of the earliest UK cases raising the question of internal relocation to an IDP camp, the United Kingdom Asylum and Immigration Tribunal positioned the putative refugee as a prospective IDP. It considered evidence of the difficulties faced by IDPs in the man's homeland and the relevant authorities' ability to provide protection. This 2002 case concerned whether a 22-year-old man from eastern Sierra Leone could internally relocate to Freetown.[28] The Tribunal noted that, if he did, he would 'be thrown into the general mele [sic] of expecting support from international agencies, along with the mass of other [IDPs] and returnees'.[29] Despite being a 'young, independent and fit man',[30] he would be 'at best, placed in a camp where conditions are described as "sub-human" and face medical conditions described as some of the worst in the world'.[31] The Tribunal ruled that he would not have '*meaningful* protection' in an IDP camp.[32]

Taking a categorical approach does not mean that the prospective IDP's individual circumstances are ignored. In early UK jurisprudence, decision-makers examine the difficulties faced by all IDPs but also demonstrate an understanding of how factors such as age and health concerns can exacerbate challenges associated with internal displacement. For example, in a 2002 decision, the United Kingdom Asylum and Immigration Tribunal considered whether a Kurdish man from Iraq could internally relocate to the Kurdish Autonomous Area, where it was likely that he would end up living in an IDP camp.[33] The Tribunal considered evidence of the situation for IDPs in the autonomous area and highlighted that '40% of [IDPs] in the region under Kurdish administration live in

[25] *Refugee Appeal No 76191* (New Zealand Refugee Status Appeals Authority, 12 August 2008), [56] ('*Refugee Appeal No 76191*').
[26] Ibid [56].   [27] Ibid [57] (emphasis added).
[28] *PO (Risk-Return-General) Sierra Leone CG* [2002] UKIAT 03285.   [29] Ibid [27].   [30] Ibid [27].
[31] Ibid [27].   [32] Ibid [28].   [33] *YJ (Non-Kurdish Speakers in KAA) Iraq CG* [2002] UKIAT 05271.

settlements with standards of water and electricity supplies, sanitation, drainage and road access that were below average for the area',[34] and IDPs survive only on UN rations.[35] The Tribunal ruled that there was no internal protection alternative, because he would probably end up living in an IDP camp in which the conditions were 'abominable'.[36] In coming to this conclusion, the Tribunal also took into account the man's disadvantage in accessing employment and government facilities due to his lack of Kurdish language skills, the fact that he would have no family support and had medical and psychological problems that would be exacerbated without such support networks.[37]

Another example of decision-makers taking into account both the situation for IDPs and the individual putative refugee's circumstances is a 2005 decision concerning whether an eighteen-year-old man from Southern Sudan could internally relocate to Khartoum, where he may have had no choice but to live in an IDP camp.[38] The United Kingdom Asylum and Immigration Tribunal referred to UNHCR evidence that described the conditions in the camps as 'harsh'[39] and 'precarious'[40] and stated that inhabitants faced significant threats to their physical security.[41] The Tribunal ruled that he would not have protection in a camp environment.[42] As part of its decision, the Tribunal emphasised that the putative refugee was a young man who had lost all of his family and would 'be returned to an IDP camp in Khartoum' where he would 'have no support network'.[43]

One theme that emerges across these decisions is that the putative refugee, as a prospective IDP, would be returning to a situation in which the relevant care providers are under-resourced. The Aotearoa/New Zealand decision stressed that the city of Kabul was facing challenges in providing for IDPs' basic welfare. The United Kingdom Asylum and Immigration Tribunal in the decisions discussed above highlighted that IDPs survive off UN rations and rely on assistance from international agencies. By taking this approach, decision-makers conceptualise refuge as something that involves the state or an international organisation[44] providing care. Understanding refuge as something bestowed by the state or an international organisation is not necessarily inconsistent with notions of

---

[34] Ibid [8].   [35] Ibid [10].   [36] Ibid [15]–[16].   [37] Ibid [15]–[16].
[38] *MM (Zaghawa – Risk on Return – internal Flight) Sudan* [2005] UKIAT 00069.   [39] Ibid [17].
[40] Ibid [37].   [41] Ibid [17].   [42] Ibid [46].   [43] Ibid [46].
[44] Under international human rights law, the state bears the duty to protect and uphold human rights. Accordingly, the primary focus should be whether the state is willing or able to provide protection. The Guiding Principles on Internal Displacement, UN ESCOR, UN Doc E/CN.4/1998/53/Add.2 (22 July 1998) principle 3(1) confirms that the state has 'the primary duty and responsibility to provide protection and humanitarian assistance to [IDPs] within [its] jurisdiction'. However, humanitarian organisations have the right to offer their services and states are required to grant these organisations access to IDPs: principles 25(2)–(3). Whether an international organisation as opposed to the state can be seen as a provider of protection is unsettled. Hathaway and Foster insist that the concept of protection in article 1A(2) of the Refugee Convention refers to 'the protection of a state accountable under international law': James Hathaway and Michelle Foster, 'Internal Protection/Relocation/Flight Alternative as an Aspect of Refugee Status Determination' in Erica Feller, Volker Türk and Frances Nicholson (eds), *Refugee Protection in International Law: UNHCR's Global Consultations on International Protection* (Cambridge University Press, 2003) 406, 411. O'Sullivan's position is that non-state actors that have acquired territorial control and have domestic and international protection obligations can be deemed providers of protection for the purposes of an IPA inquiry: Maria O'Sullivan, 'Acting the Part: Can Non-State Entities Provide Protection Under International Refugee Law' (2012) 24 *International Journal of Refugee Law* 85, 102. Schultz (n 22) argues that non-state actors can be understood as providing protection within the meaning of article 1A(2) of the Refugee Convention if 'they have an ability to enforce the rule of law and ensure basic rights protection–something few non-state actors can do': 210.

refuge discussed earlier in this book, which stress the role local community actors play in fostering a sense of refuge. In these cases, decision-makers acknowledge that refuge cannot be entirely self-made, but requires, as an essential ingredient, an authority able and willing to provide care and protection. If the relevant authority cannot provide adequate care, then the putative refugee does not have an internal protection alternative and is entitled to refugee status in Aotearoa/New Zealand or the UK.

As a consequence of this understanding of what refuge requires, countries in the Global North take responsibility for those with a well-founded fear of persecution who would otherwise be part of the large numbers of people relying on assistance from lower income countries or overstretched international organisations. Thus, these cases are consistent with the notion of international cooperation in the Refugee Convention's preamble. They align with Schultz's position that IPA cases must take into account 'the impact of return not only on the individual but also on the community' in the country of origin with respect to availability of resources.[45]

That decision-makers approached these cases with an ethic of international cooperation is significant in the context of debates over the correct test for IPA cases. Aotearoa/New Zealand and the UK adopt different tests when considering whether a putative refugee can internally relocate. Both agree that the putative refugee must be able to access the IPA safely[46] and their well-found fear of persecution must be negated.[47] Both jurisdictions acknowledge that there also must be affirmative state protection, but the tests for discerning this differ. In Aotearoa/New Zealand, the test is whether the putative refugee can 'genuinely access ... domestic protection which is meaningful'.[48] This includes consideration of whether 'basic norms of civil, political and socio-economic rights will be provided by the State'[49] using the rights in the Refugee Convention as a guide.[50] The test in the UK is whether it would be unduly harsh or unreasonable for the putative refugee to internally relocate.[51]

Scholars have criticised the reasonableness test on the grounds that it does not prioritise human rights considerations and can lead to inconsistent outcomes.[52] Refugee law experts advocate for states to determine internal protection alternatives with reference to the rights in the Refugee Convention[53] or a slightly broader human rights enquiry.[54] However, these

[45] Schultz (n 22) 252.
[46] Directive 2011/95/EU of the European Parliament and of the Council of 13 December on Standards for the Qualification of Third Country Nationals or Stateless Persons as Beneficiaries of International Protection, for a Uniform Status for Refugees or for Persons Eligible for Subsidiary Protection, and for the Content of the Protection Granted (Recast) [2011] OJ L 337/9–337/26, art 8(1); *Refugee Appeal No 76044* [2008] NZAR 719 [178] ('*Refugee Appeal No 76044*').
[47] *Refugee Appeal No 76044* (n 46) [178]; *SSHD v AH (Sudan)* (n 3) [21].
[48] *Refugee Appeal No 76044* (n 46) [178].   [49] Ibid [178].
[50] Ibid [178]; *Refugee Appeal No 71684/99* [2000] INLR 165 [60]. This is the approach outlined in the First Colloquium on Challenges in International Refugee Law, 'The Michigan Guidelines on the Internal Protection Alternative' (1999) 21(1) *Michigan Journal of International Law* 134, 139 ('Michigan Guidelines on the IPA').
[51] *Januzi v Secretary of State for the Home Department* [2006] 2 AC 426 [21] ('*Januzi*'). A reasonableness test is also used in Australia and Canada: *SZATV v Minister for Immigration and Citizenship* (2007) 233 CLR 18 [32]; *Rasaratnam v Canada (Minister of Employment and Immigration)* [1992] 1 FC 706, 711.
[52] James Hathaway and Michelle Foster, *The Law of Refugee Status* (Cambridge University Press, 2nd ed, 2014) 352; Mathew (n 3) 192; Bríd Ní Ghráinne, 'The Internal Protection Alternative Inquiry and Human Rights Considerations – Irrelevant or Indispensable?' (2015) 27(1) *International Journal of Refugee Law* 29, 46.
[53] Michigan Guidelines on the IPA (n 50) 139; Hathaway and Foster (n 52) 356.
[54] Mathew (n 3) 193–5; Schultz (n 22) 212–13.

rights-based approaches do not squarely address the problem of the discrepancies in levels of protection between countries in the Global North and Global South. Most of the rights in the Refugee Convention are not absolute, but relative to what the host state provides its nationals or foreigners 'generally in the same circumstances'.[55] Similarly, realisation of rights in ICESCR is measured by a state's available resources.[56] Thus, these two instruments acknowledge and permit discrepancies between levels of rights protection in lower- and higher-income countries.[57] What is noteworthy about the aforementioned decisions is that, through conceptualising refuge as something to be bestowed by an appropriate authority, they address the problem of states or international agencies having limited capacity to care for large numbers of people in need of protection. They provide that, when the relevant authorities are under-resourced, the putative refugee remains the responsibility of Aotearoa/New Zealand or the UK.

In taking this approach, these decisions are a counterpoint to Tuitt's concerns that law closes down or discourages enquiries about 'pressing humanitarian concerns'[58] and absolves itself of the 'unattended moral arena' of internal displacement. In considering a broad range of predicaments IDPs face and the challenges confronting the organisations providing protection, these decisions may be an example of the type of adjudicative reasoning some feminist legal scholars advocate for – one that gives 'due consideration to the cultural-economic-political-social context of the case'.[59] By considering which state is best placed to provide protection, these cases also have resonance with Kritzman-Amir's feminist approach to refuge. As discussed in Chapter 2, she draws on feminist ideas of ethics of care to posit that responsibility for refugees should be primarily determined by reference to states' varying capacity to care for refugees.[60]

Nevertheless, these decisions do not go so far as to acknowledge the roles that Global North states may have played in the situations now faced by those in the putative refugee's country of origin or habitual residence, a theme Tuitt[61] and most recently Achiume[62] address. Thus, just like in the previous chapter concerning article 1D of the Refugee Convention, there was an opportunity to position refuge as a form of restorative of corrective injustice that decision-makers did not take up.

There are only two UK cases from the early 2000s in which it was found that a putative refugee had an internal protection alternative in an IDP camp.[63] One used the wrong test. Instead of considering whether internal relocation to an IDP camp would be unduly harsh

---

[55] For a detailed discussion, see James Hathaway, *The Rights of Refugees under International Law* (Cambridge University Press, 2nd ed, 2021) ch 3.

[56] Art 2(1).

[57] The Michigan Guidelines on the IPA (n 50) 139 acknowledge that the standards in the Refugee Convention are 'affirmative, yet relative' and stress that the 'relevant measure is the treatment of other persons in the proposed site of internal protection, not in the putative asylum country'.

[58] Tuitt (n 5) 155.

[59] Alice Edwards, *Violence against Women under International Human Rights Law* (Cambridge University Press, 2010) 336.

[60] Tally Kritzman-Amir, 'Not in My Backyard: On the Morality of Responsibility Sharing in Refugee Law' (2009) 34(2) *Brooklyn Journal of International Law* 355, 362, 372.

[61] Patricia Tuitt, *Race, Law, Resistance* (Glasshouse Press, 2004) 59–60.

[62] Tendayi Achiume, 'Migration as Decolonization' (2019) 71(6) *Stanford Law Review* 1509.

[63] *Appeal No HX51798-2000 14 (Kabul – Pashtun) Afghanistan CG* [2002] UKIAT 05345; *AE (Relocation, Darfur, Khartoum an option) Sudan* [2005] UKAIT 00101.

or unreasonable, the United Kingdom Asylum and Immigration Tribunal used the much higher threshold of whether it would present a risk of persecution or treatment contrary to article 3 of the ECHR.[64] The other case concerned a Pashtun man from Mazar, Afghanistan. The issue was whether he could relocate to Kabul or an area in the south of Afghanistan which was in an exclusively Pashtun area. One issue that arose was that, if he internally relocated, he might have no option but to live in a UNHCR refugee camp for Pakistani refugees that also provided protection to Afghani IDPs. The United Kingdom Asylum and Immigration Tribunal reasoned that 'it would be difficult to regard being under UNHCR protection in a UNHCR camp as being unduly harsh', because it would be 'difficult to believe that people would be invited to make use of those camps if they were not basically humanitarian'.[65] The Tribunal accepted these camps as 'basically humanitarian' without considering any evidence regarding the actual conditions in these camps.[66] Nevertheless, the focus in this decision was whether the prospective IDP would have protection and there is identification of an international organisation that provided such protection. Thus, this decision relied on an understanding of the nature of refuge as something that must be bestowed by the state or international community.

With respect to the scope of refuge, in none of these cases did the decision-makers discuss what is meant by 'meaningful protection' in great depth. This may be because they accepted almost without question that an IDP camp is not a viable internal protection alternative. They did not need to justify their decision beyond reference to the 'abominable' and 'subhuman' conditions in the camps.

Nevertheless, the types of protections identified in the judgments cover a spectrum of breaches of civil and political as well as socio-economic rights such as physical security; social welfare; access to food, water and shelter; and availability of employment and government services. This is in line with the tests Mathew[67] and Schultz[68] propose for the availability of an IPA: whether the putative refugee would have human rights protection in the proposed place of relocation. Also, the Aotearoa/New Zealand case discussed the need for there to be durable solutions to the situation of internal displacement and, in particular, that IDPs should be able to integrate into a new community.[69] Reference to this array of rights indicates an appreciation that the prospective IDP is not only entitled to a sense of safety and adequate living conditions, they must also have the ability to live a normal life through having access to employment and government services, integrating into the community and eventually finding a solution to displacement. This is a broad understanding of the scope of refuge and reflects ideas of refuge's temporality, in particular, that it must enable refugees to imagine and work towards a better future. If a prospective IDP will not enjoy these protections because the relevant authorities are already overburdened with providing care to large numbers of IDPs, they can remain in and lay claim to a place of refuge in Aotearoa/New Zealand or the UK. While there were no female putative refugees in these cases, this approach is flexible enough to take into account gendered harms that arise in IDP camps from sexual violence to lack of employment or education opportunities for women and girls.

---

[64] *AE (Relocation, Darfur, Khartoum an option) Sudan* (n 63) [36].
[65] *Appeal No HX51798-2000 14* (n 63) [56].
[66] This can be contrasted with decisions that have found the conditions in UNHCR-run refugee camps to present a real risk of inhuman and degrading treatment: see *Sufi and Elmi v UK* [2012] 54 EHRR 9.
[67] Mathew (n 3) 193–5.   [68] Schultz (n 22) 212–13.   [69] *Refugee Appeal No 76191* (n 25) [56].

When decision-makers take this approach, the figure of the IDP is able to disrupt the boundaries between the Global North and Global South in a way that permits large numbers of putative refugees (also prospective IDPs) to continue their quest for refuge in a higher-income country. In these cases, decision-makers position the prospective IDP not as the rightless figure Tuitt describes in her scholarship, but as a rights-bearing subject. They are entitled to live a safe and normal life under the care of an authority that has capacity to provide them with protection. This approach does not address the problem that many people with a well-founded fear of persecution cannot leave their homeland to seek international protection, but it does circumscribe the Refugee Convention's operation as a containment mechanism. These decisions indicate that refugee law can operate as an instrument that helps to achieve a fairer distribution of refugee responsibility. In their determination of these protection from refuge cases, decision-makers treat the fact that there are many people in the country of origin who do not have adequate protection in line with Mathew's observation that this 'simply confirms the sad reality that there are many IDPs who are unable to exercise their right to seek asylum'.[70] In the next section, I show that, in later jurisprudence, the fact that there are large numbers of people in the refugee's homeland without protection takes on a different significance and one that shifts judicial understandings of the nature and scope of refuge for putative refugees.

7.4   Refuge as the Chance of Mere Survival

There has been a change in the ways UK decision-makers approach the question of whether an IDP camp can serve as an IPA. This has produced a narrow and impoverished understanding of refuge and entrenched the Refugee Convention as a mechanism to contain those in need of protection in the Global South, impeding refugees' journeys in search of refuge.

This turnaround occurred in 2006 and is partly attributable to the 2006 United Kingdom House of Lords decision of *Januzi v Secretary of State for the Home Department* ('*Januzi*').[71] This case concerned four putative refugees whose claims for protection had been denied on the grounds that they had an IPA.[72] The common issue on appeal was whether decision-makers must examine the prospective IPA with reference to the standards espoused in leading international human rights instruments, including the Refugee Convention. The prospect of an IDP camp serving as an IPA was an issue relevant to three of the appellants, but the United Kingdom House of Lords did not make any ruling on this aspect of their case.

Lord Bingham gave the lead judgment. He considered the approach adopted in Aotearoa/New Zealand, which involves examining whether the putative refugee would have access to Refugee Convention rights in the IPA.[73] Lord Bingham compared this to the approach adopted by the England and Wales Court of Appeal, which involved 'a comparison between the conditions prevailing in the place of habitual residence and those which prevail in the safe haven, having regard to the impact that they will have on a person with the

---

[70] Mathew (n 3) 204.   [71] *Januzi* (n 51).
[72] The first appellant was an Albanian Kosovan from Mitrovica in Kosovo. The other three appellants were from Darfur in Sudan. In relation to the appeals, the United Kingdom House of Lords rejected the first appellant's appeal. The House of Lords upheld the three Sudanese appellants' appeal and remitted the matters back to the United Kingdom Asylum and Immigration Tribunal for further consideration.
[73] *Januzi* (n 51) [9].

characteristics of the asylum-seeker'.[74] Lord Bingham preferred the England and Wales Court of Appeal's approach. He reasoned that there is no logical reason for importing all of the Refugee Convention rights into the test for internal relocation – these rights apply to refugees in a host state, not to those within their homeland.[75] Lord Bingham also expressed concern that a broad human rights enquiry may have the 'unintended' and 'anomalous' consequence of providing a pathway for migration from the Global South to the Global North:

> Suppose a person is subject to persecution for Convention reasons in the country of his [or her or their] nationality. It is a poor country. Standards of social provision are low. There is a high level of deprivation and want. Respect for human rights is scant. He [or she or they] escapes to a rich country where, if recognised as a refugee, he [or she or they] would enjoy all the rights guaranteed to refugees in that country. He [or she or they] could, with no fear of persecution, live elsewhere in his [or her or their] country of nationality, but would there suffer all the drawbacks of living in a poor and backward country. It would be strange if the accident of persecution were to entitle him [or her or them] to escape, not only from that persecution, but from the deprivation to which his [or her or their] home country is subject.[76]

The United Kingdom House of Lords held that decision-makers are not required to undertake a broad human rights enquiry in IPA cases.[77] Rather, the test of whether internal relocation would be unduly harsh or unreasonable only requires consideration of whether the putative refugee would be free from persecution and would have the 'most basic of human rights',[78] such as the right to life and right not to be subjected to cruel or inhuman treatment.[79] The Court stressed that, if the putative refugee could 'lead a relatively normal life' in the IPA 'judged by the standards that prevail in his [or her or their] country of nationality generally', it would 'not be unreasonable to expect him [or her or them] to move there'.[80]

There are a number of critical examinations of the United Kingdom House of Lords' decision in *Januzi* that, argue that the test it established for internal relocation is not a good faith interpretation of article 1A(2) of the Refugee Convention.[81] The question for this book is how it has affected decision-makers' conceptualisation of the nature and scope of refuge for putative refugees resisting the prospect of seeking refuge in an IDP camp. As already discussed, when the question of an IDP camp serving as an IPA first arose in the UK, decision-makers positioned the prospective IDP as a person in need of protection who is entitled to be under the care of an authority that has the capacity to provide that protection. Immigration judges conceived of refuge as something that must be bestowed and accepted that, if the relevant authority is under-resourced, there was no internal protection available. These decisions are also imbued with an ethic of international cooperation. However, in post-*Januzi* jurisprudence, these understandings of the IDP and ideas of refuge have diminished and decision-makers have determined that an IDP camp is an acceptable IPA in almost all cases in which the issue has been arbitrated.[82]

---

[74] *E v Secretary of State for the Home Department* [2003] EWCA 1032 [24] cited in *Januzi* (n 51) [13].

[75] *Januzi* (n 51) [15].

[76] Ibid [19]. For a discussion of this issue, see Mathew (n 3) 205; Ní Ghráinne (n 52) 44.

[77] *Januzi* (n 51).   [78] Ibid [54], [59].

[79] Ibid [54]. For a critique of limiting the focus to non-derogable rights, see Mathew (n 3) 204.

[80] *Januzi* (n 51) [47] (emphasis added).

[81] Hathaway and Foster (n 52) 351–61; Mathew (n 3) 201–6; Ní Ghráinne (n 52) 44–5.

[82] There is a 2008 decision in which the United Kingdom Asylum and Immigration Tribunal accepted that, for putative refugees from Somalia, it is likely that having to spend substantial time in an IDP camp would

This change was first evident in *HGMO (Relocation to Khartoum) Sudan CG ('HGMO')*,[83] which concerned the three Sudanese appellants who had their matters remitted back to the United Kingdom Asylum and Immigration Tribunal by the United Kingdom House of Lords in *Januzi* and one other Sudanese asylum seeker from Darfur. One issue for the Tribunal was whether the putative refugees could relocate to Khartoum where they may have had to seek refuge in an IDP camp. Expert evidence indicated that the Sudanese government provided no protection to those living in IDP camps,[84] denied humanitarian groups access to the camps,[85] actively destroyed the camps[86] and forcibly relocated their inhabitants.[87] One of the expert witnesses concluded that 'IDP camps and squatter settlements in Khartoum state provide no security for IDPs'.[88] Other evidence concerning the IDP camps before the Tribunal attested to arbitrary arrest,[89] arbitrary detention,[90] acts of violence[91] and lack of access to education[92] and employment.[93] However, the Tribunal determined that internal relocation to an IDP camp would not be unreasonable or unduly harsh, because the living conditions in the camps were 'not markedly different from the living conditions in Sudan as a whole'.[94] The Tribunal noted that 'we particularly bear in mind the fact that most people in Sudan live at subsistence level and that over 70% of those who live in urban conurbations are slumdwellers'.[95]

Comparing the putative refugee/prospective IDP to the population at large disregards the idea that putative refugees are entitled to a special form of refuge that must be bestowed by the state. In this decision, the Tribunal ignored the relationship between the state and prospective IDP. Focussing instead on the conditions experienced by the general population and using this as the comparator removes the potential for these decisions to promote ideas of cooperative refuge between the Global South and Global North. That others in the country of origin similarly do not receive protection is no longer a reason to provide the putative refugee with protection, but grounds on which to expel them back to their homeland. Comparison to the rest of the population also diverts judicial attention away from the setting of the camp and whether it can provide a sense of refuge.

Instead of examining whether the state is willing and able to provide protection to the prospective IDP, decision-makers sometimes consider if the putative refugee has family that can provide assistance.[96] This morphs understandings of refuge from something granted by the state or an international organisation to, at best, something provided privately through

---

render internal relocation unreasonable: *AM & AM (armed conflict: risk categories) Somalia CG* [2008] UKAIT 00091 [190]. However, the issue did not arise on the facts. The Tribunal determined that the first appellant was not entitled to refugee or complementary protection: [207]. The second appellant's claim for complementary protection was upheld and the Tribunal concluded that he did not have an IPA but did not consider the prospect of him living in an IDP camp: [208]–[209].

[83] [2006] UKAIT 00062. The asylum seekers in *HGMO* appealed the United Kingdom Asylum and Immigration Tribunal's decision to the Court of Appeal: *AH, IG and NM v Secretary of State for the Home Department* [2007] EWCA Civ 297. The appeal was successful. The Secretary of State for the Home Department then appealed to the United Kingdom House of Lords: *SSHD v AH (Sudan)* (n 3). The Secretary of State for the Home Department's appeal was successful and the United Kingdom Asylum and Immigration Tribunal's decision in *HGMO* was reinstated.

[84] *HGMO* (n 83) [74].   [85] Ibid [30].   [86] Ibid [29].   [87] Ibid [17], [73].   [88] Ibid [74].

[89] Ibid [22].   [90] Ibid [74].   [91] Ibid [134].   [92] Ibid [74].   [93] Ibid [77].   [94] Ibid [265].

[95] Ibid [265].

[96] For other examples of IPA cases where the family was deemed to provide protection, see Schultz (n 22) 205–7.

family members. This is evident in *SK (FGM – ethnic groups) Liberia CG*,[97] a 2007 case concerning whether a Liberian woman could internally relocate from a rural to an urban area where she may have had no choice but to live in an IDP camp. The United Kingdom Asylum and Immigration Tribunal noted that there was evidence of sexual violence perpetrated against IDPs living in the camps.[98] However, the Tribunal did not enquire as to the type and level of protection provided (if any) against the risk of sexual violence in IDP camps. The Tribunal concluded that '[w]hilst these may occur, we are unaware of any evidence that suggests that in general, lone women within such camps are as such at real risk of rape'.[99] One reason the Tribunal ruled that it would not be unduly harsh to expect her to live in an IDP camp was because her partner in the UK would send her money.[100] Thus, the Tribunal did not focus on the protection that Liberia provides to IDPs, but what protection the woman could access through family connections.

A similar line of reasoning is evident in cases concerning internal relocation and IDP camps in Somalia.[101] The 2011 case of *AMM and Others (Conflict; Humanitarian Crisis; Returnees; FGM) Somalia CG*[102] concerned whether a Somali putative refugee could intern- ally relocate to an IDP camp in Somalia's Afgoye Corridor. The United Kingdom Asylum and Immigration Tribunal stated that relocation to an IDP camp would be unreasonable 'unless there is evidence that the person concerned would be able to achieve the lifestyle of those better-off inhabitants of the Afgoye Corridor settlements'.[103] Whether a returnee could achieve such a lifestyle would depend on the putative refugee 'having family or other significant connections with such better-off elements'.[104] Without the protection of family or significant connections, the returnee would not be able to 'eliminate the risks inherent in IDP camps'.[105] In this case, the Tribunal did not consider what (if any) state protection is available to IDPs in camps in the Afgoye Corridor, but the availability of family support. In the 2014 case of *MOJ & Ors (Return to Mogadishu) Somalia CG v Secretary of State for the Home Department*,[106] the United Kingdom Upper Tribunal accepted that conditions in IDP camps in Mogadishu 'fall below acceptable humanitarian standards' and would not be an acceptable IPA.[107] However, the Tribunal found that each of the appellants would be able to provide for themselves through employment, family support or remittances and would, thus, be able to avoid life in an IDP camp.[108]

Focussing on the putative refugee's family dilutes the concept of refuge. The presence of family members in the proposed internal protection alternative should be a relevant con- sideration with respect to whether the putative refugee will be able to rebuild social and cultural networks and enjoy family unity.[109] However, decision-makers are instead approaching the presence of family as a substitute for state protection. Unlike state protec- tion, which is grounded in a state's international legal obligations, family support and remittances are voluntary. These approaches remove the idea of refuge as a duty the state must honour and deliver a precarious form of refuge hinged on private individuals'

---

[97] [2007] UKAIT 00001 ('*SK (FGM)*').   [98] Ibid [63].   [99] Ibid [63].   [100] Ibid [64].

[101] These cases also considered whether conditions in IDP camps present a risk of treatment contrary to article 3 of the ECHR. As outlined in Chapter 1 and in this chapter (n 2), these aspects of the decisions are outside the scope of this book. A discussion of jurisprudence on whether IDP camps in Somalia present a risk of treatment contrary to article 3 is provided in *SB (refugee revocation; IDP camps) Somalia* [2019] UKUT 00358 (IAC).

[102] [2011] UKUT 00445 (IAC) ('*AMM*').   [103] Ibid [602].   [104] Ibid [501].   [105] Ibid [501].

[106] [2014] UKUT 00442 (IAC) ('*MOJ*').   [107] Ibid [425].   [108] Ibid [440]–[441], [462], [478].

[109] Schultz (n 22) 217, 225.

unpredictable generosity. This is also a problematic understanding of refuge from a gender perspective, because it ignores the fact that the family is sometimes the source of protection concerns.[110] A person may not be able to leave a dangerous family situation if their family members are the only ones providing protection against the dangers of life in an IDP camp.

Decision-makers' approaches to these protection from refuge claims have also narrowed the scope of refuge. As noted earlier, while early 2000s jurisprudence in the UK concerning internal relocation to an IDP camp did not specifically outline the appropriate scope of refuge, decision-makers took into account a range of civil and political and socio-economic rights, including physical security and access to employment and government services. In later decisions, the scope has been narrowed to adequate living conditions. This is an understanding of refuge akin to humanitarian assistance in the immediate aftermath of events such as conflict or natural disaster.[111] This minimalist conceptualisation of refuge is far removed from the more comprehensive ideas of refuge for putative refugees or IDPs outlined in Chapter 2.

A narrow scope of refuge is evident in *HGMO*, in which the United Kingdom Asylum and Immigration Tribunal focussed only on living conditions and ignored the many other human rights concerns raised in the evidence. As noted earlier, it ruled that relocation to an IDP camp would not be unreasonable or unduly harsh because 'the living conditions' in the camps were 'not markedly different from the living conditions in Sudan as a whole'.[112] This truncates the ambit of refuge for putative refugees and prospective IDPs. In particular, human rights violations that are of particular concern to IDPs such as forced relocation and restrictions of freedom of movement remain outside the judicial lens.

Another example of UK decision-makers shrinking the scope of refuge is the United Kingdom Asylum and Immigration Tribunal's decision in *SK (FGM – ethnic groups) Liberia CG*.[113] The Tribunal placed weight on a US State Department Report that 'paints a picture of the camps which, whilst clearly not without problems, shows that they generally provide *reasonable living conditions*'.[114] Crucial to the Tribunal's decision was that the living conditions in the camps were acceptable, and the risk of sexual violence was of secondary importance. Thus, the Tribunal's conceptualisation of adequate refuge was a place where a person can survive because they have access to adequate food, water and shelter.

Another change in the jurisprudence is the disappearance of an underlying ethic of international cooperation. Unlike earlier cases in which decision-makers took account of the difficulties facing international organisations and NGOs in providing protection to IDPs, decision-makers now accept that these organisations are overstretched and enquire whether the putative refugee can nevertheless fend for themselves. For example, in a case concerning whether Iraqi Kurds can internally relocate to the Iraqi Kurdish Region, the United Kingdom Upper Tribunal noted that the IDP camps were already overcrowded and full.[115] The Tribunal found that the putative refugee would, therefore, not gain access to a camp and would face living in a 'critical housing arrangement'.[116] This meant 'living in abandoned and or unfinished buildings, makeshift shelters erected on spare ground, or

---

[110] Ibid 219.
[111] Durieux argues that this emergency model of refuge is essential to ensure 'basic rescue' in the aftermath of a crisis, but 'too many refugee situations freeze over in emergency mode': Jean-François Durieux, 'Three Asylum Paradigms' (2013) 20(2) *International Journal on Minority and Group Rights* 147, 167.
[112] *HGMO* (n 83) [265].   [113] *SK (FGM)* (n 97).   [114] Ibid [63] (emphasis added).
[115] *AAH (Iraqi Kurds – internal relocation) Iraq CG* UKUT 00212 (IAC) [125].   [116] Ibid [146].

squatting in government or religious buildings'.[117] The only assistance was in the form of organisations such as UNHCR and the World Health Organization providing '"emergency" items such as blankets and jerry cans'.[118] The Tribunal reasoned that, despite having 'limited education and no qualifications', he was 'physically able, literate, experienced' and had the required documentation.[119] Taking this into account, the Tribunal held that his life would not be unduly harsh as an IDP in a 'critical housing arrangement' because he could 'secure some form of employment'[120] that would enable him to 'feed and clothe himself'.[121]

As a result of decision-makers' dilution of the concept of refuge in these cases, the figure of the IDP has lost its ability to disrupt state boundaries and the Refugee Convention's effect of containing those in need of protection in the Global South is entrenched. By pitting the putative refugee against the country of origin's population at large, the image of the IDP decision-makers conjure up is a threatening one: they are one of hundreds and possibly thousands who could travel across international borders and claim refuge in the UK. Decision-makers rein in the IDP's ability to pierce the boundary between the Global South and Global North by positioning them close to the 'classic instance' of the rightless person Tuitt describes in her scholarship. The IDP is disenfranchised from their state of origin due to having a well-founded fear of persecution, but also disenfranchised from law: they are not understood to be a rights-bearer, but only entitled to the same living conditions as the rest of the population in their homeland.

The prospective IDP in these protection from refuge decisions is even further disenfranchised than the IDP Tuitt describes. Tuitt investigates the IDP's situation before she leaves her homeland. While Tuitt emphasises that travelling across international borders is only possible for a select few, it is at least still a potential recourse. The IDPs in these cases have already exercised this option. Next, I discuss how the act of travelling in search of refuge, which is exactly what a person must do to secure refugee status, weakens putative refugees' legal claims to secure a place of genuine refuge.

7.5   The Resilient Refugee

By narrowing the scope of refuge to adequate living conditions and using the country of origin's population at large as a comparator, immigration judges in the UK sidestep the need to examine the availability of state protection in IDP camps. The prospective IDP with no state protection has nothing but their own abilities, or in some cases family connections, to defend and make a life for themselves in the hostile conditions of an IDP camp. This moves decision-makers' focus to the prospective IDP's personal circumstances. To resist the prospect of life in an IDP camp, the putative refugee must prove that they are exceptionally vulnerable. For example, in *HGMO*, the United Kingdom Asylum and Immigration Tribunal accepted that, while it would generally not be unreasonable for a Sudanese putative refugee to internally relocate to an IDP camp, this may not be the case for those with an 'extreme and exceptional' health condition,[122] or for single women or female-headed households.[123]

There is one case in which decision-makers accepted that a prospective IDP's personal circumstances might render refuge in an IDP camp unreasonable. In *KH (Sudan) v Secretary*

---

[117] Ibid [127].   [118] Ibid [132].   [119] Ibid [147].   [120] Ibid [147].   [121] Ibid [148].
[122] *HGMO* (n 83) [260].   [123] Ibid [307].

of State for the Home Department,[124] the England and Wales Court of Appeal considered whether it would be unreasonable for a twenty-year-old Sudanese putative refugee to internally relocate to Khartoum where it was likely that he would live in an IDP camp. The case was on appeal from the United Kingdom Asylum and Immigration Tribunal, which had ruled that it would not be unreasonable for him to seek protection in an IDP camp because he was a 'young apparently healthy adult'.[125] The England and Wales Court of Appeal acknowledged that *HGMO* indicated that, as a general rule, it would not be unreasonable for a putative refugee to find refuge in an IDP camp in Khartoum.[126] However, the Court confirmed that this general finding must be tempered by the individual's particular circumstances.[127] The Court described the appellant's circumstances as 'stark', because he had 'lost all his living relatives, killed by those responsible for conditions in those camps'.[128] The case was remitted back to the United Kingdom Asylum and Immigration Tribunal with the instruction that the decision as to whether internal relocation to an IDP camp would be unduly harsh must take into account the fact that the man would live with 'the everyday knowledge that those responsible for such conditions are also responsible for the death of his every living relative'.[129] Any reconsideration of this case has not been reported. Nevertheless, the England and Wales Court of Appeal's judgment reflects the idea that refuge must have a palliative role and that a place that would re-traumatise a putative refugee is not a place that can provide genuine sanctuary.

However, in most cases involving the prospect of having to seek refuge in an IDP camp, immigration judges refer to the putative refugee's personal circumstances in a way that substantiates the decision that internal relocation to an IDP camp is not unreasonable or unduly harsh. In particular, decision-makers refer to personal circumstances in a way that positions the prospective IDP as a person with the talent or fortitude to endure the most hostile conditions. For example, in *SK (FGM – ethnic groups) Liberia CG*, the United Kingdom Asylum and Immigration Tribunal confirmed that it would be unreasonable to expect most single women to internally relocate in Liberia, because they would face economic destitution.[130] Nevertheless, the Tribunal found that internal relocation was not unreasonable in this case, because the putative refugee was a 'healthy and obviously resourceful woman of some intelligence'.[131] Due to her good health, capabilities and being a woman 'of some intelligence', the Tribunal was satisfied that it was possible that she may not have to resort to living in an IDP camp and she would not have to prostitute herself to survive financially.[132] Thus, the Tribunal portrayed the putative refugee as having the personal strength and ability to survive in hostile conditions.

A similar approach is evident in *Petition of GAO*,[133] concerning a Sudanese woman who faced the prospect of life in an IDP camp if she internally relocated. The immigration judge reasoned that she may not need to live in an IDP camp, because she was a 'single woman who is fit, able to work and able to support herself in a relatively troubled environment'.[134] However, in the event that she had to live in an IDP camp, it would not be 'such a traumatic change of lifestyle that she would be unable to adapt to life in an IDP camp, should that prove necessary'.[135] The judge also took into account that 'she has previously traded in the market' and this 'would give her a wider experience than those who were only farmers'.[136]

---

[124] [2008] EWCA Civ 887.   [125] Initial decision cited in ibid.   [126] Ibid [36].   [127] Ibid [36].
[128] Ibid [36].   [129] Ibid [36].   [130] *SK (FGM)* (n 97) [69].   [131] Ibid [64].   [132] Ibid [63]–[64].
[133] [2010] CSOH 92.   [134] Initial decision cited in *Petition of GAO* [2010] CSOH 92 [5].   [135] Ibid [5].
[136] Ibid [5].

The judge relied on the petitioner's previous trade experience in determining that 'refuge in an IDP camp, should it be required, would not be unreasonable'.[137] Again, the decision-maker depicted the prospective IDP as different from and more capable than other single women in Liberia due to her prior work experience and being 'fit'.

Further examples of this type of reasoning are evident in cases involving male putative refugees who face the prospect of life in an IDP camp if they internally relocate. Decision-makers often refer to male refugees' gender and innate or acquired abilities in justifying why it would not be unduly harsh for them to endure even the most brutal camp environments. For example, in *JK (Serbia) v Secretary of State for the Home Department*, the United Kingdom Asylum and Immigration Tribunal found that a putative refugee could relocate to an IDP camp in Kosovo and this ruling was upheld on appeal.[138] The decision-maker emphasised the putative refugee's 'marketable skills' (a metalworking qualification and fluency in several languages) and that he was 'single and in good health'.[139]

In some cases, decision-makers deem an IDP camp an appropriate IPA for male putative refugees solely on the grounds of youth and gender. For example, in *NO v Secretary of State for the Home Department*,[140] it was held that a thirty-year-old Sudanese man could internally relocate to an IDP camp in Khartoum despite conditions being 'grim'.[141] The immigration judge reasoned that he was 'a young man with no dependants [sic]' who must have had considerable resources to come to the UK.[142] While not having any education, he could survive economically in a camp environment by performing physical labour.[143] Another example is a case concerning whether a Chechen putative refugee could internally relocate to Ingushetia, where many Chechens were living in IDP camps.[144] Evidence in the case attested to human rights abuses in the camps occurring on a 'significant scale'[145] and that the living conditions 'vary from difficult to unbearable, with many inhabiting over-crowded, dank, dilapidated buildings that enable diseases like tuberculosis and pneumonia to flourish'.[146] Nevertheless, the United Kingdom Asylum and Immigration Tribunal found that the conditions in the camps were not 'so severe as to render internal relocation for a *young Chechen male* unreasonable or unduly harsh'.[147] In another case, a Sudanese man was deemed to have an IPA because 'IDP camps in and around Khartoum were difficult and harsh, but not unduly harsh' and he did not have any acute vulnerabilities such as continuing health problems.[148]

When decision-makers characterise putative refugees, of all genders, as young, healthy and strong, this serves to justify and sanitise the act of refusing international protection to people who may have no choice but to seek refuge in an IDP camp. The subtext of these

---

[137] Ibid [5].
[138] *JK (Serbia) v Secretary of State for the Home Department* [2007] EWCA Civ 1321 [34] ('*JK Serbia*').
[139] Initial decision cited in ibid [20].   [140] [2008] CSIH 19 XA152/06.
[141] Initial decision cited in ibid [5].   [142] Ibid [5].   [143] Ibid [5].
[144] *RM (Young Chechen Male – Risk – IFA) Russia CG* [2006] UKAIT 00050.   [145] Ibid [42].
[146] Ibid [41].
[147] Ibid [47] (emphasis added). Three years later, the Tribunal considered a case concerning whether it was unreasonable for a Chechen woman to internally relocate to an IDP camp in Ingushetia: *OY (Chechen Muslim women) Russia CG* [2009] UKAIT 00005. The Tribunal found that a Chechen woman 'could not now relocate to an IDP camp', because the local Ingush authorities were no longer accepting new IDPs in the camps and were pressuring Chechen IDPs to return to Chechnya: [68]–[70]. Therefore, the distinguishing factor in this case was not the conditions in the camps, but that the putative refugees would no longer be able to access the camps.
[148] *KK (Unreported decisions – Practice Directions) Sudan* [2006] UKAIT 00008 [24].

judgments is that, while life in an IDP camp would be insufferable for most, we are only returning those with the resilience and fortitude to protect and provide for themselves. This is the antithesis of Tuitt's contention that it is the moving entity (a person who crosses international borders) who is seen as 'synonymous with humanitarian need and suffering'.[149] In these cases, decision-makers depict those who have travelled to the Global North as courageous and resilient and, on this basis, able to forge protection for themselves in even the most adverse and hostile environments. This removes the main way in which those with a well-founded fear of persecution can trigger refugee protection – crossing international borders. It creates a double bind similar to the one present in article 1D cases identified in Chapter 6: a putative refugee will only be protected from an IDP camp if they have no ability to protect themselves, but the very act of travelling long distances to make an asylum claim is demonstrative of fortitude and resilience.

Female refugees are especially disenfranchised by this conundrum. They are less likely than men to be able to make the journey to the Global North to seek protection (as Tuitt highlights), but those who do are deemed strong and capable enough to protect themselves. While decision-makers have issued country guidance stating that single-women or female-headed households may not have internal protection in an IDP camp,[150] they have found reasons why the particular female putative refugee putting forward her case is not 'vulnerable'. In doing so, decision-makers have downplayed the risk of sexual violence in IDP camps,[151] and stressed that female putative refugees can be protected by family members without considering if those family members themselves pose a protection risk.[152] Spijkerboer's insight that 'the fate of women may provide a compelling illustration of the brutal nature of the Third World, and it may well elicit the chivalrous impulse to save them by granting asylum'[153] is not played out here.

The dichotomy created in this jurisprudence between 'vulnerable woman in need of protection' and 'strong woman capable of looking after herself' undermines agency and obscures the complex interplay between a person's actions and structural constraints. There is resistance to portraying female refugees as vulnerable or victims because it does not highlight the choices they have made and the ways in which they have actively resisted persecution and oppression.[154] Nevertheless, depicting women who have experienced grave human rights abuses as heroines who are the masters of their own destiny ignores the fact that their options for protecting themselves and others are often heavily circumscribed by structural factors such as lack of access to finance and safe spaces.[155]

The assumption that men who are young and healthy can endure life in an IDP camp is equally problematic. By focussing on women and why they may be vulnerable, the gendered

---

[149] Tuitt (n 5) 14.   [150] *HGMO* (n 83) [307].   [151] *SK (FGM)* (n 97).

[152] Ibid; *AMM* (n 102); *MOJ* (n 106).

[153] Thomas Spijkerboer, *Gender and Refugee Status* (Ashgate, 2000) 999.

[154] Alice Edwards, 'Transitioning Gender: Feminist Engagement with International Refugee Law and Policy 1950–2010' (2010) 29 *Refugee Survey Quarterly* 21, 32.

[155] Chris Coulter, 'Female Fighters in the Sierra Leone War: Challenging the Assumptions?' (2008) 88 *Feminist Review* 54, 61; Katherine Irwin and Meda Chesney-Lind, 'Girls' Violence: Beyond Dangerous Masculinity' (2008) 2 *Sociology Compass* 837. I explore these themes in the context of article 1F of the Refugee Convention in Kate Ogg, 'Separating the Persecutors from the Persecuted: A Feminist and Comparative Examination of Exclusion from the Refugee Regime' (2013) 26(1) *International Journal of Refugee Law* 82.

harms men may face are ignored.[156] For example, men are often more at risk of forced recruitment than women in IDP camps.[157] The lack of attention to gender in IPA cases involving men is indicative of a greater problem in refugee law jurisprudence where there is an assumption that only specific cases, such as domestic violence or sexual orientation, raise gender concerns.[158]

7.6   Internal Protection and Cessation of Refugee Status

While this chapter has focussed on IPA decisions as part of refugee status determinations, as this book was being written, the IPA test was being applied in cessation decisions. In 2019, the United Kingdom Court of Appeal held that refugee status could cease pursuant to article 1C(5) of the Refugee Convention if 'refugee status has been granted because the person cannot reasonably be expected to relocate' and then due to a significant and non-temporary change in circumstances 'that person could be reasonably expected to relocate'.[159] This was based on a 2018 Court of Appeal decision which held that a 'cessation decision is the mirror image of a decision determining refugee status'.[160] The issue of whether refugee status can be revoked because the refugee can return to their homeland and internally relocate to an IDP camp has been raised in a number of 2019 and 2020 cases but, at the time of writing, no final determinations had been made.[161] The application of the IPA test to cessation decisions may be part of a pattern Shultz identifies in which 'European states are reviving the Refugee Convention's cessation provisions in service of their return-oriented refugee policies'.[162]

While there is some academic support for employing the IPA test in cessation decisions,[163] the weight of commentary indicates that it is inconsistent with the ordinary

---

[156] Carpenter makes this point with respect to humanitarian evacuations. She highlights that, of all civilians in the former Yugoslavia, adult men were most likely to be killed but international organisations prioritised the evacuation of women and children: R Charli Carpenter, '"Women and Children First": Gender, Norms, and Humanitarian Evacuation in the Balkans 1991–5' (2003) 57(4) *International Organization* 661.

[157] Internal Displacement Monitoring Centre, *Sex Matters: A Gender Perspective on Internal Displacement* (February 2019) 1.

[158] Spijkerboer (n 153) 9.

[159] *Secretary of State for the Home Department v MS (Somalia)* [2019] EWCA Civ 1345 [49]. See Maria O'Sullivan, *Legal Note on the Cessation of International Protection and Review of Protection Statuses in Europe* (2021) 16–18 <www.ecre.org/wp-content/uploads/2021/02/Legal-Note-7-Cessation-February-2021.pdf>.

[160] *Secretary for the Home Department v MA (Somalia)* [2018] EWCA Civ 994 [2].

[161] In *SB Somalia* (n 101) [76], the United Kingdom Upper Tribunal remitted to the First-tier Tribunal for determination, among other issues, whether article 1C(5) of the Refugee Convention applied to a Somali refugee on the grounds that he could now internally relocate to Mogadishu, including the possibility of living in an IDP camp. In *Secretary of State for the Home Department v MSC* [2020] UKAITUR RP000722018, the United Kingdom Upper Tribunal remitted for rehearing a case involving cessation and whether a Somali refugee could internally relocate even if he would have no option but to live in an IDP camp. See also *IMA v Secretary of State for the Home Department* [2020] UKAITUR RP001312018; *Mohamed Ali Nassir v Secretary of State for the Home Department* [2020] UKAITUR RP001302018. These cases were instigated after the refugee had been convicted of a criminal offence.

[162] Jessica Schultz, 'The End of Protection? Cessation and the "Return Turn" in Refugee Law' (31 January 2020) Immigration and Asylum Law and Policy <http://eumigrationlawblog.eu/the-end-of-protection-cessation-and-the-return-turn-in-refugee-law/>.

[163] Chao Yi, 'The Applicability of the Internal Relocation Principle to Cessation of Refugee Status: The Surrogate Nature of International Refugee Protection' (Paper 76, FICHL Policy Brief Series, 2017)

meaning of the words in article 1C(5) and the Refugee Convention's object and purpose. The use of the IPA test is inconsistent with UNHCR guidance on the application of the cessation clause, which provides that 'changes in the refugee's country of origin affecting only part of the territory should not, in principle, lead to cessation of refugee status'.[164] Further support for this position comes from Hathaway and Foster's approach to article 1C(5). Contrary to the Court of Appeal's position that a 'cessation decision is the mirror image of a decision determining refugee status', they stress that the words 'cease to exist' in article 1C(5) are 'a more demanding standard than risk below a well-founded fear'.[165] Article 1C(5) requires 'a more complete and definitive transformation' of the refugee's country of origin or habitual residence[166] such as 'reversion to democracy'[167] as opposed to merely the absence of a well-founded fear of persecution.[168]

Including the IPA test in cessation decisions also skewers one of the fundamental aspects of refuge – hope for the future. Hathaway and Foster explain that article 1C(5) of the Refugee Convention aims to balance fairness to asylum countries with 'a clear commitment to avoid the constant uncertainty that would plague a refugee if her protected status were subject to ongoing reassessment'.[169] They stress that, once a 'refugee has begun to remake her life', the question of cessation must be approached with 'real caution'.[170] Ceasing refugee status merely on the grounds that an IPA has become available, as opposed to the higher and correct threshold outlined earlier, means that those with international protection live under the sword of Damocles. Instead of building a future, they live with the ever-present prospect of being returned to their homeland and for some, as UK jurisprudence is indicating, the prospect of life in an IDP camp.

Employing an IPA test in cessation decisions is also a concerning development with respect to international cooperation. Higher-income countries host disproportionately small numbers of refugees, and the UK is likely to increase the rate of return through this legal development. That an IDP camp can serve as an IPA for the purpose of a cessation determination, a notion currently being entertained by immigration judges in the UK, means that a higher-income country can hand over responsibility for providing protection to already overstretched international organisations and NGOs operating in these settings.

7.7 Conclusion

This chapter contained the book's final case study examining how decision-makers approach and determine protection from refuge claims. Similar to previous chapters, I observed that decision-makers have employed a categorical approach to conceptualising refuge by first considering the position or predicament of the person seeking protection. As shown in this chapter, in Aotearoa/New Zealand and early UK jurisprudence,

---

<www.toaep.org/pbs-pdf/76-chao/>. O'Sullivan encourages greater congruity between the IPA concept and article 1C(5) but only to introduce a concept of reasonableness in cessation decisions, not to advocate for article 1C(5) to be applied once an IPA may become available: Maria O'Sullivan, 'Territorial Protection: Cessation of Refugee Status and Internal Flight Alternative Compared' in Satvinder Juss (ed), *The Ashgate Research Companion to Migration Law, Theory and Policy* (Ashgate, 2013) 209, 226–9.

[164] UNHCR, *Guidelines on International Protection No 3: Cessation of Refugee Status under Article 1C(5) and (6) of the 1951 Convention Relating to the Status of Refugees (the 'Ceased Circumstances' Clauses)*, UN Doc HCR/GIP/03/03 (10 February 2003) [17].

[165] Hathaway and Foster (n 52) 478.   [166] Ibid 480.   [167] Ibid 481.

[168] Hathaway and Foster set out a five point test: ibid 481–5.   [169] Ibid 477.   [170] Ibid 478.

decision-makers position the putative refugee as a prospective IDP and imagine what their life would be like in an IDP camp. This gives rise to a broad understanding of the scope of refuge, but also a sensibility of international solidarity.

In line with all other case studies in this book, there has been a transition in which decision-makers produce rudimentary notions of refuge, remove the place of refuge from consideration and focus on the particular protection from refuge litigant and ask whether they are exceptional in some way. In the UK, where the overwhelming majority of these protection from refuge claims have arisen, protection from the prospect of life in an IDP camp will only be granted when the putative refugee can establish that they are exceptionally vulnerable. However, decision-makers characterise the putative refugees in the cases before them as resilient because they have made long journeys to claim asylum.

Portraying the protection from refuge claimant as strong and courageous denotes an understanding that refuge can be self-made and obscures the perversity of expecting a putative refugee to seek refuge in an IDP camp. It also solidifies the boundaries between the Global North and Global South by distorting the one method available to those with a well-founded fear of persecution to secure a remedy: mobility. For decision-makers in these protection from refuge claims, the refugee as a moving entity is not, as Tuitt has written, 'synonymous with humanitarian need and suffering'. Rather, the fact that the putative refugee has travelled to the UK and provided for themselves as an asylum seeker is evidence that they can contend with the vicissitudes of life in an IDP camp. This ignores the gendered harms in IDP camps for people of all genders.

Perhaps the most significant observation in this chapter was that adjudicative decision-makers can, and have, approached protection from refuge claims in a manner consistent with the reference to international cooperation in the Refugee Convention's preamble. Refugee law, as it is currently framed, cannot address the problem that many people in need of international protection cannot leave their homeland. Nevertheless, by taking into account that many international organisations and lower-income countries simply cannot provide protection, this jurisprudence takes a step towards more equitable responsibility sharing. That decision-makers have resiled from this approach entrenches the Refugee Convention as a containment mechanism. It also has significant implications for refugee journeys. In the cases discussed in this chapter, those with a well-founded fear of persecution face the prospect of being returned back where their journey in search of refuge began.

8

Elusive Refuge

8.1 Introduction

I began this book by discussing refugees' journeys in search of refuge. Some of these journeys are relatively short ones, where those in need of international protection seek refuge in a neighbouring country. Others are much longer and involve multiple international border crossings and transcontinental travel. Refugees' voyages to find places of refuge are often 'fragmented'[1] due to containment mechanisms and challenges imposed by factors such as gender, age, care responsibilities and disability. To be able to continue their quests for refuge, many refugees and asylum seekers turn to courts or other adjudicative decision-making bodies to seek protection, not from persecution in their homeland, but from a place of ostensible refuge. This book uniquely investigated the role 'protection from refuge' litigation plays in refugees' searches for a place of genuine refuge. By drawing on jurisprudence from four continents over a two-decade period, I examined the extent to which courts enable or hinder refugees' (or particular refugees') journeys. While there is a large body of literature on how adjudicative decision-makers approach refugee definitions, this book is the first dedicated and comparative study of how they approach the remedy: refuge.

This book has highlighted that in each protection from refuge context, there is a period or moment in which adjudicative decision-makers engage with the concept of refuge. Through adopting what I identified in Chapter 2 as categorical reasoning (sometimes in conjunction with experiential and rights-based reasoning), decision-makers use domestic, regional and international legal frameworks as prisms to outline robust ideas about refuge's functions, nature, threshold and scope. These conceptualisations of refuge prevail over states' desires to constrain refugees' movement within and across borders. These judicial approaches provide grounds for large numbers of refugees to continue their quest for refuge, but decision-makers also demonstrate an understanding of particular refugees' needs.

However, these protection from refuge victories are ephemeral. In each type of protection from refuge scenario, decision-makers transition from a categorical approach to exceptionality reasoning and remove or partially remove the place of refuge from the judicial lens. This produces minimalist and impoverished notions of refuge and means that protection from refuge challenges are determined in a way that defers to states' interests. Not only do these decisions obstruct refugees in their searches for refuge, decision-makers often neglect difficulties faced by women, children and refugees with care responsibilities and disabilities.

---

[1] Michael Collyer, 'Stranded Migrants and the Fragmented Journey' (2010) 23(3) *Journal of Refugee Studies* 273, 275.

Nevertheless, a handful of 2019 and 2020 decisions provide a glimmer of a shift back to more protection-sensitive approaches.

In this concluding chapter, I highlight the significance of these findings for refugee law scholarship and the international protection regime more broadly, as well as indicate the questions they raise for future research. First, in Section 8.2, I discuss how my analysis of judicial approaches that give a rich meaning to the concept of refuge responds to scholars' identifications of current dilemmas in refugee law. Second, in Section 8.3, I consider how the judicial dilution of the concept of refuge poses risks to the future directions of refugee law. Finally, in Section 8.4, I highlight how the analysis in this book adds new dimensions to scholarly assessments of decision-makers' understandings of gender and intersectionality. Overall, I argue that the trajectory of decision-makers' approaches to protection from refuge claims has rendered refuge elusive, but recent jurisprudence provides some hope that courts can, once again, assist refugees in their journeys in search of refuge.

8.2   Robust Refuge

In Chapter 1, I noted that scholars have expressed concern that refugee law is becoming 'relentlessly local' and that scholars 'tend to frame questions and answers within national or regional frameworks'.[2] The analysis in this book indicates that, despite divergent legal frameworks in protection from refuge challenges, there are similarities in judicial ideas of refuge across international borders. One pattern evident throughout each type of protection from refuge scenario is that when decision-makers approach the concept of refuge in a purposive manner, or give it a broad or rich meaning, they start their reasoning by focussing on refugees' or IDPs' predicament or position. I labelled this approach to protection from refuge claims as 'categorical', because it is informed by the categories of people who need international protection. This type of reasoning is not unique to adjudicative decision-makers. As outlined in Chapter 2, scholars from a number of disciplines use this as a starting point to outline and defend ideas of refuge. However, it is powerful and significant in the judicial context, because it enables decision-makers to mould legal frameworks in a way that responds to refugees' needs and entitlements. Through this approach to protection from refuge claims, decision-makers across the globe understand refuge to have restorative, regenerative and palliative functions that address refugees' present, future and past; as a remedy, right, duty, process and shared responsibility; to have an identifiable threshold; as having a broad scope encompassing a range of civil and political and economic, social and cultural rights; and as a flexible concept that can take into account particular refugees' needs.

Some aspects of these judicial understandings of refuge cement or advance ideas of what refuge is or should be when compared to scholarly literature on refugee protection (discussed in Chapter 2). With respect to refuge's functions, African and European decision-makers have recognised that one of refuge's objectives is to enable refugees to heal from past trauma. This palliative aspect of refuge is present in studies in psychology, anthropology and history, but it is not a central idea in legal understandings of refuge. The decision-makers in the protection from refuge victories discussed in Chapters 3 and 4 made the palliative function of refuge a primary consideration in protection from refuge claims. In relation to the nature of refuge, Kenyan courts understood refuge as a process between the refugee and host country. This is a notion of refuge common in anthropological literature, but Kenyan decision-makers made it part of legal understandings of refuge. In relation to refuge's threshold, the High Court of Australia is the only court to have suggested that a third country must guarantee all of the rights in the Refugee Convention in law and practice.

Perhaps the most significant way in which courts furthered notions of refuge was in Chapters 6 and 7, where decision-makers conceptualised refuge as a responsibility that must be equitably shared between the Global South and Global North. International cooperation has been a principle of international refugee law since at least the 1933 Convention Relating to the International Status of Refugees,[3] where it was referenced in the preamble. While, as noted in Chapter 2, there is a large literature on international solidarity in international refugee law, scholars bemoan the lack of reference to the concept in refugee jurisprudence.[4] The protection from refuge decisions discussed in Chapters 6 and 7 bring an ethic of international cooperation into jurisprudence by indicating that Global North states must provide refugee protection when the relevant authorities in the Global South are already overstretched. This approach is akin to Kritzman-Amir's scholarship that draws on feminist ideas of ethics of care to argue that responsibility for hosting refugees should primarily be determined by which state is best resourced to care for them.[5] As discussed in Chapter 1, courts alone cannot solve the problem of inequitable burden sharing, but they can have a role in helping to create a fairer system. That adjudicative decision-makers in two jurisdictions (the UK and Aotearoa/New Zealand), in the context of article 1D and internal protection decisions, have embraced a sensibility of global solidarity indicates that it may be possible to foster stronger judicial engagement with the concept. What was absent in these cases, and may be a development to agitate for in future litigation, is a recognition that the conditions in the resisted place of refuge are partly attributable to Western states' political and policy decisions.

Ethnographic studies indicate that, for refugees, a sense of refuge is something gradually attained through the refugee building relationships in the host country – it is not achieved immediately upon entering a country of refuge.[6] Therefore, in this book, I am not suggesting that the refugee litigants who were successful in their protection from refuge claims would have immediately achieved a feeling of refuge. This is unlikely as there is evidence of human rights concerns for asylum seekers and refugees in countries many refugees are trying to access such as Australia, Canada and the UK.[7] Nevertheless, by determining protection

[3] 28 October 1933, League of Nation Treaty Series Vol. CLIX No 3663.
[4] See, e.g., Eleni Karageorgiou, 'The Distribution of Asylum Responsibilities in the EU: Dublin, Partnerships with Third Countries and the Question of Solidarity' (2019) Nordic Journal of International Law 315.
[5] Tally Kritzman-Amir, 'Not in My Backyard: On the Morality of Responsibility Sharing in Refugee Law' (2009) 34(2) Brooklyn Journal of International Law 355, 362, 372.
[6] Catherine Besteman, Making Refuge: Somali Bantu Refugees and Lewiston, Maine (Duke University Press, 2016); Georgina Ramsay, Impossible Refuge: The Control and Constraint of Refugee Futures (Routledge, 2018).
[7] See, e.g., Jennifer Allsopp, Nando Sigona and Jenny Phillimore, 'Poverty among Refugees and Asylum Seekers in the UK: An Evidence and Policy Review' (Working Paper No 1/2014, Institute for Research into Super Diversity Working Paper Series, 2014); Australian Human Rights Commission, Asylum Seekers, Refugees and Human Rights: Snapshot Report (Second Edition) (2017) <www.humanrights.gov.au/our-work/asylum-seekers-and-refugees/publications/asylum-seekers-refugees-and-human-rights-snapsho-0>; Cécile Rousseau

from refuge challenges in a way that enables, rather than impedes, refugees' journeys, decision-makers enliven the prospect that refuge can be realised. These decisions empower refugees to continue to work towards a different and better future, which is an important aspect of refuge.

Overall, these findings raise a number of questions for further research. First, how do decision-makers conceptualise refuge in other contexts? I have focussed on cases in which a refugee was seeking rescue from or transfer to a place of refuge. This is because I wanted to explore the ways judicial ideas of refuge facilitate or impede refugees' journeys. However, ideas of refuge may also be embedded in other types of claims refugees bring before courts and other decision-making bodies. For example, when refugees challenge changes to their host states' laws and policies on access to healthcare or welfare.[8] What ideas of refuge are reflected in these decisions? Do they differ from the concept of refuge emerging in protection from refuge challenges? Do they respond to the particular needs of refugees from more marginalised backgrounds? Also, I only examined protection from refuge decisions in cases where reasons for decision are publicly available. Whether unreported first instance judgments or initial decision-makers (often public servants) adopt a similar approach is an issue for future investigation.[9]

The identification of categorical reasoning and decision-makers' construction of the 'abstract' refugee or IDP may provide the basis for future enquiries in the field of refugee law and other areas more broadly. Can this judicial approach provide an antidote to refugee law's parochialism in other contexts? Is it an approach observable in rights claims made not by refugees but others who may have shared experiences, and does it deliver similar legal advances? Further, is the adoption of categorical reasoning influenced by the ways advocates or amici curiae frame their submissions or engage in legal argument with decision-makers?

8.3   Rudimentary Refuge

The robust ideas of refuge adopted in the decisions summarised above and discussed throughout the book have been replaced with minimalist notions of refuge. Kenyan decision-makers switched from approaching refuge as a legal remedy designed to enable refugees to rebuild a meaningful life and heal from past trauma to one that is reserved for those judged the most vulnerable or most deserving. In protection from refuge claims made in the European context, decision-makers' conceptualisations of refuge changed from a legal remedy that has restorative, regenerative and palliative functions to a scarce commodity to be given to the 'peculiarly vulnerable'. In direct challenges to regional containment instruments, ideas about the nature of refuge shifted from a duty to a discretion, and the idea that there needs to be a threshold for adequate refuge dissipated from the jurisprudence. For Palestinian refugees, the concept of

---

et al, 'Health Care Access for Refugees and Immigrants with Precarious Status: Public Health and Human Rights Challenges' (2008) 99(4) *Canadian Journal of Public Health* 290; John Van Kooy and Dina Bowman, '"Surrounded by So Much Uncertainty": Asylum Seekers and Manufactured Precarity in Australia' (2019) 45 (5) *Journal of Ethnic and Migration Studies* 693.

[8] See, e.g., *Canadian Doctors for Refugee Care, The Canadian Association of Refugee Lawyers, Daniel Garcia Rodrigues, Hanif Ayubi and Justice for Children and Youth v Attorney General of Canada and Minister of Citizenship and Immigration* [2014] FC 651.

[9] Arbel, Dauvergne and Millbank (n 2) highlight that this is a methodological challenge in researching decision-making in refugee law: 7–8. This would most likely arise with respect to the case law discussed in Chapters 4, 6 and 7.

refuge was diluted from a right to an act of charity, and the ambit of refuge was narrowed from broad human rights considerations to protection of physical security. For prospective IDPs, notions of refuge withered to encompass only living conditions and the idea that refuge requires a state or international organisation willing and able to provide protection and that refuge is a shared duty also disappeared. Another aspect of these protection from refuge challenges that promulgate impoverished notions of refuge is that decision-makers partially or completely excise the resisted place of refuge from the judicial lens. It is only in the Australian context that these shifts are partly due to legislative change. In all other protection from refuge situations, decision-makers disengage with ideas of refuge and move away from a full examination of the resisted place of refuge without legislators' influence.

   Decision-makers' dilution of the notion of refuge risks refugee law developing in an asymmetrical fashion by widening the categories of people entitled to international protection, but diminishing the protection to which they are entitled.[10] Over the past few decades, courts and other decision-making bodies have demonstrated 'extraordinary judicial engagement with the [Refugee] Convention definition'.[11] For example, courts have declared that women and sexual minorities can constitute a particular social group;[12] that harm by non-state actors can amount to persecution if the state cannot or will not provide protection;[13] and that persecution can encompass denial of economic, social or cultural rights.[14] There are some developments that limit the reach of the refugee definition, such as the increased use of the internal protection alternative[15] and focus on credibility, especially in gender and sexuality-based claims.[16] Nevertheless, the overall trend is that the jurisprudence has evolved understandings of who is a refugee and enabled a wider range of people to enjoy refugee status.[17] While courts have contributed to a dynamic interpretation of the refugee definition, this book suggests that, subsequent to initial protection from refuge victories,

[10] Kate Ogg, 'Protection from "Refuge": On What Legal Grounds will a Refugee be Saved from Camp Life?' (2016) 28(3) *International Journal of Refugee Law* 384, 414.
[11] James Hathaway and Michelle Foster, *The Law of Refugee Status* (Cambridge University Press, 2nd ed, 2014) 4–5.
[12] *Islam v Secretary of State for the Home Department; R v Immigration Appeal Tribunal ex parte Shah* [1999] 2 All ER 545 at 556–7 (Lord Steyn), 563–4 (Lord Hoffman), 569 (Lord Hope); *Minister for Immigration and Multicultural Affairs v Khawar* (2002) 210 CLR 1 at [32] (Gleeson CJ), [130]–[131] (Kirby J) ('*Khawar*').
[13] *Khawar* (n 12) [29]–[31] (Gleeson CJ), [112]–[114] (Kirby J).
[14] For example, in *RRT Case No N94/04178* (Refugee Review Tribunal, 10 June 1994) discriminatory denial of healthcare was found to constitute persecution. See also *Chen Shi Hai v Minister for Immigration and Multicultural Affairs* [2000] HCA 19 [31]; *BG (Fiji)* [2012] NZIPT 800091 [90]; *MK (Lesbians) Albania v Secretary of State for the Home Department CG* [2009] UKAIT 00036 [353].
[15] The internal protection alternative 'occupied a relatively modest place in the asylum practice of Western states' until the 1990s: Jessica Schultz, 'The Internal Protection Alternative and Its Relation to Refugee Status' in Satvinder Juss (ed), *Research Handbook on International Refugee Law* (Edward Elgar, 2019) 126, 128.
[16] Jenni Millbank, 'From Discretion to Disbelief: Recent Trends in Refugee Determinations on the Basis of Sexual Orientation in Australia and the United Kingdom' (2009) 13(2/3) *International Journal of Human Rights* 391; Debora Singer, 'Falling at Each Hurdle: Assessing the Credibility of Women's Asylum Claims in Europe' in Efrat Arbel, Catherine Dauvergne and Jenni Millbank (eds), *Gender in Refugee Law: From the Margins to the Centre* (Routledge, 2014) 98.
[17] Hathaway and Foster (n 11) 4–5; Jane McAdam and Tamara Wood, 'The Concept of "International Protection" in the Global Compacts on Refugees and Migration' (2021) 23(1) *Interventions: International Journal of Postcolonial Studies* 2, 7; William Worster, 'The Evolving Definition of Refugee in Contemporary International Law' (2012) 30 *Berkeley Journal of International Law* 94.

there has not been the same approach to the remedy – refuge. What can be observed are the beginnings of a misaligned development between questions of who qualifies for protection and the nature and extent of protection states must provide. A dynamic approach to the refugee definition alongside a minimalist approach to the idea of refuge risks expanding the circumstances in which international protection is triggered, but narrowing and truncating the protection owed.

The reason why courts and other decision-making bodies across various jurisdictions have made this about-turn is an important question for future research and throughout the book I have offered some speculations and suggestions with respect to underlying motivations. While the reasons for this shift in judicial approaches to protection from refuge claims are beyond the scope of this book, the fact that there has been a pronounced change is significant. In Chapter 1, I highlighted that legal concepts do not only serve pragmatic ends, but they are also a reflection of norms and values. There are always 'conflicting visions' about how a state and the international community should treat refugees and asylum seekers.[18] Adjudicative bodies (and courts in particular) play an important role in contributing to both the legal and normative debate, because they often clash with the executive and legislature[19] and provide an 'alternative narrative'.[20] That decision-makers have shifted from broad and comprehensive to minimalist understandings of refuge suggests that courts and other adjudicative bodies are becoming less inclined to counter states' positions on appropriate standards of refugee protection. What has occurred through this transition is the loss of a powerful conflicting vision or alternative narrative on how a state or the international community should respond to those who come in search of sanctuary.

An issue for future research is the role strategic litigation has played in protection from refuge challenges. Strategic litigation is a relatively new topic in the field of refugee studies and scholars have so far focussed on its role in securing legal accountability for violations of refugee rights.[21] But what about situations in which a failed case results in positive policy change due to mobilisation of civil society, such as occurred in *Plaintiff M68* (discussed in Chapter 5)? Duffy refers to such situations as successful losses.[22] Conversely, victories in the courtroom do not necessarily lead to positive outcomes for refugees because they can prompt regressive legal and policy change.[23] Perhaps the most poignant example in this book is the production of situations of 'relative refuge' (Chapters 3 and 5), in which, after a long saga of litigation, refugees went to court to fight to remain in places of refuge from which they initially fought to leave. In 2017, refugees in Kenya litigated to be able to remain in a refugee camp and they are doing so again in 2021. In Papua New Guinea, refugees used litigation to close the Manus Island detention centre and then, later, to keep it open. Studies of the factors that influence the ultimate outcome of litigation for refugees beyond the

---

[18] Mary Crock, 'In the Wake of the Tampa: Conflicting Visions of International Refugee Law in the Management of Refugee Flows' (2003) 12(1) *Pacific Rim Law and Policy* 49.

[19] Mary Crock, 'Judging Refugees: The Clash of Power and Institutions in the Development of Australian Refugee Law' (2004) 25(1) *Sydney Law Review* 51.

[20] Marinella Marmo and Maria Giannacopoulos, 'Cycles of Judicial and Executive Power in Irregular Migration' (2017) 5(1) *Comparative Migration Studies* 1, 4.

[21] See discussion in Cathryn Costello and Itamar Mann, 'Border Justice: Migration and Accountability for Human Rights Violations' (2020) 21 *German Law Journal* 311, 325–7.

[22] Helen Duffy, *Strategic Human Rights Litigation: Understanding and Maximising Impact* (Hart, 2018).

[23] Ibid; Itamar Mann, 'Dialectic of Transnationalism: Unauthorized Migration and Human Rights' (2013) 54(2) *Harvard International Law Journal* 315.

courtroom (in particular the role of civil society and other non-legal actors) are crucial for understanding the efficacy of strategic litigation.

8.4   The Gendered Exceptional Refugee

As noted in Chapter 1, Arbel, Dauvergne and Millbank provide the most recent collection of scholarship on gender, refugee law and decision-making in their 2014 'international comparative project on gender-related persecution and [refugee status determination]'.[24] They suggest that jurisprudence concerning refugee status determinations has moved on from a situation where women's experiences are ignored.[25] The authors highlight that, in the 1980s, decision-makers understood the 'classic refugee' to be a political dissident fleeing state oppression, which 'was a much better fit for men than for women'.[26] After decades of sustained feminist engagement with refugee law, policy-makers and decision-makers now 'put gender on the tick-box list of topics for consideration'.[27]

By switching the focus from the refugee definition to the remedy (refuge), this book illustrates that, in some contexts, refugee law decision-makers have not made the basic progression from gender-blind decisions that create legal tests more fitting for men than women to including gender as an important unit of analysis. For example, in their employment of the exceptional refugee trope in protection from refuge claims made by Palestinian refugees, decision-makers reproduce the archetypal refugee fleeing physical harms emanating from the public sphere. These judgments are gender blind in the sense that they ignore or discount risks women are more likely to face in places of so-called refuge such as forced marriage. They are also gendered in that they create precedents more likely to assist male Palestinian refugees in their searches for refuge. There are also gender-blind decisions in Dublin System jurisprudence, where judges do not consider factors such as gender, pregnancy and previous experience of sexual violence in their consideration of whether a transfer would pose a risk of inhuman or degrading treatment.

While some protection from refuge challenges are arbitrated in this manner, in others, decision-makers acknowledge that gender as well as factors such as sexuality, youth and disability are important factors that must be considered. This puts these protection from refuge decisions in line with judicial considerations of refugee definitions where decision-makers 'routinely' consider questions of gender.[28] However, this book reveals that many decision-makers are not engaging with questions of gender in any substantive way, but are approaching them in a perfunctory manner. This comes across most strongly in the chapters on European protection from refuge claims (Chapter 4) and the prospect of internal protection in an IDP camp (Chapter 7). In these cases, decision-makers acknowledge that, for example, single women may be more vulnerable in certain places of refuge, but determine that they will have adequate protection because of assistance provided by NGOs or family members. There is no assessment as to the nature of assistance provided and whether and how this may insulate the woman from the particular risks to which she may be exposed.

---

[24] Arbel, Dauvergne and Millbank (n 2) 9. As noted in Chapter 1, there is only one chapter in Arbel, Dauvergne, and Millbank's edited collection concerning what I call protection from refuge challenges, Arbel's study of litigation on the bilateral agreement between Canada and the US, which I drew on in Chapter 5.
[25] Ibid 3.   [26] Ibid 3.   [27] Ibid 1.   [28] Ibid 1.

These desultory approaches to gender in protection from refuge claims raise the same query Arbel, Dauvergne and Millbank ask in the refugee status assessment context: when 'the argument can no longer be for jurisprudential inclusion', how do we facilitate 'more meaningful, more complicated, more substantive analysis'?[29] This book provides some insights on this question. As discussed earlier, protection from refuge claims are more successful for all refugees (including refugees from more marginalised backgrounds) when decision-makers start their reasoning by considering the irreducible aspects of refugeehood, rather than focussing on the specific refugee litigant's circumstances. This finding is a controversial one in the context of scholarship on refugee jurisprudence. Scholars and the UNHCR encourage refugee law judges to take account of factors such as gender, sexuality, age and disability in their decisions,[30] and this is a position I have advocated for in previous research.[31] However, in most of the jurisprudence examined in this book, I show that decision-makers address considerations of gender and other intersectional factors such as youth and disability in almost a competitive manner. They require the refugee to prove why their circumstances are worse or more exceptional than other refugees. Thus, when decision-makers move directly to these considerations without first considering the notion of refugeehood, this results in 'invidious comparisons between categories', of which Arbel, Dauvergne and Millbank warn.[32] Reflecting on litigation designed to bring refugee children in France to the UK (discussed in Chapter 4), Starfield warns that arguments invoking vulnerability can be a double-edged sword: while it may increase the chances of a win for your client, it can reduce the utility of the precedent for others not quite in such extreme circumstances.[33]

One example of this phenomenon is the notion of exceptionally or 'peculiarly' vulnerable refugees that has arisen in European protection from refuge decisions (Chapter 4) and cases concerning whether an IDP camp can provide an internal protection alternative (Chapter 7). This disadvantages male refugees, because, by virtue of their gender, decision-makers do not deem them to be peculiarly vulnerable. Further, even refugees whom jurisprudence identifies as vulnerable often cannot make successful protection from refuge claims, because decision-makers do not consider them as vulnerable as others. For example, in Chapter 7 I highlighted that, despite country guidance that most

---

[29] Ibid 6.

[30] See, e.g., Deborah Anker, 'Refugee Law, Gender, and the Human Rights Paradigm' (2002) 15 *Harvard Human Rights Journal* 133; Alice Edwards, 'Age and Gender Dimensions in International Refugee Law' in Erica Feller, Volker Türk and Frances Nicholson (eds), *Refugee Protection in International Law: UNHCR's Global Consultations on International Protection* (Cambridge University Press, 2003) 46; Constance MacIntosh, 'When "Feminist Beliefs" Became Credible as "Political Opinions": Returning to a Key Moment in Canadian Refugee Law' (2005) 17(1) *Canadian Journal of Women and the Law* 135; UNHCR, *Guidelines on International Protection No 1: Gender-Related Persecution Within the Context of Article 1A(2) of the 1951 Convention and/or Its 1967 Protocol Relating to the Status of Refugees*, UN Doc HCR/GIP/02/01 (7 May 2002); UNHCR, *Guidelines on International Protection No 9: Claims to Refugee Status Based on Sexual Orientation and/or Gender Identity Within the Context of Article 1A(2) of the 1951 Convention and/or Its 1967 Protocol Relating to the Status of Refugees*, UN Doc HCR/GIP/12/01 (23 October 2012).

[31] Kate Ogg, 'Separating the Persecutors from the Persecuted: A Feminist and Comparative Examination of Exclusion from the Refugee Regime' (2013) 26(1) *International Journal of Refugee Law* 82.

[32] Arbel, Dauvergne and Millbank (n 2) 6.

[33] Gina Starfield, 'Forging Strategic Partnerships: How Civil Organisers and Lawyers Helped Unaccompanied Children Cross the English Channel and Reunite with Family Members' (RSC Working Paper Series 133, 19 October 2020) 15.

single women would not be expected to seek refuge in an IDP camp, decision-makers find
reasons why the particular female refugee bringing the claim would not be vulnerable in
a camp setting.

Conversely, in cases where decision-makers start from a general understanding of the
predicament of refugeehood and then add to that an appreciation of the ways factors such as
gender and age heighten the risks intrinsic to seeking refuge, decision-makers engage with
a person's gender, age or disability in more meaningful, substantive and complicated ways.
This is particularly evident in Kenyan case law, where courts start their analysis by reflecting
on what it is to be a refugee and consider factors such as gender, age and disability simply to
build a picture of how the dangers and deprivations in sites of so-called refuge affect
refugees differently. They do not take account of these factors to determine which refugees
should be saved from such places.

Another issue for future research this book points to is the lack of decision-maker
guidance on questions of gender, age, sexual orientation and disability for situations in
which refugees are using courts and other decision-making bodies to seek rescue from or
transfer to a place of refuge. The UNHCR has published guidance for decision-makers on
questions of gender and sexual orientation in refugee status assessments.[34] Canada has also
published gender guidelines for decision-makers when interpreting the refugee definition.[35]
Creating decision-maker guidance for protection from refuge scenarios would be challenging due to the different legal frameworks governing these actions. Nevertheless, the
UNHCR's guidance on effective protection,[36] bilateral and multilateral containment
agreements,[37] the internal protection alternative,[38] all of which are relevant to the legal
challenges in this book, do not mention gender. Similarly, the Michigan Guidelines on
Protection Elsewhere[39] and Michigan Guidelines on the Internal Protection Alternative[40]
are silent on gender. The only guidance given to decision-makers on the role gender can
play in protection from refuge challenges are the UNHCR's guidelines on article 1D (which
briefly mention that gender and sexual orientation and sexual and gender-based violence

[34] UNHCR, *Guidelines on International Protection No 1* (n 30); UNHCR, *Guidelines on International Protection No 9* (n 30).
[35] Canadian Immigration and Refugee Board, *Chairperson Guidelines 4: Women Refugee Claimants Fearing Gender-Related Persecution* (13 November 1996).
[36] UNHCR, *Summary Conclusions on the Concept of 'Effective Protection' in the Context of Secondary Movements of Refugees and Asylum Seekers (Lisbon Expert Roundtable, 9–10 December 2002)* (February 2003) <www.unhcr.org/en-au/protection/globalconsult/3e5f323d7/lisbon-expert-roundtable-summary-conclusions-concept-effective-protection.html>; UNHCR, 'Statement by Ms Erika Feller, Director, Department of International Protection, UNHCR, at the Fifty-Fifth Session of the Executive Committee of the High Commissioner's Programme' (7 October 2004) <www.unhcr.org/en-au/admin/dipstatements/429d6f8e4/statement-ms-erika-feller-director-department-international-protection.html>; UNHCR, *Legal Considerations Regarding Access to Protection and a Connection between the Refugee and the Third Country in the Context of Return or Transfer to Safe Third Countries* (April 2018).
[37] UNHCR, *Guidance Note on Bilateral and/or Multilateral Transfer Arrangements of Asylum-Seekers* (May 2013) <www.refworld.org/docid/5acb33ad4.html>.
[38] UNHCR, *Guidelines on International Protection No 4: 'Internal Flight or Relocation Alternative' Within the Context of Article 1A(2) of the 1951 Convention and/or 1967 Protocol Relating to the Status of Refugees*, UN Doc HCR/GIP/03/04 (23 July 2003).
[39] Fourth Colloquium on Challenges in Refugee Law, 'The Michigan Guidelines on Protection Elsewhere' (2007) 28(2) *Michigan Journal of International Law* 207.
[40] First Colloquium on Challenges in International Refugee Law, 'Michigan Guidelines on the Internal Protection Alternative' (1999) 21 *Michigan Journal of International Law* 134.

should be relevant to article 1D decisions)[41] and UNHCR guidance on responding to irregular onward movement (which note that women in particular may be exposed to violence and exploitation).[42] It is important to provide guidance to decision-makers about refugee protection and the ways it must take account of different refugees' needs.

A further question for future research that this book raises is the role of gender in decision-makers' approaches to men's protection from refuge claims. There is some scholarly consideration of male refugee law litigants from a gender perspective, but these publications focus on refugee definitions.[43] In Chapters 4 and 7 (European protection from refuge claims and international protection alternative jurisprudence), I unearthed a number of cases where decision-makers' characterisation of the refugee or asylum seeker as a young, healthy, single man is part of the reasons why the claim is rejected. This reflects Spijkerboer's observation that 'in both academic and non-academic (refugee) legal discourse, the dominant view is that gender is relevant only to a particular set of cases, if at all. That is, only a limited number of "gender specific" applications for asylum are assumed to raise issues of gender'.[44] Spijkerboer's plea to consider gender and male claims has largely gone unheeded. Decision-makers' reference to a person being a 'young, single and healthy male' as a reason to conclude that he can be sent to or kept in a place of ostensible refuge that poses serious harms is a concerning development. It is also antithetical to feminist engagements with refugee law, which aim to develop a more gender-sensitive interpretation of refugee law for people of all genders, sexualities and ages. In resetting the agenda for analysis of gender in refugee law, Arbel, Dauvergne and Millbank outline a number of important issues for future research.[45] I would add to this agenda an increased focus on decision-makers' approach to gender in men's claims for protection beyond gender-related persecution claims.

8.5   Conclusion

This book has explored how decision-makers approach and determine protection from refuge claims and whether they facilitate or undermine refugees' (or only certain refugees') searches for places of genuine sanctuary. Scholars of refugee and forced migration studies often use metaphors or images to reflect the ways law positions refugees. Refugees are described as 'between sovereigns',[46] 'beyond the pale of law',[47] in a situation of 'liminality'[48]

---

[41] UNHCR, *Guidelines on International Protection No 13: Applicability of Article 1D of the 1951 Convention Relating to the Status of Refugees to Palestinian Refugees*, UN Doc HCR/GIP/16/12 (December 2017) [22], [24].

[42] UNHCR, *Guidance on Responding to Irregular Movement of Refugees and Asylum Seekers* (September 2019) [3] <www.refworld.org/docid/5d8a255d4.html>.

[43] See, e.g., Thomas Spijkerboer, *Fleeing Homophobia: Sexual Orientation, Gender Identity and Asylum* (Routledge, 2013); Millbank (n 16); Caitlin Steinke, 'Male Asylum Applicants Who Fear Becoming the Victims of Honor Killings: The Case for Gender Equality' (2013) 17(1) *City University of New York Law Review* 233.

[44] Thomas Spijkerboer, *Gender and Refugee Status* (Ashgate, 2000) 9.

[45] Arbel, Dauvergne and Millbank (n 2) 11–14.

[46] Emma Haddad, *The Refugee in International Society: Between Sovereigns* (Cambridge University Press, 2009).

[47] Emma Larking, *Refugees and the Myth of Human Rights: Life Outside the Pale of Law* (Ashgate, 2014).

[48] Efrat Arbel, 'Shifting Borders and the Boundaries of Rights: Examining the Safe Third-Country Agreement between Canada and the United States' (2013) 25(1) *International Journal of Refugee Law* 65, 83.

or in a 'state of exception'.[49] These depictions do not capture the relationship between law and refugee journeys unearthed in this book. Refugees searching for safe havens are not suspended in an in-between space, placed in a legal vacuum or outside law's reach. Rather, there are instances in which decision-makers approach protection from refuge claims in ways that build a powerful picture of refuge. In doing so, they deliver refugees significant legal victories that enable them to continue their search for refuge within and across borders. However, there has been a shift in decision-makers' approaches to these claims, atrophying ideas of refuge and inhibiting refugees' ability to seek a place of genuine sanctuary.

An image or metaphor that encapsulates this trajectory is the character of Tantalus from Greek mythology. As punishment for his crimes, Zeus condemned Tantalus to stand in a pool of water underneath the branches of a fruit tree. Perpetually hungry and thirsty, every time he reached for the fruit, the branch would retract just out of reach, and each time he bent down to drink the water, it would recede.

While refugees have not committed any crimes by searching for safe havens, like the figure of Tantalus, they are reaching for something that they can envisage, but remains elusive. Decision-makers play a role in elucidating vivid images of refuge through judgments in which they outline powerful ideas about its functions, nature, threshold and scope. However, when refugees approach courts and other decision-making bodies, adjudicators position refuge just out of grasp. This is first brought about by ephemeral protection from refuge victories: while decision-makers initially create powerful precedents that overturn or disrupt containment policies and practices, they claw them back in later decisions. Just when refugees and their advocates think that the pathway to refuge has been opened, decision-makers circumscribe these legal avenues for facilitating refugees' searches for refuge. Second, decision-makers remove the possibility of realising refuge through their shift to impoverished ideas of what refuge is. This means that, while robust notions of refuge exist in jurisprudence, refugees cannot take hold of them when they come to courts and other decision-making bodies. Third, this image arises because even those refugees who should be in a position to make successful protection from refuge claims (those whom jurisprudence identifies as exceptional in some way) are rarely able to use these legal frameworks to continue their search for a place of genuine refuge. Decision-makers create tests that indicate that refugees from more marginalised backgrounds can use litigation to seek protection from a place of so-called refuge, but in individual cases find reasons for why these refugees cannot avail themselves of these legal protections. Finally, Tantalus is an apt simile because decision-makers approach these challenges in a way that cements the current global inequities in refugee responsibility. For many refugees, the place of refuge is achingly close – across a land border, over a stretch of water or outside the confines of a camp. Decision-makers' approaches to these refugees' legal claims diminish, rather than enliven, the prospect of realising refuge in these places.

With a handful of protection from refuge victories in 2019 and 2020, it will be imperative to watch whether, at least in some parts of the world, courts will set a new trajectory or, once again, apply legal frameworks in a way that frustrates refugee journeys.

---

[49] Giorgio Agamben, *State of Exception*, tr Kevin Attell (University of Chicago Press, 2005).

INDEX

Footnotes are indicated by n following the page number.

Milton Keynes UK
Ingram Content Group UK Ltd.
UKHW050004260124
436414UK00019BB/69